y of

S

Most “devotional” books anc one a day and you will feel better. But neither vitamin pills nor devotional books were ever meant to replace balanced diets; they are meant to be supplements. Hence, most devotional material is light on doctrine, designed to give the reader a spiritual lift more than to instruct in truth. Enter Dr. Watson’s excellent book. Ignoring the normal lighthearted paradigm of this genre of literature, Dr. Watson offers biblical meat and potatoes. I can think of no other book of this type that so meticulously enlightens the mind as it encourages the heart. I recommend it highly.

—Dr. Gary E. Gilley
Pastor-teacher of Southern View Chapel, Springfield, IL
Author of *This Little Church Went to Market*

These meditations draw from the deep wells of New Testament vocabulary and theology. Here is daily grace for every reader.

—R. Kent Hughes
Pastor of College Church, Wheaton, IL

Here is a gold mine of theologically-rich words, drawn from the quarry of Scripture, that will enhance the daily walk of every believer. This book is a wonderful resource that will cultivate a deeper knowledge of biblical words and stimulate a passionate heart for the Lord.

—Dr. Steven J. Lawson
Pastor of Christ Fellowship Baptist Church
Mobile, AL

Pastor Watson has done us an outstanding service in putting together this devotional book based on various important words of Scripture. Every word of the Bible is vital to our understanding of spiritual truth, and each is loaded with significant lessons for daily living. This unique work will be like an adventure, a road to travel with heavenly thoughts and concepts to help the Christian begin each day. There is nothing quite like it for believers on the market today.

—Dr. Mal Couch, Scofield Ministries
Author, and Founder of Tyndale Theological Seminary

In my early morning devotional reading, I prefer red meat to cold cereal and milk. In ***A Word for the Day,*** Dr. Watson provides rare steak for breakfast with his wonderful daily devotional, an excellent means for a deeper understanding of Truth through the original language of God’s Word. I highly recommend this book.

—J. D. Wetterling
Presbyterian (PCA) Elder
Author of “*No one...*”

A Word for the Day delivers pithy Greek "word study" gems to devotionally enrich Christians in understanding and obeying Scripture. The biblical treasures extracted from this unique volume will prove eternally priceless for its regular reader.

—Richard Mayhue, Th.D.
Executive Vice President
The Master's College and Seminary

I am passionately in favor of "real" devotional books (you know, the ones that actually teach the Bible) and am passionately opposed to fluff, such as: "God loves, loves, loves you, oh yes He does. He loves you lots and lots and lots and thinks you're really cool, too!" You are what you eat. It's hard to be healthy eating processed sugar for breakfast. Word studies provide a solid foundation for understanding the Scriptures. Doc Watson has produced a quality product for the church-good food to grow on. A good subtitle for this book would be "Healthy Food for Faithful Shepherds and the Sheep They Feed."

—Dr. Jim Bearss
Founder and Director of "On Target Ministry"
Teaching Faithful Men through International Education

Every word that God speaks is pure (Prov. 30:5), tested and refined in the fire of divine sovereignty. Thus, it behooves God's people to carefully consider every single word that God employs in expressing His will and way to us in His Scriptures. Why should selecting one synonym over another in the writing of Scripture make any difference to us? It made a difference to the divine Author which word He chose, therefore it ought to make a difference to us. His Holy Spirit superintended the penning of each and every word. J. D. Watson's ***A Word for the Day*** enables the reader to understand the different aspects of meaning even between synonyms. In this way we begin to perceive the intricate beauties of the wonderfully crafted written Word of the omniscient God.

—Dr. William D. Barrick
The Master's Seminary

Most devotional books with which I'm familiar have conformed to modern-day pressures by sacrificing content for brevity. Dr. Watson's ***A Word for the Day*** represents a vast departure from the norm by providing remarkable substance in a daily devotional format. This is the way to start your day.

—Mr. Mitch Bettis
Publisher, Rio Blanco Herald Times
Meeker, Colorado

a WORD for the DAY

KEY WORDS from the NEW TESTAMENT

J.D. "Doc"
WATSON

A Word for the Day

Published by AMG Publishers
6815 Shallowford Rd.
Chattanooga, Tennessee 37421

ISBN–13: 978-0-89957-686-2
ISBN–10: 0-89957-686-9

First printing-October 2006
Cover designed by Market Street Design, Chattanooga, Tennessee
Edited and Proofread by Christy Sterner, Dan Penwell, Sharon Neal, and Warren Baker

Printed in the United States of America
12 11 10 09 08 07 –R– 8 7 6 5 4 3 2

Library of Congress Cataloging-in-Publication Data

Watson, J. D. (Jeffrey Dane), 1953-
A word for the day / Jeffrey D. Watson.
p. cm.
Summary: "Each day of the year a different Greek word is examined by presenting a brief word study and then offering application to make that word real for practical living. Each day also includes other related verses for the reader's personal study"--Provided by publisher.
Includes bibliographical references and indexes.
ISBN-13: 978-0-89957-686-2 (pbk. : alk. paper)
ISBN-10: 0-89957-686-9 (pbk. : alk. paper)
1. Bible--Language, style. 2. Bible--Terminology. 3. Bible--Criticism, interpretation, etc. 4. Bible--Indexes. 5. Devotional calendars. I. Title.

BS525.W38 2006
225.4'87--dc22 2006024992

Dedication

This work is dedicated first to my dear Savior and Lord,
Jesus Christ, and also to my son,

Paul C. Watson,

who teases about my preaching, "To make a Greek word, just add os to the end of the English word." His mother and I praise the Lord for his maturity and spirituality.

Son, you have never disappointed us, and our only prayer is that you will please the Lord in all you do and will "grow in grace, and in the knowledge of our Lord and Saviour Jesus Christ. To him be glory both now and for ever.
Amen."

Acknowledgments

I want to thank my friend of many years, Bob Dasal, former editor-in-chief of *Pulpit Helps,* for "hand carrying" the idea for this book to Dan Penwell, manager of product development/acquisitions at AMG. I then thank my new friend, Dan, for his guidance through the project (and for answering all my dumb questions).

Thanks also to the entire new product committee at AMG for their excitement over this book. (I had no idea that publishers got excited!)

Many thanks also go out to all the editors who diligently labored to make this book readable: Christy Sterner, Sharon Neal, Warren Baker, and Dan Penwell, with special thanks to Dr. Baker for penning the preface.

Among all the other things my loving help-meet, Debbie, does, I thank her for the countless hours of work she saved me by preparing the indexes and doing other proofing.

Finally, much thanks goes to Dr. Spiros Zodhiates for his many wonderful books that make Greek study so much easier and productive.

Preface

The building blocks of life play an important role in understanding our universe. It was not until our knowledge of atoms increased, that our understanding of the elements that make up our world became more accurate and more meaningful. Armed with this new knowledge, scientific research and our understanding of life itself grew by leaps and bounds. One discovery led to another, as the glorious creation of God was revealed under the microscope.

The same is true with the Word of God. It is likewise a whole made up of small parts—the very God-breathed words of the Lord Himself. In order to come to a richer understanding of the Bible, we must research these small building blocks; we must learn about the words of Scripture.

Some go about this task by studying the various words of an English translation of the Bible, which is, within its limits, a valuable aid to the study of Scripture. However, at this point, one is only studying the words someone else used to translate the languages of the original text. In the case of the Greek New Testament, even the best of translations is unable to reveal the nuances, idioms, and treasures of the words of the original text. If the study of the words of an English translation is equivalent to the study of creation under a microscope, then the study of the words from the original languages is as revealing as viewing created matter under a scanning tunneling microscope, which is capable of three-dimensional images at an atomic level. So rich is the study of the vocabulary of the Greek New Testament.

AMG has, for many years, provided tools to allow believers to dig deep into the riches of the Greek New Testament, without having to learn Greek to do so. Yet, these tools, like any others, require time and effort. In ***A Word for the Day,*** "Doc" Watson has already done all the work. In this book, he reveals the dimensions of key words from the vocabulary of the Greek New Testament in 366 daily studies. One day at a time, he will share the images he found in his own personal studies, and give suggestions on how to dig even deeper into the treasure that is God's Word.

Dr. Warren Baker
Chattanooga, TN

Contents

Introduction

Words matter! After all, we use words every day. They convey our thoughts, feelings, attitudes, ideas, purposes, goals, joys, sorrows—in short, *everything*. Without words, without language, humans would not be very far above animals. That point, in fact, is still a puzzle for the evolutionist, who simply cannot explain why or how humans "evolved" language. He scoffs even at the thought that words and language are gifts from God.

The English language, with its over one million words, is rich and diverse, and there is a reason for that splendor and variety. "In the simplest of terms," write the authors of the fascinating book, *The Story of English,* "the language was brought to Britain by Germanic tribes, Angles, Saxons, and Jutes, influenced by Latin and Greek when St. Augustine and his followers converted England to Christianity, subtly enriched by the Danes, and finally transformed by the French-speaking Normans."[1]

As the same authors also point out, "English has a few rivals, but no equals" and has "become a *second* language" in many countries, "where it is used for administration, broadcasting, and education."[2] Having a background in computers, I have witnessed the same phenomenon in that field as well. I've heard people speaking their native language, such as Spanish or even Polish, when all of a sudden, words such as *hard drive* and *Internet* pop out of their mouths.

While English is an amazing language, compared to Greek (the language of the New Testament), English falls short in some significant ways. We'll come back to that in a moment, but first, let's pause for a short history lesson, which will give us a much greater appreciation for the words on which we will meditate throughout the year.

Greek was actually in use centuries before the existence of recorded history (about 1400 BC). The Greek of the Classical Period (sixth to fourth century BC) was based upon Athenian dialects and finally fell out of use. It was during the "Hellenistic Age"—the period when Greek culture dominated the Mediterranean region (300 BC to AD 300)—that another form of Greek arose and became the language of the world. It was, as William Barclay notes, a simplified form of Greek, which, while in no way inferior, removed certain irregularities and oddities of dialect and ironed out some subtleties of certain moods and tenses[3]. The resulting marvel of language was called *Koinē*, which is short for *hē koinē dialektos*, "the common dialect," "language" (Acts 2:6), or "tongue" (Acts 1:19; 2:8; 21:40; 22:2; 26:14).

The most fascinating aspect of this story, however, is how Greek came to be the universal language of that day. While Aramaic was the common language of Palestine, that changed dramatically because of the conquests of Alexander the Great. He marched from modern day Greece, through Turkey (ancient Asia Minor), down through Syria into Egypt, back across through Iraq, Iran, Afghanistan,

Pakistan, and to the borders of India. By the time of his death in 323 BC, the Greek language and culture had permeated the known world. While the *empire* soon fell to the Romans, Greek *culture* still dominated.

What an example of the sovereignty and providence of God! He wanted Greek to be the language of the New Testament. Why? Primarily because of its universality. With Greek being the common language of a vast area and uncounted people, there was no language barrier to hinder the spreading of the Gospel. Gleason Archer well says:

> Greek was the most ideally adapted linguistic medium for the World-Wide communication of the Gospel in the entire region of the eastern Mediterranean, Egypt and the Near East. Accurate in expression, beautiful in sound, and capable of great rhetorical force, it furnished an ideal vehicle for the proclamation of God's message to man, transcending Semitic barriers and reaching out to all the Gentile races. It is highly significant that the 'fulness of times,' the first advent of Christ, was deferred until such time as Greek opened up channels of communication to all the Gentile nations east of Italy and Libya on a level not previously possible under the multilingual situation that previously prevailed.[4]

Which brings us back to English *vs.* Greek. While English is even more universal in our day than Greek was in New Testament times, the wealth in studying the Greek is inestimable. For example, English has only one word for *love*, but we use that word to express many types of love. As much as I loved a family dog we once had, it would be very unwise for me to say to my wife, "I love you as much as I loved my dog." Greek, in dramatic contrast, has four words for love (*eros, stergō, philōs,* and *agapē*), which we will explore in coming days. Also, while English has only two "voices," active and passive, Greek has another, the middle voice, which expresses nuances of meaning that English cannot; we will see examples of that as well.

The purpose of this book, therefore, is to share with you the richness of some of the Greek words used in the New Testament and to help you make them practical in your Christian living. Since words matter, the words of the New Testament matter most. And in a day when words don't seem to mean much, the need for precision in Christian doctrine and practice has never been more critical.

The well-known, nineteenth-century scholar Richard Trench wrote specifically about Greek synonyms—the comparing of various words with similar, yet still distinct, meanings—but what he wrote applies to any study of Greek words: "Studying synonyms trains the mind by developing precise and accurate habits of thought, and it provides a wealth of knowledge. . . . Because the words of the New Testament are God's words, it is important that we understand every delicate variation in an author's meaning. Increasing our intellectual riches through the study of New Testament synonyms will increase our spiritual wealth as well."[5]

I would like to interject here an encouragement to preachers and Bible teachers. It has grieved me deeply when I've heard some preachers and Bible teachers say such things as, "It's not necessary to use the Hebrew and Greek; the English is good enough." In the same vein, I was preaching in one church several years ago and used a couple of Greek words and their explanation in a normal exposition of a particular point. After the service, a Bible college student approached me and said, "I truly enjoyed your message, but I've been taught that I should *never* use a Greek word from the pulpit." That shocked me, to say the least.

Granted, it's certainly not good preaching and teaching when we overuse the languages and bury our listeners in technicalities. We submit, however, that neither is *ignoring* the languages good; in fact, doing so is *bad* preaching and teaching. Martin Luther was well aware of the central importance of the languages. His counsel to preachers was: "While a preacher may preach Christ with edification though he may be unable to read the Scriptures in the originals, he cannot expound or maintain their teaching against the heretics without this indispensable knowledge."[6]

Is that position biblical? Absolutely. As we'll make reference to on December 19, after seventy years of captivity in Babylon, most of the Israelites no longer spoke Hebrew, but rather Aramaic. When the Hebrew Scriptures were read, therefore, it was necessary for Ezra and the other scribes not only to "read in the book in the law of God distinctly," but also to "[give] the sense, and [cause] them to understand the reading" (Neh. 8:8). That is precisely what expository preaching involves, and a basic knowledge of the languages is absolutely essential to that end.

Each day of the year, therefore, we will examine a particular Greek word by first presenting a brief word study and then a practical application to make that word real in your life. For reinforcement, each day also includes other related verses that you can study on your own ("Scriptures for Study"). Finally, we would encourage you to use each day's study to generate "promptings for prayer." Meditate on each day's study and allow the Holy Spirit to prompt you in the four basic aspects of prayer: thanksgiving, praise, self-examination, and petition as emphasized in "The Model Prayer" in Matthew 6:9–13 (see also May 28–29 for a study of prayer).

It has been my desire for many years to write a daily devotional that would not only contain deep spiritual Truth but also be easy to read. In our day of relativism, the absolutes of God's Word (and *words*) are desperately needed. I pray that this book will bless your heart, enrich your mind, stir your soul, and empower your life. It should prove useful to pastors, teachers, and all Christian believers who desire a deeper understanding and application of "God's *words*."

Nothing frustrates a writer more than not being able to find the words that will precisely express his thoughts or feelings, but that is the case here. Words simply fail to convey what the writing of this book has meant to me. It's been one of the greatest joys of my life and one of the most profitable exercises of my ministry for our Lord. I pray it will likewise be a joy and profit to you. Most of all I pray:

εἰς ἔπαινον δόξης τῆς χάριτος αὐτοῦ

(eis epainon doxēs tēs charitos autou)

"To the praise of (the) glory of the grace of him. . . ."—Eph. 1:6

Conventions and Abbreviations

ASV – *American Standard Version* (1901)

AV – *Authorized King James Version* (unless noted otherwise, all Scripture quotations are taken from the AV).

Bold text – a primary word examined in a daily reading.

CEV – *Contemporary English Version*

Classical (ancient or secular) Greek – Greek prior to New Testament times. References to that include, for example, the Greek used by Plato (c. 427–435 BC) and the Greek of the poet Homer (eighth-century BC), who is famous for his epic poems, *The Illiad* and *The Odyssey*.

ESV – *English Standard Version*

GWT – *God's Word Translation*

NASB – *New American Standard Bible*

NCV – *New Century Version*

NKJV – *New King James Version*

NIV – *New International Version*

NLT – *New Living Translation*

NRSV – *New Revised Standard Version*

NT – New Testament

OT – Old Testament

Septuagint – the Greek translation of the Hebrew OT; translated in the third and second centuries BC, probably in Alexandria, for the Library of Ptolemy Philadelphus, king of Egypt, by a delegation of seventy Jewish scholars; hence the name *Septuagint* (seventy), and the use of the abbreviation LXX.

Westminster Seminary, Harvard, and Yale educated textual scholar Edward F. Hills well sums up the significance of the LXX to the NT student: "From Alexandria the use of the Septuagint rapidly spread until in the days of the Apostles it was read everywhere in the synagogues of the Greek-speaking Jews outside of Palestine. Then, at length, converts from these Greek-speaking synagogues brought their Septuagint with them into the Christian Church. When one studies the Old Testament quotations in the New Testament, one is struck by the inspired wisdom which the Apostles exhibited in their attitude toward the Septuagint. On the one hand, they did not invariably set this version aside and make new translations from the Hebrew. Such an emphasis on the Hebrew would have been harmful to the gentile churches which had just been formed. It would have brought these gentile Christians into a position of dependence upon the unbelieving Jewish rabbis, on whose learning they would have been obliged to rely for an understanding of the Hebrew Old Testament. But on the other hand, the Apostles did not quote from the Septuagint invariably and thus encourage the notion that this Greek translation was equal to the Hebrew Old Testament in authority. Instead, they walked the middle way between these two extremes. Sometimes they cited the Septuagint verbatim, even when it departed from the Hebrew in non-essential ways, and sometimes they made their own translation directly from the Hebrew or used their knowledge of Hebrew to improve the rendering of the Septuagint."

Hills goes on to write how the LXX applies to the controversy of Bible translations: "Do we believing Bible Students 'worship' the King James Version? Do we regard it as inspired, just as the ancient Jewish philosopher Philo (d. 42 AD) and many early Christians regarded the Septuagint as inspired? Or do we claim the same supremacy for the King James Version that Roman Catholics claim for the Latin Vulgate? Do we magnify its authority above that of the Hebrew and Greek Old and New Testament Scriptures? We have often been accused of such excessive veneration for the King James Version, but these accusations are false. In regard to Bible versions we follow the example of Christ's Apostles. We adopt the same attitude toward the King James Version that they maintained toward the Septuagint. . . . Just as they recognized the Septuagint as the providentially appointed translation of the Hebrew Old Testament into Greek, so we recognize the King James Version and the other great historic translations of the holy Scriptures as providentially approved. Hence we receive the King James Version as the providentially appointed English Bible. Admittedly this venerable version is not absolutely perfect, but it is trustworthy. No Bible-believing Christian who relies upon it will ever be led astray. But it is just the opposite with modern versions. They are untrustworthy, and they do lead Bible-believing Christians astray" (*The King James Version Defended* [Des Moines: The Christian Research Press, 1956, 1973, 1984], pp. 229-230).

(Strong's Number) – For easy cross-referencing to many Greek tools, Greek and Hebrew words in the readings also include the universally used Strong's number enclosed in parentheses. An "H" following a number indicates a reference to a Hebrew word.

Greek Pronunciation Guide

Single Vowel Sounds

Name	Transliteration	Pronunciation
alpha	*a*	a in father
bēta	*b*	b in baboon
gamma	*g*	g in gag
delta	*d*	d in dawdle
epsilon	*e*	e in egg
zēta	*z*	z in zoo
ēta	*ē*	a in gate
thēta	*th*	th in thug
iōta	*i*	i in picnic
kappa	*k*	k in kumquat
lambda	*l*	l in lump
mu	*m*	m in mud
nu	*n*	n in nonsense
xi	*x*	x in vex
omicron	*o*	ough in ought
pi	*p*	p in pepper
rho	*r*	r in rarity
sigma	*s*	s in success
tau	*t*	t in tight
upsilon	*u*	u in full
phi	*ph*	ph in phosphorus
chi	*ch*	ch in German ach, ich
psi	*ps*	ps in tipsy
ōmega	*ō*	o in oaf

Double Vowel (Diphthong) Sounds

Name	Transliteration	Pronunciation
alpha+iōta	*ai*	as in hair
alpha+upsilon	*au*	as in waft or lava
epsilon+iōta	*ei*	as in see
epsilon+upsilon	*eu*	as effort or every
ēta+upsilon	*ēu*	as in reef or sleeve
omicron+iōta	*oi*	as in see
omicron+upsilon	*ou*	as in group
upsilon+iōta	*ui*	as in see

Consonant Combinations

Name	Transliteration	Pronunciation
gamma+gamma	*gg*	as in go
gamma+kappa	*hk*	as in go
gamma+chi	*gch*	as in ghost

What Thy Word Has for Me

(A Sonnet of Prayer)

Father, may I seek Thy beloved face
    in the early hours of the morning;
May Thy written Word I ever embrace
    with a loving fervor all-absorbing.
Is there an example I should follow
    as I travel along life's troubled way?
Is there an error I should overthrow,
    or is there a command I should obey?
Or perhaps there is merely a new thought
    about Thy mighty person and power,
Which having not as yet pondered or sought,
    I now meditate hour-by-hour.
Oh, Father, may I every day see
    What Thy blessed, Holy Word has for me.

New Man

kainos anthropos

In keeping with the start of a new year, nothing could be more appropriate than to consider what the apostle Paul calls the **new man** (Eph. 2:15; 4:24). The two Greek words are *kainos anthropos*, and they are truly significant.

One word translated **new** is *neos* (3501), which "refers to something new in *time*, something that recently has come into existence." The one here, however, is *kainos* (2537), which "refers to something new in *quality*," as it would be distinguished from something that is old and worn out.[7] This word is used, for example, to refer to the "new tomb" in which Joseph of Arimathea laid the body of Jesus (Matt. 27:60). It was not a new tomb that had recently been hewn from the rock (*neos*), rather one that had never been used and was therefore new in the sense of quality.

Man is not the Greek *anēr* (435, "a male person"), but rather *anthropos* (444), the word that speaks of man as a "species,"[8] man as a race. It also refers not to a mere "part" of a man, but the whole man, every aspect of him.

Putting it all together, the picture is graphic. The new man is something that has not existed before. He has been inwardly transformed, which produces new character and new habits.

Another key verse is 2 Corinthians 5:17: "Therefore if any man be in Christ, he is a new [*kainos*] creature: old things are passed away; behold, all things are become new [*kainos*]." The Christian is, therefore, a "new creature," not new in the sense of *time*—as in the date he received Christ as Savior—rather new in *quality*, a creature that has never existed before, a creature with a new character. (See Mar. 30 for deeper study.)

As you start this new year, fully realize that you are a new man (or "woman"), a new creature in Christ with a new character and a new way of life.

Scriptures for Study: Keeping in mind the difference between *kainos* and *neos*, consider what is new in the following verses: Matthew 26:28; John 13:34; 1 Corinthians 11:25; Hebrews 8:8, 13; 9:15; 2 Peter 3:13.

Adoption

huiothesia

The Eastern concept of adoption goes deeper than our Western concept. Only Paul uses this word in the NT. He no doubt borrowed it from Roman culture since the Jews knew nothing of it.

The Greek *huiothesia* (5206) literally means "son-placing." While a child possessed nothing and had no rights, during the teenage years there was a public ceremony declaring a child to be an official member of the family. After this "son-placing," he had full privileges and responsibilities. This was not necessarily a change in *relationship*—for a Roman father could be just as loving as any other father, and no doubt many fathers had a close relationship with their children. Rather what we see here is a change in *position*. He was no longer a *child*; he was a *son*.

Adoption also occurred between a man and a child *who was not his by birth*. Augustus Caesar (the Roman ruler at the time of Christ), for example, was adopted. His original name was Octavian, the son of Atia, the niece of Julius Caesar, and thereby Caesar's grandnephew. Octavian was eighteen years old when Caesar was assassinated (March 15, 44 BC), who in his will adopted Octavian, bestowing upon him the official name of Gaius Julius Caesar. The Senate conferred the honored title "Augustus" (The Exalted) on him in 27 BC.

An adopted person was in a true sense "a new person," legally and practically. He had all the rights of a son by birth and even any old debts were cancelled.

That is the picture of the adopted child of God. We were of our father the devil (John 8:44; 1 John 3:8–10). Under him we were, indeed, slaves, slaves to sin, under a sentence of death, already dead in trespasses and sins (Eph. 2:1–3). But we have been adopted into the family of God. We are members of a new family, all the old debts are paid, and we are new people with a new Father.

Scriptures for Study: Because of our adoption, what emotion do we need never feel again, according to Romans 8:15? 🕮 In Ephesians 1:5, what is the basis of our adoption and its result?

Father (1)

patēr

In keeping with yesterday's look at **adoption**, it follows that we should today and tomorrow consider two words translated **Father**. The first is *patēr* (3962), from which are derived English words such as *paternity* and *paternal*. In Greek philosophy it referred to the patriarchal head of the family. Most notably, however, the Jews of the OT saw five basic principles concerning God's Fatherhood.

First, they saw God's Fatherhood in terms of His begetting. 1 Chronicles 29:10 gives Him a title, "Lord God of Israel our Father," and views Him as the One Who has begotten the nations.

Second, OT Jews saw God's Fatherhood in terms of His nearness to them. They saw that, as a Father, He is closer than any relative or friend. In Psalm 68, God is viewed riding through the clouds with His 20,000 chariots and angels. But then the psalmist pulls back from this mighty grandeur to view the personal thrust—"a father of the fatherless" (v. 5). What a contrast!

Third, OT Jews saw God's Fatherhood in terms of His loving grace. The Jews saw God's Fatherhood as something forgiving, tenderhearted, merciful, and gracious. "Like as a father pitieth his children, so the Lord pitieth them that fear him" (Ps. 103:13).

Fourth, OT Jews saw God's Fatherhood in terms of His guidance. Jeremiah wrote, "They shall come with weeping, and with supplications will I lead them: I will cause them to walk by the rivers of waters in a straight way, wherein they shall not stumble: for I am a father to Israel" (Jer. 31:9).

While those first four views might on the surface seem to sentimentalize God, the fifth view proves that that was not the case with the Jews.

Fifth, OT Jews saw God's Fatherhood in terms of their obedience to Him. Here is the capstone, the view that balances the others. After much rebellion and corruption, Moses said to Israel: "Do ye thus requite the Lord? . . . Is not he thy father that hath brought thee?" (Deut. 32:6). "After all that God has done for you," Moses thunders, "this is how you repay Him? You dare to rebel and disobey His Word?"

Those views serve as great reminders of how we view our Heavenly Father.

Scriptures for Study: How many times does the word **Father** appear in Matthew 6? 🕮 What observations can you make from studying them?

Father (2)

Abba

In spite of the great view OT Jews had of God as a **Father**, tragically they lost sight of the intimacy of relationship between God and His people. By Jesus' day God's Fatherhood was thought of more in terms of His overall care for Israel; the intimacy of personal relationship was gone. It even became blasphemous to mention His name—Yahweh.

Abba (5) is actually from the Aramaic *'ab* (2H). While the Greek *patēr* (3962) is usually used to translate *abba*, *abba* itself appears three times in the NT (Mark 14:36; Rom. 8:15; Gal. 4:6). It was used among Jews as the familiar term children used for their fathers, and is used even today in Hebrew speaking families, not only by small children but by adult sons and daughters. An unfortunate English equivalent that has been popularized today is "Daddy." This term has taken on a too sentimental tone and has given way to a somewhat "buddy-buddy" relationship with God. More precisely it means, "my father," "Father, my Father," or "Dear Father," which emphasize the necessity of reverence. Historically, in fact, the childish word (*daddy*) receded.

That provides us with both a comfort and a challenge.

First, the comfort is that we do have an intimacy with the Father. The Jews of Jesus' day would never have used this term, thinking it too familiar and inappropriate. But it's quite possible that Jesus used it often, which would have astounded the Jews. He demonstrated that the true believer, as a son or daughter, does, indeed, have an intimate relationship with the Father. Paul captured this when he, too, used the term.

Second, *abba* also provides a challenge. While there certainly is an *intimacy* with the Father, there must also be a *respect* for who He is. This was, of course, the expression the Lord Jesus used as He prayed in the Garden of Gethsemane (Mark 14:36), so both intimacy and respect are present. Yes, our Lord had an intimate relationship with the Father and made requests of Him, but there was still respect and reverence as He came into submission to the Father's will. This challenges us to be very careful not to barge into God's presence demanding our desires. (We'll continue this theme over the next three days.)

Scriptures for Study: Read Romans 8:15 again (see Jan. 2) and Galatians 4:6. 📖 What makes the *abba* relationship possible?

Boldness

parrēsia

Ephesians 3:12–13 declares: "In whom we have boldness and access with confidence by the faith of him. Wherefore I desire that ye faint not at my tribulations for you, which is your glory." In a larger context on prayer (vv. 12–21), Paul gives us here three basic attitudes concerning prayer. The first is **boldness** (*parrēsia*, 3954).

In Classical Greek this word was important in political situations. It meant "the right to say anything, an openness to truth, candor." Taken to extremes, it took on the negative sense of "insolence," being disrespectful. This word is used some thirty-one times in the NT and is used for the speech of the Lord Jesus, the apostles, and other believers. In each case, the basic idea was that the person had the right to speak and spoke the truth openly. The word is actually made up of two words, *pas* (3956, "all") and *rēsis* (not in NT; "the act of speaking"), so the most literal idea is "to tell all." In other words, we can come before our Father with total freedom of speech, pour out our hearts, and tell him everything. What a blessed privilege God has granted us!

It is because of Jesus Christ that we can speak to God without fear and may speak openly and candidly. Hebrews 4:14–16 and 10:19 are most vivid. In Judaism only the High Priest could enter God's presence in the Holy of Holies, and he could only do so once a year on the Day of Atonement. But now, because of the blood of Christ, we can come directly to God and speak openly to him at any time.

At this point we must sound a warning: *boldness* does not mean *insolence* (the negative sense of *parrēsia*). There is a growing disrespect of God in today's various teachings on prayer. While boldness *does* mean that we need not have any inhibitions as we come before God, we must still never forget that God is God. The "buddy-buddy" attitude that many have of God and man is truly blasphemous as it brings God down to man's level. God must be respected and worshiped as God. He is not our "buddy" or our "pal"; He is our Father and our God. We may indeed come before Him openly, candidly, and without fear, but we must also come before Him in reverence, respect, and worship.

Scriptures for Study: Read Hebrews 4:14–16. What two results come from boldness in prayer? 🕮 Read Acts 4:31. What other activity are we to do with boldness?

Access

prosagōgē

The second basic attitude of prayer in Ephesians 3:12–13 is **access**. The Greek is *prosagōgē* (4318), which means "to open a way of access" and appears only here and in two other places in the NT (Eph. 2:18 and Rom. 5:2). A similar word was used in ancient times to describe a person who gave someone else admittance to see the king. The person who wanted to see the king had no right to do so; rather someone else had to give him admittance, had to make the introduction. So, while we have no *right* to come before God (how arrogant!), we have been granted the *privilege* of doing so.

To go one step deeper, it's significant that the Greek text has the definite article ("the") before both *boldness* and *access*.[9] Literally, the verse says, "In whom we have *the* boldness and *the* access." Only the true Christian has the distinct privilege to come before God. Other religions claim they have access to God, but only those who come through Christ can truly do so (John 14:6).

With all that in mind, we must also expand our warning from yesterday: *boldness* does not mean *insolence*, and *access* does not mean *impetuosity*. To be impetuous means to be impulsive, doing things hurriedly, or rushing about. Many of us are guilty of hastily and hurriedly coming before the Lord in prayer. We often rush before Him and ask, or even demand, something from Him. And, may we say again, often we think we have a right to be before Him.

May we cease such dreadful actions! May we see that we have no right to come before God, but rather we have a marvelous privilege granted us by the introduction of our Savior. Let us never again rush into His presence, hurriedly making our desires known. Rather, in our communion with Him, let us come quietly, humbly, slowly, and deliberately before Him.

Scriptures for Study: Read Ephesians 2:18 and Romans 5:2. Who gives us our "introduction" to the Father?

Confidence

pepoithēsis

The third basic attitude of prayer in Ephesians 3:12–13 is **confidence**. The Greek (*pepoithēsis*, 4006) gives the idea of "trust, confidence, and total persuasion." All these ideas are vitally important. In what are we to place our trust and confidence? About what are we totally persuaded? *We are totally persuaded that we can come to the Father, trust Him to do His will, and be confident of the result.* Note, this is not *our* will, but *God's* will (John 14:13; 1 John 5:14–15).

Prayer is, indeed, a mystery that we do not *understand*, but it's also a mystery that we know *works*. Exactly how prayer works we do not know, but we do know that God uses it. Does something depend upon my praying for it? No. It depends upon the sovereignty of God. Does God still use prayer? Yes. "But I don't understand," you say. Neither do I, but God does. All we need to know is that it is all based upon God's sovereignty, glory, and love for His children.

This completes the warning from our last two studies: *boldness* does not mean *insolence*, *access* does not mean *impetuosity*, and *confidence* does not mean *arrogance*. There is today, without doubt, a lot of arrogant prayer. There are many who twist verses such as Philippians 4:13: "I can do all things through Christ which strengtheneth me." Many bend the meaning of the verse to say: "I can do anything I want because Christ gives me the strength," when what it proclaims is that we shall always be given the power to do what God desires of us. Many today turn to this verse, and others, to prove their "self-image" teaching and their "Christian success-motivation" philosophies. But all that is nothing but humanistic arrogance with a Christian label pasted on it. Our trust and confidence must never lie in "self." Rather our trust and confidence lies only in Christ.

Scriptures for Study: According to Philippians 3:3–4, in what do we not have confidence? 🕮 In 1 John 5:14, what confidence do we have? 🕮 See May 28–31 for more on prayer.

Faint

ekkakeō

In light of the **boldness, access,** and **confidence** that we examined in the last three days, Ephesians 3:13 offers an example of that truth: "Wherefore I desire that ye faint not at my tribulations for you, which is your glory."

Paul endured tremendous persecution, as he outlines in 2 Corinthians 11:23–33. As he wrote the letter to the Ephesians, in fact, he was under house arrest in Rome. He knew that some believers might become fearful by his extended imprisonment. He, therefore, encourages them not to **faint**. Sadly, some modern translations miss the real point of *ekkakeō* (1573) by translating it as "discouraged" (NIV) or "lose heart" (NASB and NKJV). Both of those are weaker than the actual meaning, "to turn out to be a coward, to lose one's courage, to faint or despond in view of trial,"[10] or even stronger, "to be utterly spiritless."[11] It's one thing to be *discouraged*, but quite another to faint in *despondency*.

With those words, then, Paul challenges believers not to faint, not to sink into despondency, not to become so dispirited and cowardly that they just quit. *Ekkakeō* is also used in the Septuagint in such verses as Proverbs 24:10: "If thou faint in the day of adversity, thy strength is small." So, how can we not faint? By being confident in the Lord, trusting in His sovereignty, trusting in the fact that God is using even adversity to bring about His plan and purpose.

What confidence Paul had in God! What if Paul had relied on self-confidence? What would the result have been if Paul had said, "I'll just keep a stiff upper lip and willpower will see me through?" What person could go to his death armed only with that attitude? Likewise, how could that early Reformer John Huss say, "You need not tie my hands to the stake; I will stand in the flames on my own?" It is because Paul, Huss, and many others had a power far beyond their own.

Every one of us gets discouraged at some point in our Christian walk, even to the point of total despondency. But, as Paul goes on to say, trials are actually "our glory." As he wrote to the Romans: "For I reckon that the sufferings of this present time are not worthy to be compared with the glory which shall be revealed in us" (Rom. 8:18). To memorize that verse is to transform our Christian living.

Scriptures for Study: Read Luke 18:1. What activity keeps us from fainting? 🕮 What reason for not fainting does Paul give in 2 Corinthians 4:15–16?

Saint

hagios

How right Warren Wiersbe is when he writes, "No word in the NT has suffered more than this word *saint.* Even the dictionary defines a *saint* as a 'person officially recognized for holiness of life.'"[12]

In secular Greek the word *hagios* (40) meant "to stand in awe of or be devoted to the gods." This word came right out of pagan Greek religion, but Paul had to use it since there was no other word to use. So, the word was originally used of a person who was devoted to a god. One such as that was looked upon as a "holy one" or a "holy man."

That view is true of Roman Catholicism, which teaches that to become a "saint," one first has to die. The person is then nominated for the position, after which one or more "judicial inquiries" take place, where the nominating advocate pleads the virtues of the nominee and gives proof of his or her worthiness. One such proof is that the nominee had to be responsible for at least two (and, in some cases, as many as four) miracles. Then his life is examined to see if it was "holy enough to be officially recognized by canonization." But all that flies in the face of Scripture and denies a fundamental principal of being a Christian.

Paul, by the inspiration of the Holy Spirit, lifted the word *hagios* to a new level of meaning: "to set apart or be separate." The same word is also translated *holy* and *sanctification.* While some say a saint is *dead*, God says a saint is *alive.* Being a saint is not a matter of *achievement* or *performance*; it is a matter of *position.* It's not based on what we have *done*, but who we *are* in Christ. It's not dependent upon *our works*, but upon *His grace.*

We can probably safely assume that **saint** was Paul's favorite term for the Christian since he used it some *forty-two times* in his epistles. How he loved that word! He loved saying, "Every one of you who has trusted Christ as Savior and Lord is a saint, one who has been set apart."

Scriptures for Study: Read the following verses: Acts 26:10; Romans 8:26–27; 15:25–26; 1 Corinthians 6:2; Ephesians 4:12. What are the saints of God receiving in each instance?

Sufficiency

hikanos

In our day, man views himself as the measure of all things. We see it everywhere. Man is self-sufficient, self-directed, self-motivated, and self-centered. All we hear about is man's self-esteem and self-worth. But God says something a little different. Second Corinthians 3:4–5 declares: "And such trust have we through Christ to God-ward: Not that we are sufficient of our selves to think any thing as of ourselves; but our sufficiency is of God."

Paul declares here that he is nothing in himself, that he is insufficient for anything, whether it be ministry or personal living. He says that his **sufficiency** is God alone. The Greek for sufficiency is *hikanos* (2425), which speaks of something being adequate, or large enough. It's used in Matthew 3:11, where John the Baptist declares, "He that cometh after me is mightier than I, whose shoes I am not *worthy* [*hikanos*] to bear" (emphasis added). In the same way, the centurion in Capernaum "sent friends to him, saying unto him, Lord, trouble not thyself: for I am not *worthy* that thou shouldest enter under my roof: Wherefore neither thought I myself *worthy* to come unto thee: but say in a word, and my servant shall be healed" (Luke 7:6–7, emphasis added). How we need this kind of humility and dependency in our day instead of the self-elevating philosophies that have captured the church.

What a challenge that is! May we stop trying to be sufficient in ourselves. Strength awaits us in Christ alone. Instead of self-sufficiency, may we have a *Christ*-sufficiency. Instead of self-direction, may we seek a *Christ*-direction. Instead of self-motivation, may we have a *Christ*-motivation. Instead of being self-centered, may we be *Christ*-centered. Instead of having high self-esteem, may we have high *Christ*-esteem. To be in Christ means that *only He is sufficient*.

Scriptures for Study: In 1 Corinthians 15:9, how did Paul view himself ("meet" is *hikanos*). 📖 In 2 Timothy 2:2, what should a pastor be "able" (*hikanos*) to do?

Peace

eirēnē

The Greek *eirēnē* (1515) appears some ninety-three times in the NT and means, as it did in the time of Homer, "a state of tranquility; the opposite of rage and war." This word is related to the Hebrew word *shalom* (7965H), a common Hebrew greeting, which is translated *eirēnē* over 250 times in the Septuagint. *Shalom*, however, means not so much the opposite of war but the opposite of any disturbance in the tranquility of God's people. So when Paul uses this word, for example, in Ephesians 2:14—"For [Christ] is our peace"—he is saying that because of Christ the Christian has tranquility and harmony.

In that same verse, however, is another truth, that *Christ is actually* ***peace*** *itself.* The most literal translation of Ephesians 2:14 is, "For He Himself is the peace of us." Men hold "peace-talks," where they try to "achieve" peace, "promote" peace, and "enact" peace. But the Lord Jesus Christ *is* peace. It's also significant that Paul did not use the Greek word *eirēnopoios* (1518), which means "peacemaker." What a great truth! There are many peacemakers today, those who try in vain to bring peace to the world. But the Lord Jesus is far more than a "peacemaker;" He is peace.

This is further indicated by the fact that *eirēnē* is preceded by the definite article ("the"). Christ is "*the* peace," the one and the only peace there is. According to the *Canadian Army Journal*, a former president of the Norwegian Academy of Sciences, aided by historians from England, Egypt, Germany, and India, came up with some startling facts and figures. Since 3600 BC, the world has known only 292 years of peace. During that period, there have been 14,531 wars, large and small, in which 3,640,000,000 people have been killed. The monetary value of the destruction would pay for a golden belt around the world 97.2 miles in width and about thirty-three feet thick. Why can't man ever achieve peace outside of Christ? *Because there isn't any peace outside of Christ!*

Scriptures for Study: Read Romans 5:1 and Philippians 4:6–7. What are the two major kinds of peace indicated by the prepositions? 🕮 As Colossians 3:15 commands, where should peace rule?

Blessed

makarios

There are two words commonly translated **blessed** in the Greek NT. One such word is *makarios* (3107), which appears some forty-nine times, and which our Lord used nine times in the Beatitudes (Matt. 5:3–11). Many preachers and teachers come to this word, say it means "happy," and then just move on. But this word means *much* more. The word *happy*, in fact, comes from the Middle English *hap*, which in turn comes from the Old Norse *happ*, meaning "good luck."

First, *makarios* speaks of "contentedness." The idea is an inward contentedness that is not affected by circumstances. This is indeed the kind of happiness and contentedness that God desires for His children—a state of joy and wellbeing that does not depend upon physical, temporary circumstances (cf. Phil. 4:11–13). This certainly deepens the meaning of our Lord's words, "It is more blessed to give than to receive" (Acts 20:35).

Second, *makarios* goes even deeper, as Greek scholar Spiros Zodhiates points out, to refer to "possessing the favor of God, that state of being marked by fullness from God."[13] As Romans 4:7–8 declares, "Blessed are they whose iniquities are forgiven, and whose sins are covered. Blessed is the man to whom the Lord will not impute sin." What contentedness and fullness that is!

Third, deeper still, one who is blessed is "one who becomes partaker of God's nature through faith in Christ" (see 2 Pet. 1:4). Zodhiates again offers, "To be *makarios*, blessed, is equivalent to having God's Kingdom within one's heart." Finally he adds, "*Makarios* is the one who is in the world yet independent of the world. His satisfaction comes from God and not from favorable circumstances."[14] Understanding this wonderful word enables us to read the Beatitudes, and many other verses, with a whole new understanding. How all this transcends mere happiness! In the next two days, we'll examine two related words: *hope* and *joy*.

Scriptures for Study: In Titus 2:13, what is the "contented" hope for which the believer is looking? 🕮 In James 1:12 and 25, what two things bring "contentedness"?

Hope

elpis

Consider a moment the concept of **hope** as it's viewed in the world today. Hope expresses a wish or a want, such as, "I sure do hope I get that promotion," or "I sure hope I get that raise," or "I hope we can get that new house we want." There's no certainty in the word as we use it today. The exact opposite, however, is true in Scripture. The Greek *elpis* (1680) speaks of a "desire of some good with expectation of obtaining it." Likewise, the verb *elpizō* (1679) means "to expect with desire."[15] So *hope always means certainty*; it expresses an attitude of *absolute assurance* and *rest* in that assurance.

It's amazing that Greek philosophy is glorified in the minds of many people when in truth it displays the depths of despair. As one Greek authority observes, "Living hope as a fundamental religious attitude was unknown in Greek culture," as "Theognis said, 'As long as you live by honoring the gods, hold on to hope!'" Likewise, "Seneca called hope the definition of 'an uncertain good.'"[16] In the Homeric Hymns of the eighth century BC, the assembly of Olympus is charmed by the Muses who sing "of the deathless gifts of the gods and the sorrows of men, even all that they endure by the will of the immortals, living heedless and helpless, nor can they find a cure for death, nor a defence against old age."[17]

Why such despair? Because without Christ, there is no hope (Eph. 2:12). First Corinthians 15:19 is wonderfully significant. Paul says, "If in this life only we have hope in Christ, we are of all men most miserable." Truly our hope (certainty) of resurrection and eternal life are only in Christ. First Thessalonians 5:8 also speaks of "the hope of salvation," which declares our salvation to be absolutely certain. Without that, men are miserable indeed. As the old hymn declares:

My hope is built on nothing less
Than Jesus' blood and righteousness;
I dare not trust the sweetest frame,
But wholly lean on Jesus' Name.
On Christ the Solid Rock, I stand;
All other ground is sinking sand.

Tomorrow we'll look at a verse that couples hope with **joy**.

Scriptures for Study: What else brings certainty according to Romans 15:4? 🕮 What else does our hope in Christ promise according to Colossians 1:27?

Joy

chara

The people of this world look in many ways to experience what they think is **joy**. No matter what they try, however, they manage only to capture fleeting moments of "happiness" and "feeling good." In dramatic contrast, the Greek *chara* (5479), which means "gladness and rejoicing," goes infinitely beyond mere human feelings of happiness, joy, or exuberance. In Scripture, especially in Paul's epistles, we discover the paradox that real joy is found even in the midst of pain, suffering, and affliction.

The key to understanding this great truth is that "happiness" is temporary, while joy is absolute. I have never forgotten what I once heard J. Sidlow Baxter say many years ago: "When happenings happen to happen happily, you have happiness; when happenings happen to happen unhappily, you have unhappiness; happiness, then, is merely circumstantial happenness. But joy is independent of circumstances."

In light of yesterday's look at **hope**, Romans 15:13 couples hope with joy: "Now the God of hope fill you with all joy and peace in believing, that ye may abound in hope, through the power of the Holy Ghost." How is joy possible? Only through hope, that is, *certainty*. Joy is impossible when everything around us is uncertain and we live by that uncertainty.

Philippians is especially significant, for joy is its main theme. *Writing from prison*, Paul uses *chara* no less than five times (1:4; 1:25; 2:2; 2:29 ["gladness"]; 4:1). Additionally, he uses several other words to express his joy, which are variously translated "rejoice" (eight times) and "glad" (three times). As one commentator puts it, "In Philippians joy is thus a continuous defiant *nevertheless*." No matter what happens, joy never *forgets*, never *fades*, and never *fails*. Why? Because our joy is in the Lord.

Scriptures for Study: In what do we have hope and joy according to 1 Thessalonians 2:19? 🕮 Like Philippians, what does James 1:2 encourage us to do?

Election

Eklegō (eklektos)

Here is a word that causes all kinds of troubles, but that's the last thing it should do. It is actually one of the most soothing words (and doctrines) of the Bible. The Greek for **election** (or "chosen" in verses such as Eph. 1:4) is a wonderful word, indeed. The verb is *eklegomai*, (1586; noun *eklektos*, 1588), which means "to pick or choose out for oneself." Most importantly, in Ephesians 1:4—"According as he hath chosen us in him before the foundation of the world, that we should be holy and without blame before him in love"—this word is in the aorist tense and the middle voice. The aorist tense is used for simple, undefined action. When used in the indicative mood, as it is here, it usually denotes a simple act occurring in the past.

We can best understand the middle voice by contrasting it with active and passive voice. While the active voice pictures the subject of the verb doing the acting, and the passive voice pictures the subject being acted upon, the middle voice pictures the subject acting in its own interest, that is, it receives the benefit of the action. So, the aorist middle here shows that God did the choosing independently in the past and did so *primarily* for His own interest, that is, His glory. As J. Sidlow Baxter puts it: "Think of it—chosen *out of* the world, *once for all*, to be God's *own* as a peculiar treasure!"[18] Verses 6, 12, and 14 bear this out, for they all emphasize the words "*His* glory."

Another important point concerning *eklegō* is that while it speaks of choosing for oneself, it does *not* necessarily imply the rejection of what is not chosen. A common criticism of the doctrine of election is that God's choosing of certain ones to salvation means that He, therefore, chooses the rest to condemnation. But there is no foundation for that accusation. Nowhere does the Word of God teach that God chooses (or "predestines") unbelievers to eternal damnation (what some call "double-predestination"). A person goes to hell for one reason: he rejects God and His way of salvation. A person is condemned by his own unbelief, not God's predestination.

While there certainly are some puzzling aspects of the doctrine of election, it is nonetheless a comfort to know that God chose us for Himself "before the foundation of the world, that we should be holy and without blame before him in love."

Scriptures for Study: Because we are God's chosen ones, what behavior should characterize our living (Col. 3:12–13)? 🕮 In the Parable of the Judge (Luke 18:1–8), what will God do for the elect who have suffered for Him?

Predestination

proorizō

Here is another term that causes many people to become defensive. When the term is mentioned, some react with words such as, "Oh, that whole **predestination** thing. Let's not go there!" But we do, indeed, need to "go there," for there we find wondrous truth.

Proorizō (4309) is a fascinating word. Its simple meaning is "to designate before," but we see the real depth of it in the fact that it's a compound word. *Pro* (4253), of course, means "beforehand," but *horizō* (3724) speaks of a "boundary or limit," and is actually where our English word *horizon* comes from. So, just as the horizon marks a limit between what we can and can't see, God has placed us within a certain limit, a certain "horizon." He has put us in a place where we can see and comprehend many things but where many other things are hidden from our sight and understanding, many things that are beyond our horizon. Further, even if we walk closer to the horizon, and understand things we never understood before, a new horizon appears. We will never understand it all this side of heaven.

This word graphically demonstrates that *God has marked out something for each of His elect; He has marked out a destiny*. Much of that destiny is hidden from us; it is beyond the horizon. But, praise be to God, he reveals more of it with each new step we take toward it.

What is that destiny? What is that purpose? While we don't know it all, we do know some of it. The primary purpose in God's predestination is "that [Christ] might be the firstborn among many brethren" (Rom. 8:29), that is, that *Christ* might be made preeminent. Scripture reveals that the firstborn always had preeminence. God's ultimate object, therefore, is to glorify His Son. Further, Ephesians 1:5 likewise tells us that God predestined us to **adoption** (see Jan. 2), making us Christ's brethren. Think of it! Each of us is either a brother or sister to our dear Savior. Then in Ephesians 1:11 we read that we are predestined to an inheritance, that is, spiritual riches, in Christ. *That* is our destiny.

So, we would submit that no controversy is warranted. *Predestination is simply God's marking out a destiny befitting His foreknown people.*

Scriptures for Study: In Acts 4:26–28, what events did God determine to occur? 🕮 In 1 Corinthians 2:1–8, what was Paul proclaiming that was ordained before the world began?

Foreknowledge

proginōskō

Here is one more of those "controversial" terms, but there is again no need for debate. A common belief is that **foreknowledge** simply means "prior knowledge," just knowing something before it happens. But that simply is not so. The Greek word *proginōskō* (4267) also carries the idea of *foreordination*.

A good example is found in Acts 2:23, where Peter is preaching on the Day of Pentecost and reminding the Jews about Jesus: "Him, being delivered by the *determinate counsel and foreknowledge* of God, ye have taken, and by wicked hands have crucified and slain." Now, is Peter saying that God foreknew in eternity past that Christ would die on the cross? Is he saying that God simply looked down through time and said, "Oh, yes, I see that they will put my Son to death." Obviously not. What Peter is saying is that Christ died on the cross because God purposefully sent Him to do so. The construction of the verse further bears this out. "Determinate" is from *horizō* (which we studied yesterday), and "counsel" is from *boulē* (1012), which in Classical Greek referred to an officially convened, decision-making council. Therefore, God, who is His own "decision-making council," purposefully set up boundaries in which men could act.

Deeper and more blessed, however, is that the root *ginōskō* means "to know by experience" and often is practically synonymous with love and intimacy. Matthew 1:25, for example, says that Joseph "did not know" Mary before Jesus was born, that is, they had not yet been physically intimate. Jesus used the same word in Matthew 7:23 where He speaks of those who have professed to be believers but are not: "And then will I profess unto them, *I never knew you*: depart from me, ye that work iniquity" (emphasis added).

This is exactly what we see in 1 Peter 1:1–2: "Peter, an apostle of Jesus Christ, to the strangers scattered throughout Pontus, Galatia, Cappadocia, Asia, and Bithynia, Elect according to the foreknowledge of God the Father." Some insist this just means prior knowledge, but now notice verse 20: "[Christ] verily was *foreordained* before the foundation of the world, but was manifest in these last times for you." This is significant because the Greek for *foreordained* is the same word for *foreknowledge* in verse 2. Therefore, it's obvious that this doesn't mean that God simply foresaw that Christ would be manifested. Rather, He was, as we are, foreordained and foreknown by *an intimate relationship before the foundation of the world*. What a staggering truth!

Scriptures for Study: In Romans 8:29–30, which action of God is first in the progression? In light of today's study, how does that action strike you? 📖 In Romans 11:1–24, what people has God not "cast away"? What will He do in the future?

Blameless

amōmos

Here is a word that provides us with a practical feature of what "holy living" means. Ephesians 1:4 declares, "According as he hath chosen us in him before the foundation of the world, that we should be holy and without blame before him in love." In light of our last three studies (especially Jan. 15), the reason God saves us is to make us holy, and the best way to test ourselves is see if we are "without blame," that is, **blameless**.

The Greek *amōmos* (299) is derived from the root *mōmos* (3470), "spot, blemish," and the prefix *a* (1), the "alpha-negative" (see Apr. 1) that means "without." It, therefore, means "without blemish; spotless; free from faultiness." In Classical Greek, it means that nothing is amiss in a sacrifice that would render it unworthy. Likewise, it's used in the Septuagint to show that a sacrificial animal was to have no spot or blemish (e.g., Lev. 22:21). That, then, is how we are to live—pure in attitude and action. The word shows that a Christian lives above reproach; that is, no one can look at his life and see an unholy, ungodly life.

That is the force of 1 Peter 1:16: "Be ye holy; for I am holy." Yes, that is a tall order. Quoting Leviticus 11:44–45, Peter commands that we be holy just as God is holy. Why did God choose us in Christ before the foundation of the world? So we *could* be and *would* be holy in *position* and *practice*.

We're reminded of those nowadays who preach the false Gospel of "easy-believism" without an emphasis on sin. *But sin is the issue*. The point of salvation is to make us holy.

Why must we live holy? Because our whole lives are lived before God; we are an open book "before Him," which is the Greek *katenōpion autou*, which literally means "to see down in." This pictures the searching, penetrating gaze of the Spirit of God into our lives. But that is not so much negative as it is positive. Its greatest significance is the intended closeness and intimacy with the Father that He desires for us to have. So, God not only has *made* us holy; He has also given us the capacity to *live* holy. He does not expect us to do it in the flesh; rather He empowers us to live out holiness by the Spirit.

Scriptures for Study: In Ephesians 5:27, what do the words "without blemish" (*amōmos*) refer to in the future? (See also 1 Thess. 3:13 and Jude 1:24). How does that motivate you to holiness? 📖 In Revelation 14:1–5, who are those who are "without fault?"

Love (1)

agapē

One of the most violent attacks on the doctrine of **election** (see Jan. 15) is the accusation that it is cold and hard and ultimately makes a mockery of the **love** of God. "This view," it is charged, "paints God as sitting on His throne spinning the wheel, arbitrarily picking and choosing people as if He were choosing up sides for a ball game."

On the contrary, in Ephesians 1:4, Paul writes that God "hath chosen us in [Christ] . . . in love," showing us that love is at the very root, the very heart of God's election. Perhaps the best translation of the Greek *agapē* (26) is "a self-emptying self-sacrifice." God does not deal with us only according to His sovereignty and holiness; if He did, we would be hopelessly doomed. He also deals according to love.

That God's election flows from His love is apparent throughout the Scriptures. Why did God choose Israel? "The Lord did not set his love upon you, nor choose you, because ye were more in number than any people; for ye were the fewest of all people: But *because the Lord loved you*" (Deut. 7:7–8, emphasis added). Why did He love that stiff-necked people (Deut. 31:27; Jer. 17:23)? More importantly, why did He love *me*, who is just as stiff-necked, depraved, rebellious, and self-centered? We don't know.

Christian friend, why did God choose you? Because He loves you. Deuteronomy 10:15 declares, "Only the Lord had a delight in thy fathers to love them, and he chose their seed after them, even you above all people, as it is this day." That is clearly implied in John 15:19: "If ye were of the world, the world would love his own: but because ye are not of the world, but I have chosen you out of the world, therefore the world hateth you." But does not even a simple verse such as 1 John 4:19, "We love Him because He first loved us," show us this wonderful truth?

What a blessed truth, indeed! God loved us before the foundation of the world. He loved us according to His gracious purpose, His good pleasure. We'll continue these thoughts tomorrow.

Scriptures for Study: In Romans 5:8, what is the result of God's love? 🕮 What can separate us from that love, according to Romans 8:38–39?

Great Love

polus agapē

Let's go a little deeper into God's *agapē* (26). God's love is often viewed today as some sort of shallow sentimentality, but God's love is deeper than we can even begin to comprehend. When the average person today says "love," they do not even know what they are saying because they do not mean "a self-emptying self-sacrifice." Love today is more "self-gratifying" than "self-emptying."

It's interesting to note that in secular Greek, *agapē* was actually rather colorless. As one Greek authority explains, *agapē* originally carried an element of sympathy and spoke of the love of a person of higher rank for one of a lower rank; it even went so far as to speak of a love that was not self-seeking.[19] But the Lord Jesus transformed the word; it took on the much deeper meaning of being *totally sacrificial*. As the same authority says, "[It] thus creates a new people who will tread the way of self-sacrificing love that [Christ] took."[20] We, therefore, humbly offer the following definition of God's love: "A self-emptying self-sacrifice in which God gave of Himself in the form of His only begotten Son Who gave His life for us."

But Paul is not satisfied with using just *agapē* in Ephesians 2:4; he speaks of God's "***great*** **love** [*pollēn agapēn*] wherewith he loved us." The basic meaning of the Greek *polus* (4183, great) is "much or great." But when used figuratively, as it is here, it conveys the idea of *intensity*.[21] In other words, Paul is not speaking so much of the *volume* of God's love as much as he is its *passion*. Many of us enjoy doing certain things in life; at times we all pursue a hobby or other interest "intensely." But if we could multiply this by infinity, we would even then only scratch the surface of the great love of God.

This truth again immediately begs the question, "Why does God love us?" In all my years of ministry, the only answer I have ever come to is this: *I don't know*. When we look at Ephesians 2:1–3 from the human perspective, there is no reason God should or would love us, but He does. This is not some syrupy sentimentality about "Jesus loving everybody," but rather it is a deep, incomprehensible passion for those who are totally undeserving of love.

Scriptures for Study: Meditate again on the verses studied yesterday. Write down the thoughts that they generate in your heart and mind.

Love (2)

phileō

While English has only a single word for **love**, Greek has four. *Eros* speaks of sexual passion (English "erotic") and never appears in the NT. *Stergō* speaks of mutual love between parents and children, a god and its people, and even a dog for its master, and also is not used in the NT (except for compounds such as *astorgos* [794], Rom. 1:31, and *philostorgos* [5387] Rom. 12:10). *Agapē*, which we've studied already, speaks of sacrificial love.

We turn now to *phileō* (verb, 5368) and *philos* (noun, 5384, see Nov. 18). While there's a little disagreement among scholars of the differences between this and *agapē*, *phileō* seems to be clearly distinct and speaks of esteem, high regard, and tender affection and is more emotional. While passionate, however, it does not imply a loss of reason.[22]

By far, the most vivid example of the difference appears in John 21, where our Lord and Peter speak after Peter's denial and the Lord's resurrection. The picture of Peter is that of a broken man who is ashamed of what he has done. Interestingly, our Lord doesn't rebuke Peter for that or ask why he did it, rather He simply asks his passionate disciple (v. 15), "Peter, do you *agapaō* Me more than these other disciples?" But in his shame, and knowing his Lord could see in his heart, Peter could not bring himself to say that he loved the Lord in an all-giving, sacrificial way, so he answers, "Yea, Lord; thou knowest that I *phileō* thee." In verse 16, Jesus asks again using *agapaō* and Peter again responds with *phileō*.

But then something extraordinary happens (v. 17). The Lord comes down to Peter's level and asks, "Peter, do you *really phileō* Me?" I have always imagined the tears streaming down Peter's face as he answered in his grief and cracking voice, "Lord, thou knowest all things; thou knowest that I *phileō* thee."

A key to understanding this scene is that in all three exchanges, the Lord recommissions Peter to service, telling him to feed His people. The blessing here is that even our tender affection qualifies us for service. As we grow, that affection will turn to *agapē*, as it did in Peter (for he uses *agapaō* in 1 Pet. 1:8).

My dear Christian friend, do you love the Lord? How much?

Scriptures for Study: In 1 Corinthians 16:22, what is to be declared of the person who does not love (*phileō*) the Lord? (see also Feb. 6). 📖 In Revelation 3:19, the Lord does what because He loves (*phileō*) us?

Redemption (1)

agorazō [and] *exagorazō*

Redemption! What a word we have before us today and tomorrow! Here is the word that is, indeed, the heart of our salvation. There are several graphic words in the Greek that precisely describe what salvation involves. One word is *agorazō* (59), which appears thirty-one times and means "to buy." This word is used, for example, in 1 Corinthians 6:20: "For ye are bought with a price: therefore glorify God in your body, and in your spirit, which are God's." Referring to the tribulation saints, Revelation 5:9 declares, "And they sung a new song, saying, Thou art worthy to take the book, and to open the seals thereof: for thou wast slain, and hast redeemed us to God by thy blood out of every kindred, and tongue, and people, and nation."

Another word is *exagorazō* (1805), which occurs only four times, and means "to buy out of." We find this word in Galatians 3:13: "Christ hath redeemed us from the curse of the law, being made a curse for us: for it is written, Cursed is every one that hangeth on a tree."

The source of both of these words is *agora* (58), which means "marketplace" and is the key to understanding redemption. The *agora* was the marketplace where goods were bought and sold, and it is that picture Paul wants to paint. That is where we were outside of Christ—in the marketplace, the slave market of sin. All those verses vividly demonstrate that we were "bought at a price," and therefore no longer belong to ourselves or our father the devil, but are to "glorify God in [our] body, and in [our] spirit, which are God's" (1 Cor. 6:19–20). That is also Paul's point in Galatians 2:20: "I am crucified with Christ: nevertheless I live; yet not I, but Christ liveth in me: and the life which I now live in the flesh I live by the faith of the Son of God, who loved me, and gave himself for me."

Let us rejoice in our redemption! We will look at one other word for redemption tomorrow.

Scriptures for Study: What beautiful picture does *agorazō* ("buyeth" and "bought") paint in Matthew 13:44–46? 📖 In Galatians 4:5, what spiritual reality do we have as a result of being redeemed ("redeem" is *exagorazō*)?

Redemption (2)

apolutrōsis

Continuing our meditations on **redemption**, there is another word that should strike us profoundly. The root of *apolutrōsis* (629) is *lutroō* (3084), which means "to release on receipt of a ransom." The prefix *apo* means "from," which intensifies *lutroō*. One Greek authority tells us that this expresses the *completeness* of our redemption and is one that keeps us from further bondage in the future.[23] In other words, redemption is a once-for-all transaction. We will never be enslaved again.

In our day we don't readily understand the full force of the word redemption, as did Paul's readers. When he uttered this word, they knew *exactly* what he was talking about, for it was rooted in Greek and Roman culture. In NT times, there were approximately six million slaves. Slave-trading was a major business and was an accepted part of society. It was very common, in fact, for a person to have a relative or friend who had been sold into slavery (see **servant**, Feb. 11). A slave could be freed only if someone paid the purchase price and then declared him free. *There was no way the slave could redeem himself.*

So Paul's readers clearly understood what a slave was. A person sold into slavery had no will of his own; he was in bondage; he had nothing. Unlike today, Paul's readers completely understood total depravity because they fully understood slavery. While some people think they have a problem with the doctrine of **election**, what they don't realize is that their real problem is with the doctrine of *depravity* that makes election necessary. Our nature simply does not want to accept the totality of our depravity. But a slave was not "partly free." No, he was a slave. Slavery was such a low position, that for all practical purposes, a slave was "dead."

That is precisely the picture of depravity that is painted in Scripture. As Paul writes in Ephesians 2:1–3, without Christ we "were dead in trespasses and sins" and lived according to "the lusts of our flesh, fulfilling the desires of the flesh and of the mind; and were by nature the children of wrath." In our day, sin has been redefined to mean virtually anything we want it to mean, such as "not perfect but still basically good" or simply a "low self-esteem." But the picture in Scripture is one of a spiritual corpse that God must redeem and regenerate, and that is the work of God's grace alone. And it is from that that we have been redeemed.

Scriptures for Study: In Romans 3:24, what is the sole source of redemption? 🕮 In Colossians 1:14, what else do we have as a result of redemption?

Blood

haima

In keeping with our meditations on **redemption**, it is vital that we see what the *price* was for that redemption. That price was the **blood** (*haima*, 129) of the Lord Jesus Christ. Many false teachers advocate Jesus as "a good example to follow" or speak of Him as "a good moral compass." They tell us that Adam was the bad example and Jesus was the good example and then conclude that by following Jesus' good example we can be "rescued" from sin. "If we just follow Jesus' moral example and live a good life," they insist, "we will be delivered from our shortcomings, frailties, and low self-esteem."

In contrast to this redefined Gospel, Scripture constantly speaks of the blood of Christ, that is, not His *life* but His *death* that redeems us. It was His blood that paid the purchase price. Here, indeed, is the epicenter of our salvation.

Granted, no one likes to talk about blood. It truly is a sticky, messy, graphic thing; in today's language, it's really "gross." Most people abhor the picture of a bloody Savior. Occasionally they are willing to speak of His *death* but never His *blood*. They do not want to think of a Savior hanging on a cross with blood pouring out of His body and dripping into puddles on the ground.

Some hymnbooks even remove the hymns that speak of His blood. Some modern Bible translations do the same. *Good News for Modern Man* (*Today's English Version*), for example, mistranslates *haima* (or *haimatos*) as "death" when it clearly means "blood." This Greek word, in fact, forms the basis for several English medical terms, such as, *hemoglobin, hemorrhage, hemostat,* and others, all of which relate to blood. Today we want to "soften the blow" by changing the meaning so as not to offend our sensitivities.

But just as life has always been identified with blood (Gen. 9:4; Lev. 17:11), our life is only in the blood of Christ. As Paul wrote, "But now in Christ Jesus ye who sometimes were far off are made nigh by the blood of Christ" (Eph. 2:13). We are not "made nigh" (i.e. "brought near") to God by Jesus' "moral teachings" or His "ethical standards." We are made nigh only by His blood.

Scriptures for Study: Hebrews 9:22 declares that there cannot be what without "the shedding of blood"? 🕮 What did Christ's sacrifice fulfill and replace according to Hebrews 9:12–14?

Forgiveness

aphesis

One of the direct results of **redemption** (see Jan. 22 and 23) is the **forgiveness** of sins. The Greek is *aphesis* (859), which literally means "release, pardon, or cancellation." In Classical Greek it means "the voluntary release of a person or thing over which one has legal or actual control."[24] This powerful word actually has three aspects.

First, in *legal* terms, forgiveness is a judicial release from the guilt and punishment of sin, which is death. *Primarily, forgiveness is a legal transaction*. This is a vitally important point, for we who were under the legal sentence of death according to the Law, are now forgiven by legal transaction. The Law can never save; it can only reveal guilt and condemn us, "for by the law is the knowledge of sin" (Rom. 3:20), and "no man is justified by the law" (Gal. 3:11). This is, in fact, Paul's thrust throughout the first half of the epistle to the Romans, to first show man's *guilt* and then show God's *grace*.

Second, in *ethical* terms, forgiveness is a release from the terribleness of sin that affects the conscience. Salvation changes the sinner ethically. The Christian no longer desires the things he or she used to desire (2 Cor. 5:17).

Third, in *personal* terms, forgiveness is a cessation of God's intended wrath upon the sinner. A vivid illustration of this is in the OT scapegoat in Leviticus 16. On the Day of Atonement (Yom Kippur), the High Priest chose two unblemished goats, one of which he killed and sprinkled its blood on the mercy seat (see Dec. 11). Verses 21–22 go on to describe the High Priest laying his hands on the live goat, confessing the sins of the nation, and then sending it into the wilderness.

That was a wonderful picture, but as beautiful as it was, *it was still only a symbol*. It did not *take sin away*. It was not a perfect sacrifice. It was merely a *symbol* of what only God could do through the coming Messiah. Jesus Christ would not only be the perfect *sacrificial lamb*, but He would also be the perfect *scapegoat*. He would not only *redeem* His people with His blood, but He would also *remove* their sin forever. *That* is forgiveness.

Scriptures for Study: In Matthew 26:26–28, what observance pictures our forgiveness ("remission")? 🕮 According to Hebrews 9:22, what is the only thing that brings forgiveness ("remission") of sins?

Wisdom [and] Prudence

sophia [and] *phronēsis*

In contrast to man's empty philosophies, the apostle Paul declares that the second result of **redemption** is that God, through Christ, has given us **wisdom** and **prudence**—or "knowledge and insight" (Eph. 1:8). How profound! Only through Jesus Christ can we have true knowledge and insight. Men have been groping for both for millennia, when all they have to do is open the pages of God's Word.

The Greek for **wisdom** is *sophia* (4678), a very important word to the Greeks. It spoke of a quality or attitude rather than an action. Its basic meaning, according to Aristotle, is "knowledge of the most precious things." While Aristotle didn't fully know what the most precious things were, he did have the main concept right. It referred to deep knowledge and learning, "implying cultivation of mind and enlightened understanding."[25] In other words, *sophia* speaks of the knowledge of the things that really matter, the things that matter most.

Prudence, then, is *phronēsis* (5428), another important concept to the Greeks. Its basic meaning was "way of thinking, frame of mind, intelligence, good sense," but it often had the fuller idea of "discernment and judicious insight."[26] It was being able to see beyond just the knowledge of a thing, to see how that thing applied and how it was practical. Aristotle called this the knowledge of human affairs and of things in which planning is necessary. Plutarch called this the practical knowledge of the things that concern us. We could, therefore, translate this as "insight" or even **discernment** (see July 15ff.).

Paul, therefore, uses these two terms to show that the believer has been given both wisdom and insight to thoroughly equip him for life. *Sophia* emphasizes a deep knowledge of things that really matter, that is, the truths of God, truths such as: life and death, God and man, righteousness and sin, heaven and hell, and so on. Does the world have knowledge of such subjects? No, but the believer does. *Phronēsis*, then, emphasizes how to make all of this practical, how to make these things that matter most apply to daily life. Depth is important, but what good is deep knowledge if it is not practical?

Scriptures for Study: How deep is God's wisdom, according to Romans 11:33? 🕮 If we lack wisdom (and we do), how do we get it, according to Colossians 3:16 and James 1:5?

Inheritance

eklērōthēmen

Another direct result of **redemption** (see Jan. 22 and 23) is **inheritance**, as in Ephesians 1:11. The words we find there—"we have obtained an inheritance"—translate a single word in the Greek, *eklērōthēmen* (aorist passive indicative of *klēroō*, 2820) This unique word appears only here in the NT.

In Classical Greek, from the time of Homer, the noun root *klēros* (2819) referred to "the fragment of stone or piece of wood which was used as a lot." Lots were drawn to discover the will of the gods. Since land was divided by lot, probably in the framework of common use of the fields, *klēros* came to mean a share, land received by lot, plot of land, and finally inheritance.[27] Similarly, in the OT, the same basic concept of casting lots (the Urim and Thummin) was used to discover God's will (Num. 27:21, 1 Chron. 24:5ff., etc.) and to divide land (1 Chron. 6:54–81).

So the idea Paul conveys here is that *the lot of inheritance has fallen upon us, not by chance, but by the sovereign will of God.*

Also, because *eklērōthēmen* is in the passive voice (the subject being acted upon), it can also be translated "we were made a heritage" (as it is in the *Revised Version* and the *American Standard Version*). So, instead of saying that we obtained an inheritance, this says that we were made Christ's heritage. Now, while that does fit *grammatically*, and even *theologically*, it does not fit *contextually*. And may we interject, the NIV misses the point by a mile with the mistranslation, "in Him we were also chosen," for that is not what the text says.

Our AV is correct here. Verse 14 explicitly speaks of our inheritance, which the Holy Spirit guarantees. Paul's point in the entire passage (vv. 3–14) is to outline *our* riches in Christ. Specifically, the idea of inheritance really carries us back to being predestined to **adoption** in verse 5; *the believer cannot be predestined to sonship without being predestined to inheritance*. Inheritance was, in fact, a primary reason for sonship. Paul also says in Romans 8:17, we are "joint-heirs with Christ." As theologian and commentator Charles Hodge put it: "We have not only been made *sharers* of the knowledge of redemption, but are actually *heirs* of its blessings."[28]

We'll continue these thoughts tomorrow as we meditate on the word **riches**.

Scriptures for Study: Read Ephesians 5:5. Who has no inheritance "in the kingdom of Christ?" 🕮 In Hebrews 9:15 and 1 Peter 1:4, what are some characteristics of our inheritance (*klēronomia*)?

Riches

ploutos

Yesterday we meditated on our **inheritance** in Christ. Specifically that inheritance is spiritual **riches**. Many of us view our future inheritance as pots of gold sitting in various places throughout our heavenly mansion, but this is because our minds have been polluted by the world's ideas of wealth. Our true inheritance is the salvation Paul describes in Ephesians 1:3–14.

Riches translates the Greek *ploutos* (4149), from which we get English words such as *plutonic* and *plutocrat*. A little word history is valuable here. Originally, ancient secular Greek viewed riches as simply "an abundance of earthly possessions of every kind." Later, however, a few centuries before Christ, the meaning divided into two aspects: riches in the *material* sense and riches in the *abstract* sense, as illustrated in concepts such as riches of wisdom, honor, mercy, and so forth. Plato (c. 427–347 BC) and Aristotle (384–322 BC) in particular judged riches by the effect they had on society. To them riches were to be rejected if they didn't serve the community. Most significantly, while Aristotle considered wealth as always something material, Plato distinguished "material riches from true riches which consist of wisdom, virtue, and culture."[29]

Now, while Plato and Aristotle were most certainly pagans, they had the right idea. True **riches**, true wealth, is not in *material* things but are, as Paul would write a few centuries later, in *spiritual* things. And this is nowhere greater than the wealth of true and total forgiveness of sin in the **redemption** of Christ.

Perhaps even more important, however, are the words *according to* in Ephesians 1:7: "according to the riches of his grace." The Greek is not *ek* (1537), meaning "out of," rather *kata* (2596), which literally means "down" and shows domination. God has not given "out of" His riches, but rather He has given "according to" or "dominated by" His riches.

We'll continue these thoughts tomorrow as we meditate on the word **earnest** ("first installment").

Scriptures for Study: Read Ephesians 1:3–14. List all the spiritual riches you have in Christ. 🕮 Based on Philippians 4:19, what does God promise to do according to his riches?

Earnest

arrabōn

In the last two days, we've meditated on our **inheritance** and **riches** in Christ. Right in line with those is the "earnest of our inheritance" (Eph. 1:14), which is the indwelling Holy Spirit (v. 13).

One of the saddest realities in Christianity today is the fact that many deny the biblical doctrine of the security of the believer. This doctrine has been called "that damnable doctrine that gives people license to sin." It's also argued, "If you are eternally secure, you can go out and live any way you want to and just ask God to forgive you." But this doctrine says no such thing, for anyone who has that idea of salvation cannot possibly be a Christian. Salvation involves a new person, a new creature in Christ (2 Cor. 5:17). We no longer want the things we once desired.

What this verse tells us is exactly where our security lies—*in the Holy Spirit.* We would be forced to agree with those who deny security if it were not for the Holy Spirit. But our text tells us that He is the **earnest** of our inheritance. That wonderful word earnest is *arrabōn* (728), which came into the Greek from Phoenician traders and means "first installment, down payment, deposit."

This earnest is not just a *pledge* or promise (as in the Catholic *Douay-Rheims* translation and the *Revised Standard Version*); it's actually a *portion* of the inheritance, the first installment. As one commentator puts it, "The earnest, in short, is the inheritance in miniature."[30]

So it was that this term was used in secular Greek as a legal term in business and trade; it was with this advance payment that a contract became lawfully valid, binding, and unbreakable. In fact, even today we use the term "earnest money." The same Greek word is used in modern Greek for an engagement ring; it is more than just a promise to marry; it is the first installment of the coming marriage.

What a blessing to know that God has not just *promised* us riches, but rather He has already *provided* them! And the indwelling, empowering Holy Spirit of God is the first installment.

Scriptures for Study: In 2 Corinthians 1:22, what other spiritual reality do we have besides the earnest of the Holy Spirit? We shall examine this tomorrow.

Sealed

sphragizō

Yesterday we pondered the **earnest** (first installment) of our riches in Christ, which is the indwelling Holy Spirit. This reality is actually the result of another work of the Holy Sprit—*sealing* (Eph. 1:13).

The Greek behind **sealed** is the verb *sphragizō* (4972), which means "to set a seal" or "to mark with a seal." This comes from the noun *sphragis*, which refers to a signet ring that possessed a distinctive mark. There are many illustrations of a seal, both from ancient and modern times. We can see many of these by showing the four pictures sealing provides.

First, sealing pictures *acquisition*. By this we mean that sealing pictures a finished transaction. First and foremost, sealing paints a legal picture; it shows the completion of a *legal transaction*. A modern illustration of a seal is a "notary public." A notary signs and seals a document, thereby finishing the transaction and sealing the agreement. Spiritually, the indwelling Holy Spirit is proof of the finished transaction of our **redemption**.

Second, sealing pictures *absolute ownership*. The ancients would put their seal on animals and even slaves to prove ownership. In fact, the branding of animals is thought to have begun as early as 2000 BC. Of course, branding cattle and horses is still done today. A brand is registered with the particular state in which the owner lives and that brand shows legal ownership. The same is also true today of a patent or a copyright. Spiritually, the indwelling Holy Spirit proves that we belong to Christ.

Third, sealing pictures *authenticity*. A seal attests to the authenticity of a signature; likewise, a signature proves the genuineness of a letter. Again, spiritually, the indwelling Holy Spirit proves that the believer is genuine. Think of it! The Spirit's presence within us is "God's signature."

Fourth, sealing pictures *assurance*, absolute security. The spiritual application is clear: *We are sealed eternally in Christ by the Holy Spirit's sealing*. One of the most important aspects of sealing is this one concerning assurance. All three NT references to sealing are in the aorist tense, a once-for-all past action.

Indeed, the doctrine of the sealing of the Holy Spirit is among the most blessed and reassuring doctrines of the Bible.

Scriptures for Study: In 2 Corinthians 1:21–22, what other guarantee do we have besides sealing? 🕮 In Ephesians 4:30, what should we endeavor to do in light of our sealing?

Confess

homologeō

What are we to do when we sin? Some teachers insist that we lose our salvation, but such a thought is not only sad but contradictory to the principle of "eternal salvation" (Heb. 5:9) taught throughout the NT.

Therefore, when we *do* sin, we are forgiven by *confessing* our sin. As the apostle John writes, "If we confess our sins, He is faithful and just to forgive us our sins, and to cleanse us from all unrighteousness" (1 John 1:9). What a wonderful verse that is! It is a verse we need to claim every day.

The Greek for **confess** is *homologeō* (3670). The root *logeō* (3004) means "to say," and the prefix *homo* (3674) means "same," yielding the literal meaning "to say the same words." Therefore, to confess *sin* means "to say the same thing about sin that God says," or in short, "to call sin, sin." The same word is used in Romans 10:9–10: "That if thou shalt confess with thy mouth the Lord Jesus, and shalt believe in thine heart that God hath raised him from the dead, thou shalt be saved. For with the heart man believeth unto righteousness; and with the mouth confession is made unto salvation." In other words, to be saved, we must say the same words about Christ as Scripture, that He is God and that He is the only way to salvation.

So, to confess is to join the ranks of David who said, "I have sinned" (Ps. 51:4). To confess means that we do not make excuses, we do not blame others, but rather we "acknowledge" our sin (v. 3) with "a broken and a contrite heart" (v. 17). When we do truly confess our *known* sin, God cleanses us from *all* sin. What grace that is! We no longer require ***redemption***, only *cleansing*.

Confession shows a relationship, a relationship of a child to a **Father**, and we can rejoice in that wonderful relationship.

Scriptures for Study: Both Romans 10:9–10 and 1 Timothy 6:12 speak of what kind of profession? 🕮 What is a characteristic of false teachers, according to 2 John 7?

Truth (1)

alētheia

We live in a day when the concept of **truth** is more and more challenged. Never before has there been such a redefining of truth. Many, in fact, deny that there is any truth at all. In stark contrast, however, the Word of God, in no uncertain terms, makes it clear that there *is* truth and that truth is to be found *only* in God and His Word.

The English words *truth* and *true* speak of what is real, what really is, what is factual. It's not opinion, it's not conjecture, it's not hypothesis or theory. Rather, it is, like the old expression, "telling it like it is." If something is true, it is absolutely reliable, totally secure. It cannot change because to do so would mean it's not true, not reliable.

The Greek *alētheia* (225) means basically the same thing as the English. As one Greek authority puts it: etymologically *alētheia* means "nonconcealment." It thus denotes what is seen, indicated, expressed, or disclosed, i.e., a thing as it really is, not as it is concealed or falsified. *Alētheia* is the real state of affairs.[31]

Alētheia, along with its related words, appears no less than 187 times in the NT. It appears, for example, in John 1:14, where it refers to the incarnate Christ: "And the Word was made flesh, and dwelt among us, (and we beheld his glory, the glory as of the only begotten of the Father,) full of grace and truth." In 16:13, our Lord promised, "Howbeit when he, the Spirit of truth, is come, he will guide you into all truth," that is, all that is reliable, constant, sure, and unchanging. In both cases, and in all others, the concept of truth is that which is not concealed, what really is.

So again, the fundamental concept to understand about truth is that it is that which is absolute, that which is incontrovertible, irrefutable, incontestable, unarguable, and unchanging. If something is true, it's *always* true and can *never* be untrue, no matter what the circumstances.

We will continue our study of this word over the next two days. The desire of the true Christian is absolute truth in all things and every area of life.

Scriptures for Study: What does John 14:6 declare? 🕮 In John 16:13, what is one ministry of the Holy Spirit? 🕮 In John 17:17 and 19, what is a result of truth?

Truth (2)

alētheia

There are numerous claims to **truth** in the world, but are they really sources of truth? Do they offer that which is sure, reliable, and unchanging? Let's take a look at three of the world's best claims of how to discover truth.

By far the greatest claim to being a source of truth in our day is made by *science.* But honestly, is science really a source of truth? Is it always reliable, constant, sure, and unchanging? For example, it was once accepted fact that light travels in a straight line, but it was then discovered that gravity actually bends light. We could cite many other examples of, as one writer puts it, "the rapid rate at which previous laws of science are discarded and replaced by new ones." So, for a scientist today to say, "Well, the old laws were wrong, but we now know the truth," would be the height of folly, but that is, in fact, what science claims.

Another claim to being a source of truth in our day is made by *philosophy. Philosophy* directly transliterates the Greek *philosophia*, literally, "love of wisdom." There are those who believe that ultimate knowledge can be found in man's own thinking. Philosophy, therefore, has historically been man's attempt to explain the universe around him and the meaning of his own existence. But is philosophy truth? Hardly. Why? Every philosopher says something different. In fact, in a sense, every person is a philosopher because he or she holds to some system of "truth." So, who's right?

Finally, one other claim to being a source of truth is made by *religion*, which is basically just another philosophy. Of course, in a sense, biblical Christianity is a religion. But in the five verses where the word *religion* appears in the NT, it's *always* qualified by a modifier. Speaking as a Pharisee, Paul refers to "our religion" in Acts 26:5, that is, the works-oriented religion that Judaism had become. He does so again in Galatians 1:13–14, where he uses the term "the Jew's religion." James uses two modifiers, calling one religion "man's religion" and the other "pure religion" (James 1:26–27).

So there is a marked difference between "religion" per se and "pure religion." The word pure translates *katharos* (see Aug. 22), which means that which is genuine, or that which is free from any improper mixture. Biblical Christianity is, therefore, *the genuine article*, in contrast to just "religion."

Scriptures for Study: In Romans 1:18 and 25, what do ungodly people do with the truth? What is upon them as a result? 📖 Second John is about false teachers. Read that letter and note each time John mentions the word *truth*.

Truth (3)

alētheia

If science, philosophy, or religion cannot give us **truth**, as we saw yesterday, what can? In John 18:37–38, Pontius Pilate asked the Lord Jesus, "Art thou a king?" Our Lord responded, "Thou sayest that I am a king. To this end was I born, and for this cause came I into the world, that I should bear witness unto the truth. Every one that is of the truth heareth my voice." What a powerful statement! "If you would have truth," He was saying, "you will listen to Me." To that Pilate spoke three words—probably in at least a cynical if not contemptuous tone—that have echoed through the millennia: "What is truth?"

The most noteworthy thing about that scene is that while Pilate asked a legitimate and pivotal question, he did not wait for an answer, rather "when he had said this, he went out again." Think of it—he was standing in front of Truth Incarnate but walked away. And people have been walking away from the truth ever since.

What, then, is true? What is factual? What is absolutely reliable, totally secure, and unchanging? We are left with only one answer—*God and His Word*. How sad it is that so many today are "ever learning, and never able to come to the knowledge of the truth" (2 Tim. 3:7). No matter what man discovers, no matter what he learns, no matter what advances he makes, he still misses the truth.

Ponder these two wonderful verses: "Then said Jesus to those Jews which believed on him, If ye continue in my word, then are ye my disciples indeed; And ye shall know the truth, and the truth shall make you free" (John 8:31–32). Will science make us free? No, we're ever learning but never discovering. Will philosophy make us free? No, it drove Nietzsche mad. Will even religion make us free? No, the Law keeps us in bondage.

It is only the Gospel of Christ that makes us free, and it is only in His Word that we find truth.

No matter what the question, no matter what the issue, let our motto ever be, "What saith the Scripture?" (Rom. 4:3; Gal. 4:30). Why? Because only it is truth.

Scriptures for Study: What is the pivotal mission of the church in 1 Timothy 3:15? (We'll examine this tomorrow.) 📖 What do we turn from when we turn to the truth (Titus 1:14; 2 Pet. 2:2; cf. 2 Tim. 3:8)?

Pillar [and] Ground (of the Truth)

stulos [and] *hedraiōma*

Paul makes an extraordinary statement to Timothy: "That thou mayest know how thou oughtest to behave thyself in the house of God, which is the church of the living God, the pillar and ground of the truth" (1 Tim. 3:15). Timothy was at that time the pastor of the Ephesian church. Paul had left him there to deal with several problems that had arisen. While we don't readily understand this statement, Timothy and the Ephesians immediately recognized the imagery Paul used.

The impressive temple of the goddess Diana (Artemis), one of the seven wonders of the ancient world, was located in Ephesus. William Barclay gives the following description of it: "One of its features was its pillars. It contained 127 pillars, every one of them the gift of a king. All were made of marble, and some were studded with jewels and overlaid with gold."[32] Each **pillar** (*stulos*, 4769) acted as a tribute to the king who donated it. The honorary significance of the pillars, however, was secondary to their obvious function of holding up the immense structure of the roof. Here, then, Paul says that *the church's mission is to hold up the truth.*

But Paul adds something else—the church is also the **ground** of the truth. *Ground* translates *hedraiōma* (1477), which appears only here in the NT and refers to "a stay, a prop, or a support." While the NIV translation and some commentators maintain that the idea here is "foundation," that is actually a very serious error. The church is *not* the foundation of the truth; it didn't invent the truth. That is, in fact, the very error of the Roman Catholic Church; it maintains that it dictates what is true, not Scripture alone. Rather the church is the mainstay, the prop, the support, the propagator of the truth. As the pillars of the temple of Diana were a testimony to the error of pagan false religion, so the **church** is to be a testimony to God's truth. That is its mission, *its very reason for existence.*

In direct contradiction of Paul's imagery, the mission of many of today's churches is to be "user-friendly," "purpose-driven," and "seeker-sensitive," but God said to just preach the truth. It's the solemn responsibility of every church, led by the pastor, to solidly, immovably, unshakably, uncompromisingly uphold the truth of God's Word.

Scriptures for Study: What is the responsibility of pastors (Acts 20:27–28; Eph. 4:11–12; 2 Tim. 2:15)? 📖 According to Galatians 4:16, what will sometimes happen when you proclaim the truth?

The Gospel

to euaggelion

In Ephesians 1:13, Paul speaks of "the word of truth," which is best stated and understood as "the gospel of your salvation." In other words, it is **the Gospel** that is the only **truth** that brings salvation. The real truth, which in turn forms the foundation of all other truth and is the source from which all other truth flows, is the Gospel.

Word (see also March 16) translates *logos* (3056), which means to speak intelligently, to articulate a message, to give a discourse. **Truth**, as already noted, is *alētheia* (225), which means nonconcealment, and denotes a thing as it really is, not as it is concealed or falsified. So the phrase "the word of truth" declares that there is one message that is real and unconcealed, not falsified or changing. What is that message? It is the message of the Gospel.

How profound that statement is! In a day when it is considered intolerant and divisive to say that there is only one true religion, that statement invites criticism. But such dissent does not alter the fact that God says that only His Word is truth.

The word **Gospel** has an interesting etymology. The Greek is the compound word *euaggelion* (2098): *eu* (2095), "good," and *aggellō*, "to proclaim, tell." The English, however, is even more fascinating. It comes from the Old English *gōdspel*: *gōd*, "good," and *spel*, "tale." Witches were said to cast a *spell*, that is, say certain words that supposedly had magic powers. To *spellbind* is to speak in such a way as to hold people's attention. To *spell* a word means to name or write the letters of the word. So, the Gospel is, indeed, the good spell, the good tale, the good story, the good message, the good news.

Even more significant, **the Gospel** is *the only* good tale. The definite article (the) is present quite often in the Greek. In this verse, for example, while it's present only twice in the English, we find it *three* times in the Greek. We can literally read it, "*The* message of *the* truth, *the* good news of your salvation." Paul wants to make it clear that there is *only one good news*. As we will study tomorrow, there are teachers who claim they have other "good news," but salvation is found only in the good news of Jesus Christ (John 14:6).

Scriptures for Study: What are the words of our Lord in Mark 1:15? 📖 What is our responsibility according to Mark 16:15? 📖 What is the power of the Gospel in Romans 1:16?

Accursed [and] Curse (1)

anathema

Yesterday we examined **the Gospel**, the only good news there is. There are teachers, however, who claim they have other good news. Paul deals with such teachers in Galatians 1:6–7: "I marvel that ye are so soon removed from him that called you into the grace of Christ unto another gospel: Which is not another; but there be some that trouble you, and would pervert the gospel of Christ." He makes it clear to them that a perverted Gospel is not a Gospel (a good news, a good story) at all. It is for that reason that he writes the very pointed, narrow command in the next two verses: "But though we, or an angel from heaven, preach any other gospel unto you than that which we have preached unto you, let him be accursed. As we said before, so say I now again, if any man preach any other gospel unto you than that ye have received, let him be accursed" (vv. 8–9).

Accursed is *anathema* (334), which refers to that which is "under God's curse," "devoted to destruction," or "set aside for judgment." We see a lot of tolerance in Christianity for false teachers, but this is the very opposite of what Scripture not only *teaches* but *commands*. We are not to be tolerant of false teaching; we are to consider such teaching and teachers as under God's judgment. God simply will not tolerate a perversion of the Gospel. Why? Because it's the only truth.

Today the Gospel is being retold as a new tale, a new story, a story of God's universal fatherhood, Jesus' life as a good moral example, and salvation without repentance, lordship, or even acknowledgment of sin. One today can define the Gospel in whatever terms make him feel good. Preaching against sin "puts people off, offends their sensibilities, puts them on the defensive, and makes them uncomfortable." But if we do not preach about sin and salvation from sin, we are condemned.

A theology that does not view man as "dead in trespasses and sins" (Eph. 2:1–4) is not a biblical theology. It is, in fact, false teaching. I am frightened for those who are not preaching the true Gospel; they are teaching a different Gospel, and God will judge them for it. That type of Gospel, which is no Gospel at all, must be cursed for what it is—*a lie. The only Gospel is, as the context makes clear, trust in Jesus' blood as the only redemption from sin.*

Scriptures for Study: How is the word **accursed** used in 1 Corinthians 12:3? 📖 What is the reason for being **accursed** in 1 Corinthians 16:22?

Accursed [and] Curse (2)

anathema

Today we meditate again on one of the strongest words in the Bible because of how important it is. To go a little deeper, *anathema* (331) is actually a secondary form of *anathēma* (334), and is comprised of *ana* (303), "on," and *tithēmi* (5087), "set, place, or lay." It originally meant a consecrated gift given to a god. The only NT occurrence of the old form (*anathēma*) is in Luke 21:5, where consecrated "gifts" are brought to the temple. Later *anathema* came to mean what is handed over to a god for wrath.

It appears in the Septuagint, for example, in Joshua 6:17, where the city of Jericho and everything in it was "accursed"—*anathema* translates the Hebrew *chērem* (2764H), "dedicated thing, things which should have been utterly destroyed" (Strong).

The NT occurrences reflect that meaning of "something handed over to God for judgment." As one authority specifies, "The word does not denote punishment intended as discipline but being given over or devoted to divine condemnation."[33] In other words, no corrective action is implied, only judgment and sentencing.

An amazing example of this word occurs in Romans 9:3. In a moving show of love, Paul was so burdened for his fellow Jews who would not believe the Gospel that he says, "For I could wish that myself were accursed from Christ for my brethren, my kinsmen." Perhaps Paul captured this attitude from Moses, who prayed in the same way (Exod. 32:32).

In two of the most pointed verses in the NT, Paul narrowly declares, "But though we, or an angel from heaven, preach any other gospel unto you than that which we have preached unto you, let him be accursed. As we said before, so say I now again, if any man preach any other gospel unto you than that ye have received, let him be accursed" (Gal. 1:8–9).

The Judaizers (see Apr. 2; July 4; Nov. 24; Dec. 8) had seriously perverted the Gospel, teaching that to be Christians, Gentiles had to become Jewish proselytes and obey the Mosaic Law. Such perversion and compromise was intolerable, so Paul said without equivocation that such a teacher is to be *anathema*, handed over to God for judgment.

In a day of rampant error and uncounted attacks on the Gospel, as well as widespread *apathy* about those trends in the church, we need a renewed emphasis of Paul's command. While we might be called "intolerant" and "divisive," false teaching simply cannot be tolerated.

Scriptures for Study: Read the following verses, noting the instructive use of *anathema* in each one: 1 Corinthians 12:3; 16:22.

Faith (Believe)

pisteuō

In a day when words such as **faith** and **believe** are used so loosely, it's vital that we examine them biblically. The basic meaning of *pisteuō* (4100) is "to have faith in, trust; particularly, to be firmly persuaded as to something."[34] Many teachers today insist that it simply means "mental assent" and teach that all one must do to be saved is mentally assent to a few facts about Jesus.

As one Greek authority points out, however, *pisteuō* also very clearly carries the idea "to obey": "Heb. 11 stresses that to believe is to obey, as in the OT. Paul in Rom. 1:8 [and] 1 Thess. 1:8 (cf. Rom. 15:18; 16:19 [2 Thess. 1:7–8]) shows, too, that believing means obeying. He speaks about the obedience of faith in Rom. 1:5 [6:17; 16:26], and cf. 10:3; 2 Cor. 9:13."[35] Clearly, this word immediately and fundamentally demands lordship, because it has the underlying foundation of obedience, commitment, and submission.

When someone believes something, regardless of what it is, that belief changes them and results in some action or behavior that is characteristic of the belief. Every one of the characters in Hebrews 11 had faith, but that faith *always*, without exception, resulted in an outward action. Noah did not say, "Well, if God said it's going to rain, then I believe it's going to rain, but that doesn't really affect me or demand anything from me." No, Noah built an ark as a result of believing what God said. Was Noah's action the *cause* of his salvation? No, it was an *evidence* of his salvation. Faith is a verb. It's always an action, and it must have an object.

Practically speaking, do we believe in gravity? Yes, and we act upon that belief by not jumping off tall buildings. Truly believing something, being fully persuaded of it, and trusting in it automatically demands behavior that conforms to the belief.

Applying this to salvation, to "believe in Jesus" means three things. First, it means to believe in Who He *is*, that He is God incarnate, Savior, and sovereign Lord. Second, it means to believe in what He *did*, that He died for your sins and rose again from the grave. Third, it means to believe in what He *says*, to trust Him and His Word implicitly and desire to obey Him in all respects. To obey Him means we acknowledge His lordship and submit to His authority. Any presentation of the Gospel that doesn't in some way present the essence of these three elements is a false presentation of the Gospel.

Scriptures for Study: Read Hebrews 11, noting the action that went along with faith (noun, *pistis*) in each instance.

Faithful

pistos

The Greek *pistos* (4103) is an adjective, and what an important adjective it is. Not only has a Christian put his faith in Christ, but he is now one who is **faithful**, trustworthy, consistent, constant, and reliable. God not only demands *faith*; He also demands *fidelity*.

There is a sad lack of faithfulness in Christianity today, faithfulness to the Word of God, the house of God, and service for God. We need to take a look at our *profession* and see if it is true *possession*. The true **saint**, the true *believer*, will remain faithful. True faith is evidenced by practice. Let us make it clear that this does not mean works are "part of salvation" or that works "keep us saved," as some teachers maintain. Rather it means that if we are truly born again, it will be proven by how we live. That is, in fact, the whole point of the book of James—*proof* of our *profession*.

Faithfulness is a fundamental part of Christian living. As Paul wrote to the Corinthians, "It is required in **stewards**, that a man be found faithful" (1 Cor. 4:2). As we will study tomorrow, a steward was an administrator, a house manager. Such a person would no doubt be good with money, be organized, and have business savvy. But none of those qualities are mentioned. What *really* mattered in a steward was that he was faithful, trustworthy, and reliable. A steward would be worthless if the master of the house had to be constantly looking over his shoulder to see if he was doing things right or to make sure he wasn't embezzling money.

That is a picture of the true child of God. While the context of the above verse speaks specifically of "full-time ministers," such as Paul and his colleagues, the clear application is to every Christian. We are all stewards of the truth. In Ephesians 1:1, for example, Paul addresses not only "the saints which are at Ephesus" but also "the faithful in Christ Jesus." This was also the point of the Parable of the Talents (Matt. 25:14–30), where the Lord said to the faithful stewards, "Well done, thou good and faithful servant: thou hast been faithful over a few things, I will make thee ruler over many things: enter thou into the joy of thy lord" (vv. 21, 23). Let us each be faithful in our Christian living.

Scriptures for Study: Who is the faithful woman in Acts 16:14–15? 📖 Who is the faithful *man* in 1 Corinthians 4:17?

Steward

oikonomos

In yesterday's study of faithfulness, we touched briefly on the ancient **steward**. The Greek behind this word is the compound *oikonomos* (3623), which is comprised of *oikos* (3624; "house") and *nemō* (not in NT; "to deal out, distribute, apportion"). In ancient times, a steward managed the domestic affairs of a family, business, or minor. That position still exists today in some broader ways, such as an accountant, estate manager, live-in maid or housekeeper, or even a head cook. The ancient steward, however, had far more responsibility, so it is an important metaphor for the Christian.

The metaphor is strengthened all the more by the fact that while free persons were employed as stewards (Luke 16:1, 3, 4, 8), they were usually slaves (Luke 12:42; cf. Eliezer in Gen. 15:2 and Joseph in Gen. 39:4). This applies graphically to Christians because we are spoken of as servants, or literally slaves (Rom. 1:1; etc.; see tomorrow's study).

An example, therefore, of our stewardship appears in 1 Peter 4:10: "As every man hath received the gift, even so minister the same one to another, as good stewards of the manifold grace of God." Peter tells us here that every Christian has received some "spiritual gift" (see Feb. 15, **spiritual gifts**), with which he or she serves the body of Christ. The Christian, then, is to be a steward of his or her gift, managing it and using it for the betterment of the body. And as we saw yesterday, the most essential quality of the steward is faithfulness, that is, reliability and trustworthiness (1 Cor. 4:2).

Let each of us search our hearts and ask, "Am I a faithful steward?"

Scriptures for Study: Read the Parable of the Talents (Matt. 25:14–30). Compare yourself with those stewards and make any changes that are necessary in your life.

Servant (Slave)

doulos

The most common Greek word in the NT for **servant** is *doulos* (1401) and literally means, as one Greek authority tells us, "a slave, one who is in permanent relation of servitude to another [person], his will being altogether consumed in the will of the other."[36]

As noted in our January 23 study, slavery was an integral part of society with as many as six million slaves serving in households and public works. While slaves were not usually treated horribly—they actually had medical care and other amenities—they were still slaves, with no will of their own.

We are tempted to think here, "So why is it a good thing that the Bible says we are slaves? Isn't that a horribly demeaning and dehumanizing existence?" It certainly would be if we were slaves to a fallen, sinful, unjust, and unfair master. But we are slaves of the Perfect Master, who actually redeemed us from the most horrible master of all—*sin*. As Paul declares, we have been "made free from sin" and have "[become] the servants of righteousness" (Rom. 6:18). Paul even challenged earthly masters (i.e., employers) that they should be just and fair masters (Col. 4:1).

Further, we are actually more than slaves, as Paul told the Galatians, "Wherefore thou art no more a servant, but a son; and if a son, then an heir of God through Christ" (Gal. 4:7). While our *position* is slave, our *place* is with the Father as a son (see **adoption**, see Jan. 2).

In case we might think we are above such a lowly state as a slave, let us remember what Paul said of our Lord: "Who, being in the form of God, thought it not robbery to be equal with God: But made himself of no reputation, and took upon him the form of a servant, and was made in the likeness of men: And being found in fashion as a man, he humbled himself, and became obedient unto death, even the death of the cross" (Phil. 2:6–8). If Christ could lower Himself to be a slave, is it too much to ask that we do the same?

Scriptures for Study: What does it mean to be a servant of Christ, according to Ephesians 6:6–7? 🕮 Read Philemon and note the relationship of a godly master and slave.

Dead

nekros

When you noticed today's title, perhaps you thought, "Well, this certainly won't be a good way to start the day." Please bear with me, however; I hope to change that initial reaction. We have to look at what it means to be "spiritually dead" before we can ever appreciate **grace** (which we'll turn to tomorrow).

Second only to Romans 1, Ephesians 2:1–3 is the most graphic description of man's sinful condition (and its result) in the Bible. The key to the passage is the phrase "dead in trespasses and sins" (v. 1). **Dead** is *nekros* (3498), which literally speaks of a dead body, a corpse, as in James 2:26, "For as the body without the spirit is dead, so faith without works [as an evidence] is dead also." What Paul is saying is that the unsaved person is a spiritual corpse. Life for him is a living death; even though he is physically alive, walking and breathing, he is dead while he lives. This is not a figure of speech. Paul doesn't mean they "look dead," or are "in danger of death," or are "standing on the precipice of death," or "looking death in the eye," but they are really dead. As Scottish commentator and Greek scholar John Eadie put it, it's a case of "death walking."[37]

An analogy that many of us have heard at evangelistic crusades goes something like this: "Picture a drowning man. He's struggling to stay afloat. He's already gone down twice and is now going down for the third time, with only his desperately seeking hand still above the surface. His only hope is for someone to throw him a life preserver. This is exactly what God does, but even if the preserver hits the man's hand, that's not enough. The man must close his hand around it and capture his salvation."

That's certainly dramatic and plays very well in the evangelist's emotional appeal, but it's also false. Is the lost person drowning? *No!* He's dead. He is as entombed at the bottom of the sea as are the over 1,100 men still entombed in the USS *Arizona* at the bottom of Pearl Harbor. His only hope is for God to reach down, pull his corpse to the surface, and breathe life into him. That is what God did for our dead Savior, Who "rose from the dead" (Matt. 17:9; 27:64; Rom. 6:4; etc.), and that is precisely what He does for us by His **grace**.

Scriptures for Study: Who was dead in John 12:17 but raised up by Jesus? 🕮 Who did Paul raise from the dead in Acts 20:9? These and other instances of *nekros* vividly show that spiritual death is just as literal as physical death.

Grace (1)

charis

Grace is our theology. In a sense, the word **grace** sums up all biblical theology. Of all the theological words we could discuss—*redemption*, *reconciliation*, *justification*, *sanctification*, *glorification*, *election*, and many more—none cuts to the heart of our theology like *grace*.

Incredulously, however, few words are more misunderstood, misused, or misapplied than *grace*. More and more today we hear teachers say, "Yes, salvation is by grace but good works supplement it," or, "Yes, grace is necessary, but so are works." No statement on earth could be more contradictory. Such teachers know absolutely nothing about grace.

In Classical Greek the word *charis* (5485) meant "that which affords joy, pleasure, delight,"[38] and from there several meanings developed: grace, favor, thankfulness, gratitude, delight, kindness, etc.[39] Originally, then, the word didn't carry the idea of something "unmerited" because Greek philosophy (which is at the root of our western culture) believed in human merit and self-sufficiency. Even then, however, the Greeks thought they needed "a little help," so they prayed to their gods for favors and gifts.

It was, therefore, in the NT that *charis* was transformed. While some of the meanings from the Classical Greek *are* found, the NT usage is unique because *NT grace is coupled with the person and work of Jesus Christ*. If you remove Christ, and therefore grace, all you have left is another religion. You have ten practical commandments, many ethical principles for living, but all you have is mere religion.

John 1:17 declares, "Grace and truth came by Jesus Christ." Does that say grace and truth came by religion or works? No, for the ultimate manifestation of God's grace is Jesus Christ. Throughout the NT, in fact, grace is coupled with Christ, for He is the ultimate manifestation of the grace of God. Grace can, therefore, be defined thusly: *Grace is the unmerited favor of God toward man manifested primarily through the person and work of Jesus Christ, apart from any merit or works of man*. May we lovingly, but no less boldly, say that if anyone defines grace differently than that, let him be **accursed** (Gal. 1:8–9). Anyone who does not preach that doctrine of grace is a false teacher.

We'll continue our thoughts on grace tomorrow.

Scriptures for Study: According to Romans 11:5–6, if you add works to grace, what is the result? 📖 What does Paul call grace in 2 Corinthians 9:13–15?

Grace (2)

charis

Grace (*charis*, 5485) is a hard doctrine to leave once it's been mentioned, for grace is everything to the true Christian. It is the beginning, middle, and end of salvation. Therefore, to speak of grace plus works is in essence to redefine grace as something other than grace.

Consider two passages. Second Corinthians 9:13–15 declares, "Whiles by the experiment of this ministration they glorify God for your professed subjection unto the *gospel of Christ*, and for your liberal distribution unto them, and unto all men; And by their prayer for you, which long after you for the exceeding *grace of God* in you. Thanks be unto God for his unspeakable *gift*" (emphasis added). Likewise, in 2 Thessalonians 1:12, we read, "That the name of our Lord Jesus Christ may be glorified in you, and ye in Him, according to the grace of our God and the Lord Jesus Christ."

There are some beautiful pictures of God's grace in the OT. My favorite, in fact, is the story of how King David showed kindness to Mephibosheth, the crippled son of his friend Jonathan (2 Sam. 4 and 9). In that beautiful story we read that Mephibosheth was crippled by a fall (4:4), that David desired to show him kindness, and that David did so for Jonathan's sake (9:1), just as God showed grace to man for Christ's sake. We further observe that this kindness was not earned by Mephibosheth (9:1), that he was rather sought for by the king (9:1, 5), both picturing unmerited favor, and that David sent others to fetch him (9:5), a picture of evangelism. We then see several results: Mephibosheth reverenced the king (9:6), became a servant (9:6), was given riches and security (9:7), was made a son of David the king (9:11), and that his crippled condition was hidden when he sat at the king's table (9:13).

While that is a wondrous story, it still cannot compare with the NT usage of grace because that centers in Christ. When we see the word grace in the NT, we need to realize that it is *immediately identified with Christ*, rooted in His divine person and finished work. If we add anything to that, we have negated it and even blasphemed it.

Scriptures for Study: Grace is not only a NT truth but an OT truth as well. Identify the recipient of grace in the following verses: Genesis 6:8; 19:19; Exodus 33:12–13; Ezra 9:8. Can you find some others?

Spiritual Gifts

pneumatikos charisma

We all enjoy receiving a gift, something given to us unsolicited and out of love. The greatest gift we can ever receive, however (next to salvation itself), is a "spiritual gift." The word **gifts**, as it appears in passages such as Romans 12:6–8 and 1 Corinthians 12:4–11, is the Greek *charisma* (5486), which is derived from *charis* (**grace**, 5485). In the same vein as *charis*, it is a "grace gift," an undeserved **gift** given not because of merit but just because of grace. In Romans 1:11, Paul adds the adjective **spiritual** (*pneumatikos*, 4152) to further emphasize the fact that such gifts come from the Holy Spirit (cf. 1 Cor. 12:11).

Spiritual gifts are not natural abilities or talents, but rather they are divinely endowed spiritual faculties, or abilities, given for the purpose of edifying (building up) the body of Christ. There are three lists of spiritual gifts in the NT (Rom. 12:6–8; 1 Cor. 12:8–10; Eph. 4:11). While some of those were temporary sign gifts (1 Cor. 12:8–10) and are no longer needed since the completion of the NT Scriptures (1 Cor. 13:10), there are still plenty left that God gives.

The "office gifts" of Ephesians 4:11 consist of specially gifted men that God has given to the church as leaders. While the "apostles" and "prophets" (see June 27–28) were foundational and temporary, in their place God left "evangelists" (which literally refers to "church planters," as was Paul) and "pastor-teachers" (which is the correct grammatical construction referring to one office with a two-fold purpose; see June 29–July 1). Romans 12:6–8 adds to the list: prophecy (i.e., preaching, forthtelling), ministry (serving), teaching, exhortation, and giving.

The most thrilling truth here is that "every one of us" (Eph. 4:7) has received or will receive at least one spiritual gift. And what is it that gives these gifts? The **grace** of Christ. The same grace that saved us is the same grace that bestows spiritual gifts. We did not deserve salvation; neither do we deserve spiritual gifts. These gifts are given, not to lift us up, but to lift up, to build up the body of Christ. They are not for us to *flaunt*, but for God to *facilitate* the building and care of His church.

Scriptures for Study: In 1 Timothy 4:14 and 2 Timothy 1:6, what challenges does Paul give Timothy in relation to his spiritual gift?

Injurious [Person]

hubristēs

In his first letter to Timothy, Paul writes candidly that before his conversion on the road to Damascus (Acts 9:1–9), he was "a blasphemer, and a persecutor, and injurious" (1 Tim. 1:13). A "blasphemer" (*blasphēmos*, 989) is one who slanders God, which Paul (Saul) not only did but compelled Christians to do in his persecution of them (Acts 26:11). A "persecutor" (*diōktēs*, 1376) was one who pursued someone for the purpose of persecuting them.

Most graphic, however, is the fact that Paul says he was **injurious**. The Greek *hubristēs* (5197) is rendered in various ways among Bible translations: "insolent man" (NKJV), "violent man" (NIV), and "violent aggressor" (NASB). None of those, however, completely captures the idea. *Hubristēs* denotes a person who is not just violent, but who is *driven* by violence and contempt for others. To see them humiliated and suffering actually brings him pleasure. We could almost call him a sadist, although insanity is not implied. Acts 9:1 also declares that Saul was "breathing out threatenings and slaughter against the disciples of the Lord." It is no wonder that Paul was amazed by God's will to convert him.

Hubristēs also appears in the list of sins that describe man's fallen nature in Romans 1:30, where the AV translates it "despiteful." Additionally, our Lord used the verb form (*hubrizō*) to describe the mistreatment He would suffer during His arrest and trial (Luke 18:32, "spitefully").

What an encouragement this fact is to evangelism! We have all heard people say, "I'm too great a sinner for God to save me." Paul's story enables us to respond by asking them, "Have you ever murdered someone? Have you ever dragged someone out of their home and beat them in the street?" Fortunately, most people have not, but even if they have, God can save them as He did Paul.

Scriptures for Study: Read Acts 7:55–58, 8:1–4, and 9:1–2, noting the actions of Saul (Paul).

Revelation

apokalupsis

The Greek *apokalupsis* (602) is comprised of *kaluptō* (2572, "to veil") and *apo* (575, "from") to give us the idea of "to remove the veil" or "reveal" previously hidden things. The Bible teaches that God has revealed His truth through His Spirit and has made it known to us. That is Paul's desire, for example, in Ephesians 1:17, where he prays that we will understand that God has revealed truth.

There are those today who are looking for "new revelation." Some say, "If I just 'pray through' and if I just 'get the Spirit,' God will give me a revelation." But we lovingly say, "No, He will not." That is heresy. God has already revealed all that He is going to reveal in His Word and through His Spirit who energizes that Word. If we would just concentrate on that, we will be so busy studying the depth of it all that we will have no time to "seek other revelations."

Warren Wiersbe recounts a powerful illustration of this. The famous "newspaper publisher, William Randolph Hearst, invested a literal fortune collecting art treasures from around the world. One day Mr. Hearst found a description of some valuable items that he felt he must own, so he sent his agent abroad to find them. After months of searching, the agent reported that he had finally found the treasures. *They were in Mr. Hearst's warehouse*. Hearst had been searching frantically for treasures he already owned! Had he read the catalog of his treasures, he would have saved himself a great deal of money and trouble."[40]

That graphically illustrates many Christians today, some of whom resemble the old Gnostics. Gnosticism, which came to full bloom in the second century, boasted of a deeper, superior knowledge that only certain people could acquire. Many today seek some supposed "deeper life" or "higher blessing." Some go so far as to go back to the rituals and ceremonies of the OT, thinking that they hold some deeper significance than the simple truths of the NT. How foolish. Like William Randolph Hearst, they are clueless of what they already own. And what is the "catalog" of our treasures? The Word of God. If people will only search that, they will find all the treasures God has given.

Scriptures for Study: In Romans 16:25, what does God's revelation do for us? 📖 To what final revelation does 2 Thessalonians 1:7 refer?

Knowledge (1)

ginōsis

Today we consider a very common NT word (appearing 224 times) but one that carries great significance. Few things are as important as knowledge. In Classical Greek, *ginōsis* (verb *ginōskō*, 1097, "to know") originally meant recognition, to know something or someone by sight. Later it came to refer to knowledge gained by personal experience.

One of the most vivid usages of this word occurs in Philippians 3:10, where Paul reflects, "That I may know him, and the power of his resurrection, and the fellowship of his sufferings, being made conformable unto his death" (see also July 12). Paul's greatest desire was to know the Christ, to be more deeply and intimately acquainted with His Lord and Master. He didn't just want to know things *about* the Lord, but rather to know the Lord Himself.

There are several ways of knowing someone. We can know someone *historically*, but this touches only the mind, not the heart. We can know someone *contemporaneously*; we can read so much about someone that it's almost like knowing them, but still we do not. We might also know someone *contactually*, that is, we might actually meet the person, but this is still only an acquaintance, not intimate knowledge.

In contrast, we know some people *personally*. We not only know them by *name* but also by *nature*. We know their mind, ways of thinking, feelings, reactions, disposition, temperament, habits, and idiosyncrasies. That is how Paul wanted to know his Lord.

Is knowing our Lord that way our controlling desire? Do we want to know Him above all other knowledge? But how do we get to know Him? *Through His Word.*

First, we must more and more familiarize ourselves with Him *photographically* in the Gospels. As J. Sidlow Baxter puts it, it is in the pages of the Gospels that we see the "pen-photography" of those writers. It is there that we see the *real* Jesus, the God of the universe, living and moving before us. As we read, we see His thoughts, feelings, actions, attitudes, goals, values, compassions, and dealings with men.

Second, we get to know the Lord *doctrinally* in the NT epistles. The epistles contain the direct instruction to the church and Christians on how to live and minister based upon who Jesus was and what he did in the Gospels. It is impossible for Christians to grow, mature, and be strong without the doctrinal emphasis of the epistles. We will get this primarily from doctrinal preaching.

Scriptures for Study: What does 2 Peter 3:18 command? 📖 How can we know that we know the Lord (1 John 2:3–5; 3:24; 4:7; 4:13)?

Knowledge (2)

epignōsis

Yesterday we pondered the word *gnosis*, which means "experiential knowledge." In Ephesians 1:17, however—"That the God of our Lord Jesus Christ, the Father of glory, may give unto you the spirit of wisdom and revelation in the knowledge of him"—Paul uses an intensified form of this word, *epignōsis* (1922). By adding the prefix *epi* (1909, "motion upon or toward"), the word takes on the meaning of "an experiential, personal knowledge that is full and thorough." It also speaks of "precise and correct knowledge."[41] How vital it is that we have full, precise, thorough, and correct knowledge of God.

A driving force in my own life and ministry is a passion for precision. I loathe the ambiguity and relativism that rule our day. Paul speaks here of precise doctrine, exact knowledge, not something vague and relative to each person's experience. The modern philosophies of "open-mindedness" and "tolerance" were foreign to Paul's thinking and they should be expunged from the thinking of Christians today. Many today have "a zeal of God, but not according to knowledge" (*epignōsis*, Rom. 10:2).

No, we shall never know everything, but our knowledge is full in the sense that we know what is right and necessary for Christian living. And, of course, our knowledge continues to grow with more involvement with God's Word. In other words, our knowledge can be full from moment to moment; we can right now know what God wants us to know, but tomorrow we will know more; so, each moment we are living in the full potential of our present knowledge.

That should be the prayer of every pastor for his flock, as it was Paul's prayer for the Colossian believers: "For this cause we also, since the day we heard it, do not cease to pray for you, and to desire that ye might be filled with the knowledge of his will in all wisdom and spiritual understanding; That ye might walk worthy of the Lord unto all pleasing, being fruitful in every good work, and increasing in the knowledge of God" (Col. 1:9–10).

Scriptures for Study: In 2 Timothy 3:7, what is the sad condition of the unsaved person? 📖 In 2 Peter 1:3, what comes to us through the knowledge of Christ?

Depth (Deep Things)

bathos

In the last two days we have pondered two words for **knowledge** and have touched on the importance of **depth** in our learning. We continue those thoughts today by considering Paul's words in 1 Corinthians 2:9–10: "But as it is written, Eye hath not seen, nor ear heard, neither have entered into the heart of man, the things which God hath prepared for them that love him. But God hath revealed them unto us by his Spirit: for the Spirit searcheth all things, yea, the deep things of God."

It is puzzling to me why so many Christians, and even pastors, do not want depth, but prefer to "stay in the shallows." But there is nothing more exciting than "the deep things of God." The Greek literally reads, "the depths of (the) God." "Depths" translates *bathos* (899), from which is derived such English words as *bath* and *bathysphere*. It is used in its literal sense in the Parable of the Sower, where some of the seed "fell upon stony places, where they had not much earth: and forthwith they sprung up, because they had no deepness of earth" (Matt. 13:5). Used metaphorically, however, as it is here, it refers to greatness, immensity, profoundness, inscrutability, and abstruseness.

Paul also uses *bathos* in Ephesians 3:18, where he writes of his wish that believers comprehend four dimensions of God's love: **breadth**, **length**, **depth**, and **height**. The depth of Christ's love shows us the *condescension* of His love; that is, it shows that God has reached down from His level to our level. This dimension is indeed the most wonderful of the four. As Ephesians 2:1–5 makes vividly clear, it is impossible for man to be any lower or more depraved than he already is. **But God** (see Mar. 25) has reached down and redeemed man through His **love** and **grace**.

Why did Christ die for us? *Because He loved us*. This truth is even more astounding when we remember that there was absolutely nothing lovable about us. Romans 1:21–32 and 3:10–18 are two other passages that clearly outline man's wickedness. But praise be to God that *His love* is deeper than *our depravity*.

Scriptures for Study: What is referred to as being deep in Romans 11:33? 🕮 What is the significance of *bathos* in 2 Corinthians 8:2?

Breadth

platos

As we studied yesterday, in Ephesians 3:18 Paul writes of his wish that believers comprehend four dimensions of God's love: breadth, length, depth, and height. Having examined **depth**, let us now consider **breadth**. This is *platos* (4114), which is used figuratively here (and in Rev. 20:9) to mean the great expanses of the earth,[42] so the breadth of Christ's love shows the *extent* of His love, just how all-encompassing it is.

This extent of Christ's love is also in view in Ephesians 2:11–18, where we see God's acceptance of Jew *and* Gentile equally in Christ. Jews thought salvation was only for them. They had been *told* of Yahweh's love, but they never *understood* the extent of that love. God's love is upon all people without distinction.

Revelation 5:9 also declares the breadth of Christ's love in that he "redeemed us to God by [His] blood out of every kindred, and tongue, and people, and nation." In 7:9 John again records what he saw as the result of this breadth of love, namely, *worship*: "After this I beheld, and, lo, a great multitude, which no man could number, of all nations, and kindreds, and people, and tongues, stood before the throne, and before the Lamb, clothed with white robes, and palms in their hands; And cried with a loud voice, saying, Salvation to our God which sitteth upon the throne, and unto the Lamb."

Indeed, how we should praise and worship Him for the incomprehensible extent of His love! We'll continue the examination of these four dimensions of God's love tomorrow.

Scriptures for Study: How is the word breadth used in Revelation 20:9 and 21:16?

Length

mēkos

Continuing our study of four dimensions of God's love in Ephesians 3:18, we come to its **length**. The Greek is *mēkos* (3372), which simply speaks of length and here pictures the *duration* of Christ's love; that is, it shows that His love is eternal.

The love of Christ for us spans eternity past and eternity future. Ephesians 1:4, for example, declares that God loved us in eternity *past*, and 2:4 and 7 tell us of his love in eternity *future*. What a beautiful thought God conveyed to Jeremiah the prophet: "Yea, I have loved thee with an everlasting love" (Jer. 31:3). As many scientists consider time to be the "fourth dimension," so it is that God's love for His people transcends the physical universe to include time itself. Time is a created thing, and so it is that God loved His people before time existed, and he will love them after time ceases.

Consider also Paul's discussion of this in Romans 8. In verse 35 he asks, "Who shall separate us from the love of Christ?" He then goes through a list of things that many people might think are able to separate us from this love. But Paul then concludes in verse 39, "[Nothing] shall be able to separate us from the love of God, which is in Christ Jesus our Lord."

How sad it is that there are many who refuse to accept the fact of the security of the believer when the Word of God clearly says that *nothing* can separate us from Him. As the Lord Jesus said, "My sheep hear my voice, and I know them, and they follow me: And I give unto them eternal life; and they shall never perish, neither shall any man pluck them out of my hand" (John 10:27–28). That is eternal love, from the past to the future and for that little brief period called "time."

All this truth is not only a *grand encouragement*, but it's also a *great exhortation*. How dreadfully fickle we are in our spiritual affections! Often personal desire outweighs spiritual desire. Often worldly values are allowed to overpower spiritual values. But seeing the length of Christ's love should shame us. Dear Christian, let us "love Him because He first loved us" (1 John 4:19).

We'll conclude our meditations on these four dimensions of God's love tomorrow.

Scriptures for Study: Read Romans 8:35–39, noting your security in Christ.

Height

hupsos

Concluding our study of four dimensions of God's love in Ephesians 3:18, we come finally to its **height**. The Greek *hupsos* (5311) figuratively means elevation and dignity. This word appears, for example, in James 1:9–10: "Let the brother of low degree rejoice in that he is *exalted*: But the rich, in that he is made low," which means that "the poor, in contrast to the rich, are lifted up on high by God."[43]

The height of Christ's love, then, shows the *position* to which believers have been elevated; that is, it shows God's ultimate and final purpose for us. How blessed that is! Not only has Christ's love come *down* to us, but it also *elevates* us to a new and exalted position.

Notice Ephesians 2:6: "[God] hath raised us up together, and made us sit together in heavenly places in Christ Jesus." Think of it! Christ loves us so much that He has actually joined us to Himself. May we put it this way: We have been raised from the *depth* of our *sin* to the *height* of His *glory*.

Consider one other related passage: "Behold, what manner of love the Father hath bestowed upon us, that we should be called the sons of God: therefore the world knoweth us not, because it knew him not. Beloved, now are we the sons of God, and it doth not yet appear what we shall be: but we know that, when he shall appear, we shall be like him; for we shall see him as he is. And every man that hath this hope in him purifieth himself, even as he is pure" (1 John 3:1–3). To what greater height could we possibly be elevated!

Expositor John R. W. Stott summarizes these four dimensions with this observation: "The love of Christ is 'broad' enough to encompass all mankind (especially Jew and Gentile, the theme of these chapters), 'long' enough to last for eternity, 'deep' enough to reach the most degraded sinner, and 'high' enough to exalt him to heaven."[44] Let these dimensions become real in your life.

Scriptures for Study: In James 1:9, what is a cause for our rejoicing? 🕮 In Revelation 20:1–6, what will the saints of God one day do?

Eyes

ophthalmos

Paul often emphasized in his letters that we can know God only by His Word energized through the Holy Spirit, but Ephesians 1:18 contains one of the most fascinating examples: "the eyes of your understanding being enlightened." Many today speak of "seeking enlightenment," "finding themselves," and other such concepts. But here we see what Paul had to say about the matter. Starting today, we'll examine three words.

Eyes translates the Greek *ophthalmos* (3788), from which is derived such English words as *ophthalmologist*, which is, of course, an eye doctor. Used literally, it speaks of physical eyes, as when our Lord healed the blind man (Mark 8:22–26). Used metaphorically, however, as it is here, it means "to open the eyes of the mind, [that is], cause to perceive and understand."[45] Our Lord used this word when He struck down Paul on the road to Damascus and called him to go to the Gentiles and "open their eyes, and to turn them from darkness to light" (Acts 26:18).

This word is also used in a negative sense, as in Mark 7:20–23, where our Lord says, "That which cometh out of the man, that defileth the man," and that one of those things is an "evil eye," that is, a perception and understanding of evil. Tragically, as the existence of pornography proves, there are many today who have an evil eye. Paul also writes that men's problem is that "there is no fear of God before their eyes" (Rom. 3:18).

On the positive side, however, Luke the Physician declared, "For mine eyes have seen thy salvation" (Luke 2:30). He also records our Lord's use of the word to expose the hypocrisy of the Pharisees. While they criticized the minor faults of others, pictured by a splinter in the eye, they failed to recognize their own huge faults, pictured by a timber in their eye (6:41–42).

Herein is the challenge for us to open our eyes and perceive God's truth.

Scriptures for Study: What are our eyes to see in John 4:35? 📖 What is the people's problem in Acts 28:27?

Understanding

dianoia

Yesterday we considered the spiritual significance of the word **eyes** as it relates metaphorically to perceiving God's truth. Paul uses a related word in Ephesians 1:18 to elaborate on that principle: "the eyes of your understanding being enlightened."

Understanding translates *dianoia* (1271), which means "ability to think, faculty of knowledge."[46] (See Apr. 26 for another word translated *understanding* and *understand*). As first-century Jewish philosopher Philo said, "What the eye is to the body, that is the mind to the soul."[47] In other words, while the eye *sees*, it is the mind that *understands* what is seen. Paul is, therefore, saying that our minds, our ability to think, our capacity for knowledge and understanding needs enlightenment. As we saw in our February 2 and 3 studies, people look for truth in science, philosophy, and religion, but never find it. Truth is to be found only in God's Word. So Paul is saying here that truth is to be found somewhere outside of ourselves, that we need enlightenment from an outside source.

There are several significant occurrences of *dianoia*. Our Lord uses it in Matthew 22:37–38, where He sums up the first four of the Ten Commandments into one: "Thou shalt love the Lord thy God with all thy heart, and with all thy soul, and with all thy mind [*dianoia*]. This is the first and great commandment." Paul uses it again in Colossians 1:21 to demonstrate that while we were once alienated from God in our minds (that is, our ability to think and understand), we are now reconciled and can "think straight."

Peter also uses this word in a unique way when he writes, "Wherefore gird up the loins of your mind, be sober, and hope to the end for the grace that is to be brought unto you at the revelation of Jesus Christ" (1 Pet. 1:13). "Gird up" is *anazōnnumi*, which appears only here in the NT. It's taken from the custom of that day to bind up their long garments in a girdle or belt when exerting themselves (see Oct. 3). The metaphor, then, is that our minds are to be in constant preparation for "spiritual exertion."

Scriptures for Study: In Hebrews 10:16, what does God put into the hearts and minds of His people? 🕮 In 2 Peter 3:1, what does Peter say was his purpose in writing both of his epistles?

Enlightened

phōtizō

Turning one final time to Ephesians 1:18—"the eyes of your understanding being enlightened"—we see one other word. **Enlightened** is the verb *phōtizō* (5461), which means "to give light, to shine." It, along with the noun *phōs* (5457; see June 15–16), is the source of such English words as *photo*.

The apostle John declares that, "In [Christ] was life; and the life was the light of men. And the light shineth in darkness; and the darkness comprehended it not" (John 1:4–5). Using *phōs* as a proper name, the apostle John goes on to recount how God sent John the Baptist to "to bear witness of the Light, that all men through him might believe" and that Christ alone "was the true Light, which lighteth every man that cometh into the world" (vv. 7, 9). And even though the Light is there, men "comprehended it not" (v. 5) and willfully continue to walk (John 12:35), and even "abide" (*menō*, "to remain in one place," see June 2) "in darkness" (12:46).

Paul uses *phōtizō* in 1 Corinthians 4:5 to describe coming judgment, that the Lord "will bring to light the hidden things of darkness, and will make manifest the counsels of the hearts." Men think they can hide their actions and even themselves from God, but one day everything will be exposed.

In Ephesians 1:18, then, *phōtizō* speaks of giving understanding, and culminates what Paul has been saying. Enlightenment does not come from sitting cross-legged on the floor and "contemplating the sound of one hand clapping" or other such nonsensical notions. True enlightenment comes from Christ and His Word.

I cannot begin to count how many times during in-depth study of a particularly difficult passage, verse, or word that God has enlightened me, when, as the expression goes, "the light came on" and I saw the truth. That's what God does—He brings understanding of His truth to our minds. It is through our "spiritual eyes" that we are enlightened and know God's truth.

You might not have the physical eyes of legendary fighter and test pilot Chuck Yeager who could see enemy planes fifty miles away, but God has given you perfect spiritual sight if you but use it.

Scriptures for Study: What has been brought to light by the Gospel (2 Tim. 1:10)? 🕮 What great truth does Revelation 21:23 declare?

Exceeding Greatness

huperballon megethos

Preachers talk much about God's greatness, but just how great *is* He? There are some Greek words that provide us with a glimpse. There are actually several such words in one single verse, Ephesians 1:19: "the exceeding greatness of his power to us-ward who believe, according to the working of his mighty power."

Greatness translates *megethos* (3174), which appears only here in the NT, and means "strong" or "great." This obviously wasn't good enough for Paul, so he adds *huperballō* (**exceeding**, 5235), which is a compound word from *huper* (5228, "over, above, or beyond"), and *ballō* (906, "to put or cast"). The literal meaning, then, is "to throw beyond the usual mark," so metaphorically, to excel or surpass. The full idea of the expression *huperballon megethos*, therefore, is a power that is beyond measure, super abounding or surpassing power, power that is "more than enough."

One Greek authority makes this comment: "The word *megethos* is found only here in the NT. Such Pauline *hapax legomena* (words used only once) again reflect the outreach of the great apostle's mind in seeking to describe the wonders of divine redemption. One can almost see words stretching at their seams as Paul tries to pour more meaning into them."[48]

Also notice that Paul doesn't include what God's power exceeds. The obvious implication is that it *exceeds everything*. What a thought! The God who not only spoke the universe into existence, but who raised Christ from the dead and who "put all things under [Christ's] feet, and gave him to be the head over all things" (Eph. 1:22) has power that is far beyond any possibility of measuring. What instrument could exist that could do so? Paul simply could not say enough about the greatness and majesty of God, and as exact a language as Greek is, he still had difficulty even finding words to express his thoughts. And, as we'll see tomorrow, he isn't even close to being done yet.

Scriptures for Study: How does Deuteronomy 10:17 describe God? 📖 What does Titus 2:13 tells us to do in regard to our "great" (*megas*) God?

Power (1)

dunamis

As we saw yesterday, Ephesians 1:19 uses several words to describe God's power: "the exceeding greatness of his power to us-ward who believe, according to the working of his mighty power." He heaps one word upon another to express that truth.

The first occurrence of the word **power** is *dunamis* (1411), from which are derived English words such as *dynamic* and *dynamite*. Used over 100 times in the NT, it speaks of inherent or raw power, the ability to do wonders, and that which overcomes any resistance.

There are many incredibly powerful explosives in our day, such as C-4, Petin, and many others that can overcome virtually any obstacle. One of the men in my church was in the military for many years and one day shared with me a humorous, tongue-in-cheek saying heard around explosives specialists: "There is no problem so insurmountable that it cannot be solved by the proper application of high explosives." Likewise, while explosives didn't exist in ancient times and so Paul is obviously not thinking such things, he is telling us that we have at our disposal a power that can overcome any obstruction to our Christian walk.

Now let us realize that this power is "toward us who believe." Does this mean that God wants us to have this kind of power within? *Yes!* Paul's prayer is that we will know God's power *by experience*. Are you getting the picture? We have no excuse for living in mediocrity or defeat, no excuse for living in a life of ups and downs, for this violates the very power we've been given.

As Paul wrote Timothy, for example, "For God hath not given us the spirit of fear; but of power, and of love, and of a sound mind" (2 Tim. 1:7). Like many Christians, "Timid Timothy" had a tendency to be fearful in witnessing, but Paul promises that God gives the believer power to overcome such obstacles.

Scriptures for Study: In Acts 1:8, what does the Holy Spirit's power enable you to do? 🕮 What is the power of God in 1 Corinthians 1:18?

Power (2)

ischos

Ephesians 1:19 gives us still another glimpse at God's great power: "the exceeding greatness of his power to us-ward who believe, according to the working of his mighty power." The second occurrence of the word **power** is the Greek *ischus* (2479), which speaks of strength and ability (especially physical). Does this physical ability mean we can go out and leap tall buildings at a single bound? Of course not. But God does give us physical strength and stamina beyond what we in our own weakness could ever hope to know.

Added to this is **working**, which is *energeia* (1753, English *energy*, see May 31), which speaks of power in operation or power in action; that is, it pictures something going on, a force that is actively working. Still further is the word **mighty**, which translates *kratos* (2904), "power excited into action." Greek scholar John Eadie compares them this way: "*Ischus* [power], to take a familiar illustration, is the power lodged in the arm, *kratos* [might] is that arm stretched out or uplifted with conscious aim, while *energeia* [working] is the same arm at actual work, accomplishing the designed result."[49]

What a picture! And that is what God wants us to know! These three words also occur together in Ephesians 6:10: "Finally, my brethren, be strong [*endunamoō*] in the Lord, and in the power [*kratos*] of his might [*ischus*]."

Putting all this together, Paul prays (and every pastor should pray) that we may know the surpassing, super-abounding greatness of His inherent, overcoming power, a power that is in action showing the strength of His might.

Why does Paul use so many terms? As John Eadie writes again: "The use of so many terms arises from a desire to survey the Power of God in all its phases; for the spectacle is so magnificent, that the apostle lingers to admire and contemplate it. Epithet is not heaped on epithet at random, but for a specific object. The mental emotion of the writer is anxious to embody itself in words, and, after all its efforts, it laments the poverty of exhausted language."[50]

Indeed, when it comes to describing God, words fail even the brilliance of Paul. Human language is simply too limited.

Scriptures for Study: In Acts 19:20, what "mightily [*kratos*] grew"? 🕮 In 1 Peter 4:11, what does God's power give us the "ability" *(ischus)* to do?

Power (3)

dunamis

Returning to the word *dunamis* (1411), which we examined on February 28, Ephesians 3:20 is another verse that stands out as one of the most descriptive in all of God's Word concerning His power: "Now unto him that is able to do exceeding abundantly above all that we ask or think, according to the power that worketh in us."

The first truth we should notice here is that God "is able." Scripture several times declares what God is able to do. With the threat of being cast into the furnace for not bowing to worship Nebuchadnezzar, Shadrach, Meshach, and Abednego humbly responded, "If it be so, our God whom we serve is able to deliver us from the burning fiery furnace, and he will deliver us out of thine hand, O king" (Dan. 3:17). (See today's "Scriptures for Study" for other instances.)

Because He is able, God can do "exceeding abundantly above all that we ask or think." "Exceeding abundantly" is an amazing expression. It is a very rare double compound, *huperekperissou*. The prefix *hyper* means "over, beyond, or above," the primary preposition *ek* means "out of or from," and the root *perissos* means "over and above, more than enough." It wasn't enough for Paul to say that *God can do more than enough*, but he wanted to say that He can do *above and beyond* more than enough. What a paradox! How can one do more than more than enough?

But even that is not all, for Paul adds "above" (*huper*). The full thought then is: Not only can God do *more than enough*, and *above and beyond* more than enough, but *even more* than above and beyond more than enough. In short, God can do infinitely more than what any of us can "ask" or even "think" about asking.

All that is still inadequate, however, to describe the **power** of God. Martyn Lloyd-Jones said it well: "Our greatest superlatives do not describe the power of God. Add one to another, multiply them, and add them together, and multiply again, and go on doing so 'beyond all things,' exceedingly abundantly above all things, and still you have not succeeded in describing it."[51] And let us be reminded, this is the same power "that worketh in us."

Scriptures for Study: Read the following verses, noting in each what God is able to do: Matthew 10:28; 2 Corinthians 9:8; Philippians 3:21; Hebrews 7:25; Jude 24.

Power (4)

exousia

Still another word in the Greek NT translated as the word **power** is *exousia* (1849), which is also often translated "authority." In Classical Greek, *exousia* denoted unrestricted freedom of action, power, authority, and right of action.[52] These meanings are evident throughout Scripture as well.

God's authority and right to act are evident in His absolute sovereignty. Most graphic is the picture of God in Romans 9:21: "Hath not the potter power over the clay, of the same lump to make one vessel unto honour, and another unto dishonour?" Acts 1:7 likewise declares that God has authority and control over the **times** and the **seasons** (see Aug. 27).

The authority of Christ is equally vivid. In Matthew 9:2–8, as Jesus heals and forgives sins, He states that only God has the "power" (authority) to do so. Here, in fact, is a clear claim to deity. Jesus also taught with "authority," unlike the scribes, who could teach only by tradition and human reason (Mark 1:22). It was that same "authority" that gave Him the right to cleanse the temple from those who defiled it with their merchandizing (Matt. 21:12–13, 23).

Amazingly, and by God's wondrous **grace** (see Feb. 13), the Christian has been granted *exousia*. Most notable is John 1:12, which declares that because of our faith in Christ we have the "power" (right) to be called "the sons of God." The Christian also has "liberty" in Christ to do as he wishes as long as it doesn't violate scriptural command or become a "stumblingblock to them that are weak" (1 Cor. 8:9; 4–6, 12, 13). Martin Luther put it well: "A Christian is a perfectly free lord of all, subject to none. A Christian is a perfectly dutiful servant of all, subject to all."[53]

Scriptures for Study: In Colossians 1:13, from what "power" have we been delivered? 📖 In Revelation 22:14, to what does the true believer have a right?

Fullness (1)

plērōma

The Greek words behind **fullness** (noun *plērōma* [4138] and verb *plēroō* [4137]) occur over 100 times in the NT. Ephesians 1:22–23 is a particularly striking example: "The church, which is his body, the fulness of him that filleth all in all." *Plērōma* refers to "that which is filled." It was used of a ship being filled with sailors, rowers, soldiers, and even cargo. The same basic word is then used as a verb ("filleth") later in the verse. The tense of the verb is a present participle, showing continuous action. One aspect of this is that Christ fills the church with His own life.

Another aspect, however, is that *the church is also His fullness*. In other words, as a head must have a body to complement it, so Christ must have the church to manifest His glory. John Calvin put it in these profound words: "This is the highest honor of the church that until He is united to us, the Son of God reckons Himself in some measure incomplete. What consolation it is for us to learn that not until we are in His presence does He possess all His parts, nor does He wish to be regarded as complete. Hence, in the First Epistle to the Corinthians [1 Cor. 12:12–31], when the apostle discusses largely the metaphor of a human body, he includes under the single name of Christ the whole Church."[54]

What a statement that is! To think that the sovereign Creator, perfect and complete in Himself, chooses to consider Himself, in a sense, incomplete without His Church. What a staggering thought! So, the full idea conveyed here in Paul's statement is that *Christ continues to fill the church so that the church can be the full expression of Christ.*

Another striking usage of *plērōma* occurs in Romans 13:10: "Love worketh no ill to his neighbour: therefore love is the fulfilling of the law." The last six of the Ten Commandments concern our relationship with other people. If we are filled with love, right treatment of others will be automatic. We'll look at another profound usage tomorrow.

Scriptures for Study: With what are we to be filled according to Ephesians 5:18? 🕮 How does Colossians 2:9 prove the deity of Christ?

Fullness (2)

plērōma

Adding to yesterday's study of *plērōma* (4138), another way of translating this word is "domination" or similar forms. In fact, this translation fits in all the instances of the various Greek forms used in Ephesians:

- 1:23 —"[The church], which is His body, the [domination] of Him that [dominates] all in all."
- 4:10 —"that He might [dominate] all things."
- 4:13 —"unto the measure of the stature of the [domination] of Christ."
- 5:18 —"be [dominated] with the Spirit."

With that in mind, we could translate Ephesians 3:19 this way: "That you may be filled up to all the dominance of God." To be filled with God's fullness means we are emptied of self and are totally dominated by Him. Let us express it thusly: *To be filled with the fullness of God is to be dominated by His dominance.*

At this point, we might ask, "But how is it possible to be totally dominated by God? How can our every thought, impulse, value, and goal be totally dominated by God?"

An illustration should help. If we blow air into a balloon, we can truthfully say, "This balloon is full of air." But we can then blow a little more air into the balloon and say, "It's still full, but bigger." Likewise, we can be filled with His fullness today, but we will be fuller tomorrow. This is indeed an ever-continuing process. How tragic it is when Christians, laymen and preachers alike, think they have grown enough or think they know enough! Let us each ask ourselves, "Am I being filled with all 'the fullness of God'? Am I being dominated by His dominance?"

Charles Spurgeon wrote, "The more we know the more are we conscious of our ignorance of that which is unknown." He goes on to quote Dr. Thomas Chalmers, nineteenth-century theologian, professor of theology at Edinburgh, and one of the greatest preachers of that age. Borrowing an illustration from his love of mathematics, Chalmers would tell his students, "The wider the diameter of light, the greater is the circumference of darkness." In other words, as Spurgeon concludes, "The more a man knows, he comes at more points into contact with the unknown."[55] Someone else has expressed it even more succinctly, "Knowledge is the discovery of ignorance."

We'll conclude our thoughts tomorrow.

Scriptures for Study: What promise does Romans 15:14 declare? 🕮 Even in tribulation, with what was Paul filled in 2 Corinthians 7:4?

Fullness (3)

plērōma

Yesterday we introduced the thought of being dominated by God's dominance. In practical application, how can we realistically be totally dominated by God?

First, we will be dominated by God when we read His Word. Your reading these devotionals every day certainly demonstrates your desire for growth; reading Scripture itself unlocks the door of Christian growth. Whether you read the Bible through in one year (which you can do by reading about three and a half chapters per day), read one of Paul's epistles per month by reading one chapter a day and thereby read it through several times, or follow some other method, you must avoid reading mechanically, just "to get the job done." You must read with understanding and meditate upon what you read. Reading a single verse with understanding is infinitely better than three chapters with no comprehension. You might want to jot down in a notebook lessons you learn and blessings God gives. When questions arise, write those down as well and ask your pastor about them.

Second, we'll be dominated by God when we submit to the expository preaching and teaching of God's Word as absolute truth. If you're in a church where this is not the primary ministry, find one where it is. Scripture is very clear on this issue (see May 18ff.), for no other so-called ministry will bring real growth.

Third, we'll be dominated by God when we obey what we read and hear. Knowledge without application is less than worthless—it's actually destructive. As Paul told the Corinthians, "knowledge puffeth up, but [love] edifieth" (1 Cor. 8:1). Facts alone only make us arrogant. It's application that makes us humble.

Fourth, we'll be dominated by God when we spend time in prayer. Mark it down, you will not consistently do the first three—read, listen, and apply—unless you pray. They are, in fact, impossible without prayer. Unless you commune with God (1 Thess. 5:17), you won't understand what you read, you won't want to listen to preaching, and you won't apply anything because you're not humbling yourself before God. It is through prayer that you will confess your sins (1 John 1:9), ask for wisdom (James 1:5), and pray for others (Col. 1:9; 1 Thess. 5:25).

Scriptures for Study: In Acts 12:24 and 19:20, what "grew" and "prevailed"? 📖 What is Peter's challenge to us in 2 Peter 3:18?

Trespasses

paraptōma

There are several different approaches to the "sin question" as far as man is concerned. There are, of course, people who don't recognize a "sin problem" at all. Such people view sin as an accident, mistake, or indiscretion. Others view it as merely an "amiable weakness" or simple "immaturity." Liberal theology, led by men such as Robert Schuller, views "the core of sin [as] a lack of self-esteem." In addition to those approaches, there is also a general sense of flippancy about sin nowadays. Worse is the fact that in much modern preaching, even among evangelicals, sin is not dealt with at all.

In stark contrast, there are two Greek words that very graphically reveal God's view of sin. Both of these words, in fact, appear together in Ephesians 2:1, where Paul declares that we "were dead in trespasses and sins."

We'll examine the word **sin** tomorrow, but the word **trespasses** is *paraptōma* (3900), which consists of *para* (3844), "along side of," and *piptō* (4098), "to fall." The word, therefore, pictures a deviation to one side or the other. It was used at times by the ancient Greeks to describe an error, a mistake in judgment, or a blunder. But that idea is never even implied in the NT.[56] Rather the NT usage strongly emphasizes a deliberate act with its serious consequences. In fact, the key to understanding this is to realize that **trespasses** speaks of a *willful deviation from God's requirement.*

Romans 5:15–20 uses the word *offence* (*paraptōma*) several times to describe clearly Adam's sin as a willful deviation from God's command: "through the offence of one many be dead . . . by one man's offence death reigned by one . . . by the offence of one judgment came upon all men to condemnation . . . Moreover the law entered, that the offence might abound. But where sin abounded, grace did much more abound."

What's the application? Simply that we are all willful sinners. We, just as Adam, Achan, Saul, and Israel, deliberately disobey God's commands. We don't just make mistakes; we don't just commit indiscretions; we don't just "trip up." We are *willful sinners*. We sin not because "the devil made us do it," not because it's our spouse's fault, not because we had a bad childhood. We sin because we choose to sin; we deviate from the commands of God.

Thank God for His **forgiveness**! (see Jan. 25).

Scriptures for Study: In Galatians 6:1, what two things should we do for a fellow Christian who is "overtaken in a fault" (*paraptōma*)? 🕮 What does James 5:16 add?

Sin

hamartia

A second graphic word for **sin** in the NT is *hamartia* (266), from the verb *hamartanō* (264), "to miss the mark." The verb was used in ancient Greek of a spearman missing the target at which he aimed and threw his spear. It then came to be used in the ethical sense of not measuring up to a standard, or falling short of a purpose or standard. The pivotal verse on this principle is Romans 3:23: "For all have sinned, and come short of the glory of God." What is sin? *Missing the mark.* What then is the mark for which we shoot? *The glory of God.* In other words, the mark we shoot for is to be worthy of glory, *but we miss it every time.*

In his commentary on Romans, William Barclay offers these fitting words: "We commonly have a wrong idea of sin. We would readily agree that the robber, murderer, the razor-slasher, the drunkard, the gangster are sinners, but, since most of us are respectable citizens, in our heart of hearts we think that sin has not very much to do with us. We would probably rather resent being called hell-deserving sinners. But *hamartia* brings us face to face with what sin is, the failure to be what we ought to be and could be."[57]

Indeed, a common misconception of sin is that it is something we *do*, when actually sin is something we do *not* do. And what is the thing we don't do? We do not measure up to God's standard of holiness. God is holy, perfect, absolutely pure; our sin, then, is not measuring up to that standard. All the "sins" we do are the result of what we *don't* do. How far we fall short of the glory of God!

Man's view of sin is truly distorted, and rightly so; his sinfulness distorts his view of his sinfulness and guilt. But God's view is clear—man has willfully deviated from God's law and has fallen far short of God's standard of holiness.

Once again, we thank God for His **forgiveness** (see Jan. 25).

Scriptures for Study: How many times is sin mentioned in Romans 6? Review what it means to be "dead in trespasses and sins" (see Jan. 12). 📖 Thankfully, where sin abounds, what else abounds, according to Romans 5:20 (see Feb. 13–14).

World

kosmos

Depending upon a given context, **world** (*kosmos*, 2889) can mean several things: earth, human race, etc. In its some 188 occurrences, however, it usually speaks of the "world system" or "world order," that is, the values, pleasures, inclinations, philosophies, goals, drives, purposes, attitudes, and actions of society. This system is totally man-centered and is quite vivid in the humanistic and relativistic society of today.

Ponder this contrast: Jesus' words were, "Not my will but *thine* be done"; man's words are, "Not thy will, but *mine* be done." As Martyn Lloyd-Jones put it, "They think as the world thinks. They take their opinions ready-made from their favourite newspaper. Their very appearance is controlled by the world and its changing fashion."[58]

This domination of the world over man is seen today in every area of life. The popular phrase, "I am my own person," is false and foolish, because every person is dominated by the world. For example, most people just "follow the trends," the trends of dress, hair style, morality, and countless other things. Most people think that these trends are isolated, that they are all unrelated and are without any meaning. On the contrary, they are not isolated; they are all part of an underlying philosophy—*worldliness*. Legalism teaches that worldliness is what we do or don't do, such as playing cards, going to a movie theater, or women wearing pants. Worldliness, however, is not something we *do*, but rather it's something we *believe*. Outward behavior will certainly be an outworking of this, but worldliness is an attitude, a mindset, a philosophy.

All men and women, even Christians, are in one way or another dominated by the world. Why? Because we're human; we are sinful. Only the Spirit of God can give victory over this domination. How tragic it is when Christians are dominated by the world! That is the reason for commands such as 1 John 2:15: "Love not the world, neither the things that are in the world. If any man love the world, the love of the Father is not in him."

Scriptures for Study: Read 1 John 4, noting the significance of the word **world**. 🕮 In light of that, what promise is given to the believer in 1 John 5:4?

Old Man

palaios anthropos

The very opposite of the **new man** (see Jan.1) is the **old man**. A key verse here is Romans 6:6: "Knowing this, that our old man is crucified with him, that the body of sin might be destroyed, that henceforth we should not serve sin." Oddly, this verse has been a battleground for centuries. The question has been not whether we become holy in Christ—all agree there—but rather *how* this holiness is brought about.

All misunderstanding, however, comes from the misconception that Romans 6:6 refers to something that happens in our own experience, that it is something that we do in our efforts, something that comes as a result of our own struggling against sin. *But that is the exact opposite of what the text says.*

The key to understanding this verse comes in recognizing that *all the verb tenses in Romans 6 are past tenses* (aorist or perfect). In other words, every verb tense that refers to our identification with Christ in His death refers to it being completed in the past. Romans 6:6, therefore, says that our "old man *was* crucified" way back when Christ died and that it was completed then and there. It does not say that we must each morning get up and "crucify ourselves again to sin." Rather it says that by *God's judicial act*, not by our experiential effort, the old man was "crucified" and therefore "destroyed." **Old** is *palaios* (3820), which means "old in the sense of worn out, decrepit, useless."[59] So, the old, worn out, decrepit person we used to be has been "destroyed" (past tense of *katargeō*, 2673), "to render inactive, put out of use, cancel, bring to nothing, do away with." This has been replaced by the new man.

Based on that fact of the language, the old man can refer to only one thing: *all that we were in Adam*, that is, all the guilt, penalty, power, and dominion of sin that was in Adam. Immediately we want to ask, "But I *do* still sin—why?" We'll deal with that tomorrow. The point here is that sin is not the *rule* of life like it was before. We are not dominated by sin as we once were. The old man is gone because of what Christ accomplished on Calvary. We are not *sinless*, as we'll see, but we do "sin *less*" because we are *no longer dominated and controlled by sin*. While sin used to rule, it is now Christ who rules.

Scriptures for Study: What is the contrast in Romans 7:6 ("oldness" is *palaiotes*, "antiquated")? 🕮 *Palaios* also means "not recent, what is of long standing." What is the point, then, of 1 John 2:7?

Flesh (1)

sarx

If the **old man** has been destroyed, why do we still sin? Paul knew that question would arise, so right after he writes Romans 6, he writes Romans 7, where he laments over "the flesh." While the old man is gone, while sin doesn't rule and dominate, "the **flesh**" remains.

The Greek *sarx* (4561) occurs eighty-nine times in Paul's epistles (excluding Hebrews) and refers to: the physical body thirty-seven times (e.g., Rom. 2:28), humanity or that which is human twenty-five times (3:20), and *inherent evil in the human nature* twenty-seven times (7:5). Romans 7:5, in fact, defines that third use by calling it "the motions of sins."

"Motions" is an Old English term for "impulses," which is the idea in the Greek *pathēma* (3804), from *pathos* (3806; English, *pathology*), and "describes the emotions of the soul, i.e., human feelings, and impulses which a man does not produce within himself but finds already present, and by which he can be carried away." In Classical Greek, "it acquired a predominately negative meaning, that of passion."[60] We can, indeed, be carried away by our passions.

"The flesh," then, is the selfish inclinations, self-centered perversity and propensity, the desire for self-gratification and self-satisfaction that is inherent in our moral nature. While Satan is certainly the ultimate foe, our greatest enemy is ourselves, our flesh. Martin Luther hit the nail squarely when he wrote, "I dread my own heart more than the pope and all his cardinals, for within me is the greater pope, even self."

We have two "states of mind," the *higher* and the *lower*; the higher is our spirituality, the lower is the flesh. The higher is present because of the indwelling Holy Spirit (Rom. 8), and the lower remains because we are still in the flesh. That is precisely Paul's point in Romans 7, where he says that the flesh was "another law in [his] members, warring against the law of [his] mind" (v. 23). He laments that the things he wanted to do he didn't do and the very things he didn't want to do were the things he did (v. 19). He then asks, "O wretched man that I am! who shall deliver me from the body of this death?" (v. 24). Herein is the war of the **flesh**, the sin that still remains in us (v. 18).

Thankfully, however, as we'll conclude tomorrow, God provides the victory.

Scriptures for Study: What does Romans 7:5 declare? 🕮 What is the command of Romans 13:14?

Flesh (2)

sarx

As noted yesterday, there is within us "the higher" and "the lower" (Rom. 7). The question now is, "How does 'the higher' rule? How do we deal with those passions and impulses that remain?" Indeed, if Paul had stopped with Romans 7, we would have cause for deep depression. But he *didn't* stop there. In Romans 8 he reveals the truth that the indwelling Holy Spirit provides the victory over the flesh. *In fact, "the flesh" is never mentioned in chapter 8 without the Holy Spirit also being mentioned* (vv. 1, 3–4, 5, 8–9, 12–13).

We have, therefore, been freed from sin in two ways: freed from the **old man** *positionally* by the past action of Christ (Rom. 6) and then *experientially* from the **flesh** by the indwelling Holy Spirit (Rom. 7–8).

Ponder this: *We do not have the inability to sin, but we do have the ability not to sin.* Did you get it? Have we reached sinless perfection? Have we reached the point where we no longer sin? Certainly not. But we still have the ability not to sin, we can still claim the victory over sin by the power of the Holy Spirit. No longer can we say, "I just couldn't help it." Yes, we can "help it" because of the Holy Spirit. Even though our passions and impulses are strong, we can claim the victory. Again, we are not sinless, but we do "sin *less*."

As 1 Corinthians 10:13 declares: "There hath no temptation taken you but such as is common to man: but God is faithful, who will not suffer you to be tempted above that ye are able; but will with the temptation also make a way to escape, that ye may be able to bear it." God promises that temptation to sin will never overwhelm us, that our passions and impulses do not control us.

How often do we try to run and hide from the sins that defeat us? But that is the wrong approach. We can and must face our passions and impulses. In the power of the Holy Spirit, we can say to those impulses, "I'm not afraid of you. I'm not going to run away from you. I claim God's power in my life to deliver me from myself. I'm *not* the old man, so I'm not going to *act* like the old man."

Scriptures for Study: Read Romans 8:1–13, noting how the Holy Spirit is mentioned in regard to victory over the flesh.

Put Off

apotithēmi

In light of our studies of the last three days, Ephesians 4:22 adds an important exhortation, that we **put off** the **old man**. This expression is the Greek *apotithēmi* (659), which is taken from the picture of taking off a garment and is in the aorist tense showing a once-for-all putting off of the old man. As we would take off old worthless clothes and never use them again, we take off the old man.

Commentator John Phillips recounts the time when he read the following words in the window of a dry-cleaning establishment: "If your clothes aren't becoming to you, you should be coming to us." As Phillips recognized, while that was a clever slogan, it's not what Paul is saying here. We don't send our old garments out to be cleaned; they are not becoming to a Christian so we take them off forever. That is precisely what is the problem with so-called moral reform. You cannot change people's lives until you first change their hearts. We cannot mend the old man; he must be transformed into the **new man**.

Some Christians have the mistaken idea that the old man is put off sometime during our Christian walk, but that is false. The old man was put off at salvation—the old garment was removed. The sobering application is that a person who claims to be a Christian, but whose life has not changed, is not truly born again.

A question arises here. As we've seen, Romans 6:6 declares that we are already dead to sin, that the old man, all that we were in Adam, was destroyed. So why does Paul now say to put off what has already been destroyed? The answer is simple: Romans 6:6 is *positional*, while Ephesians 4:22 is *practical*; the first is *doctrinal*, the second *experiential*. Paul is saying, "I want what has happened positionally to be true in your experience." Yes, we're dead to sin because of what Jesus accomplished in the past, which is exactly why we now willfully no longer act like sinners. We are *not* the old man, so we must not *act* like we are. Daily we put off the "remnants" of the old man (Eph. 4:22–29). In the next few days, we'll examine those remnants.

Scriptures for Study: What is Paul's similar exhortation in Romans 13:12? 🕮 Likewise, what does Hebrews 12:1 encourage using the words *lay aside* (*apotithēmi*)?

Lying

pseudos

While for decades well-meaning men have come up with various lists of "do's and don'ts" for conduct, such lists are often legalistic and without authority. In contrast, Ephesians 4:22–29 is one of God's lists. This passage lists the remnants of the **old man.** There are other such lists in Scripture—the one in Proverbs 6:16–19, for example, perhaps being the most exhaustive and all-encompassing—but the list here is unique in its *specific application to the Christian*. These sins are the sins most likely to creep back into the Christian's life.

Because **lying** is the most prominent sin of mankind, and because truth is the most essential characteristic of Christianity, Paul mentions lying first. The Greek *pseudos* (5579), where we get our English *pseudo* (as in *pseudonym*, a false name), occurs "in Greek from the time of Homer" and means "the antithesis of **truth**, *alēthei*."[61] Writing from Ephesus, the apostle John wrote to churches in Asia Minor that they knew "the truth" and "that no lie is of the truth" (1 John 2:21). There's not even the slightest bit of truth in a lie, no "gray area" as is commonly believed. Even the smallest lie negates the truth.

A lie, therefore, is "a statement that is contrary to fact offered with the intent to deceive." There are, of course, two parts to that definition. A statement that is contrary to fact is not necessarily a lie. For example, if I tell someone that I'll meet them at a certain time but am late due to car trouble, I didn't lie because I wasn't trying to deceive them. But if I said I'd be there at a certain time, knowing that I'd be late, that would be a lie.

Such things as kidding, fictional stories, figurative language, and not saying something out of politeness are not lying. There are many things, however, that *are* lying: blatant falsehoods, exaggerating or embellishing a story, cheating (because you're saying you did something on your own when you didn't), betraying a confidence, making excuses for wrong conduct, telling a half-truth, plagiarism, boasting, flattery, false humility, hypocrisy, false promises, and tragically much more. In short, when we say anything that is not true in its entirety, it's a lie.

Indeed, lying is a universal vice, a part of man's very core, and is a habit with which even the Christian will struggle. But God does give the victory.

Scriptures for Study: In John 8:44, who is the father of lies? 🕮 Read Acts 5:1–11. To demonstrate the seriousness of lying, what was the penalty for it?

Anger

orgē

A second remnant of the **old man** that can easily creep back into the Christian's life is sinful **anger**. In Ephesians 4:26, Paul commands that while we can get angry, we must not sin in that anger. The Greek is *orgē* (3709; verb, *orgizō*, 3710), which is distinct from the Greek *thumos* (2372). While *thumos* is passionate and temporary, *orgē* indicates "a more enduring state of mind."[62] The idea here then is that there is what is called "righteous anger." This is a settled state of mind in which there is an indignation and hatred of that which is offensive to and sinful against God and a desire for God's justice.

With the words "and sin not," however, Paul provides us with a check and a restraint, a test to show whether our anger is truly **righteous** (see Aug. 6). When is anger sin? When it is not directed at things that are sin against God. In short, *sinful anger is when our anger is motivated out of personal reasons, that is, when someone has offended us, not God.*

How often is our anger selfish instead of godly? How often do we get angry because we've been wronged instead of getting angry because God's Word has been violated? Even if someone's action is itself sinful, we also sin if our anger is motivated out of self, if it is motivated out of personal offense or "hurt feelings."

What horrendous destruction comes as a result of personally motivated anger! The story is told of a woman who tried to defend her bad temper by saying to preacher Billy Sunday, "Although I blow up over the least little thing, it's all over in a minute," to which Sunday replied, "So is a shotgun blast! It's over in seconds, too, but look at the terrible damage it can do."[63] Consider the results of so-called crimes of passion, where out of momentary anger someone is stabbed, shot, or just defamed by words.

The famous first-century BC Roman poet Horace wrote, "Anger is momentary insanity." How true! "Insanity" is a loss of mental capacity and reason, and that is what uncontrolled anger is. So that is not how the Christian is to live. The Christian doesn't go insane, doesn't fly off the handle, doesn't "lose it," doesn't get enraged over the least little thing. When there is anger, it is for the right reason and is controlled.

Scriptures for Study: What does Romans 1:18 declare about God's "wrath" (*orgē*)? 🕮 What does Paul command in Romans 12:19? 🕮 Likewise, what is James's counsel (James 1:19–20)?

Steal

kleptō

A third remnant of the **old man** that can easily creep back into the Christian's life is stealing, as in Ephesians 4:28, "Let him that stole steal no more." The Greek behind both the words *stole* and **steal** is *kleptō* (2813; English, *kleptomania*) and "emphasizes the secrecy, craft, and cheating involved in the act of stealing" (in contrast, *lēstēs* "includes the element of violence").[64] In other words, it's not armed robbery, but rather burglary.

This seems an odd admonition; would a Christian secretly steal? Paul's admonition must be viewed in light of the society of that day. Theft was rampant, especially on the docks and above all in the public baths. William Barclay points out, "Public baths were the clubs of the time; and stealing the belongings of the bathers was one of the commonest crimes in any Greek city." Slaves also pilfered from their masters, and even citizens practiced petty theft because it was not wholly condemned by popular opinion.

Paul feared, then, that Christians would fall back into this common practice. We can be guilty of this by pilfering from an employer, reporting more hours than were actually worked, "hiding" during working hours to avoid work, not paying a debt that is owed, an employer not paying employees fair wages, a false insurance claim, overestimating when bidding on the cost of a certain job, jacking up the price of a repair or service because the insurance company will pay for it, and keeping what a sales clerk overpays in change. All of that is stealing!

Far worse, however, is that we can steal from God. We can do that in two ways. One is by not giving as we should. While the OT practice was tithing, which was solely for the operation of Israel's government, the NT standard is: "Upon the first day of the week let every one of you lay by him in store, as God hath prospered him, that there be no gatherings when I come" (1 Cor. 16:2). We should give according to **grace** (see Nov. 27).

Another way we can steal from God is with our time. As Ephesians 5:15–17 declares, one of the characteristics of true wisdom is "redeeming the time," that is, using time wisely and advantageously. We are to use our time to glorify God. We should be faithful in our attendance to the local church, in our daily witness for Christ, and in our ministry to others.

Scriptures for Study: Review the Ten Commandments (Exod. 20:1–17) and note where lying, anger, and stealing fall. 🕮 What's the blessing of laying up "treasures in heaven" (Matt. 6:19–20)?

Corrupt Communication (Word)

sapros logos

One final remnant of the **old man** that can easily creep back into the Christian's life is **corrupt communication**, as in Ephesians 4:29, "Let no corrupt communication proceed out of your mouth, but that which is good to the use of edifying, that it may minister grace unto the hearers."

Communication translates *logos* (3056), which means to speak intelligently, to articulate a message, to give a discourse. It's derived from *legō* (3004), which originally (prior to the fifth-century BC) denoted the "activity of collecting, carefully selecting, cataloguing in succession, and arranging together in an orderly sequence."[65] This developed into the meaning "to lay before, i.e., to relate, recount" and finally "to say, speak, i.e., to utter definite words, connected, and significant speech equal to discourse."[66] How important words are! They must be carefully selected, orderly, and connected. Words matter!

So, Paul is concerned here with the words Christians use, the speech that characterizes their lives. Specifically, he's concerned that our speech not be **corrupt**, which translates *sapros* (4550), meaning "rotten, putrid." Originally this graphic word was used to describe rotten or spoiled food. Our Lord used it to warn against "false prophets . . . Ye shall know them by their fruits . . . every good tree bringeth forth good fruit; but a corrupt tree bringeth forth evil fruit. A good tree cannot bring forth evil fruit, neither can a corrupt tree bring forth good fruit" (Matt. 7:15–18). He also used it in 13:48 to refer to "bad" (rotten) fish that must be thrown away.

What must never characterize the Christian, then, is rotten, spoiled, decayed speech. Several modern translations miss the mark with the word "unwholesome," which is not as strong as **corrupt**. And how corrupt, indeed, is the speech of man today! Vulgarity, profanity, suggestiveness, and downright filth are all too common in jokes, stories, and even normal conversation.

Colossians 4:6 declares that our speech (*logos*) should be "seasoned with salt." As salt enhances the flavor of food, our speech should enhance Christ and those around us. Our words should "taste good." Let us never leave a "bad taste" in anyone's mouth.

Scriptures for Study: In Romans 13:9, what "saying" sums up the listed commandments? 📖 In 1 Corinthians 14:19, which "words" are superior?

Bitterness

pikria

As a kind of addendum to the four sins most likely to creep back into the Christian's life listed in Ephesians 4:22–29, Paul adds in verse 31: "Let all bitterness, and wrath, and anger, and clamour, and evil speaking, be put away from you, with all malice."

The Greek *pikria* (4088) simply means "harbored hostility," a smoldering resentment, holding a grudge. In his commentary on the Greek text, John Eadie puts it best: "Bitterness is a figurative term denoting that fretted and irritable state of mind that keeps a man in perpetual animosity—that inclines him to harsh and uncharitable opinions of men and things—that makes him sour, crabbed, and repulsive in his general demeanor—that brings a scowl on his face, and infuses venom into the words of his tongue."[67]

Bitterness is the end result of suppressed anger, and it defiles us, as Hebrews 12:15 declares. The Greek behind the word "defiled" is *miainō* (3392), which means "to stain with color, tinge, or pollute." Anger must not be suppressed—it must be dealt with. If it isn't, it just leads to more wrath (*thumos*) and **anger** (*orgē*; see Mar. 14.)

Several other consequences come as well: "clamour" (*kraugē*, 2906, a crying out against someone or even physical brawling), "evil speaking" (*blasphēmia*, 988; English, *blaspheme*, slanderous and damaging speech; see Nov. 23), and "malice" (*kakia*, 2549, that which is malevolent, unprofitable, useless, detrimental, poor, vice, and unsuitable).

The consequences of bitterness are horrendous! It was bitterness that drove Cain to become the first murderer and drove King Saul to try to murder David. Bitterness can hurt feelings, divide churches, and destroy reputations. Along with anger, it "give[s] place to the devil" (Eph. 4:27).

"Give place" is *didote topon*. "Give" (*didōmi*, 1325, Nov. 4) means "to give of one's own accord and with good will." "Place," then, is *topos* (5117; English, *topography* and *topology*), which, when used literally, refers to "any portion of space marked off from the surrounding territory," such as a spot, space, or room. Used figuratively, it speaks of an "opportunity, power, [or] occasion for acting." The full idea in this expression, then, is: "Here you go, devil. I'm willingly giving you a wide-open invitation to come in and work destructively through my anger."

Dear Christian friend, be careful of anger and bitterness.

Scriptures for Study: In Acts 8:23, who was "in the gall [*cholē*, 5521, 'poison'] of bitterness"? 🕮 In Romans 3:14, who is "full of cursing and bitterness"?

Good

agathos

The Greek *agathos* (18), which occurs frequently in the NT (107 times), has a wide range of meanings, including: benevolent, profitable, useful, beneficial, excellent, virtuous, and suitable. As we'll see, every one of those meanings is appropriate to all we say and do.

The whole concept of **good** was very important to the Greek philosophers, Plato in particular. To him the idea of "the good" was the highest of all ideas because it "preserves and supports in contrast to evil which spoils and destroys."[68] The universe to Plato was not mechanical at its foundation, that is, blind, impersonal, and morally indifferent, but rather it was moral, with "values and ideals [that] are supreme, and at the heart of which there is not only Reason and Purpose, but Goodness."[69]

We point this out for good reason: If goodness could be so important to a pagan, humanistic philosopher, how much more important should it be to the Christian? In light of our mediation on March 16, one of the most important aspects of good is speech, that is, *what* we say and *how* we say it. But whether it's our words, deeds, actions, or attitudes, we should strive always for the good.

With that in mind, using the meaning of *agathos* as our guide, let us test ourselves daily by asking a series of questions:

1. Is what I am about to say or do *benevolent*? Is it kind, compassionate, and caring?
2. Is what I am about to say or do *profitable*, *beneficial*, and *useful*? Will it accomplish something? Is it constructive or destructive? Will it help or hinder? Is it positive or negative?
3. Is what I am about to say or do *excellent*? Is it just *good* or *eminently* good, the best thing to say or do?
4. Is what I am about to say or do *virtuous*? Is it righteous, honorable, and moral? Does it avoid suggestiveness, vulgarity, and crudeness?
5. Is what I am about to say or do *suitable*? Does it fit the moment? Is it proper? Is it appropriate?

Scriptures for Study: What is the great truth of Romans 8:28? 🕮 What is the command of Romans 12:9? What will that, then, overcome (v. 21)?

Edify

oikodomē

Besides being **good**, what we say and do should **edify**. The Greek *oikodomē* (3619), along with its other forms, is a compound word comprised of *oikos* (3624), "house or dwelling," and *dōma* (1430), "to build." The clear idea, then, is that what we do and say should build up others around us and even ourselves. Our speech, for example, should be uplifting, encouraging, instructive, and even challenging.

A graphic example of *oikodomē* appears in 1 Corinthians 14:26–31, where we read of the chaos in the local church at Corinth. There was no order; everyone had something to say, and they all said it at the same time. They were competing to be in the spotlight and to be the most profound speaker in the church. Paul, therefore, exhorted them, "Let all things be done unto edifying" (v. 26). As on a construction site, if every worker is doing his own thing so no building could be accomplished, likewise if we are doing our own thing and trying to be prominent, the church will not be edified. There are two things involved in such building.

First, the body is built *internally*. This was, in fact, the very point Paul made in his farewell message to the Ephesian elders in Miletus: "And now, brethren, I commend you to God, and to the word of His grace, which is able to build you up [*epoikodomeō*, 2026]" (Acts 20:32). Paul gave this challenging counsel because only the Word of God can make the body strong internally. How tragic that many today strive for a big church *externally* before the church is strong *internally*. Internal growth must always come first or the work will eventually collapse of its own weight. Without a good foundation, any building will fall.

Second, the body is built *externally*. We should not overemphasize this lest we fall into the trap of the "numbers game," which is so prevalent today. But neither should we underemphasize this lest we fall into the trap of isolation and eventual stagnation. What, then, is the balance? As pastors give Christians the tools for service (Eph. 4:11–12), others are going to be brought to Christ as a result. Our Lord didn't leave church growth to our devices, such as today's "seeker-sensitive" movement. Rather, He said, "I will build my church" (Matt. 16:18). Yes, we will plant and water, but He gives the increase (1 Cor. 3:6–7).

Scriptures for Study: What principle of Christian liberty is taught in 1 Corinthians 10:23? 📖 In 1 Corinthians 14:4 and 1 Timothy 1:4, what things don't edify?

Minister Grace

didōmi charis

The expression *didōmi charis* (**minister grace** or "give grace") appears five times in the NT and is quite striking. As mentioned on March 17, *didōmi* (1325) means "to give of one's own accord and with good will." **Grace**, of course, is *charis* (5485, see Feb. 13–14), which used in the context of salvation means the unmerited favor of God toward man manifested primarily through the person and work of Jesus Christ apart from any merit or works of man.

So, what does it mean for us to give grace to others? In broad strokes, the words *grace* and *favor* paint a picture of exceptional kindness, special goodwill, friendly action in excess of the ordinary. Predominantly, that is what should characterize our speech. Paul writes in Ephesians 4:29 that "[our speech] may minister grace unto the hearers." Sometimes we say the right *things*, and even say them at the right *time*, but we say them in the wrong *way*. We must always speak with love, concern, and kindness. While we always "speak the truth" (Eph. 4:15), we never stoop to today's so-called policy of total honesty, which often hurts those around us. Our words are always kind.

There is a story in the Jewish Talmud about a king who sent two jesters on an errand. He said to one, "Foolish Simon, go and bring me back the best thing in the world," and to the other, "You, Silly John, go and find for me the worst thing in the world." Both left but were back shortly. Grinning, Simon bowed low and said, "Behold, Sire, the best thing in the world." His package contained a tongue. Silly John snickered and quickly unwrapped his bundle and said, "The worst thing in the world, Sire." It was another tongue![70]

Indeed, the tongue is the best and worst thing we each possess. It can help or hinder; it can build or destroy. May we ask ourselves throughout the day, "Is my tongue the best thing about me or the worst? Does my speech glorify and honor the Lord, and does it build up those around me?" Let us pray with the psalmist, "Set a watch, O Lord, before my mouth; keep the door of my lips" (Ps. 141:3).

Scriptures for Study: What is the measure of grace in Ephesians 4:7? 🕮 To whom does God "give grace" (James 4:6; 1 Pet. 5:5)?

Grieve

lupeō

The word *lupeō* (3076) means "to sadden, bring pain, afflict with sorrow." It appears in Matthew 26:22 and Mark 14:19, for example, where the disciples are "sorrowful" when the Lord tells them that one of them will betray Him. Peter was likewise deeply grieved when the Lord asked him the third time if he really loved Him with a tender affection (John 21:17; see Jan. 21). In 2 Corinthians 7:8–9, we read that Paul made no apology for making those believers "sorry" for their sins by what he wrote in previous letters because it was truth and because it brought them to repentance.

One particular occurrence of *lupeō*, however, is the most important of all: "And grieve not the holy Spirit of God, whereby ye are sealed unto the day of redemption" (Eph. 4:30). What a statement! It's actually an allusion to Isaiah 63:9–11, where the prophet declares that God's people "rebelled, and vexed his holy Spirit." Here is a strong reminder of the indwelling Holy Spirit and the practical result of that doctrine.

While *all* sin saddens God, not just the ones Paul lists in the next two verses, the listed sins are apparently especially painful to the Holy Spirit. Why? Because they are particularly inconsistent in the Holy Spirit-indwelt life. As we have previously studied, nothing is more inconsistent in the Holy Spirit-indwelt life than **lying**, unrighteous **anger**, **steal**[ing], **corrupt communication**, **bitterness**, and the other the sins listed here.

As we meditated on January 30, we are **sealed** with the Holy Spirit. Therefore, because we are sealed until we go home to be with the Lord, we are to *act* like it now by not grieving the Holy Spirit through sin.

We'll finish this thought tomorrow by examining what we should do with such sin.

Scriptures for Study: In John 16:17–33, what did Jesus say would turn the disciple's sorrow into joy? 🕮 According to 1 Thessalonians 4:13–18, what is the cause of sorrow? What event will turn it to joy?

Put Away

airō

The literal idea behind the Greek *airō* (142) is "to raise or lift up," and it's usually used in this way. When the Lord Jesus forgave and healed the paralytic in Matthew 9:1–8, for example, His command to the man was, "Arise, take up (*airō*) thy bed, and go unto thine house" (v. 6).

Used in the figurative sense, however, as it is in Ephesians 4:31—"Let all bitterness, and wrath, and anger, and clamour, and evil speaking, be put away from you"—it means "to pick up and carry away, to make a clean sweep."[71] As John the Baptist declared of the Lord Jesus, "The next day John seeth Jesus coming unto him, and saith, Behold the Lamb of God, which taketh away (*airō*) the sin of the world" (John 1:29). We see it again in John 2:16 as our Lord makes a "clean sweep" of the merchandizers in the temple, saying, "Take these things hence; make not my Father's house an house of merchandise."

Paul, therefore, uses it here to paint the graphic picture that we should "sweep away" the hindrances to Christian living listed in the surrounding context. Pastor and expositor Martyn Lloyd-Jones offers this solemn challenge:

> The Apostle is exhorting the Ephesians to put away all this evil. He does not say that because they have become Christians it has automatically dropped off. . . . And again we notice that he does not merely tell them to pray that these sins may be taken out of their lives. Pray by all means, but do not forget that Paul tells the Ephesians to put them off, to put them far from them, and we must do the same. It is not pleasant. It is not at all pleasant even to preach on these things; it is very unpleasant for us to face them . . . but, says the Apostle, we must do it, and if we find any vestige or trace of these things within us, we must take hold of it and hurl it away from us, trample upon it, and bolt the door upon it, and never allow it to come back.[72]

Scriptures for Study: What wonderful encouragement our Lord gives in Matthew 11:28–30 ("take" is *airō*). 🕮 In 1 John 3:5, what did Jesus "sweep away"?

Kind

chrēstos

In Classical Greek, *chrēstos* (5543) originally denoted usefulness, and therefore referred to things that were useful, suitable, and proper, such as good food or wine (e.g., Luke 5:39, "better"). The term broadened to include moral excellence.[73] When used of persons, then, it describes one who is "good-natured, gentle,"[74] "mild [and] pleasant" in contrast to "harsh, hard, sharp, [and] bitter."[75]

Our Lord used this in a verse we examined yesterday, Matthew 11:30: "For my yoke is easy (*chrēstos*), and my burden is light." Whoever heard of a "kind" yoke? They are notorious for being cruel and painful. But that is exactly what is pictured. Even though burdens will come to the Christian, they are still kind in comparison to those of the world.

Our Lord used this word, for example, to describe God Himself as one who is kind even "unto the unthankful and to the evil" (Luke 6:35). Peter declares this as well in 1 Peter 2:3, where he writes that "the Lord is gracious" (*chrēstos*). How merciful God is to allow men to continue in their indescribable wickedness!

Likewise, therefore, no matter whom we deal with, we are to do so with kindness. Our Lord gives us the same principle in the Beatitudes: "Blessed are ye, when men shall revile you, and persecute you, and shall say all manner of evil against you falsely, for my sake" (Matt. 5:11). As we saw on January 12, the word **blessed** is *makarios* (3107), which speaks of a contentedness that is not affected by circumstances. It doesn't matter how someone might treat us; what matters is how we treat them.

We'll couple this word with another tomorrow.

Scriptures for Study: In Romans 2:4 what does God's "goodness" (*chrēstos*) bring? 🕮 In 1 Corinthians 15:33, what corrupts "good" manners (*ethos*, 1485, "moral habits")?

Tenderhearted

eusplagchnos

Coupled with kindness, which we meditated on yesterday, there is tenderheartedness. In fact, the words **kind** and **tenderhearted** actually appear together in Ephesians 4:32. The Greek *eusplagchnos* (2155) appears only here and in 1 Peter 3:8. It's a compound comprised of the prefix *eu* (2095), "good or well," and *splagchnon* (4698), which literally means "strengthened from the spleen." In Classical Greek this referred to the bowels. While in our culture we think of the "heart" as the seat of emotion, in that culture it was viewed as being in the bowels. Figuratively, then, *splagchnon*, meant inward affection, pity, compassion, even **love** (*phileō*, 5368). This idea actually makes more sense than our idea of "heart," since emotions often give us "butterflies" and other feelings in the stomach.

To be tenderhearted, then, is to have good feelings, good emotions toward others, to have genuine affection for others. In the other occurrence of this word, such feelings are an integral part of unity: "Be ye all of one mind, having compassion one of another, love as brethren, be pitiful [i.e., full of pity; *eusplagchnos*, affectionate], be courteous" (1 Pet. 3:8).

Kindness and tenderheartedness are both well illustrated in this story. At one end of a truck terminal in the Midwest is a fuel supply company with a high fence around it and a railroad track running past it. Several freight trains run by each day, and a worker noticed the owner of the yard, a Christian, throwing chunks of coal over the fence at various places along the track. Curious, he asked the man why he did that. A little embarrassment at being noticed, the man replied, "A poor elderly lady lives across the street, and I know that her old-age pension is inadequate to buy enough coal. After the trains go by, she walks along and picks up the pieces of coal she thinks have fallen from the coal car behind the engine. Her eyesight is failing, and she doesn't realize that diesels have replaced steam locomotives. I don't want to disappoint her, so I throw some pieces over the fence to help her."[76]

That is Christian kindness!

Scriptures for Study: Read Philemon 1:7, 12, 20, noting the usage of "bowels" (*splagchnon*). It sounds odd (and even humorous) to our ears, but its meaning is deep. 📖 What's the command of 1 John 3:17?

But God

de theos

After reading about the horrendous depravity of man in Ephesians 2:1–3, the first two words of verse 4 declare, "**But God**." What follows through verse 10 is the description of the glorious salvation that we have in Christ by **grace** (see Feb. 13) alone, through **faith** (see Feb. 8) alone, in **Christ** (see Apr. 5) alone.

Unfortunately, however, we sometimes tend to overlook a tiny word like **but**. Here, however, it introduces the greatest contrast in the universe. In a sense, these two words contain the entire Gospel message. Why? Because they show the *ultimate contrast*: They show man's *plight*, but God's *provision*; they picture man's *impotence*, but God's *intervention*; they *describe* man's *helplessness*, but *declare* God's *hope*.

In general, *de* (1161) shows "distinction." It also serves, however, to mark a transition to something new. Therefore, as **God** (*theos*, 2316, see Apr. 3) is the subject of the sentence, He then is the distinction; He is the transition; He is the One who marks the ultimate contrast between what we *were* and what we *are!* Without God's provision, intervention, and hope, we would still be dead in our trespasses and sins, doomed forever.

Think of it! Once we were *dead* (see Feb. 12), now we're *alive* (Rom. 6:13; 1 Cor. 15:22); once we were *enemies* of God, now we're *friends* (Col. 1:21; cf. Luke 7:34; see Nov. 18); once we were *aliens*, now we are *citizens* (Eph. 2:12–13; see Dec. 2); once we were *lost*, now we are *found* (Luke 15:6, 9, 24, 32); once we were *far off*, now we are *near* (Eph. 2:13); once we were *cut off* from God, now we have *access* to him (Rom. 5:2); once we were at *war* with God, now we are *at peace* with Him (Rom. 5:1); and once we were *condemned*, now we are *justified* (Rom. 5:9).

All that because of "But God." As the psalmist declares: "Like sheep they are laid in the grave; death shall feed on them; and the upright shall have dominion over them in the morning; and their beauty shall consume in the grave from their dwelling. But God will redeem my soul from the power of the grave: for he shall receive me" (Ps. 49:14–15). And as Paul echoes in Romans 5:7–8: "For scarcely for a righteous man will one die: yet peradventure for a good man some would even dare to die. But God commendeth his love toward us, in that, while we were yet sinners, Christ died for us."

Scriptures for Study: Note the contrasts in the following: revelation (1 Cor. 2:9–10); deliverance (Acts 7:9–10); protection (1 Sam. 23:14); direction (Exod. 13:18); strength (Ps. 73:26); judgment (Isa. 17:13; Prov. 21:12; Ps. 64:6–7); ministry (1 Cor. 3:6–7); and salvation (Eph. 2:4 with Rom. 5:7–8).

Mercy

eleos

A simple definition of **mercy** is "the withholding of deserved punishment and relieving distress." The Greek *eleos* (1656) speaks of "compassion, pity." One Greek lexicon tells us, "Kindness or good will towards the miserable and afflicted, joined with a desire to relieve them."[77] Even the pagans of Greece felt pity. Aristotle wrote that tragedy aroused pity and even fear that the same tragedy might befall them.

This word appears in Matthew 23:23, for example, where our Lord calls the Pharisees hypocrites because while they fastidiously counted out a tenth of the seeds of herbs to give as tithes, they ignored the more important matters of mercy and faith. In a graphic example of mercy, after the Lord told the disciples the parable of how the Good Samaritan showed mercy (Luke 10:25–37), He then told them to "Go, and do thou likewise."

Paul also used this word often in his letters as a simple reminder of God's mercy, a reminder that none of us can hear too often (Rom. 9:23; 11:31; Gal. 6:16). In one of the most pointed verses in Scripture about salvation not being by works, Paul wrote to Titus: "Not by works of righteousness which we have done, but according to his mercy he saved us, by the washing of regeneration, and renewing of the Holy Ghost" (3:5). This word was so imbedded in Paul's thinking, in fact, that he even used it often in salutations (1 Tim. 1:2; 2 Tim. 1:2; Titus 1:4).

So mercy is obviously always to the helpless. Moreover, as Ephesians 2:1–3 show, we deserve whatever tragedy, affliction, misery, depression, heartache, and all other pain that befall us, but God relieves it by His undeserved mercy. In short, we deserve God's wrath, but He is merciful; He relieves us out of His incomprehensible compassion.

Before we close, let us note the important distinction between **mercy** and **grace**:

- Mercy – the *withholding* of what *is* deserved (e.g., death and hell).
- Grace – the *bestowing* of what is *not* deserved (e.g., life and heaven).

Or as one commentator puts it, "Mercy *pities*. Grace *pardons*."[78]

Scriptures for Study: Upon whom does God show mercy, according to Luke 1:50? 📖 As Christians, where do we continually find mercy (Heb. 4:16)?

Regeneration

paliggenesia

Like *charis* (**grace**, see Feb. 13), *paliggenesia* (3824) is one of those ancient Greek words transformed by NT usage into something far deeper than it was before. It is a compound comprised of *palin* (3825), "again," and *genesis* (1078), "birth, origin." It, therefore, meant a restoration, return to former circumstances, or revivification. The Stoics believed that the earth would periodically perish through some conflagration, so they used this word to refer to "when the earth awakened in the blossoming of springtime from its winter sleep and revived from its winter death." Philo, the first-century Jewish philosopher, often used it to refer to the world emerging out of fire in a phoenix-like resurrection, a belief also held by the Stoics. Even of Noah and his family, Philo wrote, "They became leaders of a *paliggenesia* and chiefs of a second cycle."[79]

It's significant, then, that this word is used twice in the NT to refer to a *real* rebirth. It appears first in Matthew 19:28, where our Lord Himself says, "And Jesus said unto them, Verily I say unto you, That ye which have followed me, in the regeneration when the Son of man shall sit in the throne of his glory, ye also shall sit upon twelve thrones, judging the twelve tribes of Israel." The context, of course, is our Lord's teaching of future events, so He refers to the "regeneration," the "restoration," the "re-creation," of the world that will take place after His Second Coming. Many creationists and Bible teachers believe that this will be a restoration of the primeval perfections of the earth before the Genesis Flood. In stark contrast to pagan belief, this will be a true rebirth of the original world by the one true God Who created it. As Acts 3:21 also declares, "Whom the heaven must receive until the times of restitution of all things, which God hath spoken by the mouth of all his holy prophets since the world began."

The other occurrence of *paliggenesia* is in Titus 3:5: "Not by works of righteousness which we have done, but according to his mercy he saved us, by the washing of regeneration, and renewing of the Holy Ghost." As God can restore a fallen world, He also restores those who were once spiritually *alive* and then *dead* in Adam (1 Cor. 15:22; Rom.5:17) to a *new life* in Christ (Rom. 6:4). We'll ponder a related concept tomorrow.

Scriptures for Study: Read Jesus' discourse on the "Bread of Life" in John 6:22–71, noting each occurrence of the word *life*.

Quickened

suzōopoieō

In light of yesterday's mediation on **regeneration**, let us consider a related word, which also appears only twice in the NT: "Even when we were dead in sins, hath quickened us together with Christ, (by grace ye are saved)" (Eph. 2:5); and "And you, being dead in your sins and the uncircumcision of your flesh, hath he quickened together with him, having forgiven you all trespasses" (Col. 2:13).

In Ephesians, the Greek *suzōopoieō* (4806) actually translates the entire clause "hath **quickened** us together," which literally means "to make one alive together with another." The verb is also in the aorist tense showing that at a once-for-all point in the past we were made alive "together with Christ," that is, in connection with him, associated with him in newness of life. In other words, the same power that raised him from the grave is the same power that has given us life. Think of it! The very same infinite power that could revive the *physically* dead also revives the *spiritually* dead.

A crucial truth to understand here is the picture of our identification with Christ. We need to recognize a wondrous progression:

- We have been crucified with Christ (Rom. 6:6; Gal. 2:20).
- We died with Christ (Rom. 6:8; 2 Tim. 2:11).
- We were buried with Christ (Rom. 6:4; Col. 2:12).
- Now we have been given new life with Christ (quickened).

As Romans 5:21 declares, "That as sin hath reigned unto death, even so might grace reign through righteousness unto eternal life by Jesus Christ our Lord." How we can rejoice in the new life we have with, in connection, in association with Christ! We'll examine still another related truth tomorrow.

Scriptures for Study: Read and meditate on the verses in the progression listed above. Reflect on what you used to be without Christ and what you are now.

Raised Us Up

sunegeirō

In addition to being **quickened** with Christ, as we studied yesterday in Ephesians 2:5, we also see that Christ "hath **raised us up** together" with Christ (v. 6). Again, this entire clause is a single word in the Greek, *sunegeirō* (4891). The full meaning is "to raise up together from moral death to a new and blessed life devoted to God."[80] Indeed, what God has done in us through Christ is no less than a resurrection. We have been raised from death to *life*, but even more to a *committed* life.

A key verse here is Romans 6:4: "Therefore we are buried with him by baptism into death: that like as Christ was raised up from the dead by the glory of the Father, even so *we also should walk in newness of life*" (emphasis added). Why were we baptized (*baptizō*, placed into, immersed; see June 24) in Christ? Why has God raised us up in Christ? So we will walk in newness of life. We are no longer on the level of sin; Christ has raised us up to a "new level," a "new potential." God has not raised us up so we will live like we are still dead in trespasses and sins. No, indeed! We are dead to sin; we no longer live in it.

There's a beautiful illustration of all this in the resurrection of Lazarus (John 11–12). We read there: "He [Jesus] cried with a loud voice, Lazarus, come forth. And he that was dead came forth, bound hand and foot with graveclothes. . . . Jesus saith unto them, Loose him, and let him go" (11:43–44). Even though Lazarus was now *alive*, he was still wearing the *evidences of death*—the graveclothes. That is why the Lord Jesus said, "Loose him." Since Lazarus was alive, he should look like he was alive.

How many Christians today are just like Lazarus before the graveclothes were removed! How silly it would have looked if Lazarus had tried to hop around while still wrapped in the graveclothes. But many of us do exactly that; we try to hang on to the values, purposes, and goals of the world.

Dear Christian friend, we no longer walk in trespasses and sins, governed by the flesh; rather, we walk according to the new life, the new potential, the new disposition within us.

Scriptures for Study: What is the clear implication of 2 Corinthians 5:17? (We will study this verse tomorrow.) 📖 What descriptive language did even Ezekiel use for such a transformation (Ezek. 11:19; 36:26)?

New Creature

kainos ktisis

Here is another expression that describes our new life in Christ. As mentioned on January 1, while *neos* (2537) refers to something new in *time*, something that recently has come into existence, *kainos* (2537) refers to something new in *quality*, as it would be distinguished from something that is old and worn out. In Classical Greek, *ktisis* (2937) meant the act of creation, the created thing, or the result of the act. It (and the verb *ktizō*, 2936) was often used in the Septuagint to translate the Hebrew *bara* (1254H) "to create from nothing."

While there is today a debate over so-called Lordship Salvation, such controversy is unfortunate, because the real issue boils down to one simple principle: *When Christ comes into your life, your life changes*. God's Word *everywhere* declares that a change is automatic when someone truly believes.

One of the greatest examples of this principle appears in Acts 19:8–10, where we read that Paul encountered many "hardened" (*sklērunō*, 4645, to make hard or stiff) hearts while preaching the Gospel in the synagogue for three months. But there were also those in Ephesus who believed. As verses 18–20 recount, the Gospel turned Ephesus on its ear. It changed that society. Those who were involved in occult practices burned their books on spells, sorcery, and other such things. Their life change was dramatically demonstrated by the value of those books. Five thousand pieces of silver today would be worth hundreds of thousands of dollars. We're reminded here of how even some Christians today ignorantly dabble in such things as horoscopes and Ouija boards, things that ought to be burned.

Verses 23–29 go on to say that believers no longer invested money in pagan practices or paraphernalia, which was a devastating blow to local commerce. Silversmiths were being driven out of business because people no longer bought silver shrines of Diana, which were household idols. Paul's statement that these were "no gods" at all and the stir churned up by the silversmiths combined to trigger a riot. So serious was the situation that there was the danger of Diana worship being destroyed altogether.

That is what the Gospel does. It changes lives. If one chooses to call this "Lordship Salvation," so be it, but the fact is: True *conversion* means true *change*. Christianity is not a creed, code, or a system of ethics. Christianity is a *life*, a new reality that comes when we trust Christ as Savior *and* Lord.

Scriptures for Study: How many NT examples can you list where a change of life was clearly evident after salvation?

Made Us Sit

sunkathizō

Concluding our thoughts of the last few days, there is still another word that underscores our new life in Christ. Ephesians 2:6 declares that God has "made us sit together in heavenly places in Christ Jesus." The words **made us sit** are *sunkathizō* (4776), which means "to cause to sit down together." The root is *kathizō*, "to cause to sit down." This means little to us unless we understand that sitting was often a mark of honor or authority in the ancient world. For example, a king sat to receive his subjects; members of a court sat and passed judgment on the one who stood before them; a teacher sat and taught his students.[81]

So the idea conveyed by this word is that of *honor*. In fact, this word is used of Christ in 1:20 to convey the fact that He is "seated with honor in the heavenlies." Then, when the prefix *sun* (4862) is added, we have the meaning, "to cause to sit *together in Christ*." In the spiritual sense, then, we have already been (aorist [past] tense) enthroned and exalted with Christ.

What does all that mean in practice? Simply this: *Since we are already seated with Christ in heaven, let us now act like it on earth*. Meditate on Colossians 3:1–3: "If ye then be risen with Christ, seek those things which are above, where Christ sitteth on the right hand of God. Set your affection on things above, not on things on the earth. For ye are dead, and your life is hid with Christ in God."

How plain Paul makes this in the "sister book" to Ephesians! God has given us new life and new potential; we are now to live like it. There is an old cliché that's been popular for many years. It was first uttered by a famous evangelist in the nineteenth century but is nonetheless wrong. The cliché goes, "Some Christians are so heavenly minded that they are of no earthly good." How ridiculous that is! It's impossible for a Christian to be "too" heavenly minded. Yes, there are those who act sanctimonious, self-righteous, and superior, but that is *not* heavenly mindedness. Being heavenly minded means exactly what Paul says—setting our thoughts, values, words, deeds, and all else on the things of heaven. Moreover, God cannot use us unless we *are* heavenly minded.

Scriptures for Study: What is the object of affection in 1 Chronicles 29:3? Read Psalm 119:97–168. How many times does the psalmist mention his love for God's Word? What synonyms does he use (e.g., "law" in v. 97)?

Fool (1)

aphrōn

Traditionally, of course, this is the day of practical jokes, April Fools' Day (or All Fools' Day). According to one encyclopedia, the custom probably began in France in 1564, when New Year's Day was changed from April 1 to January 1. Those who continued to observe April 1 as the beginning of the New Year were ridiculed.

The Bible, however, has much to say about the **fool**. There are some 160 references to the fool (or "fools" and "foolish") in the Bible (AV), thirty-three of which are in the NT. One Greek word for this is *aphrōn* (878). The root *phrēn* (5424) is interesting. As Greek scholar Spiros Zodhiates writes, it literally referred to "the diaphragm, that which curbs or restrains" and figuratively spoke of the "seat of all mental and emotional activity." He goes on to explain: "It was the diaphragm which determined the strength of the breath and hence also the human spirit and its emotions. It precisely refers to the ability not only to think, but also to control one's thoughts and attitudes. It is the heart as the seat of passions as well as the mind as the seat of mental faculties."[82]

When the prefix *a* (which is called the "alpha-negative;" 1) is added to a word, however, it makes it the exact opposite. We do this in English with words such as *amoral* and *amillennial*. So with the "alpha-negative," *aphrōn* means the exact opposite. In all the other ten occurrences of *aphrōn* in the NT, it is translated "fool," "fools," or "foolish."

A fool, then, is a person who not only does not think correctly, but also cannot control the thoughts and attitudes he does have. He not only doesn't think the right things, but when he does think, that's not right either. Joseph Thayer, nineteenth-century Greek scholar, defines it this way: "Without reason . . . senseless, foolish, stupid, without reflection or intelligence, acting rashly."[83] In Luke 11:40, the Lord Jesus calls the Pharisees "fools" because they thought doing something external would satisfy God. Nothing is more foolish than thinking that a Holy God could be satisfied by any works a man could do. Likewise, He called the rich farmer a **fool** in Luke 12:20 because he thought wealth and possessions were all he needed. That is, indeed, the height of folly.

Let us each thank God that we no longer need act like the fool but that we can think straight because His Word dominates our minds.

Scriptures for Study: What is a characteristic of the fool ("unwise," *aphrōn*) in Ephesians 5:17? 📖 What will silence foolish men, according to 1 Peter 2:15?

Fool (2)

anoētos

Another Greek word translated **fool** (or "foolish") is *anoētos* (453). The classic example of the foolish Christian appears in Galatians 3:1 and 3, where Paul writes, "O foolish Galatians, who hath bewitched you, that ye should not obey the truth. . . . Are ye so foolish? having begun in the Spirit, are ye now made perfect by the flesh?"

Anoētos is another "alpha-negative," which we defined yesterday. The root *nous* (3563) means "mind, intellect, understanding, reason, and thought," which is then made the opposite by the prefix *a*. The Judaizers had infiltrated the church and were undermining the very core of Christianity, namely, justification by faith alone, teaching that to be Christians, Gentiles had to become Jewish proselytes and obey the Mosaic Law. Appalled that the Galatians would tolerate, much less embrace, such heresy, Paul called them people without understanding, reason, and thought, people who had abandoned the very truth they had been taught.

That is just as true today as then. With the growing denial of justification by faith alone, the continuing onslaught against the true Gospel message, and the growing challenge to biblical ministry, there are countless "foolish" Christian teachers and followers. That type of fool can be described in several ways.

First, the fool is concerned about the *abstract* instead of the *absolute*. For many today, facts get in the way of unity. After all, it is argued, "Doctrine divides: love unites." That is the height of folly because nothing is absolute, nothing is sure.

Second, the fool is concerned about *wants* instead of the *Word*. Many churches being built today, even so-called evangelical ones, are not being founded upon a ministry of the Word of God, rather upon what people want, such as entertainment and every appealing program imaginable. But Scripture, of course, teaches none of that.

Third, the fool is concerned about *transient feelings* instead of *true faith*. Tragically, feelings drive many people's belief systems; *facts* aren't the issue, *faith* in what God says in His Word is not the issue, but rather how it makes them *feel* is the issue. It's not the *intellect* that rules, but rather it's an *impulse* that rules. There's great *zeal*, but nothing *real*. This has even kicked open the door to the growing frequency of mysticism, which teaches finding God through visions and revelations.

The challenge to each of us is to be ruled by the truth of God's Word alone.

Scriptures for Study: What is a common cause of foolish behavior, according to 1 Timothy 6:9? 🕮 In Titus 3:3, what other characteristics go along with being foolish?

God

theos

Today we begin an examination of several names and titles of God that appear in the NT. The most logical place to start, of course, is with the name **God**.

The Greek *theos* (2316), which forms such English words as *theology* (the study of God) and *theocracy* (a government ruled by God), is the most frequent designation of **God** in the NT. It meant something quite different, however, to the ancient Greeks than it did to Jews and Christians. The Greeks were polytheistic (*poly* means "many," so believing in multiple gods), so they used *theos* to refer to "the gods" as impersonal forces that sustained all that existed. By Homer's day (eighth century BC), the gods were little more than deified humans who, while powerful, still had human frailties and limitations.

In dramatic contrast, the Jews were monotheistic (*mono* means "one," so believing in only one God). The Hebrew *Elohim* (430H) was consistently translated *Theos* in the Septuagint. What's interesting is that while *Elohim* is plural (which denotes the Trinity), the Septuagint *never* uses the plural *Theoi* ("gods") because this would have given the Greeks a concept of God that was consistent with their polytheism.

Like the Jewish concept (Mark 12:32), Christians believe in the one, only, and unique God, the true God of the universe. As Paul declared, "But to us there is but one God, the Father, of whom are all things, and we in him; and one Lord Jesus Christ, by whom are all things, and we by him" (1 Cor. 8:6). Likewise, while men fashion gods according to their own image (Acts 14:11), Paul declares that there is only one "living and true God" (1 Thess. 1:9), in contrast to the dead gods of idolatry.

What a blessing it is to know that there is only one true God! As men grope in darkness, worshiping gods they have shaped to conform to their lifestyles, we worship and follow the true God of the universe.

Scriptures for Study: In the following passages, identify what we receive from God: Romans 15:13; 2 Corinthians 1:3; 13:11.

Jesus

Iesous

There have been innumerable attacks through the ages on the person of **Jesus**. His deity and humanity have always been battlegrounds. Countless cults and heretics by the hundreds have denied the "historical Jesus," and they're still doing so today.

The NT, however, mentions the name **Jesus** *by itself* some 612 times (AV) and many more times in conjunction with other names (e.g., "Jesus Christ"). Why? *Because* **Jesus** *is the name of salvation.* **Jesus** (*Iesous*, 2424) is the human name of our Lord and means **Savior** (see Apr. 6), that is, "he shall save his people from their sins" (Matt. 1:21).

It's significant that instead of choosing a name for their baby, as parents normally do, it was the angel of God who instructed Joseph and Mary as to what the child's name was to be (Matt. 1:21; Luke 1:31). God wanted no ambiguity concerning who this child would be and what He would do.

What, then, is the significance of this word? *Iesous* (both Greek and Latin) corresponds to the Hebrew *Jeshua* (3091H), which is equivalent to "Joshua," and means "the Lord is salvation." That is why men must attack and try to destroy Jesus. With Him intact, they must deny themselves, deny their religion, deny their works, and trust Him only for salvation—and that they will not do.

What power there is in that name **Jesus**! It is a call to repentance (Acts 2:38), it's the name that heals the sick (3:6), it's the name by which demons are cast out (16:18), and it's the name that saves (1 Cor. 1:2). And while men tried to *destroy* Him in His day, and while men *deny* Him in our day, there will come the day, "that at the name of Jesus every knee should bow, of things in heaven, and things in earth, and things under the earth" (Phil. 2:10). Lela B. Long, nineteenth-century hymn writer, invites us to meditate on that singular name **Jesus** with these words:

Jesus is the sweetest name I know,
    And He's just the same
    as His lovely name.
And that's the reason why I love Him so;
Jesus is the sweetest name I know.

Scriptures for Study: The gospel of John uniquely presents Jesus in His deity. This name appears there 256 times, the most times in chapter 11; read that chapter and note how many. Also, what wonderful incident is recounted there?

Christ

Christos

The Greek *christos* (5547) has an interesting derivation, which originally carried a totally secular meaning in Classical Greek. It comes from *chierin*, to rub lightly, or spread over something. Some uses were rubbing arrows with poison in preparation for battle (Homer) and applying paint or whitewash. Another common use was rubbing the body with oil after a bath.

In OT usage, this word corresponds to the Hebrew equivalent *mēsiah* (Messiah), which refers to someone who is ceremoniously anointed with holy oil for an office. The most common office for anointing was a king (e.g., David, 2 Sam. 2:7); another was of priests, such as Aaron, which is beautifully described in Psalm 133.

It is in the NT, however, that the word appears with the most power and significance. It's extremely significant that the word *Christos* is attached to the Lord Jesus **Christ** in every major event of His life and ministry. One of the most significant was in the questions He posed to His disciples. After asking, "Whom do men say that I the Son of man am?" and getting such answers as John the Baptist, Elijah, Jeremiah, or other prophets, He then asked them, "But whom say ye that I am?" It was Peter's answer that tells the tale: "Thou art the Christ, the Son of the living God." In a dramatic proof of Jesus' claim to His deity, Jesus said, "Blessed art thou, Simon Barjona: for flesh and blood hath not revealed it unto thee, but my Father which is in heaven" (Matt. 16:13–17).

Most significant in that passage, and many others, is the definite article ("the") before Christ (*ho Christos*). This demonstrates that the Lord Jesus is the one and the only Anointed One, the one and only Son of God, the one and only Savior. As John declares, "We have found the Messias, which is, being interpreted, the Christ" (John 1:41), and, "Now we believe, not because of thy saying: for we have heard him ourselves, and know that this is indeed the Christ, the Saviour of the world" (4:42). The Lord Jesus even professed Himself to be the Messiah predicted by David and the prophets (Mark 12:35; Ps. 110:1).

What a blessing it is to know that we worship the one and only Anointed One!

Scriptures for Study: As mentioned above, *Christos* is attached to Jesus in every major event of His life and ministry. Read the following scriptures and identify each event: Matthew 1:16–18; Luke. 2:11; Mark 12:35; Luke 22:67; 23:2, 35; 24:25–26.

Savior

sōtēr

The Greek *sōtēr* (4990) means **savior**, deliverer, and preserver. In Ancient Greek, *sōtēr* was actually used of both the gods and men. The gods, such as Poseidon and especially Zeus, were called "saviors from the dangers of life and also protectors and preservers." Men, however, "could also be saviors, in saving others from trouble and danger, and also in the case of doctors." The term was even applied to philosophers, such as Epicurus, statesmen, and rulers.

Sōtēr occurs twenty-four times in the NT, sixteen of which refer to the Lord Jesus (the other eight refer to God). It's never used of men (except, by application, to describe the Christian husband, who through Christ is the protector, preserver, and provider of His wife in Eph. 5:23).

In light of yesterday's study of *Christos* (**Christ**, Anointed One), we find thirteen verses in the NT where *Christos* and *Sōtēr* appear together. Luke 2:11, for example, declares, "For unto you is born this day in the city of David a Saviour, which is Christ the Lord." At the opposite end, Paul rejoiced in the future "glorious appearing of the great God and our Saviour Jesus Christ" at His Second Coming (Titus 2:13).

Most significant is Jesus' dealing with the Samaritans in John 4. Many Samaritans responded to the Gospel and testified, "Now we believe, not because of thy saying: for we have heard him ourselves, and know that this is indeed the Christ, the Saviour of the world" (v. 42). Peter also writes of "the Lord and Saviour Jesus Christ" (2 Pet. 2:20). As mentioned yesterday, the definite article ("the") is pivotal, appearing in these verses before "Christ," "Savior," and "Lord." It is, indeed, Jesus alone who is the deliverer, preserver, and Lord of men. It is He alone who provides salvation from sin (we'll examine **salvation** tomorrow).

From our perspective, of course, the greatest blessing in all this is its personal application in our experience. Because of Christ, we have absolute assurance of salvation. Not only is He the Savior of the *world*, but he is *your* Savior. As the apostle John makes clear, "These things have I written unto you that believe on the name of the Son of God; that ye may know that ye have eternal life, and that ye may believe on the name of the Son of God" (1 John 5:13).

Scriptures for Study: What should our reaction be to the thought of Christ as Savior, according to Luke 1:47? 🕮 What does Philippians 3:20 declare concerning us and Christ?

Salvation

sōtēria

Because of the importance of this form of *sōtēr* (**Savior**), which we examined yesterday, let's ponder its significance in light of our day. What exactly is **salvation**? *Sōtēria* (4991; e.g., Rom. 1:16; 10:9–10; Eph. 1:13; Heb. 5:9; etc.) means safety, deliverance, and preservation from danger or destruction.

To hear the "gospel" preached in many churches today, however, even evangelical ones, you would never know they were talking about salvation. *Deliverance* from destruction? Fewer and fewer preachers mention such an "offensive" concept. Today's "gospel" says, "Just come to Jesus and He will take care of all your problems," or "He will make you a better ballplayer," or "He will give you everything you want." The Word of God, however, clearly reveals how sinful man is and how great God is. It clearly explains that God, *solely* through His grace, mercy, and love reached down to save a dead race, a race that hated Him. As Lamentations 3:22 declares: "It is of the Lord's mercies that we are not consumed, because his compassions fail not." Why would Jeremiah use the word *consumed*? Because God is "consuming fire" (Deut. 4:24; 9:3; Heb. 12:29). Salvation is deliverance and safety from the judgment and wrath of God (cf. Rom. 1:18).

So, in contrast to the definition of **salvation** offered by today's "new theology," which is, "liberation from the oppression of this world's structures"[84] (whatever that means), I would offer this one, which I believe is soundly based on the Word of God: *Salvation is the sole act of God whereby He by His mercy and grace eternally redeems His elect believers and delivers them from their sin and the resultant spiritual death through the once-for-all redeeming work of Jesus Christ on the cross.* Any other doctrine than this should be cursed. As Paul told the Galatians (1:8–9): "Though we, or an angel from heaven, preach any other gospel unto you than that which we have preached unto you, let him be accursed. As we said before, so say I now again, if any man preach any other gospel unto you than that ye have received, let him be accursed."

Indeed, we are today hearing false gospels everywhere, and every one of them should be exposed and cursed for what it is. Salvation is not about *self-esteem*, it is not about the so-called *seeker's needs*, and it is not about *sentimentality*. It's about *sin* and the *Savior*.

Scriptures for Study: What does Romans 10:9–10 declare about salvation? 🕮 What should our attitude be toward the true Gospel (Rom. 1:16)?

Lord (1)

kurios

In early Classical Greek, while *kurios* (2962) was applied to the gods, there was no general belief of a Creator God. The word, therefore, was used in a broad way of someone who had power or authority. It was different in Eastern thought, however. To the Oriental mind, the gods were "the lords of reality." By Jesus' day, Eastern kings, such as Herod the Great (c. 73–74 BC), Agrippa I (10 BC–44 AD), and Agrippa II (27–c. 100 AD) came to be called **lord**. Most Roman emperors resisted such temptation, but others, such as Caligula (37–41 AD) and Nero (54–68) found it appealing. It was this very attitude of implied divinity that caused both Jews and Christians to refuse to use the term **lord** of the emperor.

Turning to the Septuagint, *kurios* appears over 9,000 times, some 6,156 of which translate the Hebrew *YHWH* (Yahweh, Jehovah), thus reemphasizing the meaning of divinity.

In the NT, then, *kurios* appears 717 times, the majority of which occur in Luke's gospel and Acts (210) and Paul's epistles (275). The reason for this, of course, was that they both wrote for readers who were dominated by Greek culture and language and who, therefore, understood the deep significance of this word in implying deity.

Finally, while **lord** is sometimes used as simply a title of honor, such as Rabbi, Teacher, Master (Matt. 10:24; cf. Luke 16:3), or even a husband (1 Pet. 3:6), *when used of Jesus in a confessional way, it without question refers to His divinity*. The confession *Kurios Iēsous* (Lord Jesus) is rooted in the pre-Pauline Greek Christian community and is probably the oldest of all Christian creeds.

Early Christians unarguably recognized Jesus as God, as Paul wrote to the Philippians: "And that every tongue should confess that Jesus Christ is Lord, to the glory of God the Father" (2:11). Even more significant, when Thomas saw the risen Jesus, he called Him, "My Lord and my God" (John 20:28). As we'll see tomorrow, even salvation is based on a confession of Jesus as **Lord**, as Divine Authority (Rom. 10:9–10).

Let us give our Lord glory *as* Lord! We'll continue our meditation on this truth tomorrow.

Scriptures for Study: In the following verses, note our attitudes toward God (and Jesus) as Lord: Matthew 4:10; Romans 15:11; Jeremiah 26:13; Romans 14:11; 2 Peter 3:18.

Lord (2)

kurios

Mark 12:28–34 provides a graphic demonstration of the importance of the Lordship of Christ. When a scribe asked Jesus, "Which is the first commandment of all?" Jesus answered, "Thou shalt love the Lord thy God with all thy heart, and with all thy soul, and with all thy mind, and with all thy strength." When the scribe responded that there was truly only one God whom we should love, Jesus then told Him, "Thou art not far from the kingdom of God." The profound truth in that passage is that the scribe repeated everything Jesus said *except* one word: **Lord**. He understood the importance of loving God; all that was left was to recognize Jesus Himself as Lord and believe and obey Him.

Here's the heart of the so-called (and tragic) Lordship Salvation debate (see also Mar. 30). There's something seriously wrong with a theology that teaches that there is a difference between "accepting Jesus" as *Savior* and then at some later date accepting Him as *Lord* when there's absolutely no such dichotomy or distinction in Scripture. It is, in fact, a denial of "one Lord" (Eph. 4:5) to say that all one must do is "believe in Jesus" to be saved. After all, the "the devils also believe, and tremble" (James 2:19). They believe in the facts concerning Christ, and that's exactly what many today view salvation to be, just some vague belief, where no repentance is necessary, no change of life is expected, and no responsibility is demanded. Again, Romans 10:9–10 makes it clear that salvation is based not only on a recognition of Christ as Savior but on a confession of Him as *Lord*. How could it be plainer?

What "one Lord" and therefore so-called Lordship Salvation means, is that true salvation results in an *automatic change* in the person who believes. True "conversion" (Latin *convertere*, "to turn around, transform") fundamentally speaks of a "new lordship." No longer are *we* Lord, no longer is *Satan* Lord, but rather *Christ* is Lord. That's the very essence of salvation: "Therefore if any man be in Christ, he is a new creature: old things are passed away; behold, all things are become new" (2 Cor. 5:17). There is no such thing as being *justified* without being *sanctified*, or spiritual *life* without spiritual *living*. Some object, "You're adding to the Gospel; all one must do is believe." No, we're not *adding* to the Gospel; that *is* the Gospel. Yes, all one must do is "believe," but such belief always results in obedience (Rom. 1:5; 16:26; 1 Pet. 1:2; see also **faith**, Feb. 8).

Scriptures for Study: Read Mark 8:34–38; 12:28–34; Luke 14:25–35; and Romans 10:9–10, meditating on their deep significance.

I Am

egō eimi

Here is a name for the Lord Jesus that explodes off the pages of Scripture. Speaking to the Jews, Jesus declared, "Verily, verily, I say unto you, Before Abraham was, I am" (John 8:58). At that comment, the Jews "went ballistic" and couldn't pick up stones fast enough to kill Him on the spot. Why did they react that way? Because they immediately recognized precisely what Jesus was claiming, that He was no less than God in the flesh. This was without question the most unmistakable claim to deity that Jesus made while on earth.

I Am is *egō eimi* (1510), words that actually are not very significant in themselves. The word *eimi* is simply the verb "to be" and is merely the usual word of existence. To Greeks in Jesus' day, and to our ears today, Jesus was just saying, "I exist."

Ah, but that's not what the Jews heard! They instantly noted Jesus' reference to Exodus 3:14, when Moses asked God His name and God answered: "I AM THAT I AM," which declares God "to be" self-existent, without beginning, without end. This is also expressed in the term *Yahweh*, "I Am the One Who Is," the most significant name for God in the OT. So when Jesus said, "I have always been," the Jews were enraged beyond reason or control. Similar statements on other occasions enraged the Jews because they understood that Jesus was claiming equality with God (Mark 2:5–9; John 5:16–18; 10:30–33).

That was no different, however, than it is in our day. People call Jesus "a good man," "a wise teacher," "a moral example," and other such platitudes, but flatly reject Him as God. At the core of several cults is the denial of the deity of Christ, but this truth is an absolutely cardinal doctrine of Christianity; without it, Christianity collapses of its own weight. It's also a doctrine that is clearly taught in Scripture with no ambiguity whatsoever. As John declares, "In the beginning was the Word, and the Word was with God, and the Word was God. . . . And the Word was made flesh, and dwelt among us, (and we beheld his glory, the glory as of the only begotten of the Father,) full of grace and truth. . . . No man hath seen God at any time; the only begotten Son, which is in the bosom of the Father, he hath declared him" (John 1:1, 14, 18).

Scriptures for Study: Read the following scriptures, noting Jesus' claims to deity: Mark 2:5–9; John 5:16–18; 10:30–33.

The Alpha and the Omega

to A kai to ō

Here is a fascinating title for the Lord Jesus, one that again emphasizes His deity. It appears four times in the NT, all of which are in the book of Revelation (1:8, 11; 21:6; 22:13). Most notable is 1:8: "I am Alpha and Omega, the beginning and the ending, saith the Lord, which is, and which was, and which is to come, the Almighty" (which we'll also examine tomorrow under the title **Almighty**).

Alpha (*A*, 1) and **Omega** (*ō*, 5598), of course, are the first and last letters of the Greek alphabet, which the Lord uses to emphasize that He is "the beginning and the ending" and "the first and the last" (1:11). This concept declares at least three realities about the Lord Jesus.

First, it declares His *self-existence*. The concepts of "the beginning and the ending" and "first and last" are illustrated by the fact that, as one Greek scholar puts it, "the Hebrews, the Greeks, and the Romans all used their alphabetic letters as numerals, which accounts for the ease with which alpha and omega also represent first and last."[85] "First" does not mean "first created," but rather He who already existed in "the beginning" (as in **I Am**) and who then brought all things into existence (John 1:1–3). The concept of "the beginning and the ending," in fact, is rooted in OT imagery (Isa. 41:4; 44:6; 48:12–13).

Second, it declares His *omniscience*. As the letters of the alphabet are used to create words, ideas, concepts, and therefore convey knowledge, God as the Alpha and the Omega declares His total and perfect knowledge of all things.

Third, it declares His *sovereignty*. Not only is He the one who brought all things into existence, but He is also the one who will bring all things to "the end" that He has already determined.

We should also point out once again the use of the definite article **the** (*kai*, 2532) before both Alpha and Omega. This declares that He is the one and only "beginning," the one and only "ending," and that everything in between is His.

That is the God we worship! Not some vague "life force," not a so-called Great Architect of the Universe, not some "higher power," but rather **the Alpha and the Omega**.

Scriptures for Study: Read the passages in Revelation and Isaiah noted above. What observations can you make concerning God as the First and the Last?

Almighty

pantokratōr

As noted yesterday, Revelation 1:8 declares, "I am Alpha and Omega, the beginning and the ending, saith the Lord, which is, and which was, and which is to come, the Almighty." **Almighty** translates *pantokratōr* (3841), a compound word comprised of *pas* (3956), "all or every," and *kratos* (2904; see Feb. 29), "power, strength, dominion." The idea, then, is all power, ruler over all, omnipotent.

This word appears ten times in the NT, all of which except one are in the book of Revelation (2 Cor. 6:18; Rev. 1:8; 4:8; 11:17; 15:3; 16:7, 14; 19:6, 15; 21:22). The concept, of course, is rooted in OT imagery, appearing there some forty-eight times. It flows from the Hebrew masculine noun *Sadday* (*Shaddai*, 7706H), which the Septuagint always translates *pantokratōr*, and which means "omnipotent" and "the Sufficient One." God revealed Himself to Abraham (Gen. 17:1–2), for example, to confirm that He had the power to keep His promises to make Abraham a great nation (12:2) and to make his seed as innumerable as the dust of the earth (13:16) and the stars of heaven (15:5), even though Abraham and Sarah were past the childbearing years.

It's also interesting that of the forty-eight occurrences of *Sadday* in the OT, thirty-one of them are in the book of Job (where it is always translated **Almighty**). That is significant because Job was a non-Israelite, which demonstrates that **Almighty** is a universal term for God.[86] Reading those occurrences truly gives the reader the picture of the immense greatness of God and His power over everything.

Used of the Lord Jesus, then, this word declares that He is, indeed, "the Sufficient One," "the Omnipotent, All-Powerful God," and "the Ruler of All." We do not worship a limited God, a God who can do only certain things under special circumstances. We worship God **Almighty** (Gen. 28:3; 35:11; 43:14; 48:3; etc.)

Scriptures for Study: Read the ten NT verses noted above in which *pantokratōr* appears (it's translated "omnipotent" in Rev. 19:6). What do these verses declare as characteristics and results of God's almightiness?

King

basileus

The Greek *basileus* (935) is truly ancient. It's found as early as the Mycenaean period of Greek history (1600–1200 BC). At that time it didn't refer to the sovereign of a state, but rather a subordinate prince or leader. Homer used it of a hereditary, legitimate ruler.

In the Septuagint, *basileus* became an important title for God as the only one who has the right to the title **King**. The earliest example of this term being used of God is in the dramatic scene in Isaiah 6:5: "Then said I, Woe is me! for I am undone; because I am a man of unclean lips, and I dwell in the midst of a people of unclean lips: for mine eyes have seen the King [Hebrew, *melek*, 4428H], the Lord of hosts." What a contrast this is to the attitudes today of "the Man Upstairs" and "God is my pal." Isaiah got a tiny glimpse of God as *Holy* **King**, and it totally silenced him, almost to the point of destruction (as the Hebrew indicates; "undone," *dēmēh*, 1820H).

The NT view of *basileus*, then, closely follows the OT. Most significant is the title *King of kings* (1 Tim. 6:15; Rev. 17:14; 19:16), which truly shows how He is contrasted with all other minor, insignificant earthly kings and rulers.

In his commentary, *Exploring Revelation*, John Phillips writes, "One of the most stirring pages in English history tells of the conquests and crusades of Richard I, the Lionhearted. While Richard was away trouncing Saladin, his kingdom fell on bad times. His sly and graceless brother, John, usurped all the prerogatives of the king and misruled the realm. The people of England suffered, longing for the return of the king, and praying that it might be soon. Then one day Richard came. He landed in England and marched straight for his throne. Around that glittering coming, many tales are told, woven into the legends of England—one of them is the story of Robin Hood. John's castles tumbled like ninepins. Great Richard laid claim to his throne, and none dared stand in his path. The people shouted their delight. They rang peal after peal on the bells. The Lion was back! Long live the king! One day a King greater than Richard will lay claim to a realm greater than England. Those who have abused the earth in His absence, seized His domains, and mismanaged His world will all be swept aside."[87]

What a day that will be when the **King** returns!

Scriptures for Study: Read the following passages: Isaiah 6:1–5; 43:15; 44:6; 1 Timothy 1:17; Hebrews 7:2; Revelation 15:3. What characteristics belong only to God as King? What rights are His alone?

Nazarene

Nazarēnos

Jesus was, of course, from Nazareth, a small village of farmers and artisans such as the Jewish carpenter Joseph, located on the side of a hill in southern Galilee 1,150 feet above sea level. In about ten minutes one could climb to the top of the hill and then see wonderful views for miles around. There were fertile hills and valleys and snow-capped Mount Hermon to the north; the Plain of Esdraelon, where Israel fought to survive, to the south; the blue Mediterranean and Mount Carmel, where Elijah struggled with Baal, to the west; and Tabor, where Barak led 10,000 men in battle, to the east. What a place for meditation! We can just imagine our Lord sitting in solitude, gazing on those vistas, and communing with the Father.

There's a smudge on that scene, however. In John 1:45–46 we read, "Philip findeth Nathanael, and saith unto him, We have found him, of whom Moses in the law, and the prophets, did write, Jesus of Nazareth, the son of Joseph. And Nathanael said unto him, Can there any good thing come out of Nazareth? Philip saith unto him, Come and see." Why such bigotry toward Nazareth and Nazarenes (*Nazarēnos* [3479] or *Nazōraios* [3480])? John 7:52 provides the probable answer: "They answered and said unto [Nicodemus], Art thou also of Galilee? Search, and look: for out of Galilee ariseth no prophet." Nazareth was just a backwater burg in a lackluster land that had no prophetic pertinence. He probably thought, "Surely the Messiah will come from Jerusalem."

There are at least two lessons to learn here.

First, the *real* Jesus, and His *true* disciples, will never be popular. Tragically, the Gospel today has been given a new spin. It's been diluted to appeal to the "unchurched" and made to conform to "seeker sensitivity." But the real Gospel is about sin, God's wrath, and the need for repentance and trust in Jesus' blood. No, that's not popular, and those who preach it are not popular, but that's the message of the Nazarene.

Second, Philip didn't argue with Nathanael, but rather he just said, "Come and see." Here is a picture of evangelism. There's no use trying to argue someone into the kingdom of God, or trying to prove anything to the skeptic by "apologetic evidence." The best evangelism is the *proclamation* of the truth with our *lips* and the *evidence* of Christ in our *lives*.

Scriptures for Study: Read Jesus' dealing with the Samaritan woman and notice His method of evangelism and its aftermath (John 4:1–42).

Emmanuel

Emmanouel

Emmanuel is a word with no Classical Greek background because it wasn't really Greek at all. *Emmanouēl* (1694) is actually a direct transliteration of the Hebrew *Immēnu'ēl* (6005H). It appears only once in the NT (Matt. 1:23), where it's also translated for us: "Behold, a virgin shall be with child, and shall bring forth a son, and they shall call his name Emmanuel, which being interpreted is, God with us."

What a wonderful word! It's rooted in two OT references.

First, there's Isaiah 7:14: "Therefore the Lord himself shall give you a sign; Behold, a virgin shall conceive, and bear a son, and shall call his name Immanuel." Here, of course, is a clear prophecy of the coming Messiah, who would be incarnate God in human flesh. This was to be the fulfillment of the promise God made in Genesis 3:15: "And I will put enmity between thee and the woman, and between thy seed and her seed; it shall bruise thy head, and thou shalt bruise his heel." When Messiah came, God would, indeed, be with His people "in the flesh."

Matthew 1:23, then, records the angel of God telling Joseph that his still virgin wife Mary is carrying that very promised Messiah, conceived by the Holy Spirit (see tomorrow for an examination of the word **virgin**). Interestingly, the name *Emmanuel* is not applied to Christ elsewhere in the NT. Here is a single, unique statement of who Emmanuel would be.

Second, we read in Isaiah 8:8, "And he shall pass through Judah; he shall overflow and go over, he shall reach even to the neck; and the stretching out of his wings shall fill the breadth of thy land, O Immanuel" (cf. 8:10). As one Hebrew authority tells us, this is "a cry to God Himself to be with Israel when the Assyrians threatened to destroy them."[88]

All this is instructive to the NT Christian. We each had a personal experience with the Emmanuel, who came to "seek and to save that which was lost" (Luke 19:10). Further, we now have an ongoing relationship with that Emmanuel, Who is, indeed, always "with us" through His Spirit (John 14:16).

Scriptures for Study: Read Hebrews 13:5 (cf. 1 Kings 8:57), Psalm 46:7, and 2 Chronicles 32:8. What further realities do we have besides God being with us?

Virgin

parthenos

Yesterday we examined this significance of **Emmanuel**, as it appears in Matthew 1:23: "Behold, a virgin shall be with child, and shall bring forth a son, and they shall call his name Emmanuel, which being interpreted is, God with us."

There's another significant word in this verse, however—**virgin**, which translates *parthenos* (3933). Even in all their excesses, the ancient Greeks highly valued virginity. It was, in fact, a characteristic of many of the goddesses of pagan religions. The chief examples were the Greek goddesses Artemis (Diana among the Romans) and Athene (Roman, Minerva). Athene's temple in Athens was actually named the Parthenon.

The Septuagint consistently translates two Hebrew words as *parthenos*. One is *'almēh* (5959H, maiden, young woman, a girl, a virgin). As theologian Charles Ryrie writes, "There is no instance where it can be proved that *'almēh* designates a young woman who is not a virgin" (*Basic Theology*, p. 242). The most famous verse that uses this word is Isaiah 7:14, which we also examined yesterday. The other Hebrew word is *betulēh* (1330H). While some scholars try to loosely translate this as "young woman," its use to describe Rebekah in Genesis 24:16 makes it clear that no man had "known her."

There have likewise been many false teachers through the ages who have denied the virgin birth of Christ, but the NT is very specific about this cardinal doctrine. Luke 1:27 declares that Mary was *espoused* to Joseph but that she was a virgin. She conceived by the Holy Spirit alone (Matt. 1:18). Other uses of *parthenos* appear in the Parable of the Ten Virgins (Matt. 25:1, 5, 11), as well as in Paul's teaching on marriage (1 Cor. 7:25, 28, 36ff). These and others make the meaning of *parthenos* unmistakable. As Ryrie again observes, "Thus the word means a young woman of marriageable age of whose characteristics was virginity."

Why is this doctrine important? Because the sin nature is transmitted through the earthly father through Adam, not by the mother through Eve. Adam was the representative of the race and was responsible for the Fall. If Jesus had been born of a man, he would have inherited sin, but as Paul makes clear, "For he hath made him to be sin for us, who knew no sin; that we might be made the righteousness of God in him" (2 Cor. 5:21).

Scriptures for Study: What is the lesson to be learned from the Parable of the Ten Virgins (Matt. 25:1–13; see Dec. 14)? 📖 What virgins are referred to in Revelation 14:4?

Gift (1)

dōron

Back on February 13 and 14, we examined that wonderful word **grace** (5485, *charis*). While *charis* ought to be enough to show us that salvation cannot be earned, Paul thought otherwise, for he went on to say in Ephesians 2:8–9: "For by grace are ye saved through faith; and that not of yourselves: it is the gift of God: Not of works, lest any man should boast." Let's take another look at this verse.

The Greek for **gift** is *dōron* (1435). The idea behind it, and the related word *dōrea*, is "a complimentary gift." It is used, for example, in Luke 21:1 where money is being cast into the treasury for the support of the temple and the poor (cf. Matt. 15:5). A synonym, *didōmi*, (see Mar. 17; Nov. 4) is used in that often quoted verse John 3:16, and means "to give of one's own accord and with good will."

A gift is such a nice thing to receive, is it not? The whole idea behind a gift is that it's unearned; it's given out of love. In contrast, think about the money you receive each week from your employer. Is that money a gift? Certainly not; it's that which you earned. But our salvation is a gift; it's unearned, undeserved, and given out of unfathomable love.

As we'll see tomorrow, even the **faith** (see Feb. 8) to believe was part of the gift. Spurgeon dealt with this truth in his sermon *All of Grace*:

> Even the very will thus to be saved by grace is not of ourselves, but is the gift of God. . . . I ask any saved man to look back upon his own conversion, and explain how it came about. You turned to Christ, and believed on his name: these were your own acts and deeds. But what caused you thus to turn? What sacred force was that which turned you from sin to righteousness? Do you attribute this singular renewal to the existence of a something better in you than has been yet discovered in your unconverted neighbor? No, you confess that you might have been what he now is if it had not been that there was a potent something which touched the spring of your will, enlightened your understanding, and guided you to the foot of the cross.[89]

This should, indeed, prompt us to declare *soli deo gloria*—to God alone be the glory.

Scriptures for Study: To whom does God give grace in 1 Peter 5:5? 📖 In 1 Peter 5:10, what does God's grace accomplish?

Gift (2)

dōron

In a day when the Gospel is being more and more diluted, distilled, and even denied, an emphasis on **grace** is needed like never before since the Reformation. We again consider the word **gift** (*dōron*, 1435), as Paul uses it in Ephesians 2:8.

A common teaching today says, "Christ's crucifixion is a proof of our worth." But such teaching is a heretical distortion of grace. The **cross** (see Dec. 4) is not proof of *our worth* but of *God's grace*. We were undeserving and even dead (Eph. 2:1–3). Where is the worth in a corpse? Therefore, *grace that is not ALL grace is NO grace*. Grace means that God has done everything; if He does not do everything, then it is not grace.

The key to this verse lies in the debate over the words "that not of yourselves: it is the gift of God." The debate is: To what exactly do the words *it* and *that* refer? Do they refer to **grace**, **faith**, or just the whole concept of **salvation** in general? To say they refer to grace or the whole concept of salvation results in the verse being redundant. Paul's central concept is that we have been saved by grace, which he states plainly in the first clause. Is he then going to repeat the same thing by saying "grace is a gift of God," or "salvation is a gift of God"? No, he's already said that. His point, then, is that even *faith* is a gift of God.

Ponder this: How can two unsaved people sit under the same salvation message, hear the preacher pour out his heart, listen to the Gospel message of sin, wrath, and salvation, and then one person believe and the other not? The answer is simple when we realize that left to themselves neither person would believe, but one does because God gives him the faith to do so. Because they are both dead, neither can respond until God gives them the power.

Further, faith *must* be of God, for if we say that faith is of ourselves, then faith becomes a human work, as is partaking of a sacrament or just "being a good person." *Faith* does not determine salvation; *grace* determines salvation. God has done it all. As John MacArthur rightly puts it: "When we accept the finished work of Christ on our behalf, we act by the faith supplied by God's grace." From where does our faith come? It is a gift from grace.

Scriptures for Study: In Hebrews 13:9, what is in direct contrast to the doctrine of grace? 📖 Read the following verses, noting how the ability to believe is a gift of grace: John 6:65; Acts 18:27; Philippians 1:29.

Boast

kauchaomai

Taking one last look at Ephesians 2:8–9, Paul says that salvation is of grace, "Not of works, lest any man should boast." He wants to make it very clear that no man can **boast**: "I earned my salvation," or "I bought my forgiveness."

Boast is *kauchaomai* (2744), "to boast, vaunt oneself, be proud." Paul uses it some thirty-five times in his letters. He rebuked the Corinthians, for example, "For who maketh thee to differ from another? and what hast thou that thou didst not receive? now if thou didst receive it, why dost thou glory [*kauchaomai*], as if thou hadst not received it?" (1 Cor. 4:7). In other words, what do we have that we didn't in one way or another receive? Why do we boast as if we did it ourselves?

So, Paul is telling us here that we in no way can boast that our salvation is in any way whatsoever a result of any works we can do. People boast about confirmation, **baptism** (see June 24f), church membership, Holy Communion (see Oct. 28), keeping the Ten Commandments, living the Sermon on the Mount, giving to charity, and living a moral life. Some people even boast about their **faith** (regardless of what that faith is in). But all boasting is rooted in **good works**, not grace.

Paul knew all too well about boasting. As expositor Martyn Lloyd-Jones observes, "There was never a more self-satisfied person or a more self-assured person than Saul of Tarsus."[90] Indeed, he was proud that he was a Jew, proud that he was of the tribe of Benjamin, proud that he was a Pharisee, proud of his religion, proud of his morality, proud of his knowledge, and proud of his works. But now he says, none of us have anything to boast about. As he again wrote the Corinthians, "He that glorieth, let him glory in the Lord" (1 Cor. 1:31). And to the Galatians he declared, "But God forbid that I should glory, save in the cross of our Lord Jesus Christ, by whom the world is crucified unto me, and I unto the world" (Gal. 6:14).

To say that we must add our works to God's grace is the most contradictory statement we could ever formulate. Any theology that mixes grace with works or faith with merit, no matter how sincere the motive, is heresy, plain and simple, and is to be cursed (Gal. 1:8–9).

Scriptures for Study: If we can boast in anything, in what can we boast (1 Cor. 1:31; "glory" is *kauchaomai*)? 📖 What must we never glory in (1 Cor. 3:21)?

Good Works

agathois ergois

Having studied in Ephesians 2:8–9 that works do not save, does that mean works have no place whatsoever in the believer's life? Does that mean works are meaningless and irrelevant? Absolutely not, as Paul makes clear in the very next verse: "For we are his workmanship, created in Christ Jesus unto good works, which God hath before ordained that we should walk in them" (v. 10). **Good works** do not produce salvation, but salvation most certainly produces good works.

Back on March 18, we examined *agathos* (18, **good**) and learned that it has a wide range of meanings: benevolent, profitable, useful, beneficial, excellent, virtuous, and suitable. We see here, then, the plural *agathois*. **Works** is *ergois* (plural of *ergon*, 2041), which means an act, a deed, the doing of labor, or even employment. The Christian, therefore, is now employed to do things that are good in all the ways implied by *agathos*. And that is quite a job!

Commentator Walter Liefeld relates this personal testimony that underscores the importance of these verses and this principle:

> There are few verses both more important and more misunderstood than 2:8–9. This is partly because verse 10 is often not quoted along with them. When I was a young Christian I acquired a pack of Bible verses to memorize. Among the first were Ephesians 2:8–9. I began quoting them in witnessing, but it took me years to realize that the omission of verse 10 was one reason I was having trouble persuading my morally sensitive friends that salvation is only by grace. The almost inevitable response was that if this is true, Christians can live as they please and still go to heaven. Romans 6:1 deals with this issue as well, but when we quote Ephesians 2:8–9 it should not be necessary to leave the Ephesian context, because verse 10 gives the needed corrective: we are *created in Christ Jesus to do good works*.[91]

Many Christians think that since our salvation was a gift, it, therefore, does not demand anything of us. Jesus is presented today as a "fix-it" for all our problems and someone who doesn't demand anything from us. That is serious error! *Any* gift demands a response even if it is only a simple "thank you." But truly our salvation demands much more than a "thank you" because our salvation is a life-altering reality; it transforms a depraved, hell-bound *sinner* into a blood-bought, heaven-bound *saint*.

Scriptures for Study: What prepares us for doing good works, according to 2 Timothy 3:16–17? 🕮 What's the challenge of Hebrews 10:24 in relation to good works?

Workmanship

poiēma

Ephesians 2:10 again declares, "For we are his workmanship, created in Christ Jesus unto good works, which God hath before ordained that we should walk in them."

There's a beautiful Greek word behind **workmanship**, namely, *poiēma* (4161), which refers to what is made or created. Another form of the word, *poiētēs*, refers to one who makes something or to a work of art. In ancient Greek this referred to an author or poet. In fact, our English word *poem* is derived from *poiēma*. So, we are God's workmanship, His "work of art," His "masterpiece," His "poem," if you will. While Milton's epic poems *Paradise Lost* and *Paradise Regained* are true masterpieces, they pale in comparison to the masterpiece of the true child of God.

Notice more specifically that we are *His*, that is, *God's* workmanship. There's an important contrast between the English and Greek texts. In the English, this statement begins with "we," but in the Greek it—in fact, the whole verse—begins with "Him." Literally the verse reads: "For of Him we are a product." The world says that each of us is a product of our environment or a product of our own experience. Even Christians have a tendency to think that way. But God's Word declares that the believer is actually "the product of God." Many preachers are even products of a particular Bible college or seminary (warts and all). But what we *really* are, are products of God.

Think of *poiēma* in the context of a potter. Does the pot say to the potter, "Well, you know that I had a little something to do with what I have become?" Of course not; the clay has nothing to do with the process. It's the potter who goes out and seeks the clay, brings it into his workshop, and molds it according to his own vision. Likewise, the "Divine Potter" molds us into vessels He can use. That's exactly what Paul illustrated to the Romans, in fact: "Nay but, O man, who art thou that repliest against God? Shall the thing formed say to him that formed it, Why hast thou made me thus? Hath not the potter power over the clay, of the same lump to make one vessel unto honour, and another unto dishonour?" (Rom. 9:20–21).

What a challenging thought it is to know we are each God's work of art!

Scriptures for Study: What does Romans 1:20 declare about "God's work of art" ("made" is *poiēma*)? 📖 While today's word does not appear in Philippians 2:13, what does that verse declare concerning today's meditation?

Created

ktizō

Once again, Ephesians 2:10 declares, "For we are his workmanship, created in Christ Jesus unto good works, which God hath before ordained that we should walk in them." Even more dramatic than being "God's product" (**workmanship**, *poiēma*, 4161), the Christian has been **created** in Christ.

Created is *ktizō* (2936), another word that means "to create or produce," but one that goes deeper than *poiēma*; it's the word often used in the Septuagint to translate the Hebrew word *bara* (1254H), "to create from nothing," as in Genesis 1:1. Think of this creation in light of our text. Lost men today, and tragically even some Christians, speak of "self-improvement," "self-help," "self-image," and many other "selfisms." But the principle we see here is that *God created the believer from nothing*. Think of it! What were we before Christ came into our lives? *Nothing*. Each of us was a worthless lump of clay, dead in trespasses in sins—no value, no form, no purpose. **But God** (Mar. 25) created us!

Do you see? Everything we *are* and everything we will *ever be* is because of Jesus Christ. It's not our experiences, education, training, or talents—it's **Christ**. Without Him we are nothing; without Him there is no purpose or meaning to life. How this thought again opens up 2 Corinthians 5:17: "Therefore if any man be *in Christ*, he is a *new creature*: *old things* are passed away; behold, all things are become *new*" (emphasis added).

The Christians I pastor (and I too) are somewhat biased toward the beauty of the Rocky Mountains on Colorado's western slope. And who among us has never marveled at the intricacies of the human eye or a newborn baby's fingers and toes? But there's something that is far more beautiful than all those things—*a Christian*. A child of God is the most beautiful of God's creation, for each is made in His image.

As Augustine wrote: "Men go abroad to wonder at the height of mountains, at the huge waves of the sea, at the long courses of the rivers, at the vast compass of the season, at the circular motion of the stars; and they pass by themselves without wondering."[92]

Scriptures for Study: According to Ephesians 4:24 and Colossians 3:10, what did God create? 📖 What tragedy does Romans 1:25 describe ("Creator" is *ktizō*)?

Before Ordained

proetoimazō

Let us take one more look at Ephesians 2:10, for it contains perhaps the most thrilling thought about living the Christian life: "For we are his workmanship, created in Christ Jesus unto good works, which God hath before ordained that we should walk in them."

That is a verse we should write down on a piece of paper and post in a prominent place (such as on the door of our refrigerator). It declares: *The* ***good works*** *that the sovereign God is doing in me today have already been prepared.* If we can remember that, be reminded of it daily, it will transform our living.

Why are these works "good"? Because God has dictated them; we don't produce them. God has already marked out what works are good. The reason the works of verse 9 are not called "good" is because they are *man-made* instead of *God-ordained*. Moreover, any works that man produces are "works of darkness" (Eph. 5:11; Rom. 13:12).

All that is in the words **before ordained**. The Greek *proetoimazō* (4282) is comprised of *pro* (4253), "before," and *hetoimazō* (2090), "to make ready," and so means "to prepare before, to make ready beforehand." As one Greek authority puts it, "The terms [in this word group] are used for the divine creation and preservation."[93] Another well sums up the point of our text: "God prearranged a sphere of moral action for us to walk in. Not only are works the necessary outcome of faith, but the character and direction of the works are made ready by God."[94]

Some of us walk around like "Christian boy scouts," looking for good deeds to do so we can get our "merit badge" when we get to heaven. The obvious problem with such an attitude is that it leaves man to decide which works are good. So which works *are* good? The answer is summed up in 4:24: "And that ye put on the new man, which after God is created in righteousness and true holiness." A "good work" is whatever is right and holy according to the Word of God.

Do you see the principle? God has defined good works. Just as we have nothing to boast about in our salvation, we likewise have nothing to boast of in our good works. God has ordained them, and they are now the rule of life.

Scriptures for Study: Read the following verses, noting how good works are now the rule of life for the believer: Matthew 5:16; Ephesians 4:1; 2 Timothy 2:20–21; Titus 2:7.

Draw Near (1)

proserchomai

Hebrews 10:22 declares, "Let us draw near with a true heart in full assurance of faith, having our hearts sprinkled from an evil conscience, and our bodies washed with pure water." **Draw near** is *proserchomai* (4334), to approach, accede to. It is usually used in the Septuagint to translate the Hebrew *qērab* (7126H), which also means to come near or approach but also pictures the idea of closeness to the object being approached.

The Greek likewise pictures such closeness. This word appears in Matthew 4:11, for example, where the angels "came and ministered unto [Jesus]" after Satan tempted Him and then departed. Jesus' disciples also "came to Him" often (5:1; 8:25; etc.) showing their closeness to Him. Of special note is 1 Timothy 6:3–5, where Paul writes that we should withdraw ourselves from anyone who does not "consent" to (i.e., accede or agree to) sound doctrine.

What, then, does it mean biblically to draw near to God?

First, and foremost, drawing near to God means having a sincere desire for truth. The words *true heart* are *alēthinēs kardias*. As we studied on February 1–3, both the English word **truth** and the Greek behind it (*aletheia*, 225) speak of that which is absolute, incontrovertible, irrefutable, incontestable, unarguable, and unchanging. The specific form of the Greek here also refers to "sincerity." *Kardia* (2588, **heart**, see Nov. 14) refers not just to the emotional nature, but also to the reason and to the faculty of intelligence.

While many people today say such things as, "I want to be near God," or "I want to get close to God," when confronted with the absolutes of God's Word, they rebel. That's a staggering contradiction! They don't want to draw near to God at all. They are like the Israelites, of whom Isaiah wrote, "Wherefore the Lord said, Forasmuch as this people draw near me with their mouth, and with their lips do honour me, but have removed their heart far from me, and their fear toward me is taught by the precept of men" (29:13). Yes, they say the words, but when it comes down to real truth, they reject it and live according to their own ways. The most important thing that drawing near to God means is that we sincerely want to hear, receive, and obey God's truth.

We'll continue these thoughts tomorrow.

Scriptures for Study: Where can we "come" boldly, according to Hebrews 4:16? (See also Jan. 5.) 🕮 What is a prerequisite for coming close to God (Heb. 11:6)?

Draw Near (2)

proserchomai

We continue our thoughts today on, "Let us draw near with a true heart in full assurance of faith, having our hearts sprinkled from an evil conscience, and our bodies washed with pure water" (Heb. 10:22). Drawing near to God first means having a sincere desire for truth.

Second, drawing near to God means having absolute confidence in God. The words "full assurance" translate *plerophoria* (4136), which means "entire confidence, full assurance." To be near to God, then, means that we have *total confidence* in His promises, *absolute assurance* of His provision, and *full trust* in His sovereignty. The more we doubt Him, the more we question Him, the farther away from Him we drift.

Third, drawing near to God means having a desire for holiness. The imagery in the words "having our hearts sprinkled from an evil conscience" is distinctly OT, referring to the sprinkling of the blood of the sacrifice for the cleansing of sin. But not only are we saved by this blood, but we are constantly brought back to it for daily cleansing. As the apostle John declares, "If we confess our sins, he is faithful and just to forgive us our sins, and to cleanse us from all unrighteousness" (1 John 1:9). We are forever coming back to the Cross, for it is there that our sin was dealt with and our conscience was cleared.

Fourth, drawing near to God means having a desire for His Word. While the first principle was one of *attitude*, we see here the *action*. Some interpreters view the words "our bodies washed with pure water" as a reference to **baptism** (see June 24f). But that is clearly incorrect because baptism is not a washing away of sin, but rather a symbol of identification, a public testimony of what has occurred in the heart. This phrase means that God's Word is the commodity that is going to keep us clean by our constant "bathing" in it. Paul meant this when he wrote to the Ephesians: "Christ also loved the church, and gave himself for it; That he might sanctify and cleanse it with the washing of water by the word" (5:25–26). Drawing near to God means that we are constantly involved with His Word, constantly "immersed" in it.

Dear Christian friend, are you drawing near to God each day?

Scriptures for Study: In Matthew 8:19–20, what requirement did Jesus give to the scribe who "came" to him wanting to follow? 📖 Read Exodus 3:1–6 ("nigh" in v. 5 is *qērab*, the Hebrew equivalent to *proserchomai* we noted yesterday). Note the need for our holiness.

Understand

suniēmi

Back on February 25 we considered the word *dianoia* (1271). Another word translated as *understanding* and **understand**, however, is *suniēmi* (4920), another fascinating word that was in use as far back in Greek as Homer's writings (eighth century BC). It "originally meant to bring together."[95] Greek scholar Spiros Zodhiates explains: "The comprehending activity of the mind denoted by *suniēmi* entails the assembling of individual facts into an organized whole, as collecting the pieces of a puzzle and putting them together. The mind grasps concepts and sees the proper relationship between them."[96]

A graphic example of this word appears in Acts 28:25–28. While under house arrest in Rome for two years, Paul taught those who visited him. Some believed, but some didn't. When he saw the unbelief of the Jews, He said, quoting Isaiah 6:9–10, "Go unto this people, and say, Hearing ye shall hear, and shall not understand; and seeing ye shall see, and not perceive: For the heart of this people is waxed gross, and their ears are dull of hearing, and their eyes have they closed; lest they should see with their eyes, and hear [April 28] with their ears, and understand with their heart, and should be converted, and I should heal them."

Romans 3:11 likewise declares, "There is none that understandeth, there is none that seeketh after God." In both cases the point is that the unbeliever does not understand spiritual truth; he cannot "put the pieces together" and comprehend what he is hearing. As we'll examine tomorrow, that is why Jesus used parables in His teaching.

In contrast, Romans 15:21, another quote from Isaiah (52:15), declares that Paul's word among the Gentiles fulfilled Isaiah's prophecy, that the Gentiles who had never before heard God's truth would hear and understand.

That is a great encouragement to us. After Peter's confession that Jesus was "the Christ, the Son of the living God," our Lord responded, "Flesh and blood hath not revealed it unto thee, but my Father which is in heaven." Likewise, the Holy Spirit illumines spiritual truth to us so we can understand it, so we can "put the pieces together." What a blessed gift!

Scriptures for Study: Who couldn't understand what Jesus was saying in Luke 2:50? What is the scene there? 📖 What does God want us to understand in Ephesians 5:17?

Parable

parabolē

The literal idea of the Greek *parabolē* (3850) is a placing side by side and, therefore, a comparison or similarity. "Specifically," as one Greek authority writes, a parable is "a short story under which something else is figured or in which the fictitious is used to represent and illustrate the real."[97] It's also interesting how *parabolē* is the word behind "picture" in Hebrews 9:8–9, showing that the wilderness Tabernacle was a "parable" of Christ's heavenly ministry.

It's been observed that about one-third of Jesus' teaching was couched in parables, which begs the question, Why? Why not just be literal and clear? Why be abstract? The answer lies in Matthew 13:13: "Therefore speak I to them in parables: because they seeing see not; and hearing they hear not, neither do they understand."

Our Lord uses the word **understand** (*suniēmi*; see yesterday's reading) three times in this verse and the two that follow to emphasize why He began to speak only in parables. Those who rejected Him and did not want the truth would not be able to "put the pieces together" from the stories He told. They would not be able to comprehend the fuller meaning he was trying to convey. He was actually presenting deep truths that demanded deep thinking, but the majority just wouldn't get it.

Sadly, that is true today. If our Lord were here today, He would undoubtedly speak in parables. We hear much about "loving God" and "loving Jesus," but much of such talk is nebulous at best and empty at worst. Many people who say such things, *including pastors*, abhor doctrine and deep Bible preaching and teaching. But Scripture makes clear that *only those who love the Word of God truly love the Lord*. Tragically, many books today are written about "loving God" and having a "relationship with Jesus" but never exposit Scripture. They speak of mysticism, feelings, and impressions, but never speak of doctrine and scriptural truth. Scripture, however, could not be clearer that love for God means love for His Word.

While we can, and should, greatly appreciate our Lord's parables, and while we can learn many great truths from them, let us also desire the deeper things of God's Word. Your reading this book, in fact, demonstrates that that is your desire. May God richly bless your faithfulness.

Scriptures for Study: Read the parables in the following passages, noting the contrasts our Lord draws: Matthew 21:28–32; 25:1–13; 25:14–30; Luke 10:30–37.

Hear

akouō

Probably most of us tend to think that to **hear** something simply means that sound registers in our ears and brain, but even Webster says that it goes further than that: "to perceive or apprehend with the ear; to gain knowledge of by hearing; to listen to with attention." Every parent has experienced times when their child says he or she hears what the parent is saying but doesn't really listen with attention.

The Greek *akouō* (191), however, from which we get such words as *acoustics* (the science of sound), goes even further. It not only means to hear in general (e.g., Matt. 2:3), to hear with attention (e.g., Mark 4:3, "hearken"), and to understand (e.g., Mark 4:33), but also to obey. In the Septuagint, for example, *akouō* is used to translate the Hebrew *sēma* (8085H) as in Genesis 3:17, where God said that Adam "hearkened unto the voice of thy wife" (cf. Isa. 6:9–10).

A graphic example of this word appears in the Parable of the Rich Man and Lazarus (Luke 16:19–31); when the rich man asked Abraham to send Lazarus back from the dead to tell his five brothers about the torment of hell, Abraham answered, "They have Moses and the prophets; let them hear them" (v. 29). His point was piercing. As he goes on to explain, if they would not hear (obey) God's Law as revealed, they would not be convinced by someone who rose from the dead. That truth is proven every day as people reject the resurrected Lord Jesus.

The challenges of this truth are apparent.

First, it challenges us to *truly* hear God's Word. In His messages to the seven churches in Revelation 2–3, our Lord says seven times, "He that hath an ear, let him hear what the Spirit saith unto the churches" (2:7, 11, 17, 29; 3:6, 13, 22). Like our relationship with our children, God wants us not only to hear his Word audibly, but He also wants us to *obey*.

Second, it challenges us to proclaim God's Word. It's not our carefully thought out arguments that will convince people of the Truth. Our Lord did countless miracles, even raising people from the dead, but most people still didn't believe. We are simply to proclaim the Truth, which God will use to "give the increase" (1 Cor. 3:6–7), and which will accomplish that which He pleases (Is. 55:11).

Scriptures for Study: How important is obedient hearing according to John 8:47 and 18:37? 🕮 What does Luke declare about this kind of hearing in Acts 3:22–23?

Rolled [and] Rolled Away

proskuliō, apokuliō, airō

Skeptics have for many years denied Jesus' resurrection by suggesting that the disciples just stole the body (which is the same lame story the religious leaders told in Matthew 28:12–13 and ordered the Roman guards to tell). An examination of three Greek words, however, exposes the utter foolishness of such an accusation.

First, there is *proskuliō* (4351), which is used in Matthew 27:60 and Mark 15:46 to record that a stone was **rolled** in front of Jesus' tomb to seal it. This word simply means to roll to or toward. The common practice was to use a very large, wheel-shaped stone that rolled in a channel or gutter. Such a stone usually weighed one-and-a-half to two tons.

Second, there is *apokuliō* (617), which both Mark (16:3–4) and Luke (24:2) use to paint a more graphic picture. The idea of this word is to roll up or back, indicating another common practice of a slope at the side of the opening, up which the stone had to be rolled. No doubt it had been held in place by a wedge, which Joseph of Arimathaea simply removed, allowing gravity to seal the tomb. Matthew also uses *apokuliō* to tell us that it was an angel that **rolled back** the stone (28:2). So, could the disciples have moved a one-and-a-half- to two-ton stone up a slope? Such stones required as many as twenty or more men to move. And even if the disciples could have moved the stone, could they have done so without the Roman guards (Matt. 27:65) seeing or hearing the activity?

Third, there is *airō* (142), which John (20:1) uses to give us even more information about the stone. This word means "to take up, to lift up, raise" and is translated "taken away" instead of rolled away. In other words, the stone was not just **rolled back**, but was picked up and moved a significant distance from the tomb. Again, could the disciples have performed such a superhuman feat?

While skeptics have for decades tried to discredit, destroy, and deny the Bible, historical facts, archeology, and other such evidences have confirmed the Bible's accuracy and reliability. No, we should not try to convince the skeptic of the truth, but we most certainly can show him his folly and defend the integrity of Scripture.

Scriptures for Study: In preparation for tomorrow's reading, review one or more of the resurrection accounts (Matt. 28:1–15; Mark 16:1–8; Luke 24:1–12; John 20:1–10).

Resurrection

anistēmi

What makes Christianity unique from all other religions? The **resurrection** of Jesus Christ from the dead. Every other founder of a religion is still *in* the grave, but Jesus *came out* of the grave.

Anistēmi (450) is a compound word consisting first of *histēmi* (2476), "to make to stand up, raise, awaken, or rouse (of persons lying down or sleeping)."[98] With the prefix *an* (*ana*, 303), which means "again," the full meaning of *anistēmi* is "to stand again." While secular Greek rarely used this word (and its derivative *anastasis*, [386]) to express resurrection, Plato used both for the immortality of the soul. It was used in the Septuagint, however, for when Elijah raised the widow's son from the dead in Zarephath (1 Kings 17:17–22).

One-time skeptic and critic of Christianity, apologist Josh McDowell, recounts a student at the University of Uruguay who asked, "Professor McDowell, why can't you refute Christianity?" McDowell answered, "For a very simple reason. I'm unable to explain away an event in history—the resurrection of Jesus Christ."[99]

Indeed, as mentioned yesterday, countless critics have tried to deny the facts surrounding the resurrection, but every such attempt has proven futile and foolish. The famous and brilliant British lawyer Frank Morison set out to refute the resurrection of Christ, viewing it as the greatest hoax ever propagated on humanity. With his background and training in the laws of evidence, however, the deeper he went, the more convinced he became that the resurrection was true. As a result of his quest, not only did he come to Christ, but he then wrote the best-selling book *Who Moved the Stone?* (London: Faber and Faber, 1930). Likewise, Dr. Simon Greenleaf, one of the greatest legal minds America has ever produced and famous Harvard law professor, concluded in 1874 that according to the laws of legal evidence, the resurrection was one of the best supported events in history.[100]

How we can rejoice in the resurrection! Our faith is not based on some philosophical concept or the teachings of some guru. Our faith is based upon the historical reality of the risen, living Savior.

Scriptures for Study: In Romans 6:3–5, what pictures the resurrection? 🕮 In Colossians 3:1–2, what does the new life of resurrection give us as believers (cf. 2 Cor. 5:17)?

Middle Wall

mesotoichon

On June 12, 1987, then President Ronald Reagan made the momentous speech to the people of West Berlin at the Brandenburg Gate, but which could also be heard in East Berlin. He challenged Soviet leader Mikhail Gorbachev that if he really wanted peace, he would tear down that wall. Twenty-eight months later, the Berlin Wall came down, ending the Cold War.

What a dramatic picture! The **middle wall** (*mesotoichon*, 3320) Paul refers to in Ephesians 2:14, however—"For he is our peace, who hath made both one, and hath broken down the middle wall of partition between us"—was even more daunting, dreaded, and divisive, but it, too, was eventually destroyed. It was the four-foot wall in Jerusalem that separated the court of the Gentiles from the temple area. First-century Jewish historian Josephus records that there was an inscription on the wall in both Greek and Latin "which forbade any foreigner [i.e., Gentile] to go in under pain of death."[101] Archeological discoveries in 1871 and 1934 (now on display in the Archaeological Museum in Istanbul and the Rockefeller Museum in Jerusalem) confirmed these warning inscriptions. So, while that wall fell when Jerusalem fell in 70 AD—some nine years after Paul was writing—Paul saw this wall as *already destroyed* by Christ on the cross.

All of that has a powerful application for today. There was (and still is) an arrogance and bigotry between Jew and Gentile that God never intended. God's intention was that the Jews use the "court of the Gentiles" as a place to win the Gentiles to Judaism and eventually bring them into the temple, but the Jews used the "dividing wall" to keep the Gentiles restricted, to keep them forever outside God's favor.

Sadly, we have some of the same arrogance and bigotry in today's denominations, associations, fellowships, and even local fundamental and evangelical churches. Many act as though their denomination or association was ordained of God. There's a great need today to realize the oneness that should be present in the body of Christ.

Now, we are *not* advocating a compromise of doctrine, for no church or individual believer should fellowship with those who deny foundational doctrines such as: grace alone, the deity of Christ, the virgin birth, or the inspiration of Scripture. But there is far too much "majoring on minors," which causes wicked strife in the body. Let us strive for **unity** (which we'll examine tomorrow).

Scriptures for Study: First Corinthians 1:10–3:23 is all about the disunity in the church in Corinth. Read 1:10–2:31 today, noting each example of division. Read the rest tomorrow.

Unity

henotēs

Like never before in history, we hear much about **unity** today. But much of what we hear is not based on a proper understanding of what *true* unity is. Unity, for example, is not compromise or tolerance, when we throw out all doctrine so that everyone can "get along." Neither is unity "brotherhood" or "camaraderie," which we might find in being members of the same company, union, association, or even church denomination. Nor is unity uniformity, where everyone walks, talks, acts, thinks, and even dresses alike.

The true nature of unity is found in the Greek *henotēs* (1775), which appears, for example, in Ephesians 4:3: "Endeavouring to keep the unity of the Spirit in the bond of peace." It basically means "unanimity and agreement." One Greek authority, however, provides a marvelous contrast between how the Greeks, the Septuagint, and the NT used this word: "In Greek and Roman philosophy the unity of God and the world is demanded by educated *reason*. In the OT [the Septuagint], the unity of God is a confession derived from *experience* of God's unique reality. The decisive advance in the NT, caused by God Himself, is the basing of the unity and uniqueness of God on the *unique revelation through and in the one man Jesus Christ*."[102]

To simplify, we base unity either on *reason*, *experience*, *or the person and work of Jesus Christ*. Most of today's so-called unity is based upon either *experience* ("We've all experienced the same thing, so we're in this thing together"), or *reason* ("To accomplish more, we'll get rid of our doctrinal differences"). While those sound noble, they are unscriptural. Biblical unity is this: *the unanimous agreement concerning the unique revelation of God through Jesus Christ*. Unless we can agree on the person and work of Jesus Christ, there can be no unity. It is as simple as that. That alone must be our foundation for unity.

Scriptures for Study: As noted yesterday, read the rest of 1 Corinthians 1:10–3:23, noting each example of division.

Bond

sundesmos

Another NT word that emphasizes the importance of **unity** is **bond** (*sundesmos*, 4886), as in Ephesians 4:3: "Keep the unity of the Spirit in the bond of peace." In Classical Greek, from the time of Homer onward, the root *desmos* (1199) meant "chain."[103] In the NT, it meant "band, bond, ligament."[104] With the prefix *sun* (4862, "with"), therefore, *sundesmos* means "that which binds together." In a negative sense, we see it in Acts 8:23, where someone is enslaved by a habit or attitude. Peter says of Simon the sorcerer, who was not a truly converted man, "I perceive that thou art in the gall of bitterness, and in the bond of iniquity." In Colossians 2:19, it refers to a tendon or ligament of the bones that holds the body together.

This, then, is the picture of true unity. It's not some superficial, sappy sentimentality, but rather a bond, the very ligaments of the body, that hold us together. Commentator Albert Barnes notes that the American Indians spoke of **peace** (see Jan. 11) as a "chain of friendship." That is, indeed, what the true Christian has with other Christians.

The challenge to us, then, is that a lack of peace in the body is sin, no matter what the reason (barring doctrinal purity). A vivid example appears in Philippians 4:2–3: "I beseech Euodias, and beseech Syntyche, that they be of the same mind in the Lord. And I intreat thee also, true yokefellow, help those women which laboured with me in the gospel, with Clement also, and with other my fellowlabourers." The only problem in the Philippian church was a single unnamed conflict between two women, but that one conflict threatened to do serious damage. Paul obviously doesn't tell us what the problem was because it didn't matter. Whether one woman was right and the other wrong didn't matter either. Both were wrong because they were causing disunity in the body.

When we're thinking more about what *we think* and what *we feel*, there will be division. As a pastor, I am constantly troubled (and quite honestly terrified) about what disagreements and differences of *opinion* over paint color, carpet fiber, pew design, window trim, and other such ridiculous matters can do to church unity. Such things are merely personal taste and worldly wisdom, and they are total foolishness to God (1 Cor. 3:18–20). Such things can destroy unity in a heartbeat, so we must always be on guard.

Scriptures for Study: Compare Christ's *commands* to unity (John 17:11, 21–23) and the early church's *practice* of unity (Acts 2:46–47). Around what, therefore, should we unify?

Lowliness

tapeinophrosunē

We've been meditating on **unity** for the last few days. Let's continue by pondering some attitudes that Paul gives us on how we can actually go about maintaining unity. In Ephesians 4:2–3, he writes: "With all lowliness and meekness, with longsuffering, forbearing one another in love; Endeavouring to keep the unity of the Spirit in the bond of peace."

The first attitude that will help us maintain unity is **lowliness**. The Greek *tapeinophrosunē* (5012) pictures modesty, humility, and lowliness of mind, having a humble opinion of oneself, a deep sense of one's littleness. Think of that! It's not a false humility such as, "Ah shucks, I'm not all that great," but rather a deep sense of how little we really are.

The most fascinating aspect of *tapeinophrosunē* is that, as Greek scholar Richard Trench points out, "No Greek writer employed it before the Christian era, and apart from the influence of Christian writers, it is not used later."[105] The reason this was true was that to the Greek and Roman mind, such an attitude was synonymous with weakness and cowardice. It was so abhorrent to their minds that they had no term to describe it. Likewise, in our day, when self-esteem and self-glorification are a major emphasis, even among Christians, lowliness is needed all the more.

One of my favorite stories is the one told of a group of people who went to see Beethoven's home in Germany. After the tour guide had showed them Beethoven's piano and had finished his lecture, he asked if any of them would like to come up and sit at the piano for a moment and play a chord or two. There was a sudden rush to the piano by all the people, except a gray-haired gentleman with long, flowing hair. The guide finally asked him, "Wouldn't you like to sit down at the piano and play a few notes?" He answered, "No, I don't feel worthy." No one recognized him, but that man was Ignace Paderewski (1860–1941), Polish statesman, composer, and celebrated concert pianist. While he was the only person present who really was worthy to play Beethoven's piano, he didn't think so.

That is lowliness. And if a concert pianist can think that he is lowly in the shadow of Beethoven, how little are we in the shadow of our Lord? Are our feelings, views, and opinions important enough to destroy unity?

Scriptures for Study: In Acts 20:19, what can't we do if we don't have "humility" (*tapeinophrosunē*)? 🕮 What does Philippians 2:3 have to say about "self-esteem"?

Less Than the Least

elachistoteros

Yesterday we considered the first of several attitudes Paul gives on how to maintain unity (Eph. 4:2–3). We'll return to those on May 8, but in light of the importance of **lowliness** and humility, another word that cuts to the heart of the matter is *elachistoteros*, which appears only in Ephesians 3:8, where Paul says of himself, "Unto me, who am **less than the least** of all saints."

To create the image he wanted to project, Paul forms what we would call "a comparative formed on a superlative." For example, to make a comparative out of the word *small*, we add "-er," making *smaller*. To make a superlative, we just add "-est," making *smallest*. In our text, then, for the sake of good English grammar, two words are used: *less* (the comparative) and *least* (the superlative). But in the Greek there is only one word (*elachistoteros* [1647], the superlative of *elachistos* [1646], "the least, minimal in magnitude"). We could literally translate this "lower than the lowest," or "more least," but still we have multiple words.

The most literal idea, then, is "leaster." The form of the Greek here is "designed to express the deepest abasement."[106] This was Paul's view of himself; he saw himself as the "leaster" of all saints. This wasn't false humility or fake modesty, but rather a true, biblical assessment of himself before God.

This truly flies in the face of today's virtual cult of "selfism," into which countless Christians have fallen. May we submit that any such attitude is not only the opposite of the man who is consider the greatest of the apostles, but also of our Lord Jesus Himself, as He "humbled himself, and became obedient unto death, even the death of the cross" (Phil. 2:8). Think of it! Our Lord is God, the Word that "became flesh and dwelt among us" (John 1:14), but He humbled Himself and died by crucifixion, the most agonizing and humiliating death of that day, reserved for criminals and slaves, the dregs of society.

It needs to be boldly proclaimed that the "selfism" of our day could not be farther from the NT standard of spirituality and holiness. This challenges each of us to say with Paul, "I am the leaster." The less conscious we are of self, the more Christlike we will be.

Scriptures for Study: What does Matthew 23:12 promise concerning humility? 📖 What does Peter say about God's attitude toward the proud in 1 Peter 5:5?

Pride

huperēphanos, alazoneia

Another word that comes into view when speaking of humility and **lowliness** is the word **pride**. Two common words translated "pride" or "proud" are *huperephanos* (5244) and *alazoneia* (212).

In ancient times, the *alazōn* (213) was a wandering charlatan and was a favorite comedy character in Greek plays. One Greek authority puts it this way: "It means, originally [in Classical Greek], empty, braggart talk or display; swagger; and hence an insolent and vain assurance in one's own resources, or in the stability of earthly things, which issues in a contempt of divine laws. The *vainglory of life* is the vainglory which belongs to the present life."[107] *Alazoneia* appears in 1 John 2:16, where it is one of the three categories of sin, along with the lust (see May 11) of the flesh and the **lust** of the eyes.

Huperēphanos likewise pictures arrogance and haughtiness. It appears, for example, in the list of sins that characterizes man's fall and depravity (Rom. 1:30), as well as in the list of sins that characterizes man in the last days (2 Tim. 3:2). At the very root of man's fallen condition is pride. If two words could sum up our world today, these are the ones.

It truly is amazing how often plain Bible principles and obvious Bible verses are simply ignored, even by *Christians* and Christian *leaders*. We give lip service to the Bible, but disregard what it actually says. Totally ignored, for example, is the clear fact that in the forty-nine occurrences of the word *pride* and in the forty-eight occurrences of the word *proud* in Scripture (AV), *not a single one is used in a positive way. Never* is pride tolerated, much less praised, as it is today. In spite of that, the teachings today are "positive pride" and the building up of self.

Such teaching, therefore, is blatantly wrong—it's as simple as that. It's a philosophy that is the very opposite of what God says. The clear conclusion of Scripture is that "God resisteth the proud" (James 4:6), even a supposed "positive pride." Likewise, does Proverbs 16:18 say, "Pride goeth before *exaltation*"? No, it says, "Pride goeth before *destruction*." Tragically, Christians are more and more drawn into pride and self-glory, whether it's in their jobs, in the virtual god of "sports," or even in church ministry.

Let us each be challenged every day of our lives (because it is a daily struggle) to abhor pride and avoid it as if it were the plague, for it is far worse.

Scriptures for Study: Read the following verses in Proverbs, noting the consequences of pride: 8:13; 11:2; 13:10; 16:18; 29:23.

Puffed Up

phusioō

At the risk of belaboring this subject, **pride** is an insidious enemy and should be confronted and condemned in every way possible. There is, therefore, still another term in the NT that graphically pictures this sinister foe. Paul wrote to the Corinthians that they were **puffed up**. He writes it, in fact, *five times* (1 Cor. 4:6, 18, 19; 5:2; 13:4).

At the very root of all the problems in the church at Corinth (and there were *many*!) was pride and arrogance. Paul uses *phusioō* (5448), which is derived from *phusa*, "a bellows." Just as a bellows swells up as it fills with air, the Corinthians were swollen with pride. In 4:6 they were prideful toward one another, each thinking he was better than the others. In 4:18–19 they were prideful against Paul, that he would not return to Corinth and confront them with their attitudes. In 13:4, their arrogance destroyed any possibility of love for one another. Worst of all, in 5:2 they were even prideful of a case of incest that was going on in the church, no doubt thinking they were being open-minded and practicing "Christian liberty."

I admit to a love of good movies, and one of my all-time favorites is *Patton*, in which actor George C. Scott plays the enigmatic General George Smith Patton. At the end of the movie, just before the closing credits roll, you see Patton walking alone in the countryside and hear a voice-over of the general recounting the glory of ancient soldiers that he so admired. Those words hit me so hard every time I hear them that I committed them to memory:

> For over a thousand years Roman conquerors returning from the wars enjoyed the honor of a triumph, a tumultuous parade. In the procession came trumpeters, musicians, and strange animals from the conquered territories, together with carts laden with treasure and captured armaments.
>
> The conqueror rode in a triumphal chariot, the dazed prisoners walking in chains before him. Sometimes his children, robed in white, stood with him in the chariot or rode the trace horses.
>
> A slave stood behind the conqueror holding a golden crown and whispering in his ear a warning: that *all glory is fleeting*.

Let us be challenged each day not to be puffed up. It's not only fleeting and empty, but it is also dishonoring to God. Only He deserves glory (1 Cor. 1:31; 3:21; 4:7; 9:16).

Scriptures for Study: In Deuteronomy 8:1–3, who did God humble? How did He do it? If you have a problem with pride, reflect on what God might possibly need to do to rid you of it.

Meekness

prautēs

Returning to the list of attitudes in Ephesians 4:2 that promote **unity**, there is the word **meekness**, which actually is inseparably coupled with **lowliness** (see May 4).

A common error is that **meekness** means "weakness," but that could not be farther from the truth. The Greek *prautēs* (4240, or *praotēs*) means gentleness and mildness. It has been truthfully stated many times that, "Meekness is not weakness, but strength under control." The Greek was used, for example, of horses that were broken and trained, and also of a strong but mild medicine, both of which have strength but are under control.

The ultimate example of meekness is the Lord Jesus in His humanity. As the well-known song proclaims:

> He could have called ten thousand angels,
> To destroy the world, and set Him free;
> He could have called ten thousand angels,
> But He died alone for you and me.

Our Savior had the power of the universe at His command. Is that not strength? But still Scripture says He was meek. While our Lord will one day be vindicated and glorified, instead of being vindicated at that moment, He submitted to the greater need of redeeming the lost. Additionally, our Savior was strong physically. The liberals and the world would have us believe that Jesus was weak and even effeminate, but could a weakling carry a timber weighing as much as 100 pounds after being scourged so severely? Jesus did! (see John 19:17.) But even with all that strength, Jesus was meek—His strength was under control.

Meekness, then, is the very opposite of the common attitudes of self-interest, self-assertiveness, and self-direction. What is needed today are Christians who are meek and humble, Christians who know the power they have in Christ and the Holy Spirit, and Christians who have that power under control.

Scriptures for Study: According to 1 Peter 3:15, what does meekness help us do? 📖 What do we receive with meekness in James 1:21?

Longsuffering

makrothumia

Another attitude in Ephesians 4:2 that promotes **unity** is **longsuffering**. The Greek *makrothumia* (3115) is a compound comprised of *macros* (3117), "long," and *thumos* (2372), "temper." The idea, then, is simple; we are to be *long*-tempered in contrast to *short*-tempered, to suffer long instead of being hasty to anger and vengeance.

So to maintain unity, we set aside "self," set aside our own needs, and be willing to suffer last place instead of first place, even to look like we're wrong if it will maintain unity. We're not talking doctrinal issues here—that is the point in Ephesians 4:4–6—but rather things that don't matter, the little things of personality and human interaction. What a marvelous testimony it is to be longsuffering, to have the ability to be long-tempered. "Love suffers long" (1 Cor. 13:4), and we must be "swift to hear, slow to speak, slow to wrath" (James 1:19).

When we're impatient and short-tempered with people, it's really because we're impatient with God. We are at that moment not trusting in and not leaning upon Him to give us strength. A verse that is not quoted enough and lived consistently by Christians is Isaiah 40:31: "But they that wait upon the Lord shall renew their strength; they shall mount up with wings as eagles; they shall run, and not be weary; and they shall walk, and not faint." When we wait upon God and allow Him to rule in our lives, letting Him "right the wrongs" that people do to us, then He renews our strength in three stages.

First, during the easy times we will soar like eagles. It's quite easy to live for the Lord when all goes well, but it is also during these times that we must lean upon Him lest we become puffed up.

Second, during the everyday difficulties of life, while we might not soar as eagles, we will still run and not grow tired if we are leaning on Him.

Third, it is then during the serious problems and tragedies that we will still be able to walk along without collapsing if we are leaning on Christ.

The important question now is: Are you "long-tempered"?

Scriptures for Study: What example of longsuffering do we read of in 1 Peter 3:20? 🕮 Who provides another example of longsuffering in James 5:10?

Forbearing

anechomai

One other attitude in Ephesians 4:2 that promotes **unity** is **forbearing**. The Greek *anechomai* (430) means "to hold one's self upright, to bear, to endure." This is the same word Paul uses in 2 Timothy 4:3 to describe people who will not "endure [put up with] sound doctrine" but will seek teachers who will tickle their ears. Paul also uses it in 2 Corinthians 11:4, where he is fearful that the Corinthians would "bear with," that is, put up with, tolerate, and even accept, the teaching of false teachers. How challenging both of those situations are today!

The idea here, however, is that sometimes we just put up with each other, that we bear with each other in misunderstandings, problems, and conflicts, that we **love** each other and sacrifice ourselves for each other anyway. That doesn't mean we just put up with it but still boil within, but rather we forbear *in love*. Not one of us is perfect, so we must "bear with" one another.

Without this kind of love and forbearing, unity will be destroyed and God's work right along with it. That has happened to countless churches through the ages. One of the worst examples of disunity I've ever heard of was the church that needed a new roof, but the people couldn't agree on what color shingles to use. Half the church wanted black shingles, but the other half wanted white. They fussed, fumed, and fought about it until it was about to rip the body to shreds. How did they finally resolve the controversy? They decided to put black shingles on one side of the roof and put white shingles on the other side. Did that end the disunity? Hardly. As the people filed into the church for services, those who voted for black shingles sat on the "black side" and those who voted for white shingles sat on the "white side." Was God honored? Could worship even take place in that church?

Whether it's a conflict within the entire body over some temporal issue (Acts 6:1–6) or simply a personality clash between two fussy ladies in the church (possibly the case in Phil. 4:2), **forbearing** is the answer.

Scriptures for Study: Read Acts 6:1–6, noting the conflict that arose and then the *biblical* solution.

Lust

epithumia

One of the most graphic instances of the word **lust** appears in 1 John 2:16: "For all that is in the world, the lust of the flesh, and the lust of the eyes, and the pride of life, is not of the Father, but is of the world." An often-made comment by expositors is that these three areas were the ways Satan attacked both Eve in the Garden of Eden (Gen. 3), as well as the Lord Jesus in the wilderness (Matt. 4:1–11). They are likewise the way he attacks now. Any sin we can name fits into one of those categories.

In general, **lust** (*epithumia*, 1939) refers to a strong craving, or passionate desire. While in Classical Greek it always pictures evil desire, in Scripture it can have either a good or bad connotation depending upon the context in which it is used; the context here, of course, speaks of evil cravings.

"The **flesh**" (see Mar. 10), then, refers to craving something that appeals to our fallen nature, bodily appetites that are out of control. Hunger is not evil, but gluttony is sinful. Thirst is not sin, but drunkenness is. Sleep isn't sinful, but laziness is. Sex is not sinful, but **fornication** (see July 30) is.

"The **eyes**" (see Feb. 24) refers to evil desires that are prompted by what we see. While the word *flesh* refers to our more basic desires, the word *eyes* is more sophisticated, appealing to the higher levels of sight and mind. The Greeks and Romans, for example, lived for the entertainments they could see and the intellectual thoughts they could experience.

"The **pride** of life" refers to arrogance in what one is, knows, accomplishes, or possesses. The word used here is *alazoneia* (212; see May 6).

Again, the context dictates whether *epithumia* is evil or good. For example, in 1 Thessalonians 2:17 it is used in a positive way, as Paul had a "great desire" to see that body of believers.

When, therefore, does "strong desire" turn to lust? The best definition of lust I've encountered is: "The desire to satisfy natural desires outside of the will of God." There is nothing wrong with desire—eating, drinking, sleeping, sex, etc.—but when we desire something so much that we satisfy it outside of God's prescribed way, it has turned to lust.

Let this encourage us to live a life that is **pure** (which we'll examine tomorrow).

Scriptures for Study: In Galatians 5:16, how can we avoid walking in lust? 📖 Instead of living by lust, how should we live (1 Pet. 4:2)?

Pure

hagnos

In ancient Greek, *hagnos* (53, **pure**, clean) originally carried a religious meaning and spoke of ritual cleanness, chastity, and even virginity. The same basic concept was also true of Septuagint use.

In NT usage, however, the idea of ritual purity was no longer the point, and rightly so. The NT deals with *reality*, not *ritual*. Being a Christian is not just about *how we act*, but *who we are*. It all started, of course, with the Lord Jesus. As 1 John 3:3 declares, "And every man that hath this hope in him purifieth himself, even as he is pure." Because Christ was pure (without sin), we also *are* pure and, therefore, are to *live* pure.

An interesting occurrence of *hagnos* appears in 2 Corinthians 11:2: "For I am jealous over you with godly jealousy: for I have espoused you to one husband, that I may present you as a chaste virgin to Christ." While the term *chaste* **virgin** (see Apr. 16) might seem like ritual, it's actually quite real. The setting of the verse is Paul's desire that the Corinthian believers (and by application *all* believers) would remain pure from false doctrine. He pictures this by comparing the church to a bride and Christ to the bridegroom. Just as the bride is to remain pure before the wedding, the believer is to remain pure as he or she awaits the coming of Christ. False teaching is everywhere, and it's vital that we remain **pure**.

This verse is also a great encouragement to both young ladies and young men to remain pure for marriage. Success or failure in a marriage often hinges on this. If a person remains pure before marriage, he or she will better understand "the covenant of companionship" that marriage is (Mal. 2:14; see Sept. 23). But if one is impure before marriage, there is a greater chance that he or she will be impure after marriage. Fidelity is non-existent in many marriages today often because of the sexual attitudes that were held before marriage.

There is much in the world that is impure and that will taint the Christian. We each must take care to keep ourselves pure. To that end, Paul further challenges us all to **think** on things that are pure (Phil. 4:8; see Aug. 5ff.).

Scriptures for Study: Besides things that are pure, what other things should the Christian think about and do (Phil. 4:8–9; see Aug. 5–10)? 🕮 What does James 3:17 speak of that is pure?

Reconciled

apokatallassō

The term **reconciled** is truly marvelous! The Greek is *apokatallassō* (604). The simple verb *katallassō* (2644) means "to change or exchange as coins for others of equal value."[108] The idea then is to *exchange hostility for friendship*.

In three NT references, however, the prefix *apo* (575) is added (Eph. 2:16; Col. 1:20, 21). This Greek preposition adds the idea of "back." Therefore, *apokatallassō* means "to bring back to a former state of harmony."[109] This pictures the NT principle that there was a time when there was no variance between God and man. Think of it! There was a time when there was no enmity, no warfare between us. When was that time? It was, of course, in the Garden of Eden. But sin created a barrier; it brought variance and division. The very moment that sin entered the world, Adam and Eve immediately realized they were naked, immediately tried to hide from God, immediately tried to shift the blame to someone else, and immediately denied responsibility. In that one moment, in that one act, variance was introduced.

It was the blood of Christ, however, that reconciled us; it was a "changing back" to that time of no variance. What a truth! As a believer, each of us is no longer at variance with God; we have returned to that time of walking with Him "in the cool of the day" (Gen. 3:8), communing with Him in heart and mind.

It's truly fascinating that *apokatallassō* is not found in Classical Greek. In fact, even the simple verb *katallassō* was never used in ancient pagan worship.[110] Why? Because the pagans were never reconciled to their gods; they had no concept of a god with whom they could have no variance. The gods of the ancient pagan religions were always angry, always demanding appeasement.

Moreover, neither is *apokatallassō* in the Septuagint,[111] but rather is found only in the epistles, for never before has man been brought back to a time of no variance. Only the blood of Christ could accomplish that. Even the OT sacrifices were inadequate; they were only an "atonement," that is, a covering of sin. *Only by Christ's blood could we be reconciled.*

Scriptures for Study: Read the three occurrences of *apokatallassō* (Eph. 2:16; Col. 1:20, 21), noting what God accomplished in each one.

Body

sōma

An interesting English word that contains the Greek *sōma* is *psychosomatic*, which concerns "bodily symptoms that are caused by mental or emotional disturbance" (Webster). The original meaning of *sōma* (4983) is not really certain, as one Greek authority tells us. Its first appearance was in Homer's work and referred to a corpse. It then took on the meaning of the torso and by application the whole body in the fifth century BC.[112] Gnosticism and other ancient philosophies viewed the body (and all matter) as evil and the mind (and other non-physical things) as **good** (see Mar. 18).

With the coming of the NT, however, such pagan thought was dismissed. While it is used literally, of course, to refer to the physical body (e.g., Mark 5:29; James 2:16; etc.) and even a corpse (Matt. 27:58–59; etc.), *sōma* carries a deep spiritual meaning, namely the spiritual body of Christ, the **church** (see tomorrow's reading). Paul paints a graphic picture of this truth in 1 Corinthians (12:12–27; cf. Rom. 12:5). His analogy is that just as there are many members of the physical body, all working together for the advantage and furtherance of the body, so is every Christian a member of the body of Christ.

It's extremely significant that Paul also states elsewhere that there is only "one body" (Eph. 4:4), which is also called the universal church. Some teachers do not accept this truth, such as denominations (or some groups who refuse to be even called a denomination) who maintain that their local assembly, along with other local assemblies who agree with them, are "The Church"; no one else is part of the church, no matter what they believe. That is, of course, an arrogance that is hard to fathom.

The most blatant example of false teaching concerning the body of Christ is Roman Catholicism, which teaches that it alone is the "True Church." If you're not Roman Catholic, it is taught, you are not a part of "The Church" and are, therefore, "accursed."

Biblically, however, no earthly denomination or group can be called "The Church." Every true believer who is in agreement concerning the unique revelation of God through and in Jesus Christ (see May 2) is part of Christ's body. Any other attitude destroys unity and any possibility of fellowship.

Let us rejoice in the oneness we have with other believers because we're all of one **body**.

Scriptures for Study: Read the above passages in 1 Corinthians, noting Paul's graphic picture of the physical body paralleling the body of Christ. What responsibilities do you have in view of this truth?

Church (1)

ekklēsia

What is "the church"? A study of the **church** in the NT reveals that it's not Judaism improved and continued, not the kingdom of heaven, not a denomination, and not a mere earthly organization. *Ekklēsia* (1577) is a unique word. It's comprised of *ek* (1537), "out," and *kaleō* (2564), "to call," and therefore means "a called-out assembly." It's found in Classical Greek from the fifth century BC onward and was used for the assembling of citizens of the city (*polis*, 4172) for legislation and other public business.

While *ekklēsia* occurs about 100 times in the Septuagint for the gathering of Israel for some definite purpose, the usual word is *sunagōgē* (4864, "synagogue"), which appears some 225 times to translate various Hebrew words. It's amazing that Jesus' followers didn't describe their meetings using *sunagōgē*, since this would have been the natural word for Jews to use. When it is used, it refers to the meeting place of the local Jewish community or assembly.

So *ekklēsia* is, indeed, unique, appearing some 116 times. As our Lord declared, "Upon this rock I will build my church; and the gates of hell shall not prevail against it" (Matt. 16:18). Our Lord truly transformed this word, using it to refer to *His* assembly, making it distinct from Judaism.

Our English word **church** actually comes from *kuriakos* (2960), which is derived from *kurios* (2962, Lord), and literally means "belonging to the Lord" (translated "Lord's" in 1 Cor. 11:20 and Rev. 1:10). Combining these two words, then, the church can be defined as *the called-out assembly of NT believers that belongs to the Lord.*

Ekklēsia is used first to picture the church as an *organism*. Our Lord's words above, for example, emphasize His *church*, not *churches*. Paul tells us that Christ loved the church, gave Himself for it (Eph. 5:25), sanctified it (vv. 26–27), and is the head of it (v. 23). As noted yesterday, the church is described metaphorically as Christ's body, and every believer is a member of that body.

What a miracle the church is! It's the living entity that God is using to bring about His purposes on earth. And what a blessing it is to know that each of us is an integral part of it.

Scriptures for Study: What was the reason for Paul's grief in 1 Corinthians 15:9? 📖 What does Paul call the church in 1 Timothy 3:15?

Church (2)

ekklēsia

Continuing our thoughts concerning the **church** (*ekklēsia*), not only is it described as an *organism*, but it is also called an *organization*. It's not like any other organization, however. Rather, the local church is an assembly of believers, organized and functioning according to scriptural guidelines, that carries out all outward ministry.

Several local churches are mentioned in the NT: Jerusalem (Acts 8:1), Antioch (13:1), Ephesus (20:17), Galatia (Gal. 1:2), and Judea (1 Thess. 2:14). The importance and centrality of the local church cannot be overemphasized in our day, and tragically it has been seriously altered. How vital it is that we recognized that the local church is the functioning organization of the universal church. In fact, the universal church cannot even function properly without the local church, for the local church has been ordained by God to carry on earthly ministry. That is why the apostle Paul founded local churches throughout the known world of his day. To deny the primacy of the local church is to deny the very foundation of NT ministry.

The local church, then, is for God's people to gather for worship, exercise their gifts, and equip them for service. As Paul makes clear later in Ephesians 4:11–16, God has given certain men "for the perfecting of the saints, for the work of the ministry, for the edifying of the body of Christ," and this obviously takes place in the local church, as is also made plain in the book of Acts. Paul likewise wrote to Timothy, the pastor of a local church, "But if I tarry long, that thou mayest know how thou oughtest to behave thyself in the house of God, which is the church of the living God, the **pillar and ground of the truth**" (1 Tim. 3:15 with context; see Feb. 4).

While there is a plethora of "parachurch organizations" in our day that work "alongside" (*para*) the church, and while they have certainly accomplished various works for God, they are not God's best, for they are not taught in Scripture. Many of them, in fact, are inherently weak in theology and method. God called Paul and others to found local churches, for it is through those that He wishes to perform His greatest works on earth.

Scriptures for Study: According to Acts 13:1–3, what is a demanded duty of the local church? 📖 What is another ministry of the local church and pastors, according to 2 Timothy 2:2?

Preach (1)

euangelizō, euangelion

There are two words translated **preach** (or other form) in the NT. The first is *euangelizō* (2097), "to proclaim good or joyful news." It is, of course, where we get our English word *evangelize*, and is (with the noun *euangelion*, 2098), translated by several other words: *gospel* (Matt. 4:23), *glad tidings* (Luke 1:19), *good tidings* (2:10), and *declared* (Rev. 10:7).

In ancient Greek, *euangelion* was used for a message of victory, as well as for political and private messages that bring joy. In the Septuagint it's used in several instances to proclaim God's universal victory over the world (Ps. 96:2–10; Isa. 41:27; 52:7). It's used in the NT, then, for the proclamation of the Gospel, the good news of salvation in Christ.

The English word *gospel* is even more fascinating. As mentioned on February 5, it comes from the Old English *gōdspel*: *gōd*, good; *spel*, tale. Witches were said to cast a *spell*, that is, say certain words that supposedly had magic powers. To *spellbind* is to speak in such a way as to hold people's attention. To *spell* a word means to name or write the letters of the word. So, the Gospel is, indeed, the good spell, the good tale, the good story, the good message, the good news.

Even more significant, "the Gospel" is *the only* good tale. The definite article appears quite often with "Gospel." In Ephesians 1:13, for example, we read, "In whom ye also trusted, after that ye heard the word of truth, the gospel of your salvation: in whom also after that ye believed, ye were sealed with that Holy Spirit of promise." While the article appears twice in the English, it appears three times in the Greek. We can literally read it, "*The* message of *the* truth, *the* good news of your salvation."

Paul wants to make it clear that there is only one good news. He wrote to the Galatians that anyone who perverts the Gospel is to be "accursed" (*anathema*, that which is devoted to destruction, Gal. 1:6–9; see Feb. 6–7). Today the Gospel is being defined in whatever terms each person desires. It's even being preached as not requiring repentance or even an acknowledgment of sin, but that is not the Gospel (Gal. 1:7). The Gospel, the *euangelion*, is the message of trust in Jesus' blood as the only redemption from sin. Let us not debate, philosophize, psychologize, or even "meet people's needs," all of which are typical today. Let us just proclaim the Truth, the "Good News."

Scriptures for Study: In Romans 1:16, what is the importance of the Gospel? 🕮 What is the description of those who preach the Gospel (Rom. 10:15)?

Preach (2)

kērussō

Another Greek word translated **preach** in the NT is the powerful word *kērussō* (2784). Paul used this word in his parting challenge to Timothy, telling him that in the face of apostasy (2 Tim. 3), there was only one thing to do: *Preach the Word* (2 Tim. 4:2–4).

This verb literally means "to announce or to publicly herald." The noun form *kērux* (2783; 1 Tim. 2:7; 2 Tim. 1:11; 2 Pet. 2:5) refers to the imperial herald who represented the emperor or king and announced his wishes. This word is formal, grave, serious, and authoritative. It's used of John the Baptist,[113] the Lord Jesus,[114] and the apostles and teachers.[115] The herald was not like an ambassador who might "negotiate"; he was a representative of the king and would simply announce the king's decrees. The words of the herald were to be listened to, for to ignore his words would be to ignore the king's words, and to abuse the herald was to abuse the king.

An important observation concerning this word is that while it is sometimes used to refer to others besides the full-time preacher, it is not used of *public* preaching and teaching by anyone other than those who are called, trained, and ordained to do so.

What, then, is preaching? Put simply: *Preaching is the exposition (i.e., detailed explanation) and application of God's Word from the preacher to the people*. True preaching not only explains God's Word according to: (1) the original language, (2) scriptural context, and (3) historical setting, but it also (4) *applies* that truth to Christian living, showing us what God demands from us.

Scripture over and over again demonstrates that there is absolutely nothing more important, or even equal in importance, than preaching. Tragically, however, there are countless things today that are being used to replace preaching: films, comedians, dramas and plays, so-called Bible studies that consist of people just sharing their feelings and opinions of what a given Bible text says to them, Christian music concerts, crowd-pleasing personalities and activities, panel discussions and debates, various church programs, and many others. But the Word of God is clear in showing that *preaching must never be replaced*, nor does it need man's ideas and programs to supplement it.

Whether you are a preacher or a layman, you should be committed to the preaching ministry; if you're a preacher, *practice* it; if you're a layman, *submit* to it.

Scriptures for Study: What is the importance of preaching, according to Romans 10:14? 📖 In 1 Corinthians 1:23, what is the attitude of unsaved people toward preaching?

Give Attendance

prosechō

In light of the centrality of preaching in Christian ministry, Paul wrote to Pastor Timothy, "Till I come, give attendance to reading, to exhortation, to doctrine" (1 Tim. 4:13). Sadly, most ministries today are built on entertainment, personality, crowd-gathering events, gimmicks, programs, and many other things that simply appeal to the flesh. But the truly biblical minister builds solely on the Word of God. Paul makes it very clear that until he returned, Timothy was to do one thing only: keep preaching the truth in which Paul had instructed him (cf. 2 Tim. 2:2, "And the things that thou hast heard of me among many witnesses, the same commit thou to faithful men, who shall be able to teach others also").

Give attendance translates *prosechō* (4337), which was a nautical term for holding a ship in a direction, to sail onward. The idea, then, was "to hold on one's course." And what course was Timothy to hold? Not entertainment or people's "felt needs." His course was to be the Word of God alone. Paul used the same word in his letter to Pastor Titus, "Not giving heed [*prosechō*] to Jewish fables, and commandments of men, that turn from the truth" (Titus 1:14). "Jewish fables" were a mixture of extra-biblical Jewish traditions and pagan myths. Similarly, "commandments of men" were simply man-made teachings. Paul told Titus that he was not to set his course according to those things but according to God's Word. What does all that say about many of today's methods?

Specifically, Timothy's and Titus's course was to be set on "reading," **exhortation**, and **doctrine**, and by application, this should be our course. The definite article appears before "reading," which indicates the specific practice of public reading. Because of the scarcity of manuscripts, the practice of reading and explaining Scripture in the synagogue (Acts 15:21 and Luke 4:16f) was carried over into the church (Col. 4:16; 1 Thess. 5:27). First and foremost, then, it is the reading of God's Word that should fill our churches. That should be our course.

Scriptures for Study: Read Nehemiah 8:1–8, noting the place that the reading of Scripture had. 🕮 What course are pastors to set, according to Acts 20:28 ("take heed" is *prosechō*)?

Exhortation

paraklēsis

Yesterday we considered Paul's command to Timothy in 1 Timothy 4:13: "Till I come, give attendance to reading, to exhortation, to doctrine." Not only did Paul instruct Timothy to "set his course" on the reading of the Scriptures, but He also told him to practice **exhortation**.

The Greek *paraklēsis* (3874) refers to an "admonition or encouragement for the purpose of strengthening and establishing the believer in the faith (see Rom. 15:4; Phil. 2:1; Heb. 12:5; 13:22)."[116] In short, *exhortation* is the application of the *exposition* (see May 18). It challenges God's people to obey the truth of God's Word and warns them of the consequences of not doing so.

Interestingly, while we tend to view exhortation as a negative word, *paraklēsis* is actually translated as the words *comfort* and *consolation* many times in the NT. In Romans 15:4–5, we read, "For whatsoever things were written aforetime were written for our learning, that we through patience and comfort of the scriptures might have hope. Now the God of patience and consolation grant you to be likeminded one toward another according to Christ Jesus." What really comforts and consoles? Does pop-psychology comfort? Does some little cliché or clever saying console? No. What truly brings comfort to the troubled heart and consolation to the confused mind is the Word of God.

A marvelous occurrence of *paraklēsis* appears in Acts 13:15, when Paul and his party went to Antioch in Pisidia: "And after the reading of the law and the prophets the rulers of the synagogue sent unto them, saying, Ye men and brethren, if ye have any word of exhortation for the people, say on." The verses that follow (16–52) recount how Paul preached on that day and on the following Sabbath. He reviewed some of Israel's history, spoke of David and that through him the Savior Jesus came, and then preached that only through Him is there forgiveness of sins (vv. 38–39).

What was the result? While this caused conflict among most of the Jews, which resulted in Paul being expelled from that region (v. 50), many of the Gentiles "were glad, and glorified the word of the Lord: and as many as were ordained to eternal life believed" (v. 48). Further, "the word of the Lord was published throughout all the region" (v. 49). Indeed, what truly brings comfort is to know our sins are forgiven in Christ.

Scriptures for Study: What other thing does not bring comfort, according to Luke 6:24? 📖 Whose name means "the son of consolation" in Acts 4:36?

Beseech (Exhort)

parakaleō

Today we examine a similar word to yesterday's. *Parakaleō* (3870) is a compound comprised of *para* (3844), "beside," and *kaleō* (2564), "to call," yielding the meaning "to call alongside." Originally, it spoke of summoning someone and at times "to summon to one's aid for help or encouragement." Its main three meanings in the NT, however, are reflected in the AV by three translations: *comfort* (twenty-three times), *exhort* (twenty-one times), and most importantly **beseech**, that is, to plead with or implore (forty-three times).

Paul declares in Romans 12:1–2, for example, "I beseech you therefore, brethren, by the mercies of God, that ye present your bodies a living sacrifice, holy, acceptable unto God, which is your reasonable service. And be not conformed to this world: but be ye transformed by the renewing of your mind, that ye may prove what is that good, and acceptable, and perfect, will of God." In light of the great doctrinal truths of chapters 1–11, Paul implores the Roman believers to live a life that corresponds to those truths.

Paul writes a similar command to the Ephesians: "I therefore, the prisoner of the Lord, beseech you that ye walk worthy of the vocation wherewith ye are called" (4:1). He pleaded so fervently with two ladies in the Philippian church who were causing disunity that he uses *parakaleō* twice: "I beseech Euodias, and beseech Syntyche, that they be of the same mind in the Lord" (Phil. 4:2).

There was also serious disunity in the church at Corinth, so Paul wrote: "Now I beseech you, brethren, by the name of our Lord Jesus Christ, that ye all speak the same thing, and that there be no divisions among you; but that ye be perfectly joined together in the same mind and in the same judgment" (1 Cor. 1:10). Likewise did Peter plead with his readers: "Dearly beloved, I beseech you as strangers and pilgrims, abstain from fleshly lusts, which war against the soul" (1 Pet. 2:11).

All those instances of *parakaleō*, and many more, demonstrate the seriousness of the Christian **walk** (see June 14), and they challenge us to "walk **worthy**" (see June 18). So important is this that Paul instructed Timothy and Titus that an important part of preaching is to "exhort" (2 Tim. 4:2; Titus 2:15). Thank God for pastors who obey that command.

Scriptures for Study: Read the following verses, noting what the writer is imploring you to do: Romans 15:30; 16:17; 1 Thessalonians 4:9–10; 1 Timothy 5:1 ("entreat"); Titus 1:9; Jude 3.

Doctrine

didaskalia

In 1 Timothy 4:13, Paul tells Timothy that there is one more thing he is to preach—**doctrine**. To the ancient Greeks, *didaskalia* (1319) meant imparting information and later the teaching of skills.

Didaskalia (with other forms) appears some twenty-six times in the Pastoral Epistles. Is there any doubt, then, what the preacher's job is? This is precisely why back in 3:2 Paul mentions that one of the required qualifications for the ministry is that a man is "apt to teach," which is one word in the Greek (*didaktikos*, 1317) that means "*skilled* in teaching." As one expositor puts it: "Not merely *given* to teaching, but able and skilled in it. All *might teach* to whom the Spirit imparted the gift: but *skill* in teaching was the especial office of the minister on whom would fall the ordinary duty of instruction of believers and refutation of gainsayers."[117]

I've heard certain preachers say, "I'm not really much of a teacher, but I sure love my flock," and I have heard several Christians say, "Well, he's not a good teacher, but he does have a pastor's heart." While loving God's people is commendable, if a man is not a skilled teacher, he simply is not qualified for that ministry, for he can't do the number-one thing his job requires. That is equivalent to a surgeon who does not know how to make an incision or a carpenter who doesn't know how to use a tape measure.

It's interesting, in fact, that in that entire list of qualifications, "love" is not even mentioned, while being a skillful teacher is high on the list. Of course, the pastor loves the sheep, which is understood in the shepherd/sheep analogy and certainly implied in the word *patient* (v. 3), but Paul specifically says that the candidate *must* be a good teacher.

In fact, the most outstanding facet of this qualification is that it's the only one in the list that relates specifically to a candidate's giftedness and function, the only qualification that deals specifically with what he is to do. And what does he do? *He teaches*. That is his function! He's not an entertainer, an administrator, or even primarily a counselor. He is a teacher. Men who are not doing that betray the office and bring shame to Christ.

No, doctrine and theological teaching are not *popular* today, but they are *biblical*.

Scriptures for Study: Read the following scriptures, noting the pastor's function: 1 Timothy 2:7; 4:6, 16; 5:17; 2 Timothy 1:11; 3:16–17; 4:1–4, Titus 1:9.

Sober

sōphrōn

Not only must a pastor have the ability to teach, but he must also be **sober** (1 Tim. 3:2). The Greek *sōphrōn* (4998) means "serious or prudent." It (and other forms) appear some sixteen times in the NT and are directed at several types of Christians: older women who are to teach the younger women (Titus 2:5); all Christian women (1 Tim. 2:9); aged men (Titus 2:2); younger men (2:6); and all Christians (2:12).

Two instances, however, are of special note, for they are aimed specifically at the pastor (1 Tim. 3:2; Titus 1:8). The sober pastor is serious about spiritual things. That doesn't mean he's cold and humorless, but neither does it mean that it's joke time in the pulpit. The sober man knows the seriousness of the ministry and views the world through God's eyes.

What does this say, then, about the "Christian comedians" who characterize "preaching" today? One such man I heard admitted that he went to Bible college to become a minister but turned to comedy. I do not wish to be ungracious, but that is disgraceful and impossible to justify biblically. May we add, the argument that says, "Well, if you keep people laughing, you can get your point across," is worldly nonsense. *Truly spiritual people will desire spiritual truth.* I certainly don't mind the occasional humorous comment or illustration, and use them on occasion myself, but "stand-up comedy" has no place anywhere near the pulpit. We are dealing with holy, sacred things, and we had better treat them as such. That is what God demands. So-called Christian comedy is one of the most serious errors of our day and, quite frankly, flirts with blasphemy.

Pastor and author Alan Redpath, who joined our Lord in glory in 1989, wrote: "God is trying to tell us that our current popular version of Christianity—comfortable, humorous, superficial, entertaining, worldly-wise—is exposed for the irreverent presentation of the Gospel of Christ that it really is. A preacher is commissioned to give people not what they want but what they need. No man has any business walking into the pulpit to entertain. He is there to present Calvary in all it fullness of hope and glory."[118]

Let us all be encouraged that the Gospel and all spiritual matters are serious issues, not to be trifled with or made into jokes.

Scriptures for Study: Read the Sermon on the Mount (Matt. 5–7). Do you find even the slightest hint of joke telling or other entertainment in our Lord's preaching?

Gravity

semnotēs

Yesterday we meditated on *sōphrōn* (4998, **sober**) and its importance in the life of every believer, especially pastors. A word that emphasizes a further aspect of this is *semnotēs* (4587).

In Classical Greek, as one scholar explains, *semnotēs* denotes "that which is sublime, majestic, holy, evoking reverence. . . . The [adjective] and the noun often denote the majesty of deity, but sometimes also the solemnity, serious purpose, and grandeur of a man."[119] Like *sōphrōn*, *semnotēs* (and *semnos*) are used of various types of Christians: wives (1 Tim. 3:11), deacons and their wives (1 Tim. 3:8, 11), aged men (Titus 2:2), kings and all people in authority (1 Tim. 2:2), and even for what *all Christians* should **think** about (Phil. 4:8; Aug. 6ff).

Also like *sōphrōn*, *semnotēs* is used to describe another requirement for pastors (1 Tim. 3:4; Titus 2:7). As the same Greek authority goes on to say, *semnotēs* is used in the NT to denote "an ethical and aesthetic outlook resulting in decency and orderliness," so "seriousness both of doctrine and of life is expected of the leaders of the church."[120] This man is, therefore, a serious man; he's devoted to a solemn presentation of the Scripture. As mentioned yesterday, does this leave any doubt that so-called Christian comedians and other "entertainers" are a sad disgrace? The pulpit is a place of *solemnity*, not *slapstick*.

As God declared through Isaiah the prophet, the man who God esteems is "him that is poor and of a contrite spirit, and trembleth at my word" (Isa. 66:2). John Calvin aptly writes here: "So far as relates to 'trembling,' it might be thought strange at first sight that he demands it in believers, since nothing is more sweet or gentle than the word of the Lord, and nothing is more opposite to it than to excite terror. I reply, there are two kinds of trembling; one by which they are terrified who hate and flee from God, and another which affects the heart, and promotes the obedience, of those who reverence and fear God."[121]

How many men in pulpits today tremble at the Word of God and teach their people to do the same? How many of us can say with David, "My heart standeth in awe of thy word" (Ps. 119:161)?

Scriptures for Study: Read the following verses, noting the relationship of God's Word to our hearts, that is, our thinking and feeling: Psalm 119:11; Jeremiah 15:16; 20:9; Hebrews 4:12.

Fables

muthos

The apostle Paul declares in 2 Timothy 4:1–4 that one of the major reasons why the preaching of the truth is so important is because there will come a time when people "will not endure [i.e., "put up with;" see May 10, *anechomai*, 430] sound doctrine; but after their own lusts shall they heap to themselves teachers, having itching ears; And they shall turn away their ears from the truth, and shall be turned unto fables." Those days are here!

What's worse, however, is that such people "turn away" from "the truth," which in the Greek is in the *active* voice, that is, they willfully choose to do this. Still worse is the fact that "shall be turned unto fables" is in the *passive* voice, which means that they don't choose this result; they are being acted upon and have no choice. In other words, because they *willfully* turned away, they now will *unwillingly* be deceived by **fables**.

That is a staggering truth! The Greek is *muthos* (3454), where we get the English words *myth* and *mythology*. In Classical Greek, this is a tale or fable that is "fabricated by the mind in contrast to reality."[122] Plato's myths, for example, were legendary, such as the myths of Eros, creation, the world to come, and judgment of the dead.[123] In the NT, *muthos* is always used to denote a cunning fable full of falsehoods and pretenses for the purpose of deceiving others.[124]

Let us repeat, when we *willingly* turn from God's truth, we will *unwillingly* be deceived, and how vividly we see this happening. Because most of the church won't tolerate true preaching, which proclaims truth and confronts sin, doctrinal error is everywhere: God's sovereignty has been redefined in the "Open Theism" movement; Christians seek extra-biblical revelation through mysticism and so-called prophecies; hell is denied as a reality; the roles of men and women are blurred or destroyed altogether; homosexuality, fornication, abortion, and other immorality is condoned and even defended; and on it goes. Tragically, there is virtually zero **discernment** (see July 15ff.) left in the church today. Error is rampant because we have *willingly* turned away from the truth.

May you always desire **truth** and never turn away from it.

Scriptures for Study: Read the other instances of *muthos*, noting the challenge in each one: 1 Timothy 1:4; 4:7; Titus 1:14 (see May 19); 2 Peter 1:16.

Unsearchable Riches

anexichniaston plouton

In the past few days we've been considering the importance of preaching. That being understood, then, *what exactly should we preach*? Paul tells us in Ephesians 3:8: "That I should preach among the Gentiles the unsearchable riches of Christ." What a wondrous and staggering thought!

Unsearchable is *anexichniastos* (421), "that which cannot be traced out." The root is a noun that means "a track or a trail." The verb appears only one other place in the NT: "O the depth of the riches both of the wisdom and knowledge of God! how unsearchable are his judgments, and his ways past finding out!" (Rom. 11:33). The word is also found in the Septuagint. It was one of Job's favorite words, in fact: "Which doeth great things and unsearchable; marvellous things without number" (Job 5:9; 9:10).

Riches is *ploutos* (4149), which literally means "wealth." The meaning here, however, is figurative; *it speaks of the whole wealth of salvation and growth in Christ*. It's interesting that Paul was the only Scripture writer who used the figurative meaning of *ploutos*, and that five of those fourteen usages are in Ephesians (1:7, 18; 2:7; 3:8, 16).

Putting all that together, then, we see: *The wealth we have in Christ is a pathway we cannot trace; it is unfathomable from human understanding*. Instead of the fluff and shallowness of most contemporary preaching, Paul declares that we are to preach unfathomable truths. Calvin called this "the astonishing and boundless treasures of grace."

Now, to what riches is Paul *specifically* referring? Is he implying entertainment, pop-psychology, "felt needs," or other popular notions? Hardly! He is, of course, referring back to the riches spoken of in Ephesians 1. How can any of us fathom ("trace out") redemption, forgiveness, acceptance, election, adoption, God's will, or the ministry of the Holy Spirit? We can't! From human understanding we cannot understand ("trace out") such truth; it's a path in the jungle we could never *find*, much less *follow*. Rather, it's the Holy Spirit who gives us understanding. Do you see? Paul was to *preach* all that truth, but it was the Holy Spirit who would *illumine* it to men.

So, instead of shallow sermons, motivational talks, feel-good discussions, and bad theology, every preacher should be preaching the doctrine of the unsearchable riches of Christ. Let's preach *doctrine*, not *drivel*.

Scriptures for Study: Read a few of the other occurrences of *ploutos* and identify what riches Paul is speaking of: Romans 2:4; 9:23; Ephesians 1:7, 18; 2:7; 3:16; Colossians 2:2.

Manifold

polupoikilos

In his discussion of preaching, Paul declares why we do it in Ephesians 3:10, "To the intent that now unto the principalities and powers in heavenly places might be known by the church the manifold wisdom of God." As mentioned back on January 26, **wisdom** (*sophia*, 4678) speaks of the "knowledge of the most precious things," knowledge of the things that really matter. That's why preaching is a "big deal." It's designed to make known God's understanding of the things that matter most. *And no other method of ministry will do that*. But, as if this word were not enough, Paul adds an adjective.

The word **manifold** is a marvelous word. The Greek *polupoikilos* (4182) is found only here in the NT. The literal meaning is "multi-colored," that is, marked with a great variety of colors, as in a painting. So, in our text, the word means "many-faceted" or "most varied." It's also important to note that the simple form of the word is *poikilos* (4164), meaning "various" (e.g., 1 Pet. 4:10). But Paul makes a compound verb by adding the prefix *poluso* (4183; English *poly*), "many." So, again, the idea conveyed is "multi-faceted" or "most varied."

Think of it! God's knowledge and understanding are the most varied, the most multi-faceted. It's not just that God's knowledge and understanding are deep, which of course they are, but that these take on many forms and possess infinite diversity. We can never understand anything of God unless He reveals Himself. And He does that only in His Word.

That is why we preach! Only preaching explores the depths of God; only preaching delves into who He is, what He has done, what He is doing, and what He will ultimately accomplish. It is the absolute height of arrogance to say, as many do today, "Preaching is not relevant; we've found a better method." What arrogance it is to say they we can improve on what God ordained—*the preaching of the manifold wisdom of God*.

Scriptures for Study: While *polupoikilos* appears only once in the NT, it appears twice in the Septuagint in reference to God. Meditate on Job 5:9 and Psalm 145:3, where it's translated "unsearchable."

Prayer (1)

proseuchē, eucharistia, aitēma, deēsis

When one turns to the great theme of **prayer**, he finds no less than seven Greek words that picture the concept, which, in turn, are translated by various other English words, such as *intercessions*, *supplications*, *requests*, and *giving of thanks*.

Why so many words? Probably the best explanation is that of Greek scholar Richard Trench, who writes, "These words do not refer to different kinds of prayer but to different aspects of prayer."[125] While there is a little difficulty in distinguishing these words from each other, we do see some subtle differences.

The Greek *proseuchē* (4335, with *proseuchomai*, 4336) is the most common word for prayer, appearing some eighty-five times. It's a general word that speaks of prayer to God, which underscores the obvious principle that only the true God should receive prayer. Prayer to other gods or saints is less than worthless; it's utter blasphemy against the one true God.

One vital aspect of prayer is described by *eucharistia* (2169), at the root of which is *charis* (5485, **grace**) with the prefix *eu* (2095, "good or well"). The idea, then, is to "give good grace," that is, "be thankful; give thanks." Sadly, while the Roman Catholic doctrine of the Holy Eucharist is supposedly to be the most important act of thanksgiving, it is in truth viewed as a sacrament that infuses grace into the worshiper and is part of salvation. That is not the biblical teaching concerning the **Lord's Supper** (see Oct. 28). Prayer, then, is thanksgiving, thanking and praising God for all that He does (Phil. 4:6; Col. 4:2; 1 Tim. 2:1; Rev. 7:12).

Another aspect of prayer is *aitēma* (155), "a petition, a request," as in 1 John 5:15: "And if we know that he hear us, whatsoever we ask, we know that we have the petitions that we desired of him." A synonym is the common *deēsis* (1162), "to make known one's particular need." While *aitēma* seems to be any request in general, *deēsis* appears to picture a more personal need of one's own. So, while prayer is *much more* than "asking and receiving" (as one writer wrongly defines it), we certainly can "let [our] requests be made known unto God" (Phil. 4:6).

Putting all that together paints a partial picture of prayer: *Prayer is communion with the one true God, to whom we come to praise and thank, and to whom we direct our petitions for others and ourselves*. What a privilege! We'll build on that tomorrow.

Scriptures for Study: Meditate on Philippians 4:6, where we find all four words we examined today: *prayer* (*proseuchē*), *supplication* (*deēsis*), *thanksgiving* (*eucharistia*), and *requests* (*aitēma*). What does this kind of prayer bring to our hearts and minds (v. 7)?

Prayer (2)

enteuxis, hiketēria, euchē

Continuing our meditation on seven Greek words that describe the aspects of **prayer**, we encounter *enteuxis* (1783, 1 Tim. 2:1; 4:5), which speaks of having access to someone, and even a certain amount of **boldness** (see Jan. 5) in coming to them. What a humbling privilege!

Another aspect of prayer is *hiketēria* (2428), which appears only in Hebrews 5:7, where the Lord Jesus in His humanity "offered up prayers [*deēsis*, see May 28] and supplications [*hiketēria*] with strong crying and tears." This word, along with the context, indicates humility and earnestness in prayer. Prayer is not something we do offhandedly, but rather, we practice it with all contriteness and solemnity.

This leads to one other aspect of prayer, *euchē* (2171), the basic meaning of which is a wish or vow. As one Greek authority writes, "When we pray to God, we wish that He would intervene to permit something in our lives that we feel is proper and right. . . . A Christian's wish is for God's will to take place in his life, even if it's sickness."[126]

This introduces us to perhaps the most ignored principle of prayer. Simply stated, *the plan of prayer is that our will conforms to God's will*. What shameless arrogance to say that we can make demands of God, as some teach today, such as financial prosperity. The Scripture clearly teaches that we are to pray according to God's will. The idea in the "Model Prayer" (Matt. 6:9–13) is, as Robert Young's *Literal Translation* puts it, "Thy reign come: Thy will come to pass, as in heaven also on the earth." The bottom line is, "God, do what you want." David prayed this way (Ps. 40:8), as did Jesus in Gethsemane (Matt. 26:39). Should we be any different?

Someone has wisely said: "Prayer is a mighty instrument, not for getting man's will done in heaven, but for getting God's will done on earth." Is not 1 John 5:14 clear? "If we ask any thing *according to his will*, He heareth us" (emphasis added). What is God ultimately doing? He works things according to His will, for His *ultimate glory* and our *utmost good*. May we forever abandon arrogant prayer!

So, what is prayer? *Prayer is communion with the one true God, before whom we come boldly and humbly to praise and thank and to whom we direct our petitions for others and ourselves according to His will.*

Soli Deo Gloria! (To God alone be the glory!)

Scriptures for Study: Meditate on the "Model Prayer" found in Matthew 6. Note first the word *pray* in verse 9 (*proseuchomai*) and then the petitions that follow. Most scholars agree that "there are seven *aitēmata*, though some have regarded the first three as *euchai* and only the last four as *aitēmata*."[127]

Pray Without Ceasing

proseuchomai adialeiptōs

In 1 Thessalonians 5:17 we discover another aspect of prayer, "Pray without ceasing." While *proseuchomai* (4336) speaks of prayer in general to God, the adverb *adialeiptōs* (89) adds a startling truth. It's comprised of the prefix *a* (without) and *dialeipō* (1257), "to intermit, leave an interval or gap." This word, as well as the adjective *adialeiptos*, appears several times in the NT.

In Romans 9:2, for example, Paul writes of the "continual sorrow" he had for his fellow Jews who rejected Christ. This word was used in Roman times for a nagging cough; while the person didn't cough every moment, he would still cough often, so it could be said of him, "He's still coughing."[128]

Here in our text, then, the meaning is clear—prayer is to be offered "continually, without intermission." In other words, prayer is not just those specific times when we pray, but also a constant communion with God, *a continuous consciousness of God's presence in which we view everything in life in relation to Him.*

Another writer offers, "Paul's injunction means that one should be constantly conscious of his full dependence upon God."[129] This doesn't mean we lock ourselves in a monastery where we do nothing but "pray." Rather every moment is a moment for prayer; like the cough, we're still praying.

If we meet someone, for example, we immediately consider where they stand with the Lord. If we hear of something bad happening, we pray for God to act in the situation for His glory and for people's good. If we hear of something good, we respond with immediate praise to God, for He's been glorified. In short, we view everything that comes along from a spiritual perspective. When Paul looked around his world, everything he saw prompted him to prayer in some way. When he thought of or heard about one of his beloved churches, it moved him to prayer. That is exactly the thought of Romans 1:9 and 2 Timothy 1:3.

We submit, therefore, if we do not view prayer in this way, we'll soon view God only as one we call on in time of need; we will, indeed, lose touch with His will. Our "specific times" of prayer are actually an outworking of our "constant communion." As we're continuously conscious of God's presence and our dependence, he will bring people and needs to our *minds* so that we may bring them before his *throne*.

Scriptures for Study: Read Nehemiah 2:1–5. Can you identify Nehemiah's "constant communion"?

Effectual Fervent (Prayer)

energeō

Before leaving the wondrous subject of prayer, let us ponder a phrase that often causes questions among Christians: "The effectual fervent prayer of a righteous man availeth much" (James 5:16). This has been variously translated as: "Very strong is a working supplication of a righteous man" (Young's *Literal Translation*); "The prayer of a righteous man is powerful and effective" (NIV); and, "The effective prayer of a righteous man can accomplish much" (NASB).

None of these, however, adequately reflects the central truth. Many people take this verse to mean, "If I prayer fervently and intensely, if I just pray hard enough, long enough, and often enough for a particular thing, it will happen." But such an idea flies in the face of the principle that prayer involves conforming our will to God's will.

The key to a proper understanding of this verse lies in the expression **effectual fervent**. This is only one word in the Greek, *energeō* (1754), from which is derived English words such as *energy* and *energize*, and means "to be at work, to effect something." It is extremely significant, as one Greek authority tells us, that the noun *energeia* (1753), "energy, active power, operation"; (see Feb. 29) "in the [Septuagint] (as in the NT) is used almost exclusively for the work of divine or demonic powers."[130] In Ephesians 1:19, for example, it's God's power that is "working" (*energeia*) in us, while in 2:2, Satan is said to be working (*energeō*).

Another authority agrees, adding that this usage is predominant in the *entire word group*: "Only in Philippians 2:13 does the active *energein* [present active participle of *energeō*] refer to human activity,"[131] but notice that even then it's *still God* who is working "in you both to will and to do of his good pleasure." (Note other examples in today's "Scriptures for Study.")

When we also note that the word "availeth" is *ischuō* (2480), "strength and ability," (see Feb. 29), it's then easy to see exactly what James is saying. He's not telling us that we accomplish much by our own energy in prayer, but rather that our prayers are strong because they are energized by God. We could translate this verse, "The God-energized prayer of a righteous man is strong."

Let us each pray in the energy of God and with a view to accomplishing His will.

Scriptures for Study: Read the following verses, noting in each that *energeō* refers to God's energy: 1 Corinthians 12:6, 11 ("worketh"); Galatians 2:8 ("effectually"); 3:5 ("worketh"); Ephesians 1:11, 20 ("wrought"); 3:20; Colossians 1:29; 1 Thessalonians 2:13 ("effectually").

Knoweth the Hearts

kardiognōstes

Theologians often speak of the attribute of God called "omniscience," which means that God knows all things. Twice in Scripture, however, we read of a particular application of omniscience that is sobering indeed. In Acts 1:24 we read, "Thou, Lord, which knowest the hearts of all men." We read again in 15:8, "And God, which knoweth the hearts, bare them witness, giving them the Holy Ghost, even as he did unto us." Amazingly, the words **knoweth** [or *knowest*] **the hearts** are a single word in the Greek, *kardiognōstes* (2589).

This word was unknown in both secular Greek and the Septuagint. It's a compound comprised first of *kardia* (see Nov. 14), which originally referred to the seat of emotions and spirituality but eventually came to mean spiritual and intellectual life. *Gnoskō* (see Jan. 17) means "to know by experience" and often is practically synonymous with love and intimacy. Putting these together, then, the meaning is clear and powerful. God is "the knower of hearts," or simply the "heart-knower."

Throughout Scripture, we're told that God looks into the heart and knows our thoughts and attitudes. While the Greek construction is a little different in Luke 16:15, the meaning is the same. Our Lord reveals the hypocrisy of the Pharisees and says to them, "Ye are they which justify yourselves before men; but God knoweth your hearts: for that which is highly esteemed among men is abomination in the sight of God." To the church at Thyatira, our Lord warned, "I am he which searcheth the reins and hearts: and I will give unto every one of you according to your works" (Rev. 2:23; cf. Jer. 17:9–10).

That is why the Word of God is so important. Since Jesus is the Word who became flesh, His Word is therefore the "discerner of the thoughts and intents of the heart" (Heb. 4:12). This challenges us to guard our thoughts, attitudes, motives, and all else. Knowing that God sees any pretense, any wrong motive, or any hidden agenda will help us guard our thinking.

Scriptures for Study: As a result of His knowing all things, what does God, therefore, do righteously (Jer. 11:20)? 📖 In Romans 8:26–27, what subject is Paul discussing and how does it apply to God knowing our hearts?

Abide (1)

menō

In Classical Greek, *menō* (3306) means "to remain in one place, at a given time, with someone." Metaphorically, it can mean "to keep an agreement" or "to remain in a particular sphere of life." It was also used in that sense to refer to something remaining valid in law. Finally, when used for the gods, it spoke of continuing existence.[132]

Those secular meanings are also used in the NT. Let's examine a few aspects of this word. In 1 Peter 1:23 and 25 we read, "Being born again, not of corruptible seed, but of incorruptible, by the word of God, which liveth and abideth for ever. . . . But the word of the Lord endureth [*menō*] for ever. And this is the word which by the gospel is preached unto you." We live in a day of unprecedented relativism, where opinions, ideas, and even "truth" change from moment to moment and person to person. Peter declares, however, that God and His Word continue, remain in one place, and remain valid and consistent in every situation.

Interestingly, verse 25 is a partial quotation of Isaiah 40:8: "The grass withereth, the flower fadeth: but the word of our God shall stand for ever." In the Septuagint, "stand" is *menō*. John Calvin wrote in the sixteenth century: "Nothing is more foolish than to rest satisfied with the present state, which we see to be fleeting; and every man is mistaken who hopes to be able to obtain perfect happiness till he has ascended to God. . . . But this would be of no avail, if the manner of seeking him were not pointed out; and therefore he exhibits *the word*, from which we must not in any respect turn aside; for if we make the smallest departure from it, we shall be involved in strange labyrinths, and shall find no way of extricating ourselves."[133] How much truer that is today!

We find another form of this word in the Septuagint translation of Psalm 119:89: "For ever, O Lord, thy word is settled in heaven." "Settled" is *diamenō* (1265), to remain permanently, to continue and not change. As we saw back in our study of **truth** (*alētheia*, February 1–3), God's Word is absolute, constant, and *never* changes. Oh, let us thank God that His truth "dwelleth [*menō*] in us, and shall be with us for ever" (2 John 2).

Scriptures for Study: What is true of the person who does not abide in God's truth (2 John 9)? 🕮 What, then, abides on the unbeliever (John 3:36)?

Abide (2)

menō

Another glorious application of the word **abide** (*menō*, 3306) is that God abides in the believer. In other words, as the meaning of *menō* indicates, God remains in the Christian; He's always present there, and He never leaves.

John 15 is the most graphic passage on this truth. This word appears to be one of John's favorites, in fact, as he uses it twelve times in verses 4–16, and is also translated "continue" (v. 9) and "remain" (v. 11). The picture here, of course, is our Lord's analogy of a vine that illustrates how He abides in us and we in Him. Verses 4 and 5 declare, "Abide in me, and I in you. As the branch cannot bear fruit of itself, except it abide in the vine; no more can ye, except ye abide in me. I am the vine, ye are the branches: He that abideth in me, and I in him, the same bringeth forth much fruit: for without me ye can do nothing." As a vine gives life and sends nourishment throughout the entire plant, so Christ gives us life and sustenance.

Another vivid example of this principle appears in John 14:16: "And I [Christ] will pray the Father, and he shall give you another Comforter, that he may abide with you for ever." We'll examine this verse in more detail on June 5 and 6, but the wonderful truth here is that the **Comforter** (the Holy Spirit) abides in us and will *always* abide in us (since "forever" is a long time).

God makes the same promise in Hebrews 13:5: "I will never leave thee, nor forsake thee." This is actually a quotation of Deuteronomy 31:6: "Be strong and of a good courage, fear not, nor be afraid of them [i.e., your adversaries]: for the Lord thy God, he it is that doth go with thee; he will not fail thee, nor forsake thee." What a promise! And we can be assured of the promise because "God . . . cannot lie" (Titus 1:2; cf. Num. 23:19).

What peace there is in knowing that God is always with us!

Scriptures for Study: John again uses *menō* many more times in his epistles. Read 1 John 2:6–28, for example, noting each occurrence of *abide* and *continued.*

Abide (3)

menō

One final application of the word **abide** (*menō*, 3306) is that not only does God abide in the Christian, but the true Christian also abides in God. What a relationship! But what exactly does it mean to abide in God? God's Word reveals at least four principles concerning our dwelling in God.

First, to dwell in God (or Christ) means that we walk as Christ walked. "He that saith he abideth [*menō*] in him ought himself also so to walk, even as he walked" (1 John 2:6). That means we are to *think* like Christ (Phil. 2:5) and *act* like Christ (John 13:15).

Second, to dwell in Christ means that we don't habitually live in sin. First John 3:6 declares, "Whosoever abideth [*menō*] in him sinneth not: whosoever sinneth hath not seen him, neither known him." The construction of the Greek behind both occurrences of "sinneth" is the present tense,[134] so the idea is that we do not continually, habitually sin. Sin is no longer the rule in our life; it's the exception.

Third, to dwell in Christ means that we continue in His Word. Our Lord said, "If ye continue [*menō*] in my word, then are ye my disciples indeed" (John 8:31). One of the most powerful proofs of true Christianity is that we love and obey the Word of God. Someone might claim to be a Christian, but if he doesn't obey God's Word, his profession is just that—a profession. As the apostle John says again, "He that doeth the will of God abideth [*menō*] for ever" (1 John 2:17).

Fourth, to dwell in Christ means that we bear fruit. As mentioned yesterday, our Lord again speaks in John 15:5: "I am the vine, ye are the branches: He that abideth [*menō*] in me, and I in him, the same bringeth forth much fruit." A powerful evidence of salvation is that we bear fruit, and we can bear fruit through our: *commendation* (praise and worship; Heb. 13:15); *character* (Gal. 5:22–23); *conduct* (Col. 1:10; Rom. 6:22); *charity* (Phil. 4:17); and *converts* (1 Cor. 16:15; John 4:36). Fruit-bearing also has levels: "bear fruit" (John 15:2a), bear "more fruit" (v. 2b), and bear "much fruit" (v. 5).

Scriptures for Study: Continuing yesterday's reading, read 1 John 2:24 and 4:12–16, again noting each occurrence of *abide*, *remain*, and *dwell*.

Comforter

paraklētos

Among the most blessed words in the NT is *paraklētos* (3875), which occurs only five times (John 14:16; 14:26; 15:26; 16:7–8; 1 John 2:1). The prefix *para* (3844) means "alongside of" and is used in such English words as *parallel* (lines that are alongside one another). The root *klētos* (2822, from *kaleō,* 2564, "to call") speaks of "one who is called." In Classical Greek, *paraklētos* literally means "one who is called alongside to aid" and was originally used in the court of justice to show legal assistance. Our English word *paraclete* carries much the same idea.

In the NT, however, our Savior transforms this word into an infinitely more beautiful and practical term. *First*, in the NT the "Paraclete" is not *called in*, but rather He is *sent* (John 14:16; 15:26; 16:7). *Second*, the NT "Paraclete" brings *active help* to those in need. He doesn't just "put in a good word" or "pat us on the shoulder." His comforting work involves teaching, convicting, challenging, and empowering. *Third*, and most blessed of all, the NT "Paraclete" is *personal*, not *professional*. Most defense attorneys have an underlying motive of money; they must be paid to help. But the divine Paraclete really cares; He is there with the right motive. What a beautiful term!

Sadly, modern translations miss the depth of this word, choosing to translate it "Helper" (NKJV; NASB) or "Counselor" (NIV). But **Comforter** is the best translation because it conveys the idea of personality. The Latin is *comfortis*: *com* ("alongside of") and *fortis* ("strong"). "Comforter," then, is, "One who stands with us to keep us company and give us strength." Does this not touch the heart as being personal? Is there not a sweetness and preciousness in this word?

As one commentator sums up: "*Comforter* seems to us to be the kind of help which suits best with the strain of the Discourse at this place. The comfort of Christ's personal presence with the Eleven had been such, that while they had it they seemed to want for nothing; and the loss of it would seem the loss of everything—utter desolation (v. 18). It is to meet this, as we think, that He says He will as the Father to send them *another* Comforter; and in all these four passages, it is as an all-sufficient, all-satisfying *Substitute for Himself* that He holds forth this promised Gift."[135]

We'll continue these thoughts tomorrow.

Scriptures for Study: Read all five instances of *paraklētos* (John 14:16; 14:26; 15:26; 16:7–8; 1 John 2:1 ["advocate"]), noting the personal depth of each one.

Another Comforter

allos paraklētos

Once again we meditate on John 14:16: "And I will pray the Father, and he shall give you another Comforter, that he may abide with you for ever."

The very first word we should notice is "and," for it connects verses 15 and 16. Verse 15 speaks of the *disciples'* love for Jesus; it declares that if the disciples really love the Lord, they will keep His commandments. Verse 16 then speaks of *Jesus'* love for the disciples. The evidence of His love was that when He departed He was going to send them **another Comforter**. Up to this time Jesus had been their Comforter, but He's preparing to leave them. He therefore assures them that His *departure* is not *desertion*. Verse 18 can literally be translated, "I will not leave you orphans." This thought looks back to John 13:33 where Jesus uses the term "little children." He assures His beloved disciples that He will not leave them shepherdless; He will not leave them forsaken, forgotten orphans.

The most blessed truth of all, however, is the word **another**. The Greek here is not *heteros* (2087), which means "another of a different kind" (English *heterodox* and *heterosexual*). Rather, the Greek is *allos* (243), that is, "*another of similar or identical nature*." How thrilling! The Savior is saying in essence, "When I depart, I will send another in my place who is almost identical to Me."

This One whom the Lord would send is, indeed, almost identical. There is, in fact, only a single difference between the Lord Jesus and the Holy Spirit, namely: The Lord Jesus ministered from *without*, while the Holy Spirit ministers from *within*. The Lord Jesus even warned the disciples not to expect a visible person (v. 17), but assured them nonetheless that His "replacement" would minister as He always had. Indeed, while Jesus walked *beside* them, the Holy Spirit would dwell *within* them. Many years ago, I heard the following words that I have never since forgotten:

> Oh, gift of gifts; oh, grace of grace,
> That God should condescend
> My heart His dwelling place,
> And be my bosom friend.

Meditate on that glorious truth today.

Scriptures for Study: Read all five instances of *paraklētos* again (John 14:16; 14:26; 15:26; 16:7–8; 1 John 2:1 ["advocate"]), and meditate on the personal application of each in your life.

Advocate

paraklētos

Let's take one last look at that wonderful word *paraklētos* (3875). Of its five occurrences in the NT, the four in John refer to the Holy Spirit. The final one, however, refers to the Lord Jesus: "My little children, these things write I unto you, that ye sin not. And if any man sin, we have an advocate with the Father, Jesus Christ the righteous" (1 John 2:1). The comparison is obvious: The Holy Spirit (our **Comforter**) is the *earthly* Paraclete, while the Lord Jesus (our **Advocate**) is the *heavenly* Paraclete. So, what is our Lord doing in heaven?

In 1:8–10, John says in essence, "I am not writing these things to either discourage you about holy living or to condone sinning, but rather to encourage you not to sin." The key words, then, in 2:1 are "if any man sin." The tense of the Greek verb here (*hamartē*) is aorist subjunctive, which merely means a *single* act of sin, not *habitual* sin. Literally, the phrase reads, "If any man commits an act of sin." John shows us that sin in the believer's life *cannot* be habitual (see 1 John 3:6; see also June 4).

So, there will be times when we commit *acts* of sin. There will be times when we allow the flesh to rule and will have a wrong thought, attitude, value, goal, action, or even a single word. It's for those times that God has made provision. Our text says that when we commit an *act* of sin, we have an **Advocate**. The thought here is that the Lord Jesus Christ is our "Defense Attorney," Who pleads our case before the Judge. The fascinating thing here, however, is that unlike a defense attorney on earth who *pleads our innocence*, the Lord Jesus *admits our guilt*. But in that defense, He then presents His death and resurrection as the grounds for our acquittal. *Hallelujah*!

Dear Christian friend, it's up to you whether or not you sin. Someone has put the matter this way: "We do not have the inability to sin, but we do have the ability not to sin." Did you get it? While we cannot be sinless, we can have the victory over sin. There will be times when we commit an act of sin, but those will not be the rule; rather, they will be the exception.

Scriptures for Study: What provision does 1 Corinthians 10:13 give that provides victory over sin? 📖 If needed, review the January 31 reading on **confess** (*homologeō*).

Sincere

eilikrinēs

Perhaps you've seen the old Peanuts cartoon by the late Christian brother Charles Shultz that pictures a dejected Charlie Brown standing on the pitcher's mound saying, "I don't understand how we can lose so much when we're so sincere." We also hear many people today say, "It doesn't matter what a person believes as long as he's sincere." But such people have no idea what the word **sincere** really means.

The Greek *eilikrinēs* (1506) appears only twice in the NT and means "pure, unsullied, free from spot or blemish to such a degree as to bear examination in the full splendor of the sun."[136] This is actually borne out even in our English word, which is comprised of two Latin words: *sine* (without) and *cera* (wax). In ancient times, unscrupulous dealers in porcelain ware would use wax to fill in cracks that formed when a piece was fired. An honest dealer, therefore, would describe a perfect piece using the words *sine cera*, "without wax." If a customer had a doubt, he merely had to hold the piece up to sunlight and a filled-in crack would be easily spotted.

What a beautiful picture! That was Paul's prayer, in fact, for the Philippian believers, and by application *all* believers: "That ye may be sincere and without offence till the day of Christ" (Phil. 1:10). Paul prays for the true sincerity of Christians. In other words, he prays that as we are exposed to the light of the Word of God, we will be without wax, that we truly *are* what we *appear* to be. He prays that we will be spotless and unsullied, and that others will be able to see that fact when they examine our lives.

Peter also used this word. In his second letter, he said that the reason he wrote *both* his letters was to "stir up your pure [*eilikrinēs*] minds by way of remembrance: That ye may be mindful of the words which were spoken before by the holy prophets, and of the commandment of us the apostles of the Lord and Saviour" (2 Pet. 3:1–2). In a day when impurity is everywhere and threatens to dirty up our minds at every turn, Peter's encouragement is to keep our minds pure by remembering God's truth.

Scriptures for Study: Read Philippians 4:8–9, noting the **things** we should first think about (v. 8) and then *do* (v. 9). We'll study these verses carefully starting August 5.

Dwell (1)

katoikeō

Paul prays in Ephesians 3:17, "That Christ may dwell in your hearts by faith." Paul is not speaking here of the indwelling Holy Spirit who enters at conversion (Rom. 8:9, 11, 23; 1 Cor. 6:19; 1 John 4:13) or to Christ's indwelling that also occurs at salvation (2 Cor. 13:5; Gal. 2:20; Col. 1:27).

The key lies in the Greek behind the word **dwell,** *katoikeō* (2730), a compound word comprised of *kata* (2596), "down," and *oikeō* (3611), "to inhabit a house." In the present context, however, the word is intensified. It doesn't just mean that Christ is *in* the house of our hearts, but that He is at *home* there.

This should prompt each of us to ask, "Is the Lord Jesus part of my household or just a visitor?" Several years ago there was a popular plaque that decorated many Christian homes and perhaps still does. It read: "Christ is the Head of this house, the unseen guest at every meal, the Silent Listener to every conversation." That is a nice sentiment, but He should be more than just a guest. Our Savior is a part of the family.

How, then, do we make Him feel at home? Our text gives the answer—*by faith*. Only when we trust Him and lean upon Him can He be at home. When we're living like the world, holding on to its values and attitudes, the Lord cannot feel at home in our hearts. If we are trusting in "self" instead of Him, we treat Him as merely a visitor whose presence we only tolerate.

That truth is illustrated in two incidents involving Abraham and Lot (Gen. 18–19). First, when the preincarnate Lord came with two angels to visit Abraham and Sarah, He felt very much at home. He talked with them and even sat down and ate a meal with them because Abraham was a man of faith and obedience. In contrast, however, the Lord did not go with the two angels to warn Lot of the coming destruction of Sodom. Why? Because even though Lot was a believer, he wasn't living by faith. The Lord did not feel at home in Lot's house. Indeed, how could the Lord have felt at home in an abominably wicked place like Sodom? So, let each of us ask ourselves, "Is the Lord really at home in my heart?"

We'll go a little deeper into this word tomorrow.

Scriptures for Study: What does Hebrews 11:9–10 declare about Abraham's "homes"? 🕮 What will inhabit the new heavens and new earth (2 Pet. 3:13)?

Dwell (2)

katoikeō

As noted yesterday, *katoikeō* (2730) means "to inhabit a house." There's another aspect of this word, however, that goes even deeper. We see it in Revelation 2:13: "I know thy works, and where thou dwellest, even where Satan's seat is." That is, of course, part of Jesus' letter to the church at Pergamum. While it had a serious problem with worldliness, our Lord still praises it for some things it was doing right, such as dwelling where Satan's seat was, that is, a place where paganism was part of the culture.

What's interesting is that the word usually used in Scripture to picture the Christian in the world is *paroikeō* (3939, to be a stranger, to dwell at a place only for a short time). Peter calls Christians "strangers [*paroikos*, 3941] and pilgrims" (1 Pet. 2:11), those who are temporary dwellers in a foreign land (see Dec. 2). But our Lord uses *katoikeō*, which means the exact opposite, a fixed durable dwelling. Paul prays, for example, that Christ will have permanent residence in our hearts by His indwelling Spirit (Eph. 3:17).

So, why use *katoikeō*? Why speak about the Christian taking up permanent residence in the world when our attitude should be that we are only strangers traveling through this world on our journey toward heaven? We submit that our Lord's reason is to encourage us to stay put and endure, to remain faithful witnesses where we are. While it might be easier to just go somewhere else, here is a challenge to stand firm where we are.

Commentator William Barclay (*Revelation*) tells the story of a girl who was converted in an evangelistic campaign. She was already a reporter at a secular newspaper, but the first thing she did after her conversion was to get a new job at a small Christian newspaper where she was surrounded by professing Christians. Instead of staying put and being a faithful witness, she ran away. What would have been the result if early Christians had run away every time they were met with difficult circumstances? How would the Gospel have spread? The Christian life is not about *hiding*; rather, it's about *standing*. Our Lord, therefore, commends the believers in Pergamum for their staying where He could use them.

So, while we are not of this world, we are still *in* this world; while we are *separate*, we're not to be *segregated* (John 17:15–16). God wants to use us where we are.

Scriptures for Study: What does Philippians 2:15 tell us to be in the world? 🕮 Where does Acts 1:8 tell us to go in our witnessing?

Rooted

rhizoō

Ephesians 3:17 records one of Paul's prayers: "That Christ may dwell in your hearts by faith; that ye, being rooted and grounded in love." Paul gives three pictures here that show us what spiritual depth is and how we can have it. The first, which we've already examined, is **dwell**. The second is that we are **rooted**.

The Greek *rhizoō* (4492) literally means "rooted, strengthened with roots" and figuratively "fixed and constant." In secular Greek, it was also used for the foundation of the earth and the foot of a mountain. So, the picture Paul paints here is that a Christian grows because he's rooted like a tree.

In what is the Christian to be rooted? Here is an amazing truth! A tree, of course, is rooted in the soil, from which it receives water and nutrients. The roots go deep so the tree cannot easily be uprooted and therefore destroyed. The parallel is that **love** is the soil in which we are deeply rooted. Our spiritual nutrition, all that builds us up and makes us strong, comes from the soil of the love of Christ.

Perhaps you're thinking, "But I thought the Word of God is where we get our spiritual food." Yes, but while the Word of God is the *seed*, love is the *soil*. The Word of God is placed in the soil of the love of Christ; the two are inseparable. Ponder it this way: How can we *grow* in the Word if we do not *love* the Word? Many today say they "love Jesus," but they don't love His Word. What a staggering contradiction! If we don't love the Word of God and want to grow through it, we do not love the Lord Jesus, because it is He who is the Word Who became flesh (John 1:14). "For this is the love of God, that we keep his commandments: and his commandments are not grievous" (1 John 5:3).

Psalm 119 is David's absolutely fascinating psalm on the Word of God, born out of his love for it. Of its 176 verses, all but two mention the Word of God using one of eight synonyms. David mentions four out of the eight when writing of his love for Scripture (vv. 97, 119, 127, 159). Why are Christians shallow today? Why is much church ministry geared toward entertainment? Because people don't love Scripture. Scripture alone is not enough to keep them coming back. Such people simply do not love the Lord.

Scriptures for Study: Read the following verses in Psalm 119, noting the synonyms David uses for Scripture when writing of His love for it (vv. 97, 119, 127, 159).

Grounded

themelioō

In Ephesians 3:17—"That Christ may dwell in your hearts by faith; that ye, being rooted and grounded in love"—Paul gives us one more picture of what spiritual depth is and how we can have it. He says that we must be **grounded**. From ancient Greek onwards, *themelioō* (2311) means to lay the foundation of anything. It comes from the root *thēma* (English *theme*), that which is laid down in the sense of being a fundamental.

It's interesting that Paul deliberately mixes his metaphors here. While something like, "Once you open a can of worms, they always come home to roost," is what is called an "impermissible mixed metaphor," since the two metaphors conflict because they serve different purposes, Paul uses a "permissible mixed metaphor." Yes, the first metaphor is botanical and the second is architectural, but the two serve the same purpose and exhibit a correlation with each other.

The common purpose of **rooted** and **grounded**, then, is to picture spiritual depth. They correlate because they are both in the soil of **love** for Christ. In other words, not only are we to be rooted in our love for Christ, but we are also to be grounded in our love of Christ. Here's the corollary: A tree is *stable* and *productive* in the soil, while a building is *sturdy* and *permanent* in the soil.

The most important part of a building is, of course, the foundation. Any building will only be as sturdy as its foundation. An expression in the construction world is, "If you don't go deep, you can't go high." So, the picture Paul paints here is that the Christian is to have a deep foundation. Why? *Because if we don't go deep, we can't go high*. As the Lord Jesus Himself taught, it's the wise man who "built an house, and digged deep, and laid the foundation on a rock" (Luke 6:48). If we are not firmly and deeply grounded in the things of God, then whatever we build will soon crumble. And once again, the foundation is the love of Christ and his Word.

Scriptures for Study: Read the parable of the two builders in Luke 6:46–49, which compares those who build a house on sand with those who build on rock. Can you think of some "sandy soils" on which people build their lives today?

Make Merchandise

emporeuomai

The apostle Peter predicts that false teachers and false prophets would arise within the church, that they will "bring in damnable heresies, even denying the Lord that bought them" and that many people will "follow their pernicious ways" (2 Pet. 2:1–2). We should interject that while Peter says they're *coming*, a short time later Jude writes that they are *here* (Jude 4).

Of special significance is Peter's warning that such teachers will "with feigned words make merchandise of you" (2 Pet. 2:3). **Make merchandise** is *emporeuomai* (1710) which means "to trade, to travel about as a merchant or trader," and is obviously where we get the English *emporium*.[137] (Its only other occurrence in the NT is James 4:13, where it's used in the normal sense of engaging in trade.) We should also add that "feigned" is *plastos* (4112; English, *plastic*), to mold, be artificial, false, deceptive. The complete picture, then, is that false teachers travel about and use plastic words to make money from their teachings.

Indeed, an earmark of false teachers is that they are in it for the money. Everything they do is to that end. Instead of *feeding* the sheep, they are *fleecing* the sheep. From those who sell all sorts of trinkets that have supposed spiritual benefits to those who spend a third of their television program begging for money, the false teacher is in it for the money.

This has spilled over even into evangelicalism. It's sad, indeed, that a growing trend in the church today is charging money for hearing Bible teaching. There are all sorts of seminars and conferences that charge God's people money to attend. We don't mean to imply that these are actually false teachers, but rather we are saying that they have adopted a key trait of false teachers.

The fact is that there is not a single biblical precedent for this kind of approach. Not once do we ever see God's people being charged for hearing truth. The whole idea is appalling. Yes, there are certainly needs that must be met, such as paying the electric bill, the speakers, the printing of brochures, and so forth. But whatever happened to the love offerings of God's people? If a ministry is really important, won't God provide the finances to do it?

We should be wary of any ministry that even hints at "making merchandise" of God's people. (See also **discernment**, July 15ff.).

Scriptures for Study: Read the following passages, noting other traits of false teachers: Matthew 7:15–16; 24:23–26; Acts 20:28–31; 2 Corinthians 11:3, 13–15; 1 Timothy 6:20–21; Philippians 3:2; Colossians 2:8.

Walk

peripateō

One of the key words in the Christian life is **walk**, and it appears several times in the NT. The Greek *peripateō* (4043) is a compound made from *peri* (4012), "about, around," and *pateō* (3961), "to walk," and so literally means "to walk about, to walk around, to walk concerning."

In Classical Greek, this word was used only in the literal sense and meant strolling and stopping, as someone would walk about in the marketplace. It was never used in a figurative sense as it is in the NT.[138] When used in that figurative sense, it speaks of "conduct of life," that is, how we "how we walk about," how we conduct ourselves as we walk through life.

How, then, are we to conduct ourselves? The NT actually specifies several ways we are "to walk about." Perhaps the most important way we are to walk is "in **truth**." As we studied on February 1–3, *alētheia* means "nonconcealment." It thus denotes what is seen, indicated, expressed, or disclosed, i.e., a thing as it really is, not as it is concealed or falsified. *Alētheia* is the real state of affairs.[139] In other words, truth is that which is absolute, incontrovertible, irrefutable, incontestable, unarguable, and unchanging.

Again writing about false teachers, the apostle John declares, "I rejoiced greatly that I found of thy children walking in truth, as we have received a commandment from the Father" (2 John 4), and still again, "For I rejoiced greatly, when the brethren came and testified of the truth that is in thee, even as thou walkest in the truth. I have no greater joy than to hear that my children walk in truth" (3 John 3–4).

Indeed, there is no greater joy to a true pastor than to see the sheep under his care walking in the truth. The church nowadays is literally not only *surrounded* by error but is also *filled* with error. The truth is being denied, diluted, and even destroyed on every front. The most important way Christians can conduct themselves is to *know* the truth and *live* the truth.

We'll examine another way we are to walk tomorrow.

Scriptures for Study: Read the following verses, noting how are we not to walk: John 8:12; Acts 14:16; Romans 8:1; 2 Corinthians 4:2; Ephesians 4:17.

Light (1)

phōs

In Classical Greek usage, the basic meaning of *phōs* (5457; English *phosphorus*, etc.) is **light** and brightness and conveys the ideas of sunlight, daylight, torchlight, firelight, and so forth. In other words, it refers to light itself, not the *source* of light, such as the sun, a torch, fire, or a lamp. Even early in secular usage, it was also used figuratively "to mean the sphere of ethical good, whereas misdeeds are said to take place in darkness."[140] All that was carried over into NT usage but intensified all the more by its identification with Christ.

The Christian, therefore, is to **walk** in light. Since we were once "darkness, but now are . . . light in the Lord," we are to "walk as children of light" (Eph. 5:8). In other words, we conduct ourselves according to light, the light of Christ and His Word. As He is the Light (John 1:4; 8:12) and is the Word who became flesh (1:14), then it is His Word in which we are to walk.

What seems obvious about darkness and light is that they cannot coexist. If you turn on a light in a dark room, darkness flees. But it's not as obvious in practical application. People talk much about "gray areas" of conduct, avoiding the terms *right* or *wrong* and *truth* or *error*. But the Scripture contains no such "gray areas." Conduct is either moral or immoral, good or bad, true or false.

What, then, are the "attributes" of light? Generally speaking, **light** pictures two basic thoughts.

First, in regard to the *intellect*, light pictures *truth*. So, to walk according to light means that we walk according to **truth**. No longer are we ignorant, for the truth of Jesus Christ is in us. Moreover, walking according to light means that we are growing in the knowledge of Christ day by day.

Second, in regard to *morality*, light pictures *holiness*. To walk according to light means that we live a pure, holy life; we walk as holy people. All that we say and do shines forth the light of Christ that is in us (cf. Eph. 4:17–32).

Scriptures for Study: Read the following verses, noting other ways in which we are to walk in the Christian life: Romans 4:12; 6:4; Galatians 5:16, 25; Ephesians 5:2; Colossians 4:5.

Light (2)

phōs

Taking one more look at the word *phōs* (**light**), this is one of the most glorious NT metaphors concerning the Lord Jesus Christ. Without question, the most vivid example of Christ being Light appears in John 8:12, where He declares, "I am the light of the world." But it's only when we realize where our Lord was standing when He uttered those words that we see the full significance of His statement.

The setting was the Illumination of the Temple ceremony that took place during the Feast of the Tabernacles (or Booths). That feast, which began five days after Yom Kippur (the Day of Atonement), involved the Israelites presenting offerings for seven days while they lived in huts (booths) made of palm fronds and leafy tree branches to remember their journey in Canaan (Lev. 23:43).

At the end of the feast, the illumination ceremony took place, which is described in the Mishna. The Torah was the Jews' title for the "Law" (Genesis through Deuteronomy). Questions arose, however, concerning the meanings of these laws, so over the years an oral law called "the tradition of the elders" developed, which was then put into written form around AD 200. This was called the Mishna, which means "repetition," as much of Jewish education was based on repetition; this became a principle part of what was called the Talmud, the commentaries that were written on the Law.

The Mishna tells of four tall, massive golden candleholders that stood in the temple treasury. On top of each was a large torch and bowl containing 120 logs (about twenty gallons) of oil. There was also a ladder for each candlestick; a priest would climb the ladder, pour oil into the bowl, place a wick in it made of old garments, and then light it. The Mishna records that "there was not a courtyard in Jerusalem which was not lit up from the light."[141]

So, it was on that very spot that Jesus stood when he declared, "I am the light of the world." What a scene! In essence, He said, "While these great torches light all *Jerusalem*, I light the entire *world*. Only if you know Me, will you be delivered from darkness and have light to see."

Since we are *part* of that light, we are to *walk* in that light (Eph. 5:8).

Scriptures for Study: Read the following verses and rejoice in the light: John 9:5; 12:46; Romans 13:12; 2 Corinthians 4:6; 1 Thessalonians 5:5; James 1:17. 📖 Also read 2 Corinthians 6:14–7:1, which concerns our separation from the world.

Therefore

oun

Here is another one of those Bible words that seems insignificant, but it's amazing how many times the word **therefore** appears in Scripture. We see it, in fact, 1,237 times in our AV (356 in the NT), and it's a worthwhile study in itself. The Greek is *oun* (3767) and expresses "either the merely external connection of two sentences, that the one follows upon the other, or also the internal relation of cause and effect, that the one follows from the other."[142]

The first NT occurrence is in Matthew 3:7–8, which declares, "But when he saw many of the Pharisees and Sadducees come to his baptism, he said unto them, O generation of vipers, who hath warned you to flee from the wrath to come? Bring forth therefore fruits meet for repentance." The last is in Revelation 18:8, where of Babylon, the false religious system of Rome, it is written, "Therefore shall her plagues come in one day, death, and mourning, and famine; and she shall be utterly burned with fire: for strong is the Lord God who judgeth her."

We note also our Lord's introduction to the Model Prayer, where He uses the word **therefore** twice: "But when ye pray, use not vain repetitions, as the heathen do: for they think that they shall be heard for their much speaking. Be not ye therefore like unto them: for your Father knoweth what things ye have need of, before ye ask him. After this manner therefore pray ye," followed then by the rest of the model (Matt. 6:7–9). Also, in the Great Commission, our Lord said to His disciples, "All power is given unto me in heaven and in earth. Go ye therefore, and teach all nations" (Matt. 28:18–19). Without Christ's power, there could be no "therefore."

We find this word multiple times in every one of Paul's epistles (except Titus). Of special significance in our day are Paul's parting words to Timothy. In light of growing apostasy, what did Paul challenge Timothy to do? Did he challenge Him to be an entertainer, or to be "seeker-sensitive," "user-friendly," or "purpose-driven"? No. He commanded, "I charge thee therefore before God . . . Preach the word" (2 Tim. 4:1–2). We find **therefore** also in the letters of Peter, James, and John.

We could go on for hours examining such great connections. As you read your Bible, always take note of the "therefores."

Scriptures for Study: Read the following verses, noting the connections indicated by **therefore**: Romans 5:1; 6:3–4; 9:17–18; 12:1; 1 Corinthians 5:6–7; Ephesians 5:6–7. 🕮 Make notes of other instances in your own Bible reading.

Worthy

axios

Here is another interesting word in the Greek NT. In Classical Greek, *axios* (514) carried the idea of balancing scales, of one side of the scale counterbalancing the other side.[143] A dramatic example of that idea appears in John 1:27, where John the Baptist says, "He it is, who coming after me is preferred before me, whose shoe's latchet I am not worthy to unloose." Picturing his unworthiness in comparison to Christ, John says in effect, "I don't even come close to balancing the scales."

On the other hand, in view of man's utter depravity, Paul writes that without Christ we are all "worthy of death," that is, we, like Belshazzar, have been "weighed in the balances, and art found wanting" (Dan. 5:27).

In Ephesians 4:1, Paul challenges us to "walk worthy of the vocation wherewith ye are called." In other words, we are **therefore** to **walk** in balance to something. And to what are we to walk in balance? What is the "counterbalance" on the scales? *Our calling as Christians*, that is, the way we are called upon to live. And how are we called upon to live? Another usage of *axios* answers that question: "Bring forth therefore fruits meet [*axios*] for repentance" (Matt. 3:8). Like anything that is living, the Christian is called upon to bear fruit (see June 4 for how we do that).

Paul writes another challenge in 1 Thessalonians 2:12: "That [we] would walk worthy of God." What a startling statement! How can we balance the scales when God Himself is the counter-balance? While we certainly can't compare with God in His *nature*, we can "balance the scales" in our *conduct*. That is why Peter could write that we are to "follow his steps" (1 Pet. 2:21). John adds that we are "to walk, even as he walked" (1 John 2:6). And how do we do that? We "walk after his commandments" (2 John 6).

No, we will never have the attributes of God's *nature*, such as omniscience, omnipotence, omnipresence, sovereignty, and others, but we can "balance the scales" when it comes to the Christlikeness of *character* (Gal. 5:22–23).

Scriptures for Study: Read the following verses, noting what other behavior "balances the scales" in our Christian living: Ephesians 4:1–3; Colossians 1:10–12.

Call

klēsis

One of the foundational concepts of Christianity is God's calling of men. As far back in ancient Greek as the time of Homer, *klēsis* (2821) referred to an invitation into a house or to a feast. If the "invitation conferred special honor, the word came to mean *chosen*." The full idea of *klēsis*, then, is "the act of inviting, and more often an official summons by a recognized authority."[144]

All those concepts carried over into the NT, but they were made far more significant because of what God was calling men to. With only a few exceptions,[145] Paul uses this word (and related words, such as the verb *kaleō*, "to call") to refer to the divine calling of the elect to salvation, as in: "Who hath saved us, and called us with an holy calling, not according to our works, but according to his own purpose and grace, which was given us in Christ Jesus before the world began" (2 Tim. 1:9). Likewise, Paul's prayer in Ephesians 1:18 was, "The eyes of your understanding being enlightened; that ye may know what is the hope of his calling, and what the riches of the glory of his inheritance in the saints." In other words, besides being called to salvation, we are also invited and summoned to understand the certainty of our salvation and the spiritual riches we have in Christ.

God's calling, however, also demands something from us. We are summoned, for example, to *holiness*, as Paul makes clear: "For God hath not called us unto uncleanness, but unto holiness" (1 Thess. 4:7). Peter echoes, "But as he which hath called you is holy, so be ye holy in all manner of conversation; Because it is written, Be ye holy; for I am holy" (1 Pet. 1:15–16; cf. Lev. 11:44–45).

We are also summoned to service. As *klēsis* was used as a summons to duty, Paul challenged Timothy, and therefore every pastor (and by application, every Christian): "Fight the good fight of faith, lay hold on eternal life, whereunto thou art also called [*kaleō*], and hast professed a good profession before many witnesses" (1 Tim. 6:12). Also like Paul, God calls some men to vocational service, that is, to serve Him as their full-time occupation as pastors (1 Tim. 3:1; cf. Gal. 1:15–16).

Let each of us realize what God has called us to be and to do.

Scriptures for Study: Read 2 Peter 1:3–10, noting the Christian virtues that enable us to "make [our] calling and election sure," that is, to prove the genuineness of our faith by godly living.

High Calling

anō klēseōs

Adding to yesterday's meditation on God's **call**, Paul mentions another **calling** that should bless the heart of every Christian. In Philippians 3:14, he writes, "I press toward the mark for the prize of the high calling of God in Christ Jesus." The Greek behind the words **high calling** is *anō klēseōs*. *Klēseōs* is from *klēsis* (2821), but *anō* (507) adds a whole new dimension. The literal meaning is "above or upwards." It was used in Classical Greek to "describe land or mountains in contrast to the sea, or the sky and heaven in comparison with the earth, or even the earth in contrast to the underworld."[146]

The NT, of course, takes those earthly ideas to a new level. While *anō* does not actually appear in John 11:41, the concept of the ancient world is clearly present as Jesus "lifted up his eyes" toward the Father in prayer. Even more vivid is John 8:23, where Jesus declared to the Jewish leaders, "Ye are from beneath [*katō* (2736), below, earthly]; I am from above [*anō*]: ye are of this world; I am not of this world."

This background opens up our text. Paul set his sights not on this earth but on heaven. One day he would be summoned to heaven, and he was looking forward to that day. He used this word again in Colossians 3:1–2 as a solemn challenge to every believer: "[Since] ye then be risen with Christ, seek those things which are above, where Christ sitteth on the right hand of God. Set your affection on things above, not on things on the earth" (cf. Rom. 8:6). God has given us new life and new potential; we are now to live like it.

As mentioned back on March 31, the popular old cliché, "Some Christians are so heavenly minded that they are of no earthly good," is simply incorrect. Being heavenly minded means exactly what Paul says here—setting our thoughts, values, words, deeds, and all else on the things of heaven. For God to use us, we must be heavenly minded.

We'll continue our thoughts on Philippians 3:14 tomorrow by examining what it means to "press toward" that high calling.

Scriptures for Study: Read the following verses, noting what the true believer seeks: Matthew 6:20, 33; 2 Corinthians 4:18; Hebrews 11:13–16.

Press

diōkō

Yesterday we pondered the truth of our **high calling** in Philippians 3:14—"I press toward the mark for the prize of the high calling of God in Christ Jesus." We build on that today by noticing that Paul was not casually living the Christian life or nonchalantly waiting to go to heaven. Rather he was "pressing" toward that goal.

Press is *diōkō* (1377), to chase, to pursue eagerly, to try to obtain. It's also in the present tense, showing continuous action. The Greeks used this word to speak of a hunter earnestly pursuing his prey, an attacker pursing the enemy, and an athlete endeavoring to reach the finish line.

There was once a popular teaching, which still exists in some circles, that the Christian should "just let go and let God." This teaches that Christian living is simply a passive submission to God, who will live life for us. This is called "Quietism," which the old Quakers held. Other advocates of such teaching to one extent or another were the Keswicks, Charles Finney, and Hannah Whitall Smith in her book *The Christian's Secret of a Happy Life*. To those sincere though misguided folks, passive surrender to God means an almost total absence of the Christian's actions.

On the contrary, the Christian life takes tremendous effort. In 1 Corinthians 9:24–27, Paul graphically pictures the Christian life by comparing it with the Isthmian games, which were actually held in Corinth, so his readers immediately understood what he was saying. Contestants in the games had to prove rigorous training for ten months and spent the last month of training in Corinth, where they underwent supervised workouts in the gymnasium and athletic fields every day.

The Christian, therefore, is not a *spectator* at the games, but rather a *participant*. He isn't to sit on the sidelines eating popcorn watching the Holy Spirit do all the work. The Christian life is a life of struggle, commitment, and discipline. We're in a war. That is why Paul wrote in Ephesians 6:12–20 that the Christian is to put on the spiritual armor of God to prepare for battle. Each of us should start every day with that reminder.

We'll again continue our thoughts tomorrow by examining exactly what **prize** we are pressing toward.

Scriptures for Study: What are we to "follow" (*diōkō*) in 1 Thessalonians 5:15? 📖 In 1 Timothy 6:11–12, what is involved in "[fighting] the good fight of faith" ("follow" is again *diōkō*)?

Prize [and] Crown

brabeion [and] *stephanos*

Let us take one more look at Paul's wonderful testimony and encouragement in Philippians 3:14—"I press toward the mark for the prize of the high calling of God in Christ Jesus." We are to set our sights on heaven and earnestly pursue that goal, but Paul adds something else—we're pursuing a specific **prize**.

Prize is *brabeion* (1017), and its imagery is unmistakable. In Classical Greek, it referred to the "victor's prize" in the Isthmian games mentioned yesterday. Among such things as money, fame, free meals, and front row seats at the theater in Athens, contestants in the games vied for a garland **crown** made of olive, laurel, ivy, pine, or flowers. **Crown** is *stephanos*, which in Classical Greek referred not to a kingly crown, but rather the one given at the games or for civic worth and military valor. One made of gold was awarded by the state as a mark of high honor.

Paul's challenge, therefore, could not be more graphic: Just as those contestants committed all their time and energy to acquiring temporal prizes, the Christian should be all the more committed to spiritual endeavor.

What, then, is this **prize** and **crown** toward which we **press**? There is some uncertainty here. One view is that there are five crowns that will be awarded at the Judgment Seat of Christ (Rom. 14:12; 2 Cor. 5:10; *judgment* is the Greek *bema*, which was the name of the elevated seat where a judge sat.) The *incorruptible* crown is for self-discipline (1 Cor. 9:24–27); the crown of *rejoicing* is for a faithful witness for Christ through evangelism (1 Thess. 2:19); the crown of *righteousness* is for those who are looking for Christ's coming (2 Tim. 4:8); the crown of *glory* is for pastors who have faithfully shepherded God's flock (1 Pet. 5:4; cf. James 3:1); and the crown of *life* is for those who love the Lord (James 1:12). Those five spiritual rewards will be given for faithful service unto the Lord. While not literal crowns, they might give the recipient an increased capacity to enjoy and appreciate Christ, all that He is and all that He has.

Another view is that each **crown** is simply "the acknowledged honor of the presence of [that] characteristic in the believer for eternity. So we have the crown that is life, the crown that is glory, [etc.]."[147]

Whatever the prize is, it will be glorious beyond our present comprehension. Let us press toward it.

Scriptures for Study: Read Psalm 103:4 and Isaiah 28:5, noting the same imagery as the crowns mentioned in the NT.

Prisoner

desmios

In several instances, the apostle Paul referred to himself as "the prisoner of Jesus Christ" (Eph. 3:1; cf. 4:1; 2 Tim. 1:8; Philem. 1, 9). **Prisoner** is *desmios* (1198) from the verb *desmeō* (1196) "to bind," and therefore, means "one who is bound." The tragedies of ancient Greek literature used this word to refer to one who was in chains or prison. Acts 16:25–26 recounts that as Paul and Silas prayed and sang in the dungeon in Philippi, there was suddenly an earthquake that caused their shackles (*desmon*, 1199) to fall off and the doors to open. Perhaps Paul had that incident in mind as he wrote to the Ephesians as a prisoner once more.

But while Paul certainly was a prisoner of Nero in the *physical* sense, his point was that such physical imprisonment meant nothing in the *spiritual* sense. His attitude was: "I'm not a prisoner of Nero; I'm not a prisoner of the Roman Empire; I'm not a prisoner of any earthly authority or because I've violated Roman law." Why was this Paul's attitude? *Because he did not consider man to have the final authority over the Christian's life*. Yes, man can do many things physically, but he's not the final authority; he does not have the final say. Who, then, does have final authority?

The Greek makes Paul's attitude clear. His statement is in the genitive case, which shows *originating cause*. The meaning is not just "a prisoner *belonging* to Christ," but rather "a prisoner *caused* by Christ;" neither Rome nor Nero had imprisoned Paul; Christ had imprisoned him.

The presence of the definite article, "*the* prisoner of Jesus Christ," further underscores this. Obviously Paul does not mean that he was "the one and only prisoner," or "the most important prisoner." Rather, he shows the character of his imprisonment, that is, *the distinctiveness and uniqueness of being a prisoner of Christ*. It wasn't the hopeless and terrifying imprisonment of Rome, but the assurance and peace of being in God's presence and will.

Paul also adds that he was the "prisoner of Christ for [the] Gentiles," that is, *on their behalf, for their advantage*. Why was this for their advantage? His imprisonment was a direct result of his preaching (Acts 21–22), but it was still a joy to Paul because his Gentile readers could enjoy the knowledge of what they had in Christ.

Scriptures for Study: Read Acts 5:17–20 and 12:1–19, noting how Peter, Paul, and other servants of God were imprisoned but how God delivered them.

Baptize (1)

baptizō

Few subjects invoke more controversy than baptism, but such controversy is both sad and unnecessary. As is true of most doctrines, the word itself makes the meaning clear. **Baptize** directly transliterates *baptizō* (907), which means to "immerse; place into." The verb *baptō* (911) originally referred to dipping clothes into dye or drawing water by placing the container into the water.

One of the earliest heresies to enter the church was "Baptismal Regeneration," the idea that baptism is part of salvation. Tertullian (c. 160–c. 220) was one of the earliest church fathers to teach it, and Roman Catholicism has always held it. Incredulously, even some *Protestant* churches teach this, which is especially contradictory because it is one of the doctrines they should be *protesting*! Zacchaeus (Luke 19:9), the thief on the cross (Luke 23:42–43), new believers at Pentecost (Acts 2:41), Paul (9:17–18), and Cornelius (10:47) all were declared saved *before* baptism. Salvation is by **grace** alone. Any other "gospel" is *not* the Gospel (Gal. 1:6–9).

Baptism has always signified *identification and public testimony*. The Jews used it that way; a proselyte into Judaism had to be circumcised, offer a sacrifice, and baptize himself in the presence of a rabbi to identify himself with Judaism. John the Baptist's baptism was for the purpose of identifying people with his message of the coming Christ. Christian baptism, therefore, is an identification with the death, burial, and resurrection of Christ and a public testimony that we are following Him. Even our Lord submitted to this as a picture of His future and to be our example (Matt. 4:13–17).

There's also controversy over the mode of baptism, but to argue for sprinkling or pouring is pointless if not downright silly. *Baptizō* is self-evident. Who would try dying a garment by sprinkling dye on it? I read of a Greek sea captain who after his ship was torpedoed radioed this mayday: *"Baptizō! Baptizō!"* (literally, "I'm sinking! I'm sinking!").[148] It's historical fact that the early church practiced only immersion and that other modes did not arise until about the third century and were not widely practiced until the twelfth. Those different modes simply have no biblical precedent.

Baptism by immersion is among the first steps of obedience in following Christ, which is made crystal clear in the book of Acts. If you haven't taken that step, I encourage you to talk to your pastor about doing so.

Scriptures for Study: Read Acts 2:22–47. What was the theme of Peter's sermon? What was the people's response? How many were saved and baptized?

Baptize (2)

baptizō

In addition to the NT teaching about "water baptism" we examined yesterday, there's another type of baptism taught in the NT. Sadly, this one also has caused needless controversy. Paul refers to this as the "one baptism" in Ephesians 4:5.

While some teachers think Paul is referring here to water baptism, the language simply does not allow it. "One baptism" is *en baptisma,* literally, "one placing into." But a placing into what? Not water, since the context speaks of "one body" and "one Spirit." Here is a single, definitive baptism that really does accomplish something. It's not *symbolic*; it's *actual*. This is precisely the point of 1 Corinthians 12:13: "For by one Spirit are we *all* baptized [placed, submerged] into one body, whether we be Jews or Gentiles, whether we be bond or free; and have been *all* made to drink into one Spirit" (emphasis added).[149]

What is Paul's point in both texts? The **unity** (see May 2), **bond** (see May 3), and oneness that *all* true believers have in Christ. One of the saddest teachings concerning the Holy Spirit is that "Spirit Baptism" (or "the Baptism of the Holy Spirit," a term *never* used in the NT) is a subsequent event in the Christian's life, which is then characterized by "speaking in **tongues**." But the word "baptized" is aorist indicative passive in the Greek of 1 Corinthians 12:13, which clearly shows that *we have been acted upon in the past by God* (literally, "were baptized"). He placed us into Christ's body; we do nothing to seek such "baptism" because there's nothing to seek; it's already been done.

Such teaching also results in a "spiritual elite," thereby actually dividing God's people into two classes: those who have "received the baptism" and those who haven't. I still recall riding next to a very sweet Christian gentleman on a plane trip from Denver to Indianapolis while I was still a Bible college student in 1971. At one point he asked, "Have you been baptized by the Holy Spirit?" I answered, "Yes, Sir, I have. I've been placed into the body of Christ." "Oh, no," he replied, "there's more, and I will pray that you will experience it soon." I've never forgotten that because it immediately put us into separate categories. Again, that's the exact opposite of what Paul is emphasizing, namely, *the unity of all believers in Christ.*

Scriptures for Study: Read 1 Corinthians 12:12–31, noting Paul's analogy of a body being unified. Note especially how many times Paul uses the word *all*, showing only a single category of believers in Corinth (in spite of how carnal all of them were).

Tongues

glossa

As mentioned yesterday, some teachers maintain that "the baptism of the Holy Spirit" results in speaking in **tongues**. The so-called ecstatic speech that is taught today, however, is another sad departure from both language and history.

Tongues is *glossa* (1100), which originally meant three things in Classical Greek: "the tongue of humans and animals in the physiological sense," and then figuratively either as "the faculty of speech, utterance, and also language [and] dialect," or "an obscure linguistic expression which requires explanation."[150]

Which one of those, then, is meant in a discussion of the "spiritual gift" (see Feb. 15) of tongues? The physical organ is obviously not what is referred to since Paul points out that there are "different *kinds* of tongues" (1 Cor. 12:10). Neither can this refer to some "unintelligible sound" because Paul clearly and *sharply* criticizes the Corinthians for using "unknown languages," that is, ecstatic utterances, because no one could understand them (14:2, 9, 11, 26). All gifts are for edification, so how can anyone be edified if they can't understand what's being said?

Therefore, there is no valid argument against tongues being known, earthly languages. The tongues of Acts 2:4–8 were clearly not some ecstatic speech, but rather earthly language, for "every man heard them speak in his own language." Verses 9–11 go on to list many of the regions from which these languages came. Since thousands of people from different areas gathered for the Feast of Pentecost, this was clearly the Holy Spirit supernaturally enabling certain men to speak in a language they did not already know so that every person there could hear the Gospel in his own language. This was a necessary gift in those early days but was no longer needed after the completion of God's authoritative Word. Moreover, tongues were *always* and *only* for a sign to Jews that the Gospel was true (1 Cor. 14:21–22). In *every* occurrence of tongues in the book of Acts, Jews were present.

Today's so-called practice of tongues, therefore, could not be farther from that precedent, and there is no linguistic or scriptural indication that they should have been anything different. Our desire should be to the far better gift of "prophecy" (preaching; see May 18ff.) because it edifies, exhorts, and comforts, while "an unknown tongue" edifies only the speaker (1 Cor. 14:3–4).

Scriptures for Study: Read 1 Corinthians 14:27–34. Can you note the six principles that Paul gives for the regulation of tongues, all of which are violated in today's modern "tongues movement"?[151]

Apostle

apostolos

At the close of yesterday's reading, we observed Paul's statement that Christ gave **spiritual gifts** (see Feb. 15) to the believers who remain on earth.

One such "office gift" was the **apostle**. While a few men in the NT were called "apostles" who did not actually possess the strict qualifications (see today's "Scriptures for Study"), in each context the title seems an honorary one because of each man's association with Paul and because each did the *work* of an apostle but did not hold the *office* of apostle. Far too much emphasis has been placed on this unofficial meaning of the word *apostle*. Some today go so far as to say that the office still exists in a more or less "general sense." But that is not the case; as we'll see (see June 29), the work of the apostle continues through the labor of the **evangelist**.

First, in the "official sense," the most important requirement was that the man had to have seen the resurrected Lord Jesus. Paul makes this clear in 1 Corinthians 9:1. No man can be an apostle unless he has seen the risen Lord.

Second, a man must have been called and commissioned, in person, by the Lord Jesus. Paul is the chief example; he usually began his letters by describing himself as "Paul, called to be an apostle" (or literally, "a called apostle"). Paul was indeed called and commissioned on the road to Damascus. Like the other apostles, he was also personally trained by the Lord Jesus (Gal. 1:16).

Third, an apostle received special revelation from God and, therefore, had absolute authority. Paul received direct revelation from God concerning the mystery of the church (Eph. 3:2–3). That is why "apostolicity" (i.e., the authority of apostles) became the ultimate test for the canonicity of books of NT books. A book had to have either been written by an apostle or substantiated by the teaching of an apostle.

Fourth, an apostle had the power to work miracles (Heb. 2:4), which were always for the Jews. The apostles were only for the laying of the foundation of the church (Eph. 2:20). God is no longer concerned with the *foundation*, but rather the *structure*, the continual building of the body of Christ. Once the foundation of the church was laid, and once the Word of God was completed, the office of apostle passed from the scene.

Scriptures for Study: Read the following examples of men who held the honorary title of apostle but were not officially apostles: James (Gal. 1:19), Barnabas (Acts 14:14), possibly Silas and Timothy (1 Thess. 2:6), and possibly Apollos (1 Cor. 4:6, 9).

Prophet

prophētēs

The Greek behind the word **prophet** (*prophētēs*, 4396) clearly indicates one who, along with proclaiming truth already revealed (implied in Acts 13:1), also speaks *immediately* of the Holy Spirit, that is, speaking under the direct inspiration of the Holy Spirit.[152] While the apostle had a wider ministry, the prophet was in a local assembly. Also, the prophet was subject to the apostle and his message was judged by the apostle (1 Cor. 14:37).

There is no "unofficial" meaning of *prophētēs,* as some interpreters maintain. Again, the prophet spoke *immediately* of the Holy Spirit. This was necessary before the completion of the written Word of God. In contrast, the preacher/teacher today speaks based on his careful study of Scripture and the illumination of the Holy Spirit. So, like the apostle, the prophet passed away with the completion of the Scriptures; both were only foundational (Eph. 2:20).

Martyn Lloyd-Jones well sums up this point:

> Try to imagine our position if we did not possess these New Testament Epistles, but the Old Testament only. That was the position of the early Church. Truth was imparted to it primarily by the teaching and preaching of the apostles, but that was supplemented by the teaching of the prophets to whom truth was given and also the ability to speak it with clarity and power in the demonstration and authority of the Spirit. But once these New Testament documents were written the office of a prophet was no longer necessary. Hence in the Pastoral Epistles which apply to a later stage in the history of the Church, when things had become more settled and fixed, there is no mention of the prophets. It is clear that even by then the office of the prophet was no longer necessary, and the call was for teachers and pastors and others to expound the Scriptures and to convey the knowledge of the truth.[153]

That is where we are today. With the passing of those foundational offices, we now look to two offices around which church leadership revolves. Everything in the church now rises or falls depending upon the quality of the descendants of the apostle and the prophet: the **evangelist** and the **pastor-teacher**.

Scriptures for Study: Read Exodus 7:1–2; 2 Peter 1:20, 21; and 1 Corinthians 14:32, noting how the prophet spoke only what God revealed to him while still retaining his own consciousness.

Evangelist

euangelistēs

What is an **evangelist**? We've heard this term countless times in the last century, from D. L. Moody to Billy Graham. But what exactly is it? While the precise meaning of the term *evangelist* is not easy to establish, we can deduce the meaning from its NT appearance.

The Greek *euangelistēs* (2099), "one who proclaims good news," and the contexts in which it appears, seem to indicate that this proclamation was in places where the Gospel was previously unknown. Besides Ephesians 4:11, it occurs in only two other verses. First, Philip is referred to as an evangelist in Acts 21:8. A little earlier (8:5) we're told, "Philip went down to the city of Samaria, and preached Christ unto them," which is what the evangelist did. Later in that passage we also read of Philip's dealing with the Ethiopian eunuch. The second occurrence is in 2 Timothy 4:5, where Paul tells Timothy to "do the work of an evangelist," that is, to proclaim the good news.

Like the apostle, therefore, the evangelist went about proclaiming the Gospel. The implication in Ephesians 4:11 is that they would also plant churches, which makes the evangelist the direct descendant of the apostle. This principle follows of necessity.[154]

What a position and responsibility! This is not to be confused with what is often called an "evangelist" today. To equate the NT position with what one writer calls "the modern revivalist who bears the name [evangelist], and who has little recognition in the New Testament,"[155] is to insult the biblical text. Today this is often a guy with six suits and a dozen sermons who goes all over the country preaching. While preaching the true Gospel is certainly paramount, the *biblical* evangelist did far more. He taught people the Word and grounded them in the faith over a period of time. He also, of necessity, founded a local church because that's where the new believer should be. That done, he would move on, leaving a **pastor-teacher**, the descendent of the **prophet**, in his place.

This picture of church planting is, in fact, the ideal biblical model for "missions." While "missions" today is defined as going out to do anything we want to do and getting mission support for it, NT missions involves planting churches. That is the way the apostle Paul did it, and so should we.

Scriptures for Study: Read Acts 18:18–19:10. While a fledgling church met in Priscilla and Aquila's home (1 Cor. 16:19), Paul spent a total of three years (Acts 20:31) establishing that church.

Pastor-Teacher (1)

pomenas kai didaskalous

The word **pastor** (Latin *pēstor*) translates *poimēn* (4166), "shepherd." It originally referred to the herdsman who tended and cared for the sheep. Metaphorically it referred to a leader, a ruler, or a commander. Plato, for example, compared "the rulers of the city-state to shepherds who care for their flock."[156] That meaning was carried over into the NT; a pastor is a man who cares for and feeds the flock.

Teacher is *didaskalos* (1320), a teacher or tutor, which covers "all those regularly engaged in the systematic imparting of knowledge or technical skills: the elementary teacher, the tutor, the philosopher, also the chorus-master who has to conduct rehearsals of poetry for public performance." Likewise in the NT, "men holding this office had the task of explaining the Christian faith to others and of providing a Christian exposition of the Old Testament."[157] So, the Christian teacher is one who systematically imparts divine truth and practical knowledge based upon the Word of God.

The key to understanding both these terms, however, is that *they refer to the same office*; they must not be separated. According to a rule of Greek grammar,[158] "pastors and teachers" (*pomenas kai didaskalous*, Eph. 4:11) is literally "pastor-teachers." This is a single term that refers to two functions carried on by one man. Theologian and commentator Charles Hodge well sums up this office and cites one historical example of those who deviated from the biblical precedent:

> According to one interpretation we have here two distinct offices: that of pastor and that of teacher, but there is no evidence from Scripture that there was a set of men authorized to teach but not authorized to exhort. The thing is almost impossible. The one function includes the other. The man who teaches duty and the basis of it, at the same time admonishes and exhorts. It was, however, on the ground of this unnatural interpretation that the Westminster Directory made *teachers* a distinct class of officers in the Church. The Puritans in New England endeavored to put the theory into practice, and appointed *doctors* [or "lecturers"] as distinct from preachers. But the attempt proved to be a failure. The two functions could not be kept separate. The whole theory rested on a false interpretation of Scripture. *Pastors and teachers*, therefore as most modern commentators agree, must be taken as a twofold description of the same officers, who were simultaneously the guides and instructors of the people.[159]

Scriptures for Study: Read the following verses, noting the analogy of the shepherd and sheep, on which the concept of pastor is based: Mark 6:34; John 10:2–3, 12–16.

Pastor-Teacher (2)

pomenas kai didaskalous

Concluding our look at the **pastor-teacher**, the whole point of the "shepherd" imagery (*poimēn*, 4166) is that he meets *all* the needs of the sheep: care, feeding, protecting, exhorting, etc. To divide "pastors" and "teachers" into two offices destroys the entire picture. This would have been crystal clear to readers in Paul's day. The idea of one shepherd who fed the sheep and another who tended to their needs would have been totally foreign to them because a shepherd did both.

By far, however, the most important function of the pastor-teacher is that he feeds God's flock. Nothing is more important or even equal in importance. Unlike today, Paul emphasized this over and over again in the pastoral epistles. A quick look at the statistics of those epistles, in fact, reveals how central this is.

In searching for various related terms, we find the following in the Authorized Version: *teach* (nine times); *teaching* (twice); *preach* (once); *preaching* (twice); *speak* (three times); *exhort* (seven times); *doctrine* (sixteen times); *rebuke* (five times); *reprove* (once).[160] That is a total of at least *forty-six* references to the teaching and preaching ministry of the pastor-teacher (also called "bishop" and "elder"). Is there any doubt? Should there be any question today?

Still there are those today who think that other things are more important. Today's "minister," or whatever you prefer to call him, is viewed as part administrator, part manager, part philanthropist, and even part entertainer. He is expected to be, and even desires to be, "well-rounded," that is, someone who can wear many hats, including: businessman, media figure, psychologist, and philosopher. While there's not a single word of Scripture that even implies any of those other so-called qualities for a pastor, it makes it clear that he *must* be, from beginning to end, a *teacher*. If he is not a teacher, if he cannot clearly convey God's truth, he does not belong in the ministry (1 Tim. 3:2).

If you're a pastor, your greatest challenge is to faithfully **preach** (see May 17–18) and teach the depth of God's Word. If you're a layman, your challenge is to submit to the preaching of truth.

Scriptures for Study: Read the following verses, noting Paul's emphasis on the pastor's duty to teach: 1 Timothy 4:6, 11–13, 16; 5:17; 2 Timothy 2:24; 4:1–2; Titus 2:1.

Elder

presbuteros

The NT term **elder** actually has Jewish origins. The usual Hebrew word is *zaqen* (2205H), which was used to refer to the leaders of Israel, such as the seventy tribal leaders who assisted Moses (Num. 11:16; Deut. 27:1). The NT uses the Greek *presbuteros* (4245, English *presbyterian*), which basically means "one who is advanced in years or of mature age." How old exactly we do not know, but the main emphasis in Israel and the early church was *maturity*. This word was the only commonly used Jewish term that was free from any connotation of either the monarchy or the priesthood. So, since the early church was Jewish, it was only natural for this concept to be adopted.

The term **elder**, then, refers to the man himself, to him personally, in short, his *character* as a mature man. The term has nothing to do with his responsibilities and duties, but rather his character, the fact that he is qualified to lead because he's a spiritually mature man. The term is used about eighteen times in Acts and the epistles to refer to leaders in the church.

While there's a popular teaching today that there are two classes of elders, some who rule and others who teach; Scripture simply does not support such a dichotomy. Some base this view upon 1 Timothy 5:17—"Let the elders that rule well be counted worthy of double honour, especially they who labour in the word and doctrine"—but as noted scholar M. R. Vincent writes: "The passage lends no support to the Reformed theory of two classes of elders—ruling and teaching. The special honor is assigned to those who combine qualifications for both."[161]

Puritan Matthew Henry, who was closer to the Reformation than we are today, bears this out: "Some [referring to the Reformers] have imagined that by the 'elders that rule well' the apostle means lay-elders, who were employed in ruling but not in teaching . . . but, as it is hinted before, they had not, in the primitive church, one to preach to them and another to rule them, but ruling and teaching were performed by the same persons, only some might labour more in the word and doctrine than others."[162]

As we'll see tomorrow, since **elder**, **bishop**, and **pastor** all refer to the same person, this one man has several responsibilities and needs prayer and encouragement from those he leads.

Scriptures for Study: Read Acts 20:13–31, noting the serious duties of elders.

Bishop

episkopos

The term **bishop** is one that in our day has been encumbered with a lot of ecclesiastical trappings. In the NT, however, this term (which we find, for example, in that list of leadership qualifications in 1 Timothy 3:1–7) refers to the same person as **pastor** and **elder**.

The Greek *episkopos* (1985, English *episcopal*) means "overseer, guardian." Its basic roots are in Greek culture. Emperors appointed bishops to oversee captured or newly formed cities. It's also possible that it had roots in the Essene Jews of the Qumran community. The Essenes preached, taught, presided, exercised care and authority, and enforced discipline. In either case, the idea is basically the same.

While there has been debate for centuries over these three "offices," there's absolutely no doubt whatsoever that biblically, pastor, elder, and bishop refer to the same person. While that sounds like a narrow, dogmatic statement, it's not meant to be; rather, it merely states historical fact that cannot be disproved.

We could cite many examples, but perhaps the best is the fourth-century Roman scholar Jerome, who was without argument one of the greatest students of the biblical languages in the early centuries of the church. He states quite boldly and against all the traditions of his day that bishops and elders were originally the same. He wrote: "A presbyter [elder] and a bishop are the same . . . the churches were governed by a joint council of the [elders]. . . . If it be supposed that this is merely our opinion and without scriptural support that bishop and [elder] are one . . . examine again the words the apostle addressed to the Philippians [1:1, where Paul addresses his letter to bishops and deacons]. Now Philippi is but one city in Macedonia, and certainly in one city there could not have been numerous bishops. It is simply that at that time the same persons were called either bishops or [elders]."[163] Several other early church fathers concur.

What happened, however, was that church leaders deliberately deviated from this biblical truth and ultimately formed a clerical hierarchy that continues to this day even in many Protestant and some Evangelical denominations. The resulting damage is incalculable.

The biblical picture, then, is that the word **elder** refers to the man's *character*, **bishop** refers to his *position* as leader, that is, a ruler and guardian, and **pastor** refers to his *duty* of feeding God's people (Acts 20:28).

Scriptures for Study: Read 1 Timothy 3:1–7 and Titus 1:5–9, noting the qualifications that a man must have to be a pastor (elder and bishop). Note also that Titus 1:5 speaks of appointing elders, verse 7 calls the same men bishops, and verse 9 speaks of the duty of this man, namely, teaching (cf. 1 Pet. 5:1–4).

Liberty (1)

eleutheria

A well-known radio talk show host closes his program each weekday with the words, "America is the greatest nation on God's green earth." We certainly agree. No other nation has ever known the liberties we enjoy in America, and no nation has ever had a history and heritage equal to it. And it's on this day each year that Americans celebrate their independence from the ungodly invader that England was in the eighteenth century.

The Christian, however, knows a **liberty** that is far and away superior even to American citizenship. The Greek *eleutheria* (1657) means freedom and independence. In Classical Greek, it held a primarily political sense of "the full citizen who belongs to the *polis*, city state, in contrast to the slave who did not enjoy full rights as a citizen." Citizens enjoyed free speech, could participate in public debates over civic issues, and controlled their own affairs.[164]

In contrast, *eleutheria* never refers to political freedom in the NT. While the Jews were looking for a Messiah who would deliver them from the Roman Empire (even though the OT never said such a thing of the Messiah), Jesus was not a political deliverer or a "revolutionary," as some teachers have called Him. NT usage does, however, picture the idea of freedom in contrast to slavery.

This is exactly what Christ has done for the believer—he has "made us free [*eleutheria*]" (Gal. 5:1). First and foremost, he has "made [us] free from the law of sin and death" (Rom. 8:2). While we were once in bondage to sin and prisoners of death, Christ freed us by His death, burial, and resurrection.

Another way Christ has made us free is by giving us independence from the OT **Law** (see Dec. 9). The context of Galatians 5:1 concerns the teaching of a sect called the Judaizers (see Nov. 24; Dec. 8), who taught that not only did one have to believe to be saved but one also had to obey the Law. Back in 3:1–3, he calls them foolish because while they had been saved by grace, they were now living by "legalism" (see Mar. 8).

What joy and peace there is in knowing that we are truly free in Christ. We will continue our thoughts tomorrow.

Scriptures for Study: Read the following verses, noting again the liberty we have in Christ: Romans 8:20–21; 2 Corinthians 3:17; James 1:25; 2:12.

Liberty (2)

eleutheria

Yesterday we rejoiced in the **liberty** we have in Christ, the freedom He has provided from sin, death, and legalism. Liberty, however, does have a limit. Liberty is not a synonym for *license.* The teaching that says, "Because I'm a Christian, I can live any way I wish," is not biblical. Christian liberty does not mean "antinomianism" (without law).

Peter, for example, wrote that while we are "free" (*eleutheria*, 1657), we're not to use our "liberty for a cloak of maliciousness, but as the servants of God" (1 Pet. 2:16). In other words, we do not use our liberty to mask our licentiousness.

While Paul does not specifically use *eleutheria,* he still deals with this principle in detail in his first letter to the Corinthians. The scene in 8:4–13 is that some weaker Christians in the church were offended by other Christians eating meat that had been sacrificed to idols. Understanding that such deities did not exist and that they were in no way participating in the pagan worship, stronger Christians rightly saw that there was nothing wrong with eating it; meat was just meat.

Some other Christians, however, had come out of such pagan worship and were still sensitive to the association of such meat to that false worship. Seeing other Christians eating such meat offended them and tempted them to fall back into sin. The word *offend* in verse 13 is *skandalizō* (4624, English *scandalize*), which means to cause to stumble and fall. Paul also says that such a situation was a "stumblingblock" (v. 9), which is *proskomma* (4348), an obstacle in one's path that trips him and causes him to fall.

What, then, did Paul say to the stronger Christians? He didn't say, "It's okay; just go ahead and eat that meat; those weaker Christians just need to grow up." Rather, he said, "Take heed lest by any means this liberty of yours become a stumblingblock to them that are weak. . . . If meat make my brother to offend, I will eat no flesh while the world standeth, lest I make my brother to offend" (vv. 9, 13).

The challenge to each of us is that nothing is worth offending another brother or sister in Christ. Even though there is nothing whatsoever sinful about a particular practice, we should be willing to set it aside if we know that it would cause another believer to trip and fall.

Scriptures for Study: Read our Lord's teaching on this issue in Matthew 18:6–14. How serious did He view the offending of a weaker believer?

Perfecting

katartismos

After listing the "office gifts" for the church in Ephesians 4:11, Paul goes on to say in verse 12 why God gave them: "For the perfecting of the saints." **Perfecting** translates *katartismos* (2677), which occurs only here in the NT. The root *artismos* comes from the related word *artios* (739, English *artist*) and means suitable, complete, capable, sound. With the intensifying prefix *kata* (2596), "according to," the meaning of *katartismos* is very instructive: "to put in order, restore, furnish, prepare, equip."[165]

In ancient Greek the verb form (*katartizō*, 2675) was used in a medical sense to refer to setting a broken limb or putting a joint back into place. It was also used in politics for bringing together opposing factions so that government could continue. A NT example of the verb, which appears thirteen times, is in reference to repairing fishing nets (Matt. 4:21; Mark 1:19).

It was, therefore, the responsibility of the **apostle** and **prophet**, and it is today the responsibility of the **evangelist** and **pastor-teacher**, to put in order, restore, furnish, prepare, and equip the **saints** (see Jan. 9). In many Christian circles, this has been totally turned around. Many today believe, "The pastor's job is to 'win souls' and build the church; he should spend most of his time calling on people, knocking on doors, and other 'people duties.'" But that is not the NT precedent. Many go to the phrase "house to house" (Acts 2:46; 20:20) to teach that, but in each case the context makes it clear that the teaching of *believers* is in view. The old Scottish ministers, in fact, had the right idea as they used to go from home to home catechizing. They then had an educated congregation.

The NT makes it clear that the pastor's duty is to train believers, who then go out as the outreach. The shepherd/sheep analogy makes this obvious. The shepherd feeds and nurtures the sheep so that they are healthy and capable of reproducing. Indeed, the pastor's first concern is to be for the occupied seats, not the empty ones. How does a pastor go about all that? By the teaching of the Word of God. Many today are trying to do it through programs, promotional gimmicks, and marketing strategies. But when God's people fail in service, it's not because of weak *programs*, but because of weak *teaching*.

Scriptures for Study: Read Acts 2:41–47 and 20:16–20, noting the teaching and fellowship that characterized the early church.

Witness

martus

In Ephesians 4:12, Paul declares that the **evangelist** and **pastor-teacher** are to train Christians "for the work of the ministry." But what exactly is the work of the ministry? Acts 1:8 is the most important verse to church outreach, the verse that speaks of the commission given to every believer: "But ye shall receive power, after that [i.e., when] the Holy Ghost is come upon you: and ye shall be witnesses unto me." That truly is "the Great Commission" (cf. Matt. 28:19–20).

The original setting of the Greek *martus* (3144, English *martyr*) was the legal sphere, just like today. The witness gives solemn testimony to that which he knows and offers evidence. The Christian, therefore, is one who testifies of Christ and gives evidence through his or her life. So, it's not just that we witness for Christ with our *lips*, but rather what we also do through our *life*. It's not so much that the local church evangelizes through "programs of evangelism" or "evangelistic campaigns," but rather individual believers are the outreach.

To illustrate, we see today multimillion-dollar public schools with huge gymnasiums, Olympic swimming pools, state-of-the-art science labs, cutting-edge computer technology, and ultra-competitive athletic programs. Billions of dollars are thrown at public education, but study after study shows that the quality of education continues to decline. Why? Because we have forgotten what education is. As one unknown sage has put it: "A school is a log with a teacher on one end and a student on the other."

Likewise, evangelism is not dependent upon a multimillion-dollar facility, the latest marketing technique, or some spiel we recite to manipulate someone to "believe in Jesus." Biblical evangelism (*euaggelion*, 2098, see Feb. 5) is *one* person telling *another* person about the *only* Person.

What then is the purpose of the local church in this regard? The local church is the training ground. The local church is where Christians are to be trained so they are equipped to serve, to be effective witnesses. This challenges each one of us to be the witness God wants us to be and challenges pastors to do the appropriate equipping.

Scriptures for Study: Read the following scriptures, noting the one-on-one nature of personal evangelism: John 4:5–14; Acts 8:26–35.

Deacon

diakonos

The NT mentions one other office for church government, the **deacon**. The Greek *diakonos* (1249) is used to describe a church office called "deacon" (Phil. 1:1; 1 Tim. 3:8–13). A "deacon" is one who takes care of the temporal matters in the church, thereby freeing the pastor so he can be devoted to the ministry of the Word.

In spite of what seems to be an obvious reference to deacons in Acts 6:1–6, there are a few teachers who for some odd reason make it an issue and deny it, but that is clearly the first instance of deacons. In fact, the basic meaning of "serving tables" is right in the passage. This sets the perfect precedent of what the deacon does—he takes care of temporal matters.

A minority argues, "The text nowhere calls them deacons," but we must humbly disagree. While the noun **deacon** is not used for the seven men appointed to serve, the verb *diakoneō* (1247, to serve by waiting on a table) is used twice in verse 1 and the infinitive *diakonia* (1248) is used in verse 2, both of which come from the same root. So, why doesn't Luke use the noun here? Undoubtedly because the church is still in its infancy and the office has not yet been systematically defined.

Some argue further, "The book of Acts nowhere uses the term *diakonos* (deacon), which seems strange if an order of deacons was initiated in Acts 6. Elders are mentioned several times in Acts (cf.. 11:30; 14:23; 15:2, 4, 6, 22–23; 16:4; 20:17), making the omission of any reference to deacons even more significant." But that's an argument from silence, which is always weak and often even dangerous. Just because an office is not *named* doesn't mean that it didn't *exist*. The epistles build upon the book of Acts, and the office of deacon that is *named* in the epistles seems clearly *rooted* in that early situation of Acts 6. That is the consistent position of most commentators and expositors and is the natural conclusion of plain, normal interpretation.

The application is challenging. If you're a deacon or are thinking of becoming one, God holds you to a very high standard. If you are not a deacon, pray for those who are.

Scriptures for Study: Read the qualifications for deacons in 1 Timothy 3:8–13, noting the high standard to which such men are held.

Cornerstone

akrogoniaios

In Ephesians 2:20 Paul likens the church to a building. While in modern construction we think of the foundation as the most important part of a building, Paul pictures the ancient construction technique of a **cornerstone**. While the **apostle** (see June 27) and **prophet** (see June 28) were the foundation of the church, the Lord Jesus is the Cornerstone.

Akrogoniaios (204) is a compound made of *akron* (206), "top" or "tip," and *gōnia* (1137), "an angle or corner." The literal idea then is, as one commentator puts it, "at the tip of the angle" and refers to "the stone set at the corner of a wall so that its outer angle becomes important."[166] It was this stone that became the basis for every measurement in the building. It governed every line and angle. It provided no more support to the structure than any other stone; rather, its entire value lay in its outer angle.

This is actually rooted in OT imagery. The term *cornerstone* had for centuries been a prophetic metaphor for the coming Messiah. Isaiah, for example, declared, "Therefore thus saith the Lord God, Behold, I lay in Zion for a foundation a stone, a tried stone, a precious corner stone, a sure foundation; he that believeth shall not make haste" (Isa. 28:16).

Perhaps even more significant is Psalm 118:22: "The stone which the builders refused is become the head stone of the corner." The entire psalm, in fact, is totally messianic and is actually the most quoted psalm in the NT. Verse 22 declares that the stone the Jews would reject would be the very stone that God would use to build all His work.

That is the picture Paul paints of Christ. In all respects He was the perfect cornerstone—strong, perfect in character, and exact in measurement. We, therefore, are to conform to Him in every detail for we, too, are part of the building. What if we do not conform to the Cornerstone? What if we do not measure ourselves by that standard? What if our placement is not according to that absolute? Just think of how noticeable peeling paint is on a house or how an improperly laid brick or stone sticks out. *Any such flaw either weakens, or at the very least, disfigures the building.* Likewise, we are to conform to Christ lest we weaken or disfigure the building.

We'll continue examining Paul's metaphor over the next few days.

Scriptures for Study: Compare the following verses with their source in Psalm 118: Matthew 21:9, 42; 23:39; Mark 11:9, 10; 12:10, 11; Luke 13:35; 19:38; 20:17; John 12:13; Acts 4:11; Hebrews 13:6; 1 Peter 2:7.

Fitly Framed Together

sunarmologeō

Paul continues his construction metaphor in Ephesians 2:21: "In whom all the building fitly framed together groweth unto an holy temple in the Lord." As every craftsman knows, there's something amazing about building something, taking many small parts of totally different shapes, sizes, and material, and making them fit together step by step. It's a marvel to see how it all comes together to make up the structure.

That is precisely why Paul uses the words **fitly framed together**, which translate an utterly fascinating single Greek word, *sunarmologeō* (4883), an architectural metaphor that pictures the intricate process in masonry of fitting stones together to form a structure.

It's actually comprised of three words. The key word is the noun *harmos* (719), which means "a joint." The prefix *sun* (4862) is a primary preposition that denotes union and means "together" or "together with." This intensifies *harmos*; the idea is not just "a joint," but rather, "a together-joint." It's further intensified with *logos* (3056; see Mar. 16), from the verb *logeō* ("to speak intelligently"), and therefore means, "intelligence, word as the expression of that intelligence, discourse, saying."[167] Our Lord, of course, is called "the Word," "the Logos" (John 1:1–3), for He is the very intelligence of God come in the flesh to deliver His discourse, His message. At the heart of *logos*, then, is the idea of choosing exactly the right words and fitting them together to form sentences, paragraphs, and ultimately an entire discourse.

Putting it all together, we have "together-joint-choose."[168] The picture is vivid. We can see the stonemason diligently choosing a stone, carefully chipping away a corner here, an imperfection there, trying it in the wall for fit, and then repeating the process as many times as needed until it fits exactly. This not only makes a strong wall, but one in which every stone compliments the others and the wall as a whole. Consider also that not one stone is exactly like another—each one is unique.

What a beautiful picture of true **unity** (see May 2) in the church! Every believer needs to "fit." The building of the church is an ongoing process in which each believer is being properly and uniquely cut and trimmed to be useful to the building, to compliment the whole. A beautiful bay window is no more important to the building than a single nail in a window casing; both are necessary for the glory of the building and even the designer.

Scriptures for Study: Examine the only other NT occurrence of *sunarmologeō* (Eph. 4:16). What is the end result of this great process?

Grow

auxanō

Taking one more look at Ephesians 2:21—"In whom all the building fitly framed together groweth unto an holy temple in the Lord"—Paul continues his building metaphor by saying that the structure is actually growing. Talk about mixing your metaphors! But what a marvelous mix it is!

We usually think of a building as a static thing; once done, it's done. But not so this structure. The word **grow** ("groweth" in the AV) is *auxanō* (837), which means "to grow or increase, of the growth of that which lives, naturally or spiritually."[169] It's used some twenty-two times in the NT, such as in Jesus' words, "Why take ye thought for raiment? Consider the lilies of the field, how they grow; they toil not, neither do they spin" (Matt. 6:28), and Peter's admonition, "As newborn babes, desire the sincere milk of the word, that ye may grow thereby" (1 Pet. 2:2).

But the key to understanding this word is that *growth comes from a power outside of the object.* Greek scholar Spiros Zodhiates writes this excellent explanation: "For someone or something to grow (*auxanō*), it must be acted upon by an outside power or have the element of life within him or it. This is seen clearly in the use of the verb *auxanō*. For instance, the lilies grow (Matt. 6:28; Luke 12:27); the seed is grown (Matt. 13:32); the fruit comes from the seeds (Mark 4:8); the mustard seed grew to a tree. In all these instances, it was something living that could grow because of the element of life within it. This growth, however, was not because of any special ability of the seeds, but because of the quality of life so implanted by God Himself."[170]

God's building, therefore, is a living entity that is ever growing. It grows, however, not because of its own special abilities, and certainly not because of the talents of any of the stones in it, but only because of God's power.

In what ways, then, does this building grow? It grows first by each living stone fulfilling its function and using its gifts to the glory of the building. Second, the building grows by adding new stones to the structure. As the living stones are witnesses and testimonies of the Cornerstone (Acts 1:8), He in turn adds new stones to His building (Matt. 16:18).

Scriptures for Study: What is John's point in John 3:30 ("increase" is *auxanō*)? 📖 What "increased" and "grew" in Acts 6:7, 12:24, and 19:20? What does that encourage us to do?

Dung

skubalon

Philippians 3:10 is one of the most beautiful verses in the NT. Paul ruminates, "That I may know him, and the power of his resurrection, and the fellowship of his sufferings, being made conformable unto his death." Paul's greatest desire was to know Christ. The driving force of his life was to be more deeply and intimately acquainted with His Lord and Master. He didn't just want to know things *about* the Lord, but rather, to know the Lord Himself (see Feb. 18).

But how much did he want such knowledge? How strong was that desire? Verse 8 answers: "I count all things but loss for the excellency of the knowledge of Christ Jesus my Lord: for whom I have suffered the loss of all things, and do count them but dung, that I may win Christ." The word **dung** is *skubalon* (4657). Sadly, every modern translation misses the depth of this word by rendering it *refuse* (ASV), *rubbish* (NASB, ESV, NIV, NKJV), *garbage* (NLT), or even *trash* (NCV).

But *skubalon* goes even further than those somewhat milder images. It's an extremely course, ugly, and repulsive word that also referred to excrement, and the AV correctly captures that image. Paul considered everything in this world as nothing more than the most repulsive thing he could think of in comparison to knowing the Lord Jesus Christ.

That challenges each of us to ask ourselves, "Do I really love the Lord? Do I really desire to know Him personally, not just for salvation, but for intimacy?" The only way we can do this, of course, is through His Word. Jesus Himself said, "If ye love me, keep my commandments" (John 14:15), and "He that hath my commandments, and keepeth them, he it is that loveth me" (v. 21). That is why David wrote, "O how love I thy law! it is my meditation all the day" (Ps. 119:97), and why the apostle John could write, "Whoso keepeth his word, in him verily is the love of God perfected: hereby know we that we are in him" (1 John 2:5).

The big question: How much do you love the Lord? We'll meditate on a related thought tomorrow.

Scriptures for Study: Read the following verses in Psalm 119, noting how David loved God and His Word: 113, 119, 127, 159; 163-165. 📖 I would encourage you to review our February 18 reading.

Count

hēgeomai

As we saw yesterday, in comparison with knowing the Lord Jesus more deeply and intimately, Paul considered everything else in this world as nothing better than **dung** (Phil. 3:8). But how did he come to that conclusion? What prompted such a devotion to Christ that would discount even good things as worthless in contrast? The answer lies in the word **count**, which he uses twice in verse 8 and once in verse 7: "But what things were gain to me, those I counted loss for Christ."

The Greek *hēgeomai* (2233) comes from *agō* (71), "to lead, lead along," and literally means to lead on or forward, to be a leader or chief. It's used mostly to refer to those who have influence and authority (Luke 22:26; Acts 15:22), such as those who rule in the church (Heb. 13:7, 17, 24), a chief magistrate such as Joseph in Egypt (Acts 7:10), and even the Messiah (Matt. 2:6, which quotes Mic. 5:2).[171]

Metaphorically, then, this word speaks of "leading out before the mind," that is, to think about something in order to view, regard, or esteem it. What prompted Paul's striking comparison? It was his lofty view, towering regard, and extraordinary esteem for Christ.

Another striking occurrence of this word appears in Hebrews 11:25–26, where it's said of Moses: "Choosing rather to suffer affliction with the people of God, than to enjoy the pleasures of sin for a season; Esteeming [*hēgeomai*] the reproach of Christ greater riches than the treasures in Egypt: for he had respect unto the recompense of the reward." Like Paul, Moses' esteem and regard for God outweighed anything the world could offer, and Egypt could offer anything a man like Moses could want.

A sobering warning appears a few verses before that concerning the terrible judgment that will befall those who have "trodden under foot the Son of God, and hath counted [*hēgeomai*] the blood of the covenant, wherewith he was sanctified, an unholy thing, and hath done despite unto the Spirit of grace" (Heb. 10:29).

The challenge this word makes to our hearts is obvious. What do we think of Christ (cf. Matt. 22:42)? How high do we esteem Him? Is He more important than all else? Do we value Him over anything the world can offer? In a day when *self*-esteem rules, what should we *really* esteem?

Scriptures for Study: What's the challenge of Philippians 2:3 ("esteem" is *hēgeomai*)? 🕮 What encouragement does God give us in James 1:2?

Perfect (Mature)

teleios

When we hear the word **perfect** in modern English, we take it to mean without flaw, such as a perfect diamond, for example. In old English, however, it meant "mature." The same idea is reflected in the Greek *teleios* (5046), which is derived from *telos* (5056), which in turn "originally meant the turning point, hinge, the culminating point at which one stage ends and another begins; later, the goal, the end." Several things were looked upon as being an end, or a goal, such as marriage, physical and intellectual knowledge, and, of course, death. So, anything that has reached its *telos,* its goal or end, is *teleios*, that is, "complete."[172]

Teleios occurs several times in the NT. In Ephesians 4:13, for example, Paul's desire for God's people is that "we all come in the unity of the faith, and of the knowledge of the Son of God, unto a perfect man, unto the measure of the stature of the fulness of Christ." Within the context of the following verse, where there is a direct contrast with being "children, tossed to and fro" by "every wind of doctrine," the clear idea of *teleios* is "a complete, mature adult."

What, then, does the word *mature* mean? What is maturity? The English word *mature* comes from the Latin *matūrūs* (ripe, mature, timely, and seasonable), so our word means "having completed natural growth and development, full development."

So, what, then, is *spiritual* maturity? It is to be fully developed in Christ, that is, as our text puts it, "unto the measure of the stature of the fullness of Christ." The Greek behind "stature" (*hēlikia*, 2244) originally spoke of age, lifespan, height, and even size of body. It's used, for example, to describe Zacchaeus, who was "little of stature" (Luke 19:3). Used metaphorically, as it is here, and combined with the words "measure" and "fulness," the idea is "the measure of maturity in Christ, the measure of being dominated by Him and possessing Christlikeness of character."

So, we are to measure ourselves not by the yardstick of society, or by the ruler of some legalistic list of "do's and don'ts." Rather, we are to measure ourselves according to the gauge of the stature of Christ. In short, *spiritual maturity is Christlikeness of character* (Gal. 5:22–23). God wants the church to be built in the image of Christ, according to His stature.

Scriptures for Study: In Romans 12:1–2, what brings about Christian maturity? 🕮 What ministry also promotes maturity, according to Colossians 1:28?

Sleight

kubeia

Today we begin a study of several words that speak of "discernment" (Latin *discernere*: *dis*, "apart," and *cernere*, "to sift"). Scripture constantly emphasizes the principle of "separating and distinguishing between" in order to see and understand the difference, to distinguish truth from error.

Ephesians 4:14 is probably the most graphic description in Scripture of the immature, unguided, undiscerning Christian. Paul speaks of the **sleight** of men, which is the first way false doctrine comes. The Greek *kubeia* (2940), from *kubos* (English *cube*), appears only here in the NT and literally means "playing dice." **Sleight**, then, graphically pictures the implication of the gambling, trickery, and fraud that's involved in false doctrine.

We're reminded of the old scam, Three-Card Monte. The scam artist lays three cards on the table, one of which is a queen, shuffles them back and forth, and then asks you to "find the lady." You'll win at first, but when the bet increases, you'll lose because of a sleight-of-hand trick. The dealer picks up two cards with his right hand, the upper card between his thumb and his forefinger and the lower card between his thumb and his middle finger, with a small gap between the cards. According to common sense, and, is in fact, what he did at first, the dealer should drop the lower card first, but this time his forefinger smoothly and slyly ejects the upper card first, which causes you to lose track of the queen. This is especially difficult to see if the dealer's hand makes a sweeping move from left to right while he drops the cards. The moral of the story: *You're going to lose.*

That is the false teacher. By "slight of mouth," he tricks the unwary without their even knowing it because they are gullible and overconfident in their knowledge. Pride gets the Three-Card Monte victim every time; he's confident he can follow the queen, but he can't because of the sleight of hand—the hand is quicker than the eye. Likewise, immature Christians are overconfident in their supposed knowledge and are easy prey for the false teacher.

That is precisely why Paul warned the Ephesian elders in Miletus that "grievous wolves [will] enter in among you, not sparing the flock. Also of your own selves shall men arise, speaking perverse things, to draw away disciples after them" (Acts 20:29–30).

Scriptures for Study: Begin reading several passages on discernment, which we'll continue listing over the next few days. First Kings 3:5–14 records God's dealing with Solomon. It's often observed that Solomon prayed for "wisdom," but more specifically what did he actually ask for?

Cunning Craftiness

panourgia

Continuing our study of discernment, Ephesians 4:14 declares, "That we henceforth be no more children, tossed to and fro, and carried about with every wind of doctrine, by the sleight of men, and cunning craftiness, whereby they lie in wait to deceive."

A second way false teaching comes is by **cunning craftiness**. This expression is one word in the Greek, *panourgia* (3834), a compound made from two roots, *pas* (3956, "all") and *ergon* (2041, "work"), yielding the meaning "capable of all work," or as Aristotle viewed it, "an unprincipled [capability] to do anything."[173] *That* is the false teacher. He will do anything, stoop to any level needed to manipulate error, to make something look like truth and thereby lead others away from truth.

A vivid example is how the Jehovah's Witness "bible" (*The New World Translation*) deliberately (and dishonestly) alters John 1:1 for the express purpose of denying the deity of Christ: "In [the] beginning the Word was, and the Word was with God, and the Word was a god." What is the source of that rendering? Supposedly, it's based upon the "oldest manuscripts," which is patently false and is easily shown to be so. In point of fact, it was translated thusly from German by Johannes Greber in 1937, a former Catholic priest turned spiritist who claimed the translation came from God's spirits.

Paul also uses *panourgia* in 2 Corinthians 4:2, where believers should "[renounce] the hidden things of dishonesty, not walking in craftiness, nor handling the word of God deceitfully; but by manifestation of the truth commending ourselves to every man's conscience in the sight of God."

Tragically, almost every day so-called Christian books hit the shelves—books that do not handle the Scripture rightly, but twist it to say what the writer wants it to say. Scripture is misread, misinterpreted, and misapplied to conform to the writer's preconceived ideas. While we most certainly do *not* think those authors are purposely trying to **deceive**, and still love them as Christian brothers, such developments are no less terrifying because people (even some pastors) are not recognizing obvious error.

As we'll continue to see in the next few days, we must constantly discern *everything* we read and hear.

Scriptures for Study: Read the following passages on discernment: Isaiah 8:20; Ezekiel 44:23–24.

Lie in Wait to Deceive

methodein tēs planēs

The third way false teaching comes, as Paul lists in Ephesians 4:14, is that false teachers **lie in wait to deceive** (*methodein tēs planēs*).

Lie in wait is from *methodeia* (3180, English *method*), which does not appear in Greek literature prior to the NT,[174] but means "to investigate by settled plan" or "a deliberate planning or system."[175] There is, therefore, a settled plan, an elaborate system, a deliberate scheme behind those who teach false doctrine. It's also translated as *wiles* in Ephesians 6:11 to refer to Satan's methods and tactics.

The desire of the false teacher is to **deceive**, which translates *planē* (4106), "a wandering out of the right way," and, therefore, figuratively "delusion and error." Second Thessalonians 2:10–11 speaks of the lost multitude that will believe the Antichrist, and for that very reason God will "send them strong delusion, that they should believe a lie." While that day is not yet here, delusion, error, and seduction are everywhere. So convincing is some error that our Lord Himself said, "There shall arise false Christs, and false prophets, and shall shew great signs and wonders; insomuch that, if it were possible, they shall deceive the very elect" (Matt. 24:24).

Tragically, however, there are many true believers nowadays who are gullible and will believe almost anything and follow practically anybody. As long as some teacher mentions God or Jesus, regardless of what else he (or she) says, many Christians think all is well. Even with our unequalled education, freedom, sophistication, access to God's Word, Christian books, and a multitude of Bible translations (which I'm convinced is actually part of the problem), it seems that anybody, no matter what he teaches, can get a following and even financial support from individual Christians, entire local churches, and even whole denominations, associations, and fellowships. Like little children, such Christians are captivated by something new—a new interpretation, idea, catchy phrase or term, method of "ministry," and countless other things.

In 1887, Robert Shindler, a fellow pastor and close friend of Charles Spurgeon, wrote in Spurgeon's wonderful publication, *The Sword and the Trowel*: "It is all too plainly apparent men are willing to forego the old for the sake of the new. But commonly it is found in theology that that which is true is not new, and that which is new is not true."[176] Oh, that we would recognize that in *our* day!

Scriptures for Study: Read the following passages on discernment: Matthew 7:15–16; 24:4, 5, 11, 23–26; Mark 13:22–23.

Discern (1)

diakrinō

Today we come to the actual word **discern**, as it is used in Scripture. Most people are aware of the old adage, "Red sky in morning, sailors take warning; red sky at night, sailor's delight." That is actually based on Matthew 16:2–3. The occasion was when the Pharisees tempted Jesus to perform a sign from heaven. But He turned it around on them and said, "O ye hypocrites, ye can discern the face of the sky; but can ye not discern the signs of the times?" In other words, they could discern a simple natural phenomenon, but they had no spiritual discernment of who Jesus really was.

The Greek is *diakrinō* (1252), one of several similar words that speak of judgment and discernment. It literally means "to make a distinction," something the Pharisees *could not* do and something many Christians today *will not* do.

This word also appears in the context of the regulations for **tongues** (see June 25) and other sign gifts in 1 Corinthians 14:29: "Let the prophets speak two or three, and let the other judge [*diakrinō*]." That "safety valve" guarded against false doctrine; others listened to what was being taught and "made a distinction."

A graphic picture of discernment appears in Acts 17:11. After leaving Thessalonica because of much bitter treatment from Jews there, Paul and Silas headed for Berea, about forty-five miles away. Upon entering the synagogue, they found a group of new believers who "were more noble than those in Thessalonica, in that they received the word with all readiness of mind, and searched [*anakrinō*, see tomorrow's reading] the scriptures daily, whether those things were so." While many in Thessalonica had "received the word of God which [they] heard" (1 Thess. 2:13), the Bereans were totally dedicated to the study of Scripture to see if what Paul said was true.

That is discernment and is what we need today. We must listen to every word a teacher speaks and every word an author writes. May I also interject that this most certainly includes what you're reading right now. What I write must be compared to Scripture and Scripture alone. It has been well said, "Truth says, 'Examine me,' while tolerance says, 'Leave me alone.'"

Scriptures for Study: Read the following passages on discernment: Acts 20:28–31; 2 Corinthians 11:3, 13–15.

Discern (2)

anakrinō

Another word translated **discern** is *anakrinō* (350). Paul declared to the Corinthians, who were anything but mature, discerning, or spiritual: "The natural man receiveth not the things of the Spirit of God: for they are foolishness unto him: neither can he know them, because they are spiritually discerned. But he that is spiritual judgeth all things, yet he himself is judged of no man" (1 Cor. 2:14–15).

"Spiritual" is *pneumatikos* (4152, see Feb. 15) which means "non-carnal"[177] or "dominated by the Spirit, in contrast to [the] natural."[178] To be truly spiritual, then, means that we are characterized not by our natural instincts or opinions but by the Holy Spirit. That is why Paul further says that the spiritual person "judgeth all things." Here is a crucial principle. Both "judgeth" and "discerned" are *anakrinō*. From about 400 BC onward, it expressed "the questioning process which leads to a judgment: to examine, cross-examine, interrogate, enquire, and investigate." Other concepts in the root *krinō* (2919) are to scrutinize and sift.[179]

As mentioned yesterday, to discern something means that we don't say, "Well, as long as that Bible teacher talks about God or Jesus, then he's okay." Rather, true spirituality and real maturity mean that we examine *everything*, that we investigate, question, scrutinize, and sift through every aspect of what is being taught and practiced, not from the perspective of the flesh, natural inclination, or personal opinion, but by the domination of the Holy Spirit and God's Word.

Sadly, most people are, just like the Corinthians, anything but *spiritual*; they are, in fact, the very opposite, looking at everything from *their* perspective not *God's*. The truly spiritual person simply does not accept everything that comes along; rather, he or she first examines it *biblically* to see if it's right or wrong.

As also mentioned yesterday, the Bereans in Acts 17:11 "searched [*anakrinō*] the scriptures daily" so they could discern that what Paul taught was true. How we need Bereans today!

Scriptures for Study: Read the following passages on discernment: 1 Timothy 6:20–21; Philippians 3:2 ("concision" is *katatomē*, 2699, a mutilation, a butchering).

Discern[er] (3)

kritikos

Hebrews 4:12 is among the strongest NT statements about discernment: "For the word of God is quick, and powerful, and sharper than any two-edged sword, piercing even to the dividing asunder of soul and spirit, and of the joints and marrow, and is a discerner of the thoughts and intents of the heart." Here the Greek behind the word **discerner** is *kritikos* (2924), which appears only here in the NT and which from Plato's day onward referred to "a competent, experienced judge."[180] What a perfect description of the Word of God! It's the Discerner, the Judge of men's thoughts and even their "intents," that is, intentions, ideas, notions, and purposes (Greek, *ennoia*, 1771).

We should also add a statement from the ancient *Didache*, also called the *Teaching of the Twelve*. This is an early second-century document, written by an unknown author, which contains teachings on church order. While it wasn't recognized as part of the canon of Scripture, it was very highly regarded in the early church (and still should be). Like Scripture, it also warned against false teachers: "Welcome every apostle on arriving, as if he were the Lord. But he must not stay beyond one day. In case of necessity, however, the next day too. If he stays three days, he is a false prophet. On departing, an apostle must not accept anything save sufficient food to carry him till his next lodging. If he asks for money, he is a false prophet" (11:4–6). As we saw back on June 13, there are many teachers who **make merchandise** of God's Word and people, who are "in it for the money." This ancient document recognized such teachers and strongly warned against them.

Matthew 7:1 always arises here: "Judge not, that ye be not judged." Well-meaning people argue, "See there, Jesus says we are not supposed to be critical of anyone; we should not criticize what they believe or say." But is that what the verse says? If it did, Paul contradicted the Lord Jesus many times. What such readers fail to do is *read the context* (vv. 2–5). What Jesus very clearly says is that we are not to judge and discern *hypocritically* or judge someone's motives and attitudes, which have nothing to do with what someone teaches. They might have the purest motive and sweetest attitude, but that's not the issue; *the issue is what they teach.*

Scriptures for Study: Read Matthew 7:1–5 for yourself and see what our Lord is saying about discernment.

Prove

dokimazō

Paul uses one other word to underscore the importance of discernment. He wrote to the Thessalonians, "Prove all things; hold fast that which is good. Abstain from all appearance of evil" (1 Thess. 5:21–22).

Prove is *dokimazō* (1381), which means "test, pronounce good, establish by trial." A related word, *dokimos* (1384), was originally used as a technical term for coins that were genuine. So, Paul is saying, "Examine everything, put everything to the test, verify each item to see if it's genuine or if it's a fake. If it's good, seize it and hold on to it. If not, however, withdraw from it."

As that great expositor John Gill wrote some 100 years before Spurgeon in London: "Abstain from all appearance of evil, of doctrinal evil. Not only open error and heresy are to be avoided, but what has any show of it, or looks like it, or carries in it a suspicion of it, or may be an occasion thereof, or lead unto it; wherefore all new words and phrases of this kind should be shunned, and the form of sound words held fast."[181]

The apostle John echoes Paul's mandate to discernment by also using *dokimazō* in 1 John 4:1, where it's translated "try": "Beloved, believe not every spirit, but try the spirits whether they are of God: because many false prophets are gone out into the world." How much clearer could Scripture be? *Don't believe every spirit.* There are several teachers today we could list who can say anything and people will believe it. They are, in fact, seldom, if ever, questioned. Likewise, there are countless claims to spiritual authority today, innumerable assertions that "this is what the Bible says," but every single one is to be examined, tested, and verified.

As I've shared many times with the sheep I shepherd that shepherds, too, must be tested and verified. This is why all pastors should stick with the *Scripture alone,* expositing only the Word of God. We should not seek for new and novel things, or search for new terms or new philosophies. If we stick with the Scripture alone, that leaves little room for error.

Scriptures for Study: Note the significance of the following occurrences of *dokimazō*: Romans 12:2; 1 Corinthians 3:13 ("try"); Galatians 6:4; Philippians 1:10 ("approve"); 1 Timothy 3:10.

Hymenaeus and Alexander

Humenaios kai Alexandros

Before leaving the crucial issue of discernment, we should also note carefully that Paul mentions two false teachers *by name* in 1 Timothy 1:8–20: **Hymenaeus and Alexander** (*Humenaios* [5211] *kai Alexandros* [223]). Hymenaeus had in some way shipwrecked his faith and later even denied the doctrine of future resurrection, as did another heretic, Philetus (2 Tim. 2:17). While the identity of Alexander is uncertain (cf. 2 Tim. 4:14), he fought Paul on doctrine, and Paul had no compunction whatsoever in naming him.

In today's tolerant, enlightened, and politically correct atmosphere, however, such an act is considered unloving and divisive, even if what is being taught is destroying biblical truth and hurting people spiritually. It's appalling how many Christians today would rather offend *Christ* instead of a false teacher. They are so afraid that an exposé might hurt some heretic's feelings that they will allow him (or her) to contradict or deny biblical truth.

Historically, heretics were routinely exposed for error. In the second century, for example, the first of the "great heretics" was the Gnostic teacher Marcion, who was exposed by men of the faith, Justin Martyr and Polycarp. In the fourth century, Arius was exposed for his apostasy that Jesus was not coequal with God and was, in fact, a created being. Augustine and others fought him passionately. (Arianism still lives today, the most recent form appearing in the popular novel *The Da Vinci Code* by Dan Brown.[182]) And how can so-called evangelicals today ignore the Reformers who denounced every rite, ritual, and sacrilege of Roman Catholicism? Instead, many tolerate its hellish doctrines and even promote unity with that fallen system.

One of the most obvious examples in our day of blatant apostasy is the teaching of Robert Schuller, who says that "the core of sin is a lack of self-esteem" and that salvation "means to be lifted from sin (psychological self-abuse . . .) and shame to self-esteem."[183] Similarly, teachers such as Joel Osteen and others categorically (and admittedly) refuse to preach on sin and define salvation in whatever nebulous terms that will not offend the "felt needs" of their listeners.

It has been well said, "A half truth presented as if it were a whole truth is an untruth." If we truly love Christ, we will fight untruth without apology. While we certainly will "[speak] the truth *in love*" (Eph. 4:15, emphasis added; July 25), we will never shy away from **speaking the truth,** a principle we'll explore tomorrow.

Scriptures for Study: Read the following passages on discernment: Colossians 2:8; 2 Peter 2:1–3.

Speaking the Truth (1)

alētheuō

While we examined the graphic word *alētheia* (**truth**) way back on February 1–3, we find another form of it in Ephesians 4:15 in the context of discernment: "But **speaking the truth** in love, may grow up into him in all things, which is the head, even Christ." Speaking the truth is not optional, not just "one approach to ministry among many." It is rather *the single mandated method of building and maintaining a church.*

As we recall, *alētheia* (225) is that which is reliable and unchanging. The Greek in our text, however, is the verb form *alētheuō* (226), which actually translates all three words. Some expositors view this word as hard or even "almost impossible to express satisfactorily in English."[184] Others agree and translate it in various ways: "grow up in the truth," "followers of truth," "holding or following the truth," "professing the truth," and even "adhere to the truth, that is, practice integrity."[185] Some modern Bible translations also get it wrong, such as the *New Living Translation*: "hold to the truth."

Such translations are inaccurate for three reasons:

First, one expositor, who writes that this word is "not normally translated 'speaking,'" is in error because that's precisely how it is usually translated. Based upon Classical Greek usage, one Greek authority writes: "The verb *alētheuō* usually means simply to speak the truth. For example, Plato argues that he who commends justice speaks the truth (*alētheuei*), and this is parallel to his earlier statement that such a man speaks truly, whilst he who commends injustice speaks falsely (*pseudoito*, *The Republic*, 589c)."[186] Additionally, the verb tense (a nominative plural masculine present participle) yields the idea "continually speaking the truth."

Second, the context shows that Paul has been discussing the speaking gifts and now makes the obvious assertion that the men called to those offices are to speak the truth.

Third, the only other instance of *alētheuō* in the NT is in Galatians 4:16: "Am I therefore become your enemy, because I tell you the truth?" The Greek here is another present participle (*alētheuōn*, nominative singular masculine), yielding the idea, "Have I become your enemy because I am continually telling you the truth?" Of course, the answer is a resounding "yes." Most people do not wish to be told the truth *at all*, much less *continually*. The truth, however, is the only thing the Christian should speak.

Scriptures for Study: Read Proverbs 8:7 and Zechariah 8:16 and note the mandate to speak the truth.

Speaking the Truth (2)

alētheuō

Concluding our meditation on Ephesians 4:15, we are to be constantly **speaking the truth**, that which is reliable and unchanging.

Commentator Albert Barnes makes this excellent statement, which includes not only preachers but all true Christians:

> The truth is to be spoken—the simple, unvarnished truth. This is the way to avoid error, and this is the way to preserve others from error. In opposition to all trick, and art, and cunning, and fraud, and deception, Christians are to speak the simple truth, and nothing but the truth. Every statement which they make should be unvarnished truth; every promise which they make should be true; every representation which they make of the sentiments of others should be simple truth. Truth is the representation of things as they are; and there is no virtue that is more valuable in a Christian than the love of simple truth.[187]

Sadly, however, that is anything but the norm today. The vocabulary of much of the church today is politically correct catch-phrases, sentimental expressions, and psychobabble. Instead of confronting false teachers with their error, we embrace them with such schmaltziness as, "Our brother brings up an intriguing, thought-provoking point," or "Our brother is entitled to his own ideas, and we should be open to it." No, we are supposed to speak the **truth**.

What is so difficult about this principle? Why do so many people avoid, redefine, or ignore the truth? The answer is simple: *Knowing the truth makes us responsible*. As long as we don't know the truth, we don't have to do anything with it or act accordingly. Most people don't want to hear the truth because they're comfortable in their own ideas and philosophy and want to continue in them without challenge.

On the importance of doctrinal preaching, one great preacher comments: "If you take away the doctrine you have taken away the backbone of the manhood of Christianity—its sinew, muscle, strength, and glory."[188] He then illustrates that those who wish to abandon doctrine can be compared to sailors who would go to sea without charts.

What a perfect picture of our day! Wanted today are showy churches and glitzy ministries, but shunned is the preaching of truth. Many Christian leaders think they know more than God, more than the inspired apostle Paul, more than many great leaders in church history. As a result, we are seeing the shipwrecks.

Scriptures for Study: Read the following scriptures, again noting the mandate to speak the truth: Acts 26:25; 1 Timothy 2:7.

[Speaking the Truth] in Love

en agapē

We never want to fail to mention the controlling agent in **speaking the truth**. Lest our speaking be harsh, mean-spirited, insensitive, or arrogant, Paul adds a principle in Ephesians 4:15 that must control our speaking—we are to speak the truth **in love** (see Jan. 19–21).

While Paul wrote many strong, sometimes even scathing, rebukes to the believers in Corinth, for example, no one there could have accused him of being unkind or unloving. Likewise, this will keep us from speaking rudely, unkindly, arrogantly, or overbearingly. A pastor must never "browbeat" God's people; neither should any believer be arrogant, overbearing, or use "high-pressure techniques" in personal witnessing. Our goal is to *humbly* and *lovingly* point people to the Lord and His truth.

Further, love is the balancing agent of conviction and courage. When the child of God has convictions and courageously stands on them, he will be called "closed-minded," "intolerant," "hard-nosed," and many other things, but when love is the balancing agent, people will take notice.

One commentator ably demonstrates the comparison of love and truth by pointing out that speaking the truth without love makes us *ungracious*, while speaking only love with no truth makes us *unfaithful*.[189] In other words, "raw truth" can alienate the people we are trying to reach, while "uncontrolled love" can suppress the very truth we need to share.

The famous early nineteenth-century missionary to China and Bible translator Robert Morrison (1782–1834) tells the story of when as a young student, perhaps about sixteen years of age, he once ate breakfast with Caesar Malan, a Swiss Reformed preacher in Geneva. Upon discovering that Morrison was a young student of divinity, Malan said, "Well, my young friend, see that you hold up the lamp of truth to let the people see. Hold it up, hold it up, and trim it well. But remember this: You must not dash the lamp in people's faces; that would not help them to see." Morrison adds that he remembered those words often throughout his life, and so should we.[190]

Scriptures for Study: Read 1 Corinthians 3:1–2; 12:1; 14:20, 39, noting how Paul uses the term of endearment *brethren* as he delivered the truth to those carnal Christians.

Labor

kopiaō

The Greek verb *kopiaō* (2872) and the noun *kopos* (2873) appear several times in the NT (about twenty-six and twenty respectively), and they underscore a dramatic difference between the **old man** (see Mar. 9) and the **new man** (see Jan. 1). While the old man will **steal** (see Mar. 15) and try to get money using other "shortcuts," the new man desires honest **labor** (Eph. 4:28).

We've all seen the "get-rich-quick" mentality, for example, whether it takes the form of winning the lottery, the latest system for buying real estate, or the newest "pyramid scheme." There's certainly nothing wrong with riches and money in itself, but it's "the *love* of money [that] is the root of all evil" (1 Tim. 6:10, emphasis added). And it is, indeed, that love of money that drives the "get-rich-quick" mentality.

In contrast, the godly Christian doesn't live like that. *Kopiaō* speaks of "exertion and toil," "the process of becoming tired," and the "consequent fatigue and exhaustion."[191] Peter used this word, for example, when he told the Lord that he and his companions "toiled" all night fishing and had caught nothing (Luke 5:5). Nothing more is known of a certain Mary whom Paul simply greets as one who "bestowed much labour" on Him and other servants of Christ (Rom. 16:6). He praised three others in the Roman church—Tryphena, Tryphosa, and Persis—for the same reason. All these godly servants tirelessly and sacrificially served the Lord.

Especially important is the duty of a pastor to labor in his study of the Word of God: "Let the elders that rule well be counted worthy of double honour, especially they who labour in the word and doctrine" (1 Tim. 5:17). In contrast to today's tendency to stay out of the "Pastor's Study," Paul makes it clear that the responsibility of a pastor is to exhaust himself in the study of the Word of God.

What is God's promise for faithful labor? We'll be able to say with Paul, "I may rejoice in the day of Christ, that I have not run in vain, neither laboured in vain" (Phil. 2:16; cf. 1 Cor. 15:58; Heb. 6:10).

We'll look at another word tomorrow (**working**) that again emphasizes our labor.

Scriptures for Study: What's the promise of 1 Corinthians 3:8? 🕮 Read of Paul's "labors" and "weariness" (both *kopos*) in 2 Corinthians 11:23–33 and compare it with your own service. This humbles us all.

Working

ergazomai

So important is our **labor** for the Lord that Paul is not satisfied with just using *kopiaō* (2872) in Ephesians 4:28 but adds "working with his hands the thing which is good, that he may have to give to him that needeth."

Working is *ergazomai* (2038), which speaks of work in general, such as working "in a field (Matt. 21:28) or at a trade (Acts 18:3), or even 'to do business' (Matt. 25:16)"[192] Not only are we working to the point of exhaustion (*kopiaō*), but we are doing it systematically, doing it every day in our field, trade, business, or Christian service.

At the very foundation of society is the necessity of work. *Even before the Fall*, man was required to work (Gen. 2:15), which then became even more necessary, and much more difficult, after the Fall (3:17–19). So foundational is work that Paul told the Thessalonians that "if any would not work, neither should he eat" (2 Thess. 3:10). Every Jewish rabbi was taught a trade, for as the rabbis said, "If you do not teach your son a trade, you teach him to be a thief." As always, our Lord is our model, and he was a carpenter. What a principle that is in our day when so many people have no work ethic, when many young people are not being taught how to work.

Let us also interject, the concepts of "entitlements" and "welfare" were creations of political liberalism, which is by definition socialism, "the redistribution of wealth." There are certainly cases when people need help, such as in 1 Corinthians 16:1–3, where the needs of people in the Jerusalem church were met by the believers in the churches in Galatia (cf. Gal. 6:10), but the welfare system in our society is horribly abused. People who work support millions who *can* but *won't*. This is undeniable in the countless documented cases where people say, "Why should I work when I can get money by not working?" So, not only does Scripture declare it, but even common sense tells us that if a man can work, he works, or he does not eat. Biblical *principles* always have practical *reasons*.

So, whether we're working at our secular job or working in Christian service, we work systematically and always to God's glory and to the good of those in need.

Scriptures for Study: What is promised to those who work "good" (Rom. 2:10)? 🕮 In 1 Thessalonians 4:11–12, what is to be our motive in everything we do?

Followers (1)

mimētēs

The apostle Paul says something staggering in Ephesians 5:1: "Be ye therefore followers of God as dear children." **Followers** translates *mimētēs* (3402), from which we get our English word *mimic* and which is the most literal translation and most vivid picture.

As one Greek authority tells us, this word goes as far back as the sixth century BC in secular Greek. According to Aristotle, at the beginning of civilization, man learned skills by mimicking animals. For example, weaving and spinning were learned from spiders, and house building was learned from birds. Plays, paintings, sculptures, and poetry were merely "imitations of reality." Even an actor was called a *mimos* (a "mimer").

Commentator William Barclay (*Ephesians*) also observes, "Imitation was a main part in the training of an orator. The teachers of rhetoric declared that the learning of oratory depended on three things—theory, imitation, and practice. The main part of their training was the study and the imitation of the masters who had gone before."[193]

Paul, however, brought this word to the NT and gave it deeper meaning. Think about it a moment in light of our world today; people mimic athletes, entertainers, world leaders, military figures, and the like. But the Christian is to mimic God; we are to copy His character, attitudes, and actions. As the old adage goes, "Imitation is the sincerest of flattery."[194] I've always been amazed by impressionists who can mimic famous people so perfectly. But far greater is the Christian who mimics God. *While the first certainly takes great talent, the latter takes a miracle*. It's not talent that enables us to mimic God, but rather the miracle of the Holy Spirit as He produces "the fruit of the Spirit" (Gal. 5:22–23).

Spurgeon declared: "While it thus humbles us, this precept ennobles us; for what a grand thing it is to be imitators of God! . . . Time has been when men gloried in studying Homer, and their lives were trained to heroism by his martial verse. Alexander carried the *Iliad* about with him in a casket studded with jewels, and his military life greatly sprung out of his imitation of the warriors of Greece and Troy. Ours is a nobler ambition by far than that which delights in battles; we desire to imitate the God of peace, whose name is love."[195]

We'll continue these thoughts tomorrow.

Scriptures for Study: It's amazing how many times in Scripture we read that we are to mimic God. Read the following verses, noting how we are to imitate Him: Matthew 5:48 (for "perfect," see July 13); John 15:12; Philippians 2:3–8; 1 Peter 2:21–22.

Followers (2)

mimētēs

In Ephesians 5:1, Paul provides a vivid example of what it means to be a *mimētēs* (3402) a "mimic" of God. He says that we do so "as dear children." Indeed, there is nothing more imitative than a child. This is one way in which he or she learns.

I've never forgotten a television commercial I saw many years ago. While it was short and had no dialogue, the impact was powerful. A father and his little boy, who looked to be about two years old, were sitting together under a tree. The dad reached into his shirt pocket, retrieved a pack of cigarettes, lit one, and laid the pack down between him and his son. Having seen what his father had done, the little boy picked up the pack and looked at it. The camera froze on that picture, and the point was made.

When one reads Paul's entreaty, the first reaction can easily be one of question. Is it really possible to mimic God? Isn't that somewhat naïve? Isn't that a bit exaggerated? Didn't Paul get a little carried away? How can we who are sinful and who live in a sinful world be mimics of God? The answer to those questions is found in viewing the attributes (characteristics) of God.

First, there are God's "natural attributes." These are those characteristics that describe what God is in His *nature* and include His omniscience, omnipotence, omnipresence, eternality, sovereignty, and immutability. These attributes are what are called "incommunicable," that is, unable to be passed on to man.

Second, however, are God's "moral attributes." These are the characteristics that describe God's *character* and what He does; they include His holiness, righteousness, justice, mercy, grace, and love. These attributes, on the other hand, are "communicable," that is, able to be passed on to men. God can (and does) communicate holiness, righteousness, justice, mercy, grace, and love to men so we can manifest them in their lives.

So, how can we mimic God? *By manifesting His moral attributes*. We can indeed mimic God by possessing His "character attributes."

Scriptures for Study: Read the following verses, noting one of God's moral attributes in each and the challenge for us to imitate it: 1 Peter 1:16; 1 Timothy 6:11; Philippians 4:8–9; James 2:13; Hebrews 12:28–29.

Fornication

porneia

In the last two days we examined *true* love, which is to be mimics of God. In contrast, however, is *counterfeit* love, which is impurity of life. The apostle Paul lists several characteristics of counterfeit love in Ephesians 5:3–7, which we'll examine over the next few days.

The first characteristic is **fornication**. The Greek here is *porneia* (4202). Originally it referred to prostitution. It's derived, in fact, from the related word *pornē* (4204), which means "prostitute" (Matt. 21:31; 1 Cor. 6:15). It was used in the Septuagint to refer not only to common prostitution, but religious prostitution that was part of the fertility rites of Baal worship. By sexual relations with temple prostitutes, humans, supposedly, could share in the fertilizing power of and cosmic harmony with the fertility god Baal.

In later rabbinical language, which carried over into the NT, *porneia* came to be used for any sexual relations outside of marriage, including: premarital sex, extramarital sex, homosexuality, lesbianism, sodomy, pedophilia, incest, and bestiality. This is vividly seen in the Graeco-Roman world, which had become so perverted that all these activities were indulged in without shame or scruple, not only by the common people but by the social elite as well.

Does that not sound like our own day? While there are a few weak outcries against sexual perversion, indifference is the chief attitude. "What's the big deal?" it's argued. "After all, what's done in private is up to each person's decision."

Even the word *fornication* is avoided (*even by Christians*). Instead of "fornication" or even "premarital sex," we hear phrases such as "discovering one's sexuality" and "living together." Instead of "adultery," we hear "having an affair." Instead of "homosexuality" (much less "sodomy"), we hear "gay community" and "alternate lifestyle." Instead of "pornography," we hear "art." Man changes his terminology because he does not recognize that Satan has perverted God's creation! Even modern Bible translations soften *porneia* to the word *immorality* instead of what it really means—*fornication*. What's the difference? According to Webster, *immorality* is simply that which the morals of a particular society does not approve, while *fornication* is the same no matter where it is found.

So, in contrast to that philosophy, both ancient and modern, any sexual relations outside of marriage are forbidden: "Let it not be once named among you, as becometh saints" (Eph. 5:3).

Scriptures for Study: What's the source of fornication and other evil (Matt. 15:19)? 🕮 What specific type of fornication was going on right within the church at Corinth (1 Cor. 5:1)?

Uncleanness

akatharsia

The second characteristic of counterfeit love is **uncleanness** (Eph. 5:3). The Greek *akatharsia* (167) is a broader term than *porneia* (**fornication**). Paul uses this word in Ephesians 4:19 to show that man is so far gone, so past even feeling guilt for his sin, that he's totally given over to filthy living.

Akatharsia is actually tied in with the Old Testament concepts of "clean" and "unclean." One could become "unclean" in several ways—by eating unclean meat, for example—so Paul "borrows" the term, brings it into the Christian life, and shows that everything propagated by Satan's counterfeit love is unclean, impure, and polluted. Not only are immoral acts impure, but immoral *thoughts* and *fantasies* are impure. Today there are books written about people's sexual fantasies and the world has the audacity to call such things "love"!

One insidious example of such uncleanness (if not outright fornication) is the vileness of *pornography*. In conjunction with the word *graphē* (1124), which means "writing," it's from *pornos* that this term is derived, and which means a writing or picture of sexual sin and involves all the meanings listed yesterday. But while certain types of pornography are considered "bad," other types, such as *Playboy* magazine, actually have a certain degree of respectability and are not really considered pornography by some people, but rather "art." In recent years indescribably revolting paintings and sculptures have been displayed in art galleries and are even paid for with tax money.

According to *Forbes Magazine* (5-25-01), pornographic magazines gross $1 billion annually, pornography on the Internet another $1 billion, pay-per-view movies $128 million, and adult videos add between $500 million and $1.8 billion, yielding a total of $2.6 to $3.9 billion per year. If that's not enough to appall us, how about the complicity of local and state governments that gather sales tax on such perversion? After all, it's argued, "It's just another business," and "We can't regulate morality."

Many a man (even among Christians) has started with pornography and ended up not being able to have normal relations with his wife or even being transformed into a child molester. Such conduct must "not be once named among [Christians]" (Eph. 5:3). We must constantly be on guard against uncleanness and "abstain from all appearance of evil" (1 Thess. 5:22).

Scriptures for Study: What must we do about such sins as uncleanness and fornication (2 Cor. 12:21; Col. 3:5)? 🕮 Instead of uncleanness, to what has God called us (1 Thess. 4:7)?

Covetousness

pleonexia

The third characteristic of counterfeit love is **covetousness** (Eph. 5:3). The Greek *pleonexia* (4124) means "greedy desire to have more," which is a good definition of the English *covetousness.* I recently asked a godly Christian man, a dairy farmer who was visiting our church, "How's business?" He answered, "We're paying the bills and the family is provided for. That's enough." I rejoiced in his godly attitude. The world says, "I have to have *more*," while God says, "I will supply your *needs*" (Matt. 6:33; Phil. 4:19).

Like *akatharsia* (**uncleanness**), this word is used in Ephesians 4:19, where it's translated "greediness." Man's underlying motive is greed, lust, and self-gratification. That fact is intensified all the more in sexual matters. Why? Because the human sexual drive is strong and if left to itself, becomes perverted in unimaginable ways.

It's fascinating to notice that man mistakes all of what we have seen thus far to be "love," when all of this is actually the exact opposite, *hate*. Why? Because love is self*less,* not self*ish*; because love *gives* instead of *takes*; because love *satisfies* instead of *gratifies*. True love always meets the true *need*, while gratification simply feeds *lust*.

It's also significant that **covetousness** is often an "ignored sin." I read of a Catholic priest who reported that during his many years of hearing confessions, he heard of all kinds of sin, even crimes, but not once did he ever hear anyone confess **covetousness**. Indeed, we don't think about this being sin, but it most certainly is. Paul goes on in verse 5, in fact, to say the "covetous man, who is an idolater, hath [no] inheritance in the kingdom of Christ and of God." Since Ephesus was a key city in ancient pagan worship (e.g., Diana worship), Paul's readers immediately understood what he was saying.

Here is a pointed challenge. As the Ephesian believers purged their lives of idolatry, we should do the same and not allow anything pagan to touch our lives. From horoscopes, to Halloween, to holly, *Christianity makes no peace with idolatry*. How tragic it is that many Christians, including preachers, just don't seem to recognize how much God hates idolatry and *anything* reminiscent of it! And covetousness is just another form of idolatry.

Scriptures for Study: What is our Lord's counsel in Luke 12:15? 🕮 In 2 Peter 2:1–3, who uses covetousness as a tool?

Filthiness

aischrotes

While the first three characteristics of counterfeit love involve impure *acts*, the next three concern impure *speech*. The fourth characteristic, then, is **filthiness** (Eph. 5:4). The root of *aischrotes* (151) is *aisch*, which originally referred to that which was ugly and disgraceful and came to refer to that which is simply indecent. Spiros Zodhiates summarizes its significance:

> Impropriety, a summarizing improper conduct whether in action or word or even thought and intent; indecorum of any kind; conduct which when exposed by the light makes the person ashamed of himself; ugly, shameful conduct of any kind; conduct which is contrary to a person who follows after God (only in Eph. 5:4). Attachment and conformity to God requires a conduct of which God is not ashamed and which could not bring shame to the person when it is brought to light.[196]

How filled our world is today with such filthiness! I was reminded here of Oscar Wilde's novel *The Picture of Dorian Gray*. The story describes a painted portrait of a man that ages and grows ugly to coincide with the man's life of immorality, while the man himself remains youthful and handsome. A movie was actually made from the book in 1945, and even then the special effects were good enough to show the features of the man in the portrait changing from attractiveness to revulsion.

What's interesting, however, is that while the story seems to condemn such a lifestyle, Wilde was actually defending it, and, in fact, defending his own homosexuality. In chapter 2, for example, he wrote, "The only way to get rid of a temptation is to yield to it." In defense of his writing, which critics called immoral, he wrote in the Preface of the novel, "There is no such thing as a moral or immoral book. Books are well written, or badly written. That is all."

The same attitude exists in our day, when men are amoral and everything is relative. Like the character in his novel, however, Wilde's filthiness led to his ruin. After a two-year prison term for sodomy, Wilde's health, money, fame, and even writing talent were gone. Lying on his deathbed from brain inflammation, he sought peace by converting to Roman Catholicism.

There is, therefore, whether in word or deed, no place for ugliness, indecency, and impropriety in the believer's life.

Scriptures for Study: From where did our Lord say that evil speech comes (Matt. 12:34; 15:19)?

Foolish Talking

morologia

The fifth characteristic of counterfeit love is **foolish talking** (Eph. 5:4). This term, and the next, are much more subtle and prevalent than **filthiness**. Many people would never live or speak blatant filthiness, but they would (and do) practice these other two.

Foolish talking, which appears only here in the NT, translates *morologia* (3473). The Greek *moros* (3474; English *moron*) means "silly, stupid, foolish," and *logia* comes from *log*, which means "word or discourse." The idea conveyed here, then, is the speaking of things that are foolish and pointless. Writing to a pastor, Paul uses this idea again: "But avoid foolish [*moros*] questions, and genealogies, and contentions, and strivings about the law; for they are unprofitable and vain" (Titus 3:9), which is wise counsel for a pastor. Solomon adds, "The tongue of the wise useth knowledge aright: but the mouth of fools poureth out foolishness" (Prov. 15:2).

There is no point in conversing with the lost person who babbles on about the foolishness of man. But may we also submit, neither is there any point in conversing with a Christian who does the same thing. How much talk there is today about nothing! Today's "talk shows" (secular and Christian) are filled with such pointless discussion. We hear many give their opinions, but no one presents or even wants the absolutes contained in God's Word. Indeed, many want "a forum for opinion," not a statement of truth. That was exactly what Paul declared to the Corinthians. In essence, he said, "I did not come to the Greek forum to debate some new philosophy, but rather to preach the truth of the Gospel" (1 Cor. 2:1–5).

Tragically, may we also add, there's even a lot of "moronic speech" spewing from pulpits today. From "feel-good" sermonettes to psychological babbling, truth is absent. Where the Word of God is not heeded, a Christian should not even waste his time. If people do not want the truth, if they do not want what God says, there is nothing left to say. Let us not *waste* our time on foolish talking, but rather *invest* our time in truth.

Scriptures for Study: Read 2 Timothy 2:15–17, noting what the pastor *should* do, what he should *not* do, and what will be the *consequence* if he fails in those actions.

Jesting

eutrapelia

The sixth and final characteristic of counterfeit love is **jesting** (Eph. 5:4). *Eutrapelia* (2160, only here) is a fascinating word. The prefix *eu* (2095) means "good" or "well" (English *eulogy*, "good words," and *eugenetics*, "good genes"). The root *trepō* (not in the NT) means "to turn." *Eutrapelia*, then, means "that which easily turns." Within this context about speech, the idea is to turn something spoken into a different meaning. Not only are off-color jokes and stories included, but also twisting innocent words into a double meaning.

It's significant that Paul uses this word because historically the Ephesians were masters of this and were known for producing humorous orators. An ancient expression goes, "I am a facetious cavalier because I was born in Ephesus." How prevalent that is today! Many comedians are masters of this kind of "humor." They can take something innocent, even something pure, and turn it into something filthy.

So, this is not the speech that is to be typical of the Christian. Sadly, however, this has infiltrated the church in *subtle form*. While not vulgar or suggestive, more and more the popularity of Christian speakers is gauged by how funny and entertaining they are. While we're certainly not against all humor in preaching, we must be *very* careful and sparing in its use, because we're not in church to laugh or be entertained, but rather to worship and "grow in grace, and in the knowledge of our Lord and Saviour Jesus Christ" (2 Pet. 3:18).

Isn't it significant that while few people will come to hear the exposition of Scripture, *thousands* will flock to hear a "Christian comedian" or a "preacher" who tells plenty of funny stories to spice up his "sermons." But is it not also significant that not one verse of Scripture records our Lord telling a joke?

The modern advice is, "Warm up your audience with a joke and sprinkle in others throughout your sermon." But where does Scripture even suggest such a worldly idea? Nowhere in his letters does Paul write, "You know, a funny thing happened to me when I was on the road to Damascus." Why doesn't Scripture say, "People will more easily accept truth if we make it funny?" *Because sin, salvation, and doctrine are not funny*! They are life-and-death issues that must be presented with reverence, **sobriety** (see May 23), and **gravity** (see May 24). If I may be so bold, *people who need humor do not love truth.*

Scriptures for Study: Read Peter's sermon on the Day of Pentecost (Acts 2:14–38) and Paul's sermon in Antioch in Pisidia (13:16–41). Do you find even the slightest hint of joke telling or other entertainment in their preaching?

Think

logizomai

Among his final words to the believers in Philippi, Paul wrote, "Finally, brethren, whatsoever things are true, whatsoever things are honest, whatsoever things are just, whatsoever things are pure, whatsoever things are lovely, whatsoever things are of good report; if there be any virtue, and if there be any praise, think on these things" (4:8).

What a profound statement! **Think** is *logizomai* (3049), which means "to put together with one's mind, to count, to occupy oneself with reckonings or calculations."[197] While in Classical Greek, especially in the writings of Plato, it spoke of non-emotional thinking that desires to grasp and apply facts, it later added the idea of subjective, emotional, and volitional character. As he often did, however, Paul gives this word group an even deeper significance, namely, it "must be oriented to the facts established by God," with the result that it now "becomes the term for the 'judgment of faith.'" In other words, all our thinking, pondering, and questioning are put into the context of God's standards.[198]

It's now easy to see exactly what Paul was saying to the Philippians and what he's saying to us today. How are we to think? Are we to think in the cold, calculated, detached way of the philosopher? Indeed not. While we certainly use the mind and calculate facts, those things always apply in some subjective way, they affect our will and character, and they are weighed according to the balance of God's standards.

Paul then goes one step farther to specify several specific things that we should think about, weigh, and apply. One commentator calls these "six ethical terms."[199] We have already considered three of those subjects in previous studies.

First, we should think about the things that are "true" (**truth**, see Feb. 1–3), that is, think about things as they really are, not as they are concealed, falsified, or misrepresented.

Second, we are to think about things that are "honest" (**gravity**, see May 24), things that are solemn, dignified, sublime, and majestic.

Third, we are to think about things that are **pure** (see May 12), things that are morally, and even doctrinally, holy and chaste.

In the next few days, we'll examine the other subjects Paul lists here. As Proverbs 23:7 declares: "For as he thinketh in his heart, so is he." Someone once said, "You might not be what you think you are, but *what* you think, you are."

Scriptures for Study: What great conclusion does Paul come to in Romans 3:28 ("conclude" is *logizomai*)? 🕮 What does he also conclude in Philippians 3:13 ("count" is *logizomai*)?

Just (Righteous)

dikaios

The fourth subject on which we should **think** is that which is **just** (Phil. 4:8). The Greek *dikaios* (1342) is a very common NT word and means "upright" and "righteous."

In a strictly social sense, the ancient Greeks called someone righteous if he conformed to accepted social virtues. This was transformed in the Septuagint, of course, as all virtue is based upon God's Law. There, *dikaios* translates the Hebrew *saddiq* (6662H) some 180 times (e.g., Gen. 7:1; Prov. 10:30; etc.), but also translates several other terms, such as *yēsēr* (3477H, "upright," Ps. 119:137).

The NT uses this word (and related words) in several ways. While it occurs in almost every book, it's Paul who makes the greatest and most frequent use of it. He applies it to God (Rom. 3:26), Christ (2 Tim. 4:8), man (Rom. 1:17; 3:10), and even things, as here in our text (also Rom. 7:12; Col. 4:1).

At the very foundation of man's salvation from sin is the issue of *dikaios*. Scripture first declares with blazing clarity that man's righteousness is not enough to save him. Neither is keeping the Law enough (Rom. 3:20; "justified," *dikaioō*, 1344), nor doing good works (Titus 3:5; "righteousness," *dikaiosunē*, 1343). As Jesus declared, "Except your righteousness shall exceed the righteousness of the scribes and Pharisees"—which was a practical impossibility because they knew all the Law—"ye shall in no case enter into the kingdom of heaven" (Matt. 5:20).

Scripture then declares with equal precision that it's only by the righteousness of Christ that we are saved (Rom. 3:26, 28; 5:1; Gal. 2:16), a righteousness that we receive by faith alone (Rom. 1:17).

With that foundation, since the just live by faith, they should now *think* about things that are just. As the beloved Puritan Matthew Henry writes, "Whatsoever things are . . . agreeable to the rules of justice and righteousness in all our dealings with men, and without the impurity or mixture of sin."[200]

More recently, William Hendrickson says it well: "Having received from God righteousness, both of imputation and impartation, believers should think righteous thoughts. They should, in their mind, gratefully meditate on God's righteous acts (Rev. 15:3), appreciate righteousness in others, and should plan righteous words and deeds."[201]

Scriptures for Study: What advantage does the righteous person have, according to James 5:16? 🕮 In 1 John 2:29, what does doing righteous things indicate?

Lovely

prosphilēs

The fifth subject on which we should **think** is that which is **lovely** (Phil. 4:8). The adjective *prosphilēs* (4375), which appears only here in the NT, is a compound, comprised of *pros* (4314), "to" or "toward," and *phileō* (5368), **love**. As we learned back on January 21, *phileō* speaks of esteem, high regard, and tender affection.

Most commentators say that this word means acceptable, pleasing, and amiable, so these are the things we are to think about and do. While that is certainly true, there is a deeper principle here that better drives the lesson home.

In light of the word *phileō*, the eminent nineteenth-century Scottish Greek scholar John Eadie points out that this word actually was somewhat common among classical writers and "signifies what is dear to anyone, or has in it such a quality as engages affection."[202] In other words, as another commentator explains, its "fundamental meaning is 'that which calls forth love.' . . . Thus, the Christian's mind is to be set on things that elicit from others . . . admiration and affection."[203]

What a challenge! The Christian is to think and do things that will endear him or her to others, things that not only will *express* love *to* others but also *inspire* love *from* others. William Tyndale captured the thought in his 1534 translation with "whatsoever things pertain to love."

So, how do we accomplish that? It seems pretty obvious, does it not? We certainly will not endear ourselves to others, much less to God, by lying, stealing, cursing, gossiping, losing our temper, or any other such ungodly behavior. Rather, we will elicit admiration and affection from God and others by godly behavior. And the only way we can *do* and *say* such things is to *think* about such things.

Scriptures for Study: Read 1 Corinthians 13. What actions and attitudes will endear us to others?

Good Report

euphēmos

The sixth and final subject on which we should **think** is that which is of **good report** (Phil. 4:8). *Euphēmos* (2163) is another interesting word that appears only in this NT instance. Like *prosphilēs* (**lovely**), we find here another compound, consisting of *eu* (2095), "good, well," and *phēmē* (5345), "rumor, fame."

While ancient superstitious pagans used *euphēmos* in the sense of thinking or saying only words that would be good omens, the essential idea of positive words is true. The word has, therefore, been translated in many ways by commentators and translators: *of good repute, admirable, honorable, high-toned, auspicious,* and others. Whichever word one chooses, this word suggests at least three applications.

First, we should think and talk about things that are *worth* thinking and talking about, things that are appealing. We've all sat around a dinner table, for example, when conversation that started out good slowly turned frivolous, foolish, or even inane. While there's certainly nothing wrong with talking about the weather or perhaps our favorite novelist's newest thriller, our thoughts and speech should major on high and noble things.

Second, we should think and talk about things that are likely to win others and not offend them. This brings us to our English word *euphemism*, which comes directly from *euphēmos*. A euphemism, in fact, as Webster tells us, is "the substitution of an agreeable or inoffensive expression for one that may offend or suggest something unpleasant." We often say, for example, that someone "passed away" instead of "died." Perhaps the most infamous euphemism of all was Hitler's "The Final Solution," which actually meant the extermination of all European Jews and other "inferior races." So, while we certainly don't refer here to the absurdities of certain "politically correct" phrases, our desire should always be to guard against offending.

Third, we should think and talk about things that are positive and constructive rather than negative and destructive. One way we can think destructively is by dwelling on past sin and thereby being defeated by that memory. Yes, sin should grieve us, and our desire is victory over it, but it should not depress us and rob us of joy. Such thoughts are not of "good report."

While this brings us to the end of the six ethical things that should comprise the topics of our thinking, Paul adds two other profound words, which we'll examine next.

Scriptures for Study: Read the following verses, noting things that are simply foolish and not worth thinking and talking about: 1 Timothy 1:4; 4:7; 6:4–5; 2 Timothy 2:23; Titus 3:9.

Virtue

aretē

While the apostle Paul lists six ethical values on which the Christian should think, he adds two additional words in Philippians 4:8: **virtue** and **praise**. These words might seem out of place at first. After all, aren't the other six adequate to outline what our thought life should be? But notice that we have not only "six whatsoevers" but also "two anythings." In other words, the "two anythings" seem to be added to include anything the "six whatsoevers" might not cover. Paul wants to be all-inclusive, and he does so brilliantly and practically.

Virtue is *aretē* (703), which actually has a strong foundation in Greek philosophy. Among the Classical writers, it was a very broad term that spoke of excellence of any kind, such as mental excellence, moral quality, or physical power. Especially to the Stoics it spoke of the highest good of humanity.

It's extremely interesting, therefore, that Paul would even use this word (which he does only here) because of its obvious idea of human merit and achievement. So, why would he do that? J. B. Lightfoot, a recognized authority on Philippians, no doubt has the answer when he suggests that Paul was telling his readers, "Whatever value may reside in your old heathen conception of virtue."[204]

In other words, recognizing that there is a certain amount of good in human morality, Paul is saying in essence, "If there is *anything* excellent, moral, or valuable, even in general human virtue, even in a purely secular way, even in the teachings of your old philosophical system, think on it." While he couldn't list every possible moral excellence, he could at least use a word that would encompass any *possible* good thing that he hadn't already covered.

A simple acrostic might help us with this word. Let us think on things that are: **V**aluable, **I**deal, **R**ight, **T**asteful, **U**seful, and **E**xcellent.

Scriptures for Study: Another oddity is that relatively uneducated Peter also uses *aretē* in the only other occurrences of this word in the NT (1 Pet. 2:9, "praises"; 2 Pet. 1:3, 5). Most significantly, read 2 Peter 1:3–10, noting his list of godly virtues.

Praise (1)

epainos

Yesterday we noted that Paul adds two additional words in Philippians 4:8 to describe the subjects of the believer's thought life: **virtue** and **praise**. To be all-inclusive, he adds these to cover anything that the other six terms might not include.

Praise translates the noun *epainos* (1868), a compound comprised of the prefix *epi* (1909), "upon," and the noun *ainos* (136), "praise." Its basic meaning is "applause" and speaks of commendation, approval, and public recognition. The verb *aineō* (134), for example, is used in the Gospels to describe a crowd's praise of the Lord Jesus. At His birth, we see both angels (Luke 2:13) and shepherds praising Him (2:20). Upon His "Triumphal Entry" into Jerusalem (Luke 19:37), we can easily picture the crowd waving their hands and shouting their praise.

Epainos, then, along with the verb *epaineō* (1867), is found some seventeen times in the NT. A somewhat negative example appears in the Parable of the Unjust Steward, where a rich man "commended" his steward for his shrewd business dealings (Luke 16:8). The opposite was true of Paul, as he could *not* praise the Corinthian believers for some of their activities (1 Cor. 11:22).

We then find *epainos* used many times for the praise, commendation, approval, and public recognition that belong only to God. Three times Paul uses it in Ephesians 1 to declare: "To the praise of the glory of his grace, wherein he hath made us accepted in the beloved" (v. 6; cf. vv. 12, 14).

What, then, is Paul saying in our text? We should think on things that are worthy of praise, things that deserve praise. In short, we are to think on things that give *God* praise.

So, Paul's "six whatsoevers" and "two anythings" are to be those things on which we are to think. And how can we do that? One expositor says it well: "We have to make deliberate choices to think profitable thoughts. Our minds will not automatically drift into these channels. Most of us are mentally lazy. And because of the fall, we have a bias toward the degenerate. The secret of a guided thought life is an active assertion of the will, in cooperation with the Holy Spirit, to 'think on these things.'"[205]

We'll examine another word for **praise** tomorrow.

Scriptures for Study: What is one way we can praise God, according to 1 Peter 1:7? 🕮 What does 1 Corinthians 4:5 declare about praise toward us?

Glory [and] Praise (2)

doxa

The most common word translated **praise** in the NT is *doxa* (1391), which is also translated even more often as **glory**. Like *charis* (**grace**) and other NT words, here is one of the most dramatic examples of NT usage transforming a word's meaning. In secular Greek, *doxa* means opinion or conjecture, especially favorable human opinion, which then includes an evaluation placed by others, such as fame, repute, honor, or praise.

Coming to the NT, however, we see a totally different picture. While the ideas of repute and honor are still present, the concept of opinion vanishes entirely; of the some 165 occurrences, not one speaks of this (neither do any of the post-apostolic fathers use it that way). In other words, no longer does the subjective, shifting, selfish opinion of man matter a whit. Rather, all that remains and all that matters is the eternal constant of God's fame, repute, honor, and praise.

Even more significant, however, the ideas of "radiance" and "glory" were added to *doxa*, concepts that were foreign to secular Greek. It now denotes "divine and heavenly radiance, the loftiness and majesty of God, and even the being of God."[206] As Hebrews 1:3 declares, Christ is "the brightness of his glory, and the express image of his [the Father's] person." (We'll examine that amazing word **brightness** tomorrow.)

This change of meaning is due to a transformation in the Septuagint. It's there that "opinion" disappeared and it's where *doxa* was used to translate the Hebrew *kēbōd* (3519H, "honor, glory, majesty, wealth"). Like *doxa*, it speaks of "the luminous manifestation of His person, His glorious revelation of Himself."[207]

Puritan Thomas Watson wrote: "When we praise God, we spread his fame and renown, we display the trophies of his excellency. In this manner the angels glorify him; they are the choristers of heaven, and do trumpet forth his praise. Praising God is one of the highest and purest acts of religion. In prayer we act like men; in praise we act like angels."[208]

Our English word *doxology* (an expression of praise) is derived from *doxa*, and who could improve on Thomas Ken's hymn, penned in the seventeenth century?

Praise God from whom all blessings flow;
    Praise Him all creatures here below;
Praise Him above ye heav'nly host;
    Praise Father, Son, and Holy Ghost. Amen.

Scriptures for Study: Read the following OT references, noting the roots of the Greek *doxa* in the Hebrew *kēbōd*: Exodus 33:18; 40:34; Psalm 72:19; Isaiah 6:3; Ezekiel 1:28.[209] 🕮 Now read Luke 2:9 (Jesus' birth) and 9:28–31 (Jesus' Transfiguration) and notice the same visuals. Hallelujah!

Brightness

apaugasma

As alluded to yesterday, Hebrews 1:3 declares of Christ, "Who being the brightness of [the Father's] glory, and the express image of his person." **Brightness** is *apaugasma* (541, found only here), which comes from the verb *augazō* (826, "illuminate or shine"). We find *augazō*, for example, in 2 Corinthians 4:4: "In whom the god of this world hath blinded the minds of them which believe not, lest the light of the glorious gospel of Christ, who is the image of God, should shine [*augazō*] unto them."

With the addition of the prefix *apo* (575), "from," *apaugasma* therefore pictures radiant splendor emitted from a luminous body. Here is a wonderful allusion to nature. As John Gill comments: "The allusion is to the sun, and its beam or ray: so some render it 'the ray of his glory'; and may lead us to observe, that the Father and the Son are of the same nature, as the sun and its ray; and that the one is not before the other, and yet distinct from each other, and cannot be divided or separated one from another."[210]

Think of it! The Lord Jesus Christ is the very radiant splendor of God the Father's glory. While *personally distinct* from the Father, the Son is still *essentially one* with the Father, as our Lord Himself states in John 10:30 ("I and my Father are one"). What a paradox!

Additionally, since the Son is the radiant splendor of the Father, and since the light is eternal (John 1:1–4), we have a clear demonstration that the Son is also eternal. This forever discounts anyone who rejects the *deity* of Christ or doubts the *eternal Sonship* of Christ. While there has been debate on the latter among Bible teachers, we must insist that His Sonship is from all eternity (John 8:58; 17:5, 24; Col. 1:17; Rev. 22:13).

This is further underscored in our text by the word "being." The Greek is *hōn*, which is the masculine present participle of *eimi* (1510), "to be." "This means," as one Greek authority tells us, "that there has never been a time when Jesus Christ has not been the [radiant splendor] of the Father," which not only includes eternity past, but also "even in His incarnation when He purged our sins."[211]

Meditate today on God's radiance and set your mind on His glory!

Scriptures for Study: To prepare for tomorrow's meditation, read John 1:1–9. How many times does John use the word **light**? (We'll return to Hebrews 1:3 on August 14 to examine **express image**.)

Darkness

skotos

The best way to appreciate **light** (see June 15–16) is to think about **darkness**. I remember that when I was about twelve years old, our family took a vacation out West and took a tour of the Carlsbad Caverns. At one point our tour guide told us to stand absolutely still because he wanted to show us what dark was. He then turned out the lights in the cavern. I've never forgotten that dark; it was the total, absolute absence of light.

The point of the Greek *skotos* (4655), however, goes deeper; it's "chiefly of the *effect* of darkness upon man," which is his limited ability to see and his subsequent groping in uncertainty.[212] One commentator puts it brutally, but truthfully: "Darkness is the emblem and region of ignorance and depravity."[213] Ironically, Socrates agreed, "There is only one good, knowledge, and one evil, ignorance,"[214] as did poet Robert Browning, "Ignorance is not innocence but sin."[215] Why is **ignorance** (see Aug. 16) sin? Because whatever keeps us from God is sin, and ignorance does just that.

Ignorance is, indeed, man's problem. As Alfred Lord Tennyson wrote in 1850, "Let knowledge grow from more to more."[216] But even in this age of incredible knowledge and astounding accomplishment, man is hopelessly ignorant. He is "ever learning, and never able to come to the knowledge of the truth" (2 Tim. 3:7).

Most significant of all, as most commentators observe, Ephesians 5:8—"For ye were sometimes darkness"—does not say we were *in* darkness, but rather it says we *were* darkness. To illustrate, it's not as if we used to live in a dark room and resided there like a piece of furniture, but rather, we were actually part of the darkness itself. What is the significance? Ponder these contrasts: In regard to the *intellect*, light pictures *truth*, while darkness pictures *ignorance* (see also Oct. 2); likewise, in regard to *morality*, light pictures *holiness*, while darkness pictures *impurity*.

History bears this out. For example, the "Dark Ages" (about 590–1000) was a time of great ignorance, superstition, and immorality. Likewise, because of the darkness that resides in him, man has been ignorant, superstitious, and immoral down through the ages. We need only think of the immoral practices of pagan religion, not to mention those of modern society, to see that man truly *is* darkness.

This prompts us all the more to rejoice in the Light.

Scriptures for Study: Read the following verses, noting in each the contrast of what we *were* and what we *are*: Romans 13:12; 1 Thessalonians 5:4–5; 1 Peter 2:9; 1 John 1:6.

Express Image [and] Person

charaktēr [and] *hupostasis*

Today we return to Hebrews 1:3 to meditate on another reference to the Lord Jesus. Not only is He "the brightness of [the Father's] glory," but He is also "the express image of his person." It would appear that the writer (undoubtedly Paul) was not content with saying that Christ is the radiant splendor of the Father, the very rays of glory coming from the Father as beams of light emit from the sun; he wanted to say more.

Express image is *charaktēr* (5481), which is one of those graphic words for which Greek is noted. Our English word *character* is a direct transliteration of this Greek word. *Charaktēr* is derived from *charassō* (not found in the NT), which means "to carve." In Classical Greek, it evolved in meaning. It originally referred to one who sharpens or scratches; then one who writes in stone, wood, or metal, that is, an engraver; and then to the impression itself, such as a stamp for making coins or a character in writing. It finally came to refer to (as the English word *character* also does) "the basic bodily and psychological structure with which one is born, which is unique to the person and which cannot be changed by education or development."[217]

The word **person** (*hupostasis*, 5287), then, refers to that which stands under something else, that is, the foundation of something, the true essence and substance of it. It's used again in that well-known description of faith: "Faith is the substance [*hupostasis*] of things hoped for, the evidence of things not seen" (Heb. 11:1). In other words, the foundation, the very essence of faith is an absolute confidence that while we can't see something, we still know it's real and that it's ours.

That background vividly demonstrates the "character" of our Lord. Think of it! He is the precise imprint of God's substance, the exact copy of His essence. With those terms, coupled with the term **brightness** earlier in the verse, the author's purpose is to demonstrate the glory of Christ. How can anyone doubt the deity of Christ, as does every cult? What blasphemy it is to in any way doubt, discount, or deny His glorious essence!

Scriptures for Study: Read the following verses in worship of our Lord in His glory: Romans 16:27; 2 Corinthians 4:6; 2 Thessalonians 2:14; Hebrews 13:21; 2 Peter 3:18.

Vanity

mataiotēs

Man is pretty smart. There's no denying his astounding advancements and achievements. Having taught computer science and studied its history, for example, I learned that the brilliance of its early pioneers and subsequent developers is absolutely amazing. Likewise, many other inventions—from the automobile to the airplane to the aerosol can—illustrate man's intelligence and cleverness.

Yet, in all that genius, Paul describes the unregenerate man as walking in the **vanity** of the mind (Eph. 4:17). The Greek behind the word "mind" is *nous* (3563), which speaks of intellect, thought, reason, and understanding. **Vanity**, then, is *mataiotēs* (3153), that which is aimless, futile, empty, fruitless, and worthless. In the end, all man's thinking is aimless and futile because it's totally of self, without regard for God.

How different that attitude is compared to the foundational verse of the book of Proverbs: "The fear of the Lord is the beginning of knowledge: but fools despise wisdom and instruction" (1:7), which is then amplified in 9:10: "The fear of the Lord is the beginning of wisdom: and the knowledge of the [Holy One] is understanding" (cf. Job 28:28, Ps. 111:10).

From where does knowledge come? *From a proper attitude toward God.* We must first fear Him. Unless God is acknowledged as supreme, sovereign, and sacred, unless there is the presupposition of His existence, absoluteness, and wrath, man can *never* find **truth** (see Feb. 1–3). *Science* without God creates evolution. *Philosophy* without God produces existentialism, humanistic psychology, and countless other empty notions. *Religion* without God spawns everything from the violent fanaticism of Islam, to the worship of a rock or stick by pagans, to the works-oriented "salvation" of all religious thought. *All knowledge begins with God, and that beginning is a fear of Who He is.*

It is the height of human folly to ignore the Bible and then to hope for knowledge. The **fool** (see Apr. 1) is the one who not only does not *desire* the knowledge of God, but who even treats it with *contempt*. The fool despises the Scriptures, Christ, the Gospel, and God's servants. The fool despises authority, discipline, and absolutes of behavior. As a result, even as smart as he is, he's still intellectually deficient. And that is what the Christian is not and must never be.

In the next two days we'll examine two other words that demonstrate man's deficiency.

Scriptures for Study: *Mataiotēs* appears in only two other places in the NT (Rom 8:20; 2 Pet. 2:17–18). Can you discern the author's point in each usage?[218]

Ignorance

agnoia

After writing of the **vanity** of man's thinking (Eph. 4:17), Paul goes on to write of man's **ignorance** (v. 18). In light of man's many accomplishments and obvious intelligence, such a statement seems odd at the very least. But Paul knew what he was talking about.

Ignorance is *agnoia* (52; English, agnostic). As one Greek authority tells us, this ignorance is not caused by something external, but by man himself.[219] Another points out that in ancient use, it could refer to a man who lives without knowledge either because he hasn't heard the truth or because he has refused the truth, and that if he "had received it, it would have freed him from his ignorance of his origin."[220] In other words, he just closed his eyes to the truth; he refused to believe what was right in front of him.

That certainly exposes the so-called agnostic. He says that he doesn't believe we can know if there is a God, but he says this only because he does not *want* to know. He is "willingly ignorant" (2 Pet. 3:5), or as I heard one preacher say, "stupid on purpose." If he would just believe, he would be freed from the prison of his own ignorance.

That is exactly the point of Romans 1:18: "For the wrath of God is revealed from heaven against all ungodliness and unrighteousness of men, who hold the truth in unrighteousness." "Hold" is *katechō* (2722), which is comprised of the root *echō* (2192), "to have or hold," and the prefix *kata* (2596), "down." The idea, then, is to "hold down, quash, suppress." William Tyndale's 1534 translation and the Geneva Bible both render it "withhold" and Young's *Literal Translation* has "holding down."

Man will do anything he can to suppress, hold down, and withhold God's truth. He tries to do so through evolution, philosophy, and even religion. Paul goes on to write in verse 28, "They did not like to retain God in their knowledge." "Retain" is again *echō*, "to have or hold." No longer did man want to have any knowledge of God, and he still has no such desire. He simply will not have it!

What a blessed comfort it is for the Christian to know that he or she no longer need be ignorant.

Scriptures for Study: What does Acts 17:30 declare concerning man's ignorance? 📖 What does 1 Peter 1:14 demand of the believer?

Blindness

pōrōsis

As if man's **vanity** of mind and **ignorance** were not bad enough, Paul also writes of man's **blindness** (Eph. 4:18). Here is a fascinating truth. **Blindness** translates *pōrōsis* (4457), which not only means "blindness," but also "hardness." It comes from *pōroō* (4456) and ultimately *pōros* (not used in the NT), which means "to harden, to form a callous (when broken bones heal), and thus to petrify, to become hard."[221] And may we add, the callous is harder than the bone itself.

Man was, indeed, broken at the Fall, and his heart has deliberately continued to grow calloused toward God, with the result that it is petrified, stone hard. Perhaps you have spoken to someone about spiritual things and actually saw a stone-hard look materialize on their face, and the more you told them the harder they got. That is Paul's point. As one commentator writes: "An inner petrification of the very heart itself was the cause of this inborn ignorance which caused the darkening in spite of all the light in nature and all the light inherited from Adam and from Noah, and with this darkening went the alienation. The very heart was stone-hard, unresponsive to moral and spiritual impression."[222]

Paul painted a similar picture when he wrote to Timothy that man's "conscience [has been] seared with a hot iron" (1 Tim. 4:2). "Seared" is *kauteriazō* (2743; English, *cauterize*). Just as scar tissue loses feeling because of nerve damage, man has no spiritual feeling because sin has cauterized him.

And who is at the heart of this problem? Satan himself. As Paul wrote, "The god of this world hath blinded the minds of them which believe not, lest the light of the glorious gospel of Christ, who is the image of God, should shine unto them" (2 Cor. 4:4).

Thankfully, however, the prophet Ezekiel had a vision of the salvation that would be revealed in the NT when he wrote: "A new heart also will I give you, and a new spirit will I put within you: and I will take away the stony heart out of your flesh, and I will give you an heart of flesh" (Ezek. 36:26).

And it is in that salvation, that "heart of flesh," that we rejoice.

Scriptures for Study: Read Mark 8:14–21 ("hardened" in v. 17 is *pōroō*). Jesus here rebukes His disciples for their spiritual insensitivity. This challenges us not to fall into the same error.

Unfruitful

akarpos

A few days ago (see Aug. 13), we considered the word **darkness**. Paul adds to that picture in Ephesians 5:11 by commanding, "Have no fellowship with the unfruitful works of darkness."

Unfruitful is *akarpos* (175). The root *karpos* (2590) appears some sixty-six times in the NT and primarily refers to the fruit of plants (Matt. 21:19) or the produce of the earth (James 5:7, 18). The extended meaning, however, is more significant. "The use of the term *fruit* expressly indicates that it is not a question of deliberate, self-determined action on man's part. Rather it is that 'fruit-bearing' which follows from his turning to God and the power of the Spirit working in him."[223] In other words, just as fruit automatically comes from a plant or tree because it is its nature to do so, spiritual fruit is automatic in the Christian. We don't produce fruit because of *our effort*, but because of the *Spirit's energy*. Fruit comes because that is now our nature. That is why our Lord said, "By their fruits ye shall know them" (Matt. 7:20).

When the prefix *a* (1; the "alpha-negative," April 1) is added, however, *akarpos* means the exact opposite: "unfruitful, fruitless, barren, unproductive." Among its eight NT appearances, we find it in reference to the "thorny ground hearer" in the Parable of the Sower: "He also that received seed among the thorns is he that heareth the word; and the care of this world, and the deceitfulness of riches, choke the word, and he becometh unfruitful" (Matt. 13:22). Jude uses it to refer to apostates, who are "clouds . . . without water, carried about of winds; trees whose fruit withereth, without fruit, twice dead, plucked up by the roots" (Jude 12).

So, as fruitfulness is automatic because of natural inclination, so is unfruitfulness. The unsaved man does not have to work at being unfruitful; it comes naturally. As our Lord declared, "Even so every good tree bringeth forth good fruit; but a corrupt tree bringeth forth evil fruit. A good tree cannot bring forth evil fruit, neither can a corrupt tree bring forth good fruit" (Matt. 7:17–18).

This challenges us, with Paul, to "have no fellowship with the unfruitful works of darkness" (Eph. 5:11), but rather, to bear fruit for God's glory. Tomorrow we'll discover how we bear **fruit** in the Christian life.

Scriptures for Study: What is spoken of as being unfruitful in 1 Corinthians 14:14? 🕮 In 2 Peter 1:5–8, what virtues will prevent unfruitfulness?

Fruit (1)

karpos

As we discovered yesterday, *karpos* not only speaks of the **fruit** produced by plants, but it dictates that such fruit is automatic because it is the nature of the plant to bear it. The same is true of the *true* Christian. A true believer *will* bear fruit. This is, in fact, an undeniable proof that a person *is* a Christian. But what constitutes fruit in the Christian life? The NT declares that there are no less than five types of fruit, which we'll examine in the next few days.

First, the fruit of the Christian life most often mentioned by Bible teachers is that of *witnessing for Christ*. Some Christians think that the *only* way we bear fruit is by winning converts to Christ. But not only are there other types of fruit, but it's also not just *winning* someone to Christ that makes us fruitful; but rather, we are also being fruitful when we are simply *witnessing*, whether someone believes or not.

We do see the idea that converts are fruit, for example, in Romans 1:13, where Paul writes, "Oftentimes I purposed to come unto you . . . that I might have some fruit among you also, even as among other Gentiles." That clearly implies people believing in Christ. He also mentions "the firstfruits of Achaia" (1 Cor. 16:15), which pictures converts. The Lord Jesus also spoke of the "harvest" (John 4:35), which obviously implies reaping. But in the verses that follow, He also adds, "He that soweth and he that reapeth may rejoice together. And herein is that saying true, One soweth, and another reapeth." Jesus also compared evangelism to catching fish in Mark 1:17, but as every fisherman knows, even though you don't catch fish every time you go out, you're still a fisherman.

This principle is extremely important because it's very easy to become success-motivated in evangelism. High-pressure techniques, "easy-believeism," "seeker-sensitivity," and other abuses have all been used to "get results" and make it appear that we are "successful," but they have also generated a lot of pride. In contrast, God has commanded us to go forth and be witnesses (Acts 1:8), whether or not we see converts. God blesses faithfulness, not results, because He is in charge of the results (1 Cor. 3:4–10). We can be assured, then, that we are bearing fruit as we witness for Christ.

Scriptures for Study: Read 1 Corinthians 3:4–10, noting who is in charge of *witnessing* and who is in charge of *winning*.

Fruit (2)

karpos

While the most often emphasized type of spiritual fruit is that of *witnessing for Christ*, there are several other types.

Second, there is *worship of Christ*. Hebrews 13:15 is the key verse here: "By him therefore let us offer the sacrifice of praise to God continually, that is, the fruit of our lips giving thanks to his name." While the OT Jew offered literal sacrifices on the altar, both the fruit of the herd and the field, the NT Christian offers the fruit of the lips in worship, that is, our thanksgiving and our praises.

There is actually a beautiful picture of this even in the OT: "Turn to the Lord: say unto him, Take away all iniquity, and receive us graciously: so will we render the calves of our lips" (Hos. 14:2). Sadly, most modern translations totally miss the image here. "Calves" is the Hebrew *par* (6499H), which literally refers to a young bull used in sacrifice. While "fruit" is a figurative meaning of *par* (NIV, NASB, etc.), the AV better demonstrates the full force of the word by translating it literally. The idea is that the praise of our lips is as good a sacrifice as is a literal calf. So, we bear great fruit when we worship and praise God.

Third, there is fruit in our *wholesome conduct*. To the Romans, Paul wrote, "But now being made free from sin, and become servants to God, ye have your fruit unto holiness, and the end everlasting life" (Rom. 6:22). To the Colossians he likewise declared, "That ye might walk worthy of the Lord unto all pleasing, being fruitful in every good work, and increasing in the knowledge of God" (Col. 1:10).

Most graphic of all, however, is Philippians 1:10–11: "That ye may be sincere and without offence till the day of Christ; Being filled with the fruits of righteousness, which are by Jesus Christ, unto the glory and praise of God." Though some older manuscripts read "fruit" (singular), the vast majority of manuscripts and ancient versions read "fruits" (plural). This clearly fits Paul's emphasis much better. He wishes these saints to be "filled" with these fruits, that is, these manifestations of holiness. As John Gill writes, "That they might be like trees laden with fruit . . . in large quantities."[224]

Scriptures for Study: Read Psalm 136, listing every blessing for which we should praise God. 🕮 Using OT imagery, what virtue does Paul call "a sweetsmelling savour" to God in Ephesians 5:2?

Fruit (3)

karpos

Thus far we've examined three types of fruit in the Christian life: witnessing for Christ, worship of Christ, and wholesome conduct. We conclude today with two others.

Fourth, there is fruit in our *winsome character*. The essence of Christ's own character, and therefore Christian character, is summed up in Galatians 5:22–23: "The fruit of the Spirit is love, joy, peace, longsuffering, gentleness, goodness, faith, meekness, temperance: against such there is no law."

This fruit of the Spirit is the outward indicator, *proof positive*, of salvation, and every true believer *will* possess them to one extent or the other. This, in fact, follows of necessity; since *Christ* is in us, His *character* is in us and merely needs to grow, develop, and deepen. As Jesus declared, "Ye shall know them by their fruits. Do men gather grapes of thorns, or figs of thistles? Even so every good tree bringeth forth good fruit; but a corrupt tree bringeth forth evil fruit. A good tree cannot bring forth evil fruit, neither can a corrupt tree bring forth good fruit" (Matt. 7:16–18).

Who, then, produces this fruit of Christian character? It doesn't come from self-effort, that is, from the power of the branches (John 15:4). Just as literal fruit is produced on the branches by the power of the vine, Christ is likewise "the vine [and we] are the branches" (John 15:5).

Fifth, a final type of spiritual fruit is in our *wealth-sharing with other Christians*. Twice Paul refers to a "gift" as "fruit." To the Romans he wrote, "When therefore I have performed this, and have sealed to them this fruit, I will come by you into Spain" (Rom. 15:28). The occasion was Paul's collection for the poor saints in Jerusalem. Those who gave to this offering were giving the fruit of their labor and love to others.

Years later Paul also wrote to the Philippians: "For even in Thessalonica ye sent once and again unto my necessity. Not because I desire a gift: but I desire fruit that may abound to your account" (Phil. 4:16–17). More than once the Philippians sent monetary support to Paul, and he called that "fruit."

What a blessing it is to know that as branches of the Living Vine we can produce fruit that glorifies the Vine. Tomorrow we'll take one more look at fruit-bearing.

Scriptures for Study: Read Psalm 1, noting the contrasts between the godly and ungodly person.

Purge

kathairō

Before leaving this vitally important subject of fruit in the Christian's life, it's essential that we note the levels of fruit-bearing that our Lord Himself mentions in John 15 and also how to "increase productivity."

Our Lord first mentions, of course, that there are some branches that bear no fruit at all (v. 2). This indicates lifeless branches that are taken away and burned. The spiritual application is clear: A person who does not bear fruit is not a true believer and will one day be taken away to hell.

Our Lord goes on, however, to tell us that while all true branches will produce fruit, some will produce more than others. Specifically, He says that some will produce "fruit" (v. 2), others will produce "more fruit" (v. 2), and still others will produce "much fruit" (vv. 5, 8). How, then, can we get to that third level? How can we "increase productivity" as Christians?

First, we increase fruit mainly by *purging*. In verse 2, Jesus says of "Level 1" branches that He will **purge** them so they will bear "more fruit." The verb *kathairō* (2508) means "to cleanse or prune, to free from any improper mixture." Our English words *catharsis* and *cathartic* come from this word. As the vinedresser prunes and cleanses the branches of small shoots, mildew, and fungus, the Father removes things from our lives that slow our progress, hinder growth, and prevent fruit.

Second, we increase fruit by our *permanence* in Christ. Verses 4 and 5 speak of our "abiding" in Christ. Just as a well-established plant will produce more fruit than a new plant, the longer we **abide** (see June 2) in Christ, the more fruit we'll produce.

Third, we increase fruit by *propagation*. The old adage, "Anyone can count the seeds in an apple, but no one can count the apples in a seed," says it well. As we bear fruit in the form of converts and other types of fruit, they in turn will produce fruit, and the progression continues.

Let us each examine our hearts and ask, "At what level of fruit-bearing am I? Am I glorifying the Vine as much as I could? What needs to be pruned so that I can increase my productivity?"

Scriptures for Study: What did Paul thank God for in 2 Timothy 1:3 ("pure" is the noun *katharos*). 🕮 What's involved in the "pure" (*katharos*) heart in 2 Timothy 2:22?

Reprove

elegchō

As mentioned on August 19, Paul commanded the Ephesians to "have no fellowship with the unfruitful works of darkness" (5:11). But lest we think that it's enough just to withdraw from sin, as a monk would do in the monastery, Paul adds that we are also to **reprove** "the unfruitful works of darkness."

In Classical Greek, both Plato and Aristotle used *elegchō* (1651) for "the logical exposition of the facts of a matter for the purpose of refuting the (usually sophistical) argument of an opponent." The word then developed the "principal meaning of convince, refute."[225]

That meaning is essentially the same in the NT. So strong is this word, in fact, that Greek scholar Richard Trench writes: "It means to rebuke another with the truth so that the person confesses, or at least is convinced, of his sin."[226] In his commentary on Ephesians, John Calvin adds, "It literally signifies to drag forth to the light what was formerly unknown."[227]

What a vivid picture! We must drag error kicking and screaming into the light to expose it. That is *especially* the responsibility of pastors, as Paul makes crystal clear in 2 Timothy 4:2 and Titus 1:9, 13 (cf. 2:15). To say the very least, however, this flies in the face of the attitude of our day. While the growing tendency in many churches is to avoid even the *mention* of false doctrine or sin, Paul's repeated emphasis is the *refutation* of such practices. The ruling attitude in society today is "tolerance." "How *dare* we say that something is wrong," it is argued. In stark contrast, the godly Christian will appreciate commentator Kent Hughes's blunt observation:

"According to the world, Christianity ought to be as broad and accepting as possible. And the fact is that clergy who think in this way, who baptize every form of sin as OK, become the darlings of the media. A cultured accent, a fuchsia-colored bishop's shirt, and the urging to place condoms in Gideon Bibles will get you a spot on *Good Morning, America*. Our culture loves the 'open-minded,' nonjudgmental, 'live and let live' personality."[228]

Let us pray for men who will stand uncompromisingly for the truth!

Scriptures for Study: What tool do we use for reproof (Eph. 5:13)? 🕮 In 1 Timothy 5:20, what is the purpose of reproof ("rebuke" is *elegchō*)?

Awake

egeirō

Just as no light enters our eyes when we are asleep physically, likewise no spiritual light enters when we are asleep spiritually. Paul, therefore, commands in Ephesians 5:14: "Wherefore he saith, Awake thou that sleepest, and arise from the dead, and Christ shall give thee light."

Awake is *egeirō* (1453). Used literally, it means "to rise from sleep, implying also the idea of rising up from the posture of sleep."[229] In Matthew 8:25, for example, where the terrified disciples came to Jesus "and awoke him, saying, Lord, save us: we perish," we can picture them shaking Him awake and yanking Him up to his feet to do something. Used metaphorically, of course, it speaks of waking up from lethargy or sluggishness.

I would submit, however, that both ideas are implicit. To illustrate, as most teenage boys do, I remember my parents trying to wake me up from that deep teenage boy sleep, which enabled me to peacefully sleep through a freight train thundering through my room. After finally waking me up and getting a response, one of them would, five minutes later, call again, "Are you awake?" at which time I would groggily answer, "Yes." But was I? Of course not. I was conscious, but still in the position of sleep, far from awake, alert, and ready for the day.

The same is true spiritually. Many Christians are conscious—they profess Christ, go to church, pray, and so forth. But many are not really awake, not really out of the posture of sleep, not alert and ready for the challenges and commands of Christian living.

Paul goes on to say that such Christians are actually "dead." No, this doesn't mean they are dead *spiritually*; rather, it means they are dead *effectively*; that is, such Christians are not growing and have no practical vitality or useful witness. This verse is a call to repentance and renewed devotion to the Lord. If we answer the call, Paul adds, "Christ shall give [us] light" (Eph. 5:14). The implication is that He will give us even more **light** (see Aug. 13) than we have; that is, He will illumine His Word that much more to our hearts and minds.

Scriptures for Study: Read Matthew 26:36–41 and ponder the challenge it gives us. 📖 What should we be doing instead of sleeping (1 Thess. 5:6)?

He Led Captivity Captive

ēchmalōteusen aichmalōsian

Many a Bible student has justifiably wondered what that odd phrase **"he led captivity captive"** (Eph. 4:8) means. A common teaching views **captivity** as referring to OT saints who, though saved, were held in some sort of captivity. Supposedly, then, Jesus went into hades (hell), retrieved them from their captivity, and took them to heaven. Such a teaching, however, is actually rooted in Roman Catholic *tradition*, not Scripture,[230] and doesn't even come close to the imagery of the phrase.

The Greek (*ēchmalōteusen aichmalōsian*) more literally says, "He led captive captivity." *ēchmalōteusen* is the aorist indicative active of *aichmalōteuō* (162), "to capture," and *aichmalōsian* (161), "the state of being captive," is a noun from *aichmalōtos* (164), a captive. The picture is rooted in the public triumphs of conquerors, especially as celebrated by the Romans. The language clearly describes the conqueror who took captives, led them away in chains, and then made them part of his triumphal procession.

We find the same expression in the OT. In Judges 5:12, Deborah praises the Lord for giving victory over Canaan: "Awake, awake, Deborah: awake, awake, utter a song: arise, Barak, and lead thy captivity captive." The idea is clear: You will now lead captive him who held you captive. Also, in Amos 1:3–6, God pronounces judgment on the nations around Israel because they had "carried away captive the whole captivity, to deliver them up to Edom," that is, the Philistines had handed over a large number of Israelites to the cruel Edomites.

So, what is Paul saying? As one expositor puts it, "It is a picture of the Lord Jesus Christ leading in His triumphal train the devil and hell and sin and death—the great enemies that were against man and which had held mankind in captivity for so long a time. The princes which had controlled that captivity are now being led captive themselves."[231]

What a picture! Our Lord is, indeed, the Conqueror of conquerors, the King of kings, the Lord of lords. Those who once held us in bondage are now captives of the Great Conqueror and march in chains before Him. As if that were not enough, Paul goes on to say (as we'll see tomorrow) that Christ gave **spiritual gifts** (see Feb. 15) to the believers who remain on earth.

Scriptures for Study: Ephesians 4:8 is actually a "semi-quotation" of Psalm 68:18. The scene is a victory hymn celebrating God's conquest of the Jebusites and His ascent (represented by the Ark of the Covenant) up Mount Zion (2 Sam. 6–7; 1 Chron. 13). Soldiers captured by the enemy became "re-captured captives," and the spoils of war became the property of the conqueror to give as he wished.[232]

Circumspectly

akribōs

Back on June 14 we meditated on the word **walk**, which is *peripateō* (4043), "to walk about, to walk around, to walk concerning." Paul uses this word again in Ephesians 5:15 to specify an extremely important way we are to walk, namely, **circumspectly**. What a word this is! It is absolutely crucial to Christian living.

Sadly, in their overzealousness for simplicity, modern translations miss the force of this word by replacing it with "be careful." The English *circumspectly*, however, is from the Latin *circumspectus*. The verb form, *circumspectō*, means "to look all around, be on the lookout." *Circumspectly* is clearly a far better translation; it tells us to look everywhere as we walk.

That is also the idea of *akribōs* (199; English, *accurate*), which speaks of precision, diligence, accuracy, and exactness. It's used in Matthew 2:8 where Herod sent the wise men to Bethlehem and told them to "search diligently for the young child." It also appears in Acts 18:25 to describe Apollos, who was "mighty in the scriptures" (v. 24) and "taught diligently [*akribōs*] the things of the Lord." (No better word could be said of a preacher, a word that tragically describes fewer and fewer preachers today.) So, we are to look, examine, and investigate our walk with the utmost care. To be wise is to walk watchfully, looking at and carefully examining everything with which we come in contact.

In some European countries, to protect property, owners often build a high wall, the top of which they cover with broken glass embedded in the mortar to discourage intruders who might try to climb over it. One can sometimes see a cat walking "circumspectly" along the top of such a wall. You'll see it cautiously pick up one paw and place it precisely where there's no glass. Once that paw is in place, it then moves the next one and so on.

That immediately reminds us of the principle of *discernment*, which we examined at length back in July (15–22). In a day when discernment in the church is fading into oblivion, Paul challenges us to "walk circumspectly," to investigate and examine everything. Someone has wisely said, "When the pilot does not know what port he is heading for, no wind is the right wind."

Scriptures for Study: By implication, what does 1 Thessalonians 5:1–2 encourage us to do ("perfectly" is *akribōs*)?

Time

chronos [and] *kairos*

There are two basic words in the Greek that are translated **time**. Interestingly, both appear in Acts 1:7: "And he [Christ] said unto them, It is not for you to know the times or the seasons, which the Father hath put in his own power." "Times" is *chronos* (5550; English, *chronometer*), which basically means "time, course of time, passage of time," or more precisely, "space of time whose duration is not as a rule precisely determined."[233] Acts 19:22, for example, says that Paul "stayed in Asia for a season" (i.e., "for awhile," an indefinite period). While there are examples where *chronos* is used in a more specific sense, in light of the other word used here, *chronos* speaks of a time period that is not precisely known.

Seasons, then, is *kairos* (2540), which refers to "a decisive or crucial place or point,"[234] such as a date. The point in Acts 1:7, therefore, is that it is not for us to know either the indefinite time or the definite time of Christ's return to the earth. Some teachers say that we can ascertain the "date" when Jesus will come, but that is plainly false, for any "date" is a definite time. Other teachers insist that while we can't know the *exact* time, we can still know the "year." But that, too, is false, for a year would be an *indefinite* time.

There's a reason for our Lord's statement. It's not that His earthly kingdom is not important; rather, we're not told when He is coming back because He's given us a task that is much more pressing. That task is spoken of in the very next verse: "But ye shall receive power, after [literally, when] that the Holy Ghost is come upon you: and ye shall be witnesses unto me both in Jerusalem, and in all Judaea, and in Samaria, and unto the uttermost part of the earth."

The most pressing thing for us to do today is not to try to figure out when Jesus is coming, but to be active witnesses for our Lord. There is, of course, a special blessing in studying the prophecy of Revelation (1:3), but there are some who get so absorbed in prophecy that they begin to neglect the commission God has given them, not to mention the false predictions and silly applications that some students make.

Scriptures for Study: Read 1 Thessalonians 5:1–6, noting the same basic principle we see in Acts 1:7–8.

Time [Redeeming the]

kairos

Yesterday we saw the important contrast between two Greek words translated **time**. Today we'll examine a very important NT instance of *kairos* (2540), the word that indicates "a decisive or crucial place or point." In Ephesians 5:16, Paul exhorts, "Redeeming the time, because the days are evil" (cf. Col. 4:5).

"Redeeming" is *exagorazō* (1805; see Jan. 22), "to buy up." As Christ purchased us out of the slave market of sin (e.g., Gal. 3:13; 4:5), Paul uses the same imagery to say that we are to "buy up" all our time and devote it God. God wants us to be concerned with decisive points of time and specific situations of life, to consider each and every moment to be an opportunity for growth, service, and witness. The fool *wastes* time (Eph. 5:15), but the wise man *invests* it.

Sadly, while modern translations try so hard to be relevant, they often miss the point, power, and purpose of a text. Here, for example, instead of "redeeming the time," the NIV reads, "making the most of every opportunity;" the NASB says, "making the most of your time;" and the ESV says, "making the best use of the time." *But that's not what the text says*. Saying that *exagorazō* means any of the above is patently false; it never means any of that.[235]

Modern versions are actually *interpreting*, not *translating*. The text plainly says "buy up" (or "redeeming," AV, NKJV, Tyndale, and Young's *Literal Translation*). Paul is purposely graphic. He's not just saying "make the most of your time;" he's saying more than that—to "buy it" and make it yours and use it correctly.

Recognizing that, the respected nineteenth-century commentator R. C. H. Lenski writes: "We say 'use' the opportunity; Paul says 'buy it out,' purchase all that it offers. That means: pay the necessary price in effort and exertion."[236] In other words, we don't just *use* the time; we *buy* it, no matter how much it costs. Wisdom does not come cheap. It takes time, effort, dedication, and, in fact, a lifetime of investment.

Each and every moment of our day is an opportunity, and we should guard each one. As the old Latin expression goes, *tempus fugit*, "time flies;" or as the first-century BC Greek poet Virgil elaborated, *fugit irreparabile tempus*, "Time irretrievably is flying."[237] Missed opportunities can never be recaptured.

Scriptures for Study: Read the following verses, noting each challenge: Galatians 6:9–10 ("season" and "opportunity" are *kairos*); Ephesians 6:18 ("always" is *kairos*); 1 Peter 1:5.

Drunk [and] Excess

methusko [and] *asotia*

In Ephesians 5:18, Paul commands: "And be not drunk with wine, wherein is excess; but be filled with the Spirit." Why bring up such a topic? Because in some respects there's a similarity between drunkenness and Spirit-filling, namely, both speak of *control*. While the **drunk** is controlled by alcohol and has *lost* control, the Spirit-filled person is controlled by the Spirit and *retains* control.

One scholar notes of the Greek *methuskō* (3182), "A curious use of the word occurs in Homer, where he is describing the stretching of a bull's hide, which in order to make it more elastic, is *soaked* . . . (*methuskō*) with fat."[238] So, the translation could be, "Do not be soaked with wine."

Paul wasn't satisfied, however, with using *methuskō* alone. He adds *asotia* (**excess**, 810). This interesting word refers to more than just the amount consumed. The root is *sotia*, which in turn is from *sōzō* (4982); "to save, deliver, make whole, preserve safe from danger, loss, [and] destruction."[239] The prefix *a* (1; the "alpha-negative," April 1) makes it the exact opposite—no safety or deliverance, having no preservation from danger, loss, and destruction.

The Ephesians knew precisely what Paul meant because they knew Greek mythology. Dionysus was the god of vegetation, especially the god of wine. Worship was characterized by frenzied orgies that were associated with intoxication. The use of phallic symbols, the tearing of wild animals into pieces, the eating of raw flesh, and savage dancing were also practiced, especially in Thrace and Asia Minor (the location of Ephesus). Dionysus later became known as Bacchus, the name by which he was known to the Romans.

In the month of Poseidon, there was also a festival in honor of Dionysus in Athens. During the three-day spring festival, virtually everyone was drunk, and there was a wine drinking contest. Alexander the Great held such a contest in which thirty competitors died. I was reminded here of today's New Year's Eve parties, as well as the deaths of college students during drinking binges.

So, Paul uses the term **drunk** to contrast the orgies of evil with the sweetness of Spirit-filling. Of course, the Ephesians would not identify themselves with such pagans. Neither should we "*lose* ourselves" in drink or drugs; rather, we should *immerse* ourselves in the Holy Spirit. This prepares us for tomorrow's meditation.

Scriptures for Study: Read the following verses, noting the use of *asotia*, and how it has no place in the believer's life: Luke 15:13 ("riotous" is *asotos* [811]); Titus 1:6 ("riot" is *asotia*); 1 Peter 4:3–4 ("riot").

Be Filled with the Spirit (1)

plērousthe en pneumati

This wondrous phrase (Eph. 5:18) has tragically been the subject of much debate through the years. **Spirit** is *pneuma* (4151), which lierally means breath or breeze, and figuratively, the principle (or "spirit") of life that resides in man, the very breath of God breathed into man. It's interesting, therefore, that Paul doesn't use *methuskō* (3182) here to say, "Be *drunk* with the Spirit." To be **filled** with the **Spirit** is not to lose control and be mindless, as is true of some Christians today. There are those, for example, in the "laughing revival," who begin laughing hysterically "in the Spirit," and others who roll on the floor or run around the church building. What is that if not a virtual form of "drunkenness"?

While the disciples were accused of having had too much wine on the Day of Pentecost (Acts 2:13), the charge came only from their critics who were mocking them. Other observers, however, were amazed by what they saw, which was not a frenzy or ecstatic gibberish, but rather, people who were controlled by the Spirit and who coherently proclaimed Christ in human languages they had never spoken before.

Instead of *methuskō*, then, Paul uses *pleroō* (4137; see also March 3–4), which speaks of filling a container and means "to influence fully, to control." As one Greek authority adds, "To fill up, to cause to abound, to furnish or supply liberally, to flood, to diffuse throughout."[240] It is used, for example, in Matthew 13:48, to refer to a full fishing net. The chief idea then is that we are to be permeated with, and therefore controlled by, the Spirit.

Now, all of that is fine in *theory*, but what does it mean in *practice*? Preachers often say that "filling" means "control," but what exactly does that mean? As theologian Louis Sperry Chafer puts it: "It is not a matter of acquiring more of the Spirit, but rather of the Spirit of God acquiring all of the individual."[241] It means that we are influenced by Him and nothing else. To put it succinctly: *To be filled with the Spirit is to have our thoughts, desires, values, motives, goals, priorities, and all else set on spiritual things and spiritual growth.*

We will meditate further on Spirit-filling in the next few days.

Scriptures for Study: Read Acts 6:3 and 7:55, noting the uses of *plērēs* (4134), a form of *pleroō*. In both instances "full" is *plērēs*.

Be Filled with the Spirit (2)

plērousthe en pneumati

Continuing our thoughts on being **filled** with the Holy **Spirit**, it's interesting that since some NT Christians are referred to as being full of the Holy Spirit, such as the "deacons" of Acts 6:3 (see July 8), there must have been something about them that was *recognizable as evidence*.

What, then, did people see? Can there be any doubt that it was Christlikeness of character? That's the point of Galatians 5:22–23: "But the fruit of the Spirit is love, joy, peace, longsuffering, gentleness, goodness, faith, meekness, temperance: against such there is no law." When such character is present in our lives, people will see Holy Spirit control in us. They won't have to see some emotional outburst or ecstatic experience; rather they will see Christlike behavior.

The construction of the Greek verb for "filled" (*plērousthe*) is all-important. One of the most prominent misconceptions about Spirit-filling is that it involves some "crisis experience," some "dramatic event," some so-called second blessing, which comes only because we "agonize over it in prayer" for a period of time. But Scripture says none of that. On the contrary, we need not *struggle* for it; we simply *claim* it.

First, the verb is *present tense*, which shows a continuing action. In other words, Spirit-filling is designed to be a continuing reality. A literal translation of the Greek is, "Be being filled." We are to be in the state of *constantly being* filled with the Spirit.

Second, the verb is in the *imperative mood*, which indicates a military command and something we control. Spirit-filling is not *optional*, but rather *mandatory*. As Ephesians 5:17 declares, this is the will of God. God, therefore, would not give us a command unless we were being put in charge of carrying out the command, so it's up to us to obey. While "sealing" (see Jan. 30) and "baptism" (see June 25) are done by God, and are therefore in the aorist tense, "filling" is up to us to allow. As we'll detail on September 10, the underlying principle for being Spirit-filled is *yieldedness*; we must allow the Holy Spirit to take control.

Third, this is further indicated by the verb being in the *passive voice*, the subject being acted upon. We allow the Holy Spirit to act upon us and control us. Let us each day renew our yielding to Holy Spirit control.

Scriptures for Study: Instead of the Holy Spirit, who was in control in Acts 5:3? 📖 In Romans 15:19, what will "fill" us by Holy Spirit power?

Be Filled with the Spirit (3)

plērousthe en pneumati

Another question that arises concerning Spirit-filling is, "What exactly is its purpose?" All one need do to find the answer is open the book of Acts. There are at least six instances in Acts where people are filled with the Spirit (2:4; 4:8, 31; 7:55; 9:17; 13:9). In every instance, the purpose of Spirit-filling was an empowering for service, more specifically, *an empowering to proclaim the truth of God.* That is the power spoken of in Acts 1:8: "But ye shall receive power, after that the Holy Ghost is come upon you: and ye shall be witnesses unto me both in Jerusalem, and in all Judaea, and in Samaria, and unto the uttermost part of the earth" (see July 7).

Peter is a wonderful example of this empowering for service. Rarely do we see the Lord Jesus in the gospels without Peter tagging along. He wanted to be with the Lord and do what the Lord did. As long as he was with His Lord, he felt invincible. He even drew a sword in the Garden of Gethsemane and was ready to take on all comers (John 18:3–11). But in a matter of hours, when His Lord was gone, Peter's power and boldness evaporated. He vehemently denied even knowing Jesus.

A strange thing happened, however, a few days later. On the Day of Pentecost, we see that same miserable man preaching boldly without fear or even the slightest hesitation. What made the difference? The answer appears in Acts 4:8. As he stood before the Sanhedrin after being arrested, Peter was "filled with the Holy Ghost." His Lord was again with Him in the form of the Holy Spirit who filled and empowered Him for proclamation. Even the members of the Sanhedrin marveled at his boldness (v. 13).

It is that realization of Christ's *presence* that leads to a Christ *portrait*, a Christlikeness. As Paul wrote to the Corinthians, who certainly needed the exhortation, "We all, with open face beholding as in a glass the glory of the Lord, are changed into the same image from glory to glory, even as by the Spirit of the Lord" (2 Cor. 3:18). In this way, His *work*, His *will*, His *ways*, and His *words* will all become yours.

Scriptures for Study: Read 1 Corinthians 2:1–5 and 1 Thessalonians 1:5, noting the power of proclamation the Holy Spirit gives.

SEPTEMBER **2**

Psalm

psalmos

Right on the heels of his command to Holy Spirit filling, Paul mentions several evidences of Spirit-filling. The very first is singing: "Speaking to [i.e., among] yourselves in psalms and hymns and spiritual songs, singing and making melody in your heart to the Lord" (Eph. 5:19).

Here is a truly amazing principle! *There is nothing more indicative of the Spirit-filled life than the expression of song.* Whether a person has an angelic voice or can't "carry a tune in a bucket," the Spirit-filled Christian is a singing Christian. In the next few days, we'll examine a few aspects of "church music" that Paul lists here.

The first is the *psalm* (*psalmos*, 5568). A psalm is "a sacred, inspired poem of praise." Psalms were actually designed to be sung with the accompaniment of a stringed musical instrument, such as the harp, the lute, or the lyre (all of which are in the guitar family). In fact, the word *psalm* is merely a transliteration of the Greek title of the book of Psalms (*psalmoi*), which originally meant plucking the strings of a musical instrument.[242]

Sadly, there are some today who do not want to face the facts of such musical instruments. Some years ago, a preacher friend of mine traveled and held meetings in various churches. Part of the ministry was music of which his guitar was a part. A certain pastor came to him one day and said, "I couldn't allow you to come to my church because you use a guitar." My friend asked why and the answer followed, "Oh, because it's a stringed instrument, and we feel that those are worldly." My friend lovingly asked him, "Well, then, do you have a piano in your church? It, too, is a stringed instrument." The pastor was noticeably taken off guard and blurted out his answer, "Well . . . yes, but you can't see the strings."

So, the first type of Christian music is the psalm, a sacred, inspired poem of praise. We should also point out that while new psalms are not being written today because no inspired writings are being produced, some hymn writers have *adapted* certain psalms. Robert Grant (1785–1838), for example, adapted Psalm 104 into that great hymn "O Worship the King." Likewise, Martin Luther adapted his glorious hymn, "A Mighty Fortress Is Our God," from Psalm 46.

Scriptures for Study: Read your favorite psalm. 📖 You might also want to read and compare Psalm 46 and 104 with the hymn versions mentioned earlier.

Hymn

humnos

The second type of music Paul lists in Ephesians 5:19 is the **hymn**. While a *gospel song* is "a religious exhortation to fellow man," and a *carol* is "a simple narrative in verse of some outstanding biblical event," a *hymn* is "an ode of praise to Almighty God."[243]

The word *hymn* is a transliteration of the Greek *humnos* (5215), which appears in the NT only here and in Colossians 3:16. While its origin is uncertain, the word goes as far back in secular Greek as Homer and was "a general word used to include the most varied poetical forms." Also in general, it referred "to songs to the gods, particularly a song in praise of the divinity."[244] It's interesting that because of that origin, "the word 'hymn' nowhere occurs in the writings of the apostolic fathers because it was used as a praise of heathen deities and thus the early Christians instinctively shrank from it."[245]

Nevertheless, Paul used *hymnos* for a reason. His obvious purpose was to show that instead of hymns being dedicated to pagan gods, Christians sing hymns to the one true God. According to Augustine, a hymn has three characteristics: It must be sung; it must be praise; it must be to God.

A hymn might be inspired. Some scholars believe that verses such as 1 Timothy 3:16, Philippians 2:6–11, and Hebrews 1:3 are examples of ancient hymns. While in the final analysis, that is only speculation, it might be true. First Timothy 3:16, for example, is quite poetical. It can be arranged in six lines in a series of couplets with the second line complementing the first:

> God was manifest in the flesh,
>   justified in the Spirit,
> seen of angels,
>   preached unto the Gentiles,
> believed on in the world,
>   received up into glory.

A hymn can also be "uninspired," that is, not written by a Scripture writer. Many throughout history have written new poetic lyrics that glorify God.

Hymns will be better understood in light of the last type of church music, which we'll examine tomorrow.

Scriptures for Study: Again, while it's not certain, Philippians 2:6–11 and Hebrews 1:3 might have been ancient hymns. Read and meditate on them.

Spiritual Song

pneumatikos ōdē

The third type of music Paul lists in Ephesians 5:19 is the **spiritual song**. The word **song** is *ōdē* (5603, English *ode*), which in ancient times referred to "any kind of song, as of battle, harvest, [or] festal."[246] Paul, therefore, qualifies it here with the word **spiritual** (*pneumatikos*, 4152). He didn't have to say "spiritual psalm" or "spiritual hymn" because these are already spiritual in content, but he had to qualify "songs" as being "*spiritual* songs."

What are the differences between a "hymn" and a "spiritual song"? There are actually several subtle differences. (1) A hymn is a direct praise of God, while a spiritual song is an expression to other people, as is illustrated in the song, "In My Heart There Rings a Melody." (2) A hymn is objective and presents objective facts, while a spiritual song is more subjective in expressing personal feelings. A good example of this is found in the song, "It Is Well with My Soul." (3) A hymn focuses on the attributes and majesty of God, while a spiritual song is often evangelistic, as is the song, "Have You Any Room for Jesus?" (4) The tune (or melody) of a hymn is more staid, sober, and sedate, while a spiritual song often has a catchy melody or lifted rhythm, as in the songs, "He Lives" and "Are You Washed in the Blood?" (5) A hymn usually does not have a chorus, while a spiritual song usually does.

While there certainly are many good spiritual songs, it's tragic beyond words that hymns have virtually disappeared and have been replaced with the "praise chorus" and other lighter fare. One preacher very well sums up such church services: "Hollow excitement, a lack of strong Biblical preaching, and the triviality of the service."[247] Or as Vance Havner once put it in his wonderful way: "If ever sanctified musicians were needed, it is today! The church has been invaded by gospel jazz, degenerating from hymns to hootenannies. Church music has fallen on evil days."[248]

Hymns such as the *Doxology, When I Survey the Wondrous Cross*, and many others are characterized not only by praise to God, but also by depth and doctrinal truth. In contrast, much music today is *shallow* instead of *substantive* and *trite* instead of *true*.

Scriptures for Study: Read Revelation 5:9, 14:3, and 15:3, noting the qualifying word added to specify what kind of *ōdē* is being sung.

Singing

aidō

In Ephesians 5:19, Paul adds another word that deals with church music. It's extremely significant that the emphasis in the NT is not actually on *music* but **singing**. What really matters most is what comes out of our mouths, the words we are singing.

In all five of its NT occurrences, the Greek *aidō* refers to praises to God (Eph. 5:19; Col. 3:16; Rev. 5:9; 14:3; 15:3). Therefore, the music itself is not an *element* of worship, but rather, an *aid* to an element. Music only accompanies, that is, supports the singing; *it is never the focus*. Singing is the most beautiful of musical instruments; its tones, pitch, and inflections far surpass any other instrument. The point of singing is to proclaim God and His Word.

In sad contrast, today it is the *music* that is actually prominent. It is music *style* that actually rules, and that is simply not biblical. Someone who asks of your church, "What style of music do you use in your services" has already seriously erred.

It's interesting, for example, that people of the World War II era would never have dreamed of going into a church and saying, "I'm looking for a church that has a Benny Goodman or Glen Miller style of music." But that attitude is exactly what we see today. Style of music dominates our churches, and it's usually pop music, and even rock music, that people want.

I greatly appreciated a statement I heard J. Ligon Duncan make: "Music must pass the test of the catacombs."[249] When people insist that it's good lighting and great sound that are the keys to good worship, they fail miserably. If it can't be done in the catacombs below the streets of Rome, it isn't essential or even good. He further submits: "Music must also pass the test of the stake." It's easy to picture the old Lutheran dying under Catholic persecution while singing Luther's *A Mighty Fortress Is Our God*. But can we honestly picture a martyr singing one of today's shallow praise ditties?

While church music is a touchy subject, and while music is a very subjective thing, we must take great care in choosing music that first is substantive and second is simply good music. This leads us to one other word that we'll examine tomorrow.

Scriptures for Study: Read the other four occurrences of *aidō* (Col. 3:16; Rev. 5:9; 14:3; 15:3), noting in each the praise offered to God. 🕮 Note also OT verses where the Septuagint translates the Hebrew *shiyr* (7891H) as *aidō* ("sing" in Exod. 15:21 and 1 Chron. 16:23).

Making Melody

psallō

Paul uses one other word in reference to church music, translated **making melody** in Ephesians 5:19. Obviously, *psallō* (5567) is the same basic word as *psalmos* (see Sept. 2). It literally means to twang or snap, as one would pluck the strings of a musical instrument. While essentially the same, the subtle difference in NT usage is that "*psalmos* means a hymn of praise," while *psallō* means "to sing a spiritual or sacred song."[250]

While there are some dear Christians who do not believe in using any musical instruments in the church because none are mentioned in the NT, these words make it obvious that instruments were present (although not mandatory). No NT writer made an issue of this because there was no issue to make; instruments were a part of life.

These words underscore first the importance of melody in music. Melody can be defined as "a rhythmically organized series of high and low tones which avoids unnecessary repetition and comes to a climactic and resolved end." The melody is the heart of a song and must not be obscured or overpowered by other elements. Most music of the Orient, for example, is dissonant and unresolved. Melody is nonexistent, and there's no discernable beginning or end. This fact actually reflects the religious systems of the Orient, which teach meaningless existence.

A second element of music is *rhythm*. While rhythm alone is not music at all (such as RAP, an acronym for Rhythmic American Poetry), and while rhythm that overpowers the melody is bad music, rhythm is actually the foundation of music. There's no music without it.

A third element of music is harmony, which actually didn't appear until about the ninth century AD. Of the three kinds of harmony, the best and most widely accepted is called "harmonizing in thirds" (*faux-bourdon*, false bass). This simply means playing the third or the sixth tone above or below the melody (e.g., from the note "C" on a piano, a third up is "E" and another third is "G," making the "C chord"). The purpose of harmony is to enhance the melody, which again must not be obscured or overpowered. An example in classical music would be Stravinsky's "Rites of Spring," which is full of atonality and dissonance caused by harmony run wild.

So, we say again, the point of good music is that it makes *melody*.

Scriptures for Study: Read the other NT occurrences of *psallō* (Rom. 15:9; 1 Cor. 14:15; James 5:13; "sing" occurs in all three). 📖 Note also OT verses where the Septuagint translates the Hebrew *zēmar* (2167H, "to sing with musical accompaniment") as *psallō* (2 Sam. 22:50; Ps. 9:2; 18:49; 30:4; 47:6).

Worship

proskuneō

While music is the first result of the Spirit-filled Christian, another is **worship**. The words "in your heart to the Lord" in Ephesians 5:19 paint that picture, but the Greek *proskuneō* (4352) appears many times in the NT to underscore the importance of worship.

This common word means "to kiss toward, to kiss the hand, to bow down, to prostrate oneself." None of those words are "holy" in themselves. They can refer to any recipient of worship, but we place them in the context of the worship of God, bowing down before Him to give honor, respect, praise, and adoration. While literally bowing down or lying down is not demanded, the idea of doing so "in [our] heart[s]" certainly is.

Scripture is permeated by the precept of worship. Tragically, many churches today are built on "meeting people's needs" when such an idea is foreign to Scripture and should be the farthest thing from our minds. Our thoughts should be set on worship of God. The NT, as well as the OT, is filled with examples.

In Matthew 2:2, what was the first concern of the Magi when they came to visit Jesus? *Worship*. In Matthew 4:8–10, what was the central issue of the greatest spiritual battle ever fought? *Worship*. What was Mary of Bethany's desire in John 12:1–3? *Worship*. What did the Lord Jesus discuss with the Samaritan woman immediately after telling her about salvation in John 4:20–24? *Worship*. What was the key issue that Paul emphasized to the Athenians in Acts 17:23? *Worship*. In Philippians 3:3, what is the defining characteristic of the true Christian? *Worship*. And finally, what will be the activity in heaven, according to Revelation 4:10–11? *Worship*.

We must also be careful *how* we worship. First, God will not tolerate the worship of a false god (Exod. 34:14–15). Second, God will not accept the worship of the true God in the wrong way, such as worship that is "self-defined," as illustrated by Nadab and Abihu (Lev. 10:1–2) and Uzzah (2 Sam. 6:1–9). Third, God will not accept the worship of the True God with the wrong attitude, such as ritual, habit, and tradition (Mark 7:6, quoting Isa. 29:13; Amos 5:1, 21–23).

Let us take great care in our worship of the holy God. We'll meditate on another element of worship tomorrow.

Scriptures for Study: Read the texts mentioned in today's reading (spread it over tomorrow's reading). Meditate on the centrality of proper worship in the Christian and in the church.

Reverence

entrepō

At the very heart of the concept and outworking of *worship* is the principle of *reverence*. The Hebrew word translated "reverence" in the OT is usually *shachah*, the same word used for worship. In the NT, however, we find a most remarkable word.

The Greek *entrepō* (1788) literally means "to turn into oneself, to put self to shame, to feel respect or deference toward someone else." It's graphically used, for example, in the Parable of the Wicked Vinedressers (Matt. 21:37; Mark 12:6; Luke 20:13). A vineyard owner hired men to tend his vineyard, but they were wicked. When the owner sent servants to collect the harvest, the tenants beat them and stoned them, even killing some. He finally sent his son, thinking the tenants would "reverence" him, but instead they killed him. The parable is, of course, about the Lord Jesus and the many servants of God who came before Him.

That is, indeed, the scene today, even in many churches. We simply do not reverence the Lord. Instead of putting ourselves to shame and completely bearing ourselves to God, we entertain ourselves and demand what we want, and He is thereby mistreated. How can we worship when we are laughing at the "Christian" comedian, performing a stage play, or swaying to the music of a rock band? Frankly, such things should grieve us.

This trend is really not at all new, however, for "there is no new thing under the sun" (Eccles. 1:9). There are actually biblical examples of it. One of the most profound appears in 1 Kings 18. It's noteworthy that when Elijah just *asked* the people if they were ready to follow God or Baal, not a single person responded (v. 21). But when he then asked if they would like to see a "contest" between him and the priests of Baal, they got really excited about that (v. 24). Now, I do not believe for a moment that that was Elijah's motive, but what a picture that is of the church today! People want a show, and to get crowds, to build a big church, and to appear successful. Many Christian leaders are more than happy to provide people with whatever they want. Where is the Scripture for such a philosophy of church building?

Let us again be challenged to proper worship.

Scriptures for Study: Continue reading the scriptures mentioned yesterday.

Submit

hupotassō

A third result of Spirit-filling is "submission" (Eph. 5:21–6:4). Here is one of the most misunderstood principles of God's Word, which has been greatly misapplied and abused. But this principle is actually the one that leads into Paul's deeper discussion of the family and the responsibilities of each family member, as well as that of employers and employees.

It needs to be stated clearly right from the start that submission has absolutely nothing to do with superiority, inferiority, authority, or position. Submission does not mean "slavery," nor does it imply "domination." Neither does it mean the same as "obedience."

Submit is *hupotassō* (5293). The root *tassō* (5021) originally carried the military connotation of drawing up troops (or ships) into battle array. From that came the ideas of directing or appointing someone to a task and to arrange and put things in order. The prefix *hupo* (5259), then, means "under."

To illustrate, when someone joins the military, he's no longer an individual; he no longer governs himself but voluntarily ranks himself underneath someone else. I was amazed when the army came out with the new recruiting slogan some time back: "An Army of One." How silly that is, but it does reflect the philosophy today of individualism and independence apart from submission. The whole point of *hupotassō* is not to be an army of one, but to *voluntarily get in order under someone*.

As Spirit-filled Christians, then, we rank ourselves under one another within God's predefined positions. Again, this does not imply that one person is inferior to another. Rather, it means that the Christian is humble and is willing to be "ranked underneath" as God prescribes. Without such order, there is chaos.

The Christian, for example, ranks himself underneath God-ordained human government and obeys its laws, as long as they do not demand that he disobey God's Word (Rom. 13). The Christian wife ranks herself under her husband and follows his godly leadership (Eph. 5:22; 1 Cor. 11:3). In turn, the Christian husband ranks himself under the direct headship of Christ and leads his wife by God's Word (Eph. 5:22, 25; 1 Cor. 11:3). Christian children rank themselves underneath their parents and obey them (Eph. 6:1–3). The Christian employee ranks himself under his employer and obeys in much the same way as he obeys the government (6:5; cf. Rom. 13:1ff.).

So, Spirit-filling brings proper submission, which in turn maintains proper order. This will especially transform our homes and workplaces.

Scriptures for Study: Read Ephesians 5:21–6:4, observing God's design.

Quench

sbennumi

We'll conclude our meditations on Spirit-filling today and tomorrow by observing exactly how we can be Spirit-filled. There are actually four NT commands concerning the believer's relationship to the Holy Spirit. One is that we must not **grieve** the Holy Spirit (see Mar. 21). Another is that we are to "walk in the Spirit" (Gal. 5:16; see **walk**, see June 14).

Another that we've not yet mentioned, however, is that we must not in any way **quench** the Holy Spirit (1 Thess 5:19). In the literal sense, the Greek *sbennumi* (4570) means "to extinguish by drowning with water, as opposed to smothering."[251] It's used in the literal sense in several places, such as Mark 9:46, which speaks of hell as a place "where their worm dieth not, and the fire is not quenched." We see it again in Ephesians 6:16, where Paul declares that the "shield of faith" is "able to quench all the fiery darts of the wicked." The leather-covered shield of the ancient warrior was often soaked in water to extinguish arrows that had been dipped in pitch and set on fire.

Figuratively, then, *sbennumi* means "to dampen, hinder, repress, as in preventing the Holy Spirit from exerting His full influence."[252] How do we "drown" the Holy Spirit's working? By simply saying "no" to Him, by resisting His guidance, by opposing His will.

It's significant that the original sin of Satan was rebellion against God, as declared in Isaiah 14:14: "I will ascend above the heights of the clouds; I will be like the most High." Just think, then, when a believer says, "*I* will" instead of "*thy* will," he or she is acting just like Satan and therefore quenching the Holy Spirit. How significant that is in our day of "selfism"! To put it bluntly, it's positively satanic to elevate *self* over the *Spirit*, to be concerned with *self*-esteem instead of *Christ*-esteem. The Lord Jesus Himself yielded to the Father's will in the Garden of Gethsemane with the words, "Not my will, but thine, be done," and we must do the same or we extinguish the work of the Holy Spirit in us.

This leads us to one other command, which we'll examine tomorrow.

Scriptures for Study: What graphic word did Stephen use to describe Jewish rebellion against Christ (Acts 7:51)? 🕮 What language does Isaiah 63:10 use to describe Israel's sin against His Spirit?

Yield

paristēmi

One other requirement for Spirit-filling is *yieldedness*, which is truly the key to that filling.

Paul wrote the Romans on this issue in 6:13 and 12:1, where we find the Greek *paristēmi* (3936), **yield**, in 6:13 and "present" in 12:1. This is a compound word comprised of *histēmi* (2476), "to place or stand," and *para* (3844), "near." It, therefore, means "to cause to stand near or before." It was used widely in secular Greek, such as, "to place at someone's disposal," "to bring [as a sacrifice]," and "bring before (the emperor or the court)."[253] Paul's point, then, is clear: The Christian is commanded to place himself before the Lord as a living sacrifice for God's glory and use, to yield to the total control of God's will, to conform not to the world's mold but to God's mold as revealed in His Word.

Theologian Louis Sperry Chafer says it very well:

> A yieldedness to the will of God is not demonstrated by some one particular issue: it is rather a matter of having taken the will of God as the rule of one's life. To be in the will of God is simply to be willing to do His will without reference to any particular thing He may choose. It is electing His will to be final, even before we know what He may wish us to do. It is, therefore, not a question of being willing to do some one thing: it is a question of being willing to do *anything*, when, where and how, it may seem best in His heart of love. It is taking the normal and natural position of childlike trust which has already consented to the wish of the Father even before anything of the outworking of His wish is revealed. This distinction cannot be overemphasized. . . . There must be a covenant relationship of trust in which His will is assented to *once for all* and without reservation.[254]

Indeed, the way to know God's *will* is to know His *Word*. To be yielded, then, is to **covenant** (see Dec. 27) with God to obey His Word *before we even know what it says*. Once we settle that issue, we'll accept whatever it says. The primary problem in all of us is biblical authority. We must settle that question before we can even address any other.

Scriptures for Study: What does Paul go on to say about yielding in Romans 6:16? 🕮 What was the testimony of the churches in Macedonia (2 Cor. 8:1–5)?

Stir Up

anazōpureō

The apostle Paul gave Pastor Timothy some wonderfully encouraging counsel in his final NT letter. He challenged that sometimes discouraged pastor, "Wherefore I put thee in remembrance that thou stir up the gift of God, which is in thee by the putting on of my hands" (2 Tim. 1:6).

"Stir up" translates *anazōpureō* (329), which appears only here the NT. The root *zōē* (2222; see Oct. 20) means "life," the root *pur* (4442; English *pyromaniac*) means "fire," and the prefix *ana* (303) means "up." Putting all that together paints the picture: "to kindle up the flame," or "to rekindle the fire." As one Greek authority puts it, "to stir up smoldering embers into a living flame."[255] Just as we occasionally have to stir a fire in a fireplace, fan it a little, and add some fuel, every believer needs the same, spiritually speaking. The fuel is the Word of God, and the Holy Spirit is the fan and the stirring that rekindles the warmth and passion in the believer.

Specifically, Paul says to "stir up *the gift* of God." While "gift" might refer to Timothy's "spiritual gift" (see Feb. 15), it seems more likely that it refers more specifically to Timothy's ordination into the ministry. Paul goes on to say that it was bestowed at the "laying on of hands," a metaphor for ordination into the ministry. Paul was obviously present at that ordination; note the similarity between that verse and 1 Timothy 4:14 (cf. Acts 13:3; Titus 1:5).

What, then, are the characteristics of the gift Timothy needed to stir up? The answer lies in the next verse: "For God hath not given us the spirit of fear; but of power, and of love, and of a sound mind." He challenges Timothy to remember the **power** (*dunamis*, see Feb. 28), **love** (*agapē*, see Jan. 19), and **sound mind** (*sōphronismos*, from *sōphrōn*, **sober**, see May 23) that he has in Christ.

Paul's words were addressed directly, of course, to Timothy, and therefore apply specifically to pastors; it is indeed easy for a pastor to get discouraged in the face of the great difficulties of biblical pastoral ministry. But Paul's encouragement also applies to *every* believer. Every Christian will get discouraged from time to time, and Paul's words will serve us well as a challenge to "stir up" what God has given us.

Scriptures for Study: When you're tempted to get discouraged, read what Paul suffered throughout his ministry (2 Cor. 11:23–30). Despite those hardships, he could nonetheless write the words of 12:9–10. 🕮 You might also want to review the word **faint** (Jan. 8).

Head

kephalē

Back on September 9, we alluded to the principle of "headship," which is integrally tied to "submission."

Head is *kephalē* (2776), which means exactly what it implies, "the head, top, that which is uppermost in relation to something," such as the head of a person (Matt. 8:20) or animal (Rev. 9:17). Used metaphorically of persons, then, it speaks of one who is "chief, one to whom others are subordinate."[256] Some interpreters try to get around the implications of authority by saying that *kephalē* can also mean "source or origin," but the only time this is even hinted is in secular Greek to refer to the "source of a river."[257]

Paul uses this word, for example, in Ephesians 5:23: "For the husband is the head of the wife." God has ordained the husband to be the head, the leader in the home. The wife is to voluntarily "rank herself" underneath that leadership. The analogy of the body is crucial here. The head controls the body. She, therefore, doesn't act *before* or *independently* of the head. If the body acts independently, the result is chaos, or even "convulsions." Tragically we see many families today in convulsions because of either *no* leadership or the *wrong* leadership.

In the same verse, Paul goes on to give another even more significant example: "even as Christ is the head of the church" (cf. 1:22; Col. 1:18). Christ is the Head, the Leader, the Controller of the church. If the church, and thereby each individual Christian, acts independently from Christ, there is chaos.

Writing over forty years ago, A. W. Tozer was deeply burdened by this very problem. In one of the most powerful articles he ever penned, he lamented: "Jesus Christ has today almost no authority at all among the groups that call themselves by His name. . . . [It] may be likened to that of a king in a limited, constitutional monarchy. The king (sometimes depersonalized by the term 'the Crown') is in such a country no more than a traditional rallying point, a pleasant symbol of unity and loyalty much like a flag or a national anthem. He is lauded, feted and supported, but his real authority is small. On formal occasions he appears in his royal attire to deliver the tame, colorless speech put into his mouth by the real rulers of the country."[258]

Scriptures for Study: Read the following scriptures, noting the vital importance of Christ's headship: Matthew 21:42 and Acts 4:11 (see July 9); 1 Corinthians 11:3; Ephesians 1:22; Colossians 2:10, 19.

Feet (1)

pous

As the head is used in Scripture as a powerful metaphor, so is the opposite extremity—the **feet**. The Greek here is the very common word *pous* (4228), which literally, of course, refers to the feet of men (Matt. 10:14) and animals (7:6).

It is the metaphorical uses of *pous*, however, that capture our attention. One such use is the idea of the feet referring to the whole person, which was used in Classical Greek as well as in the NT. Romans 3:15, for example, pictures sinful men as those whose "feet are swift to shed blood."

Another use of *pous* is the idea of "at the feet of someone," in the sense of respect, subordination, or worship. Jesus' followers, for example, sat at His feet for teaching (Luke 8:35; 10:39). Paul also sat at the feet of Gamaliel to learn "the law of the fathers" (Acts 22:3). Others threw themselves at Jesus' feet in worship (Luke 17:16; Rev. 1:17; 22:8). Especially touching is the woman who washed his feet with her tears and dried them with her hair (Luke 7:38).

By far the most significant metaphorical use of *pous*, however, is that of a symbol of power and dominion. A common image in ancient times was the conqueror's foot on the neck of his defeated enemy. At Joshua's command, for example, his captains put their feet on the necks of the five defeated Amorite kings (Josh. 10:24). The same image is used of Christ's victory over Satan in Romans 16:20.

There are then references to the ultimate victory of our Lord as He will rule and reign on earth. Paul looks forward to this day in 1 Corinthians 15:25, 27–28: "For he must reign, till he hath put all enemies under his feet. . . . For he hath put all things under his feet. But when he saith all things are put under him, it is manifest that he is excepted, which did put all things under him. And when all things shall be subdued unto him, then shall the Son also himself be subject unto him that put all things under him, that God may be all in all."

What a day that will be!

Scriptures for Study: Note Hebrews 1:13 and 10:13, where the Greek literally reads "footstool for His feet."

Feet (2)

pous

There is one other metaphorical use of *pous* that deserves a full day of meditation. It pictures the feet as "an instrument of moving." The most graphic example of this usage appears in Romans 10:15, a quotation of Isaiah 52:7: "How beautiful are the feet of them that preach the gospel of peace, and bring glad tidings of good things!"

About twenty-five miles northeast of Athens, there lays the famous plain "Marathon," where in 490 BC the Greek general Miltiades defeated the Persians, led by Darius I. To let Athens know of the defeat so they would not prematurely surrender to the Persian fleet, Miltiades sent a runner named Pheidippides, to report the victory. Upon arriving in Athens, he delivered the message and then promptly collapsed and died. As you might think, today's "marathon race" is named after that incident.

Such runners were used regularly in ancient times to report battles and other critical events. To keep vigilant watch for such runners, lookouts were posted at all times. These lookouts were specially trained to discern how the runner was moving. If he was moving sluggishly, this meant bad news. But if he was moving quickly, kicking up dust with his feet, the lookout knew immediately that the news was good, and he could start spreading the coming of the good news before it even arrived.

With that backdrop, Paul declares that every believer is such a runner, carrying the good news, the glad tidings of **the Gospel** (see Feb. 5) everywhere he goes. This is not an *option* for the believer; it's a *mandate*. It's our duty to proclaim the Gospel.

Among his many books, the greatest gifts to the church to come from the pen of theologian, pastor, and teacher Dr. R. C. Sproul are (in my opinion): *The Holiness of God* and *Chosen by God*. In the latter, he writes of Paul's logical progression of thought in verses 13–15: "Without sending there are no preachers. Without preachers there is no preaching. Without preaching there is no hearing of the gospel. Without the hearing of the gospel there is no believing of the gospel. Without the believing of the gospel there is no calling upon God to be saved. Without the calling upon God to be saved there is no salvation."[259]

Scriptures for Study: Read Isaiah 52:7–9 and Romans 10:13–17, meditating on your responsibility to witness for Christ.

SEPTEMBER 16

Washing

loutron

One of the greatest challenges of God's Word appears in Ephesians 5:26, a challenge aimed directly at the Christian husband. Paralleling the Lord Jesus and the church with the husband and wife, the apostle Paul writes, "That he might sanctify and cleanse it with the washing of water by the word."

Inexplicably, many commentators say that this "washing" refers to baptism, but the text doesn't say that, nor is there a single thing in the context to support that idea. Words mean things, and Paul simply does not use the word *baptism* (*baptizō*, see June 24–25). If he meant baptism, why didn't he say baptism?

We must point out, in fact, that if we hold this view here, for consistency we are compelled to hold it for Titus 3:5 as well, which is the only other place that *loutron* (3067, **washing**) appears: "Not by works of righteousness which we have done, but according to his mercy he saved us, by the washing of regeneration, and renewing of the Holy Ghost." But is our salvation based upon the "*baptism* of regeneration"? God forbid! That is the heretical doctrine of baptismal regeneration! Nowhere does the NT teach that the physical act of baptism saves us. Neither does baptism have anything to do with the doctrine of sanctification, which Paul has already mentioned.

No, Paul uses *loutron*, which does *not* mean "baptism" here or anywhere else.[260] Rather *loutron* refers to a basin or laver for washing and to the act of washing itself. It's derived from *louō* (3068), "to bathe." It's also significant that the definite article ("the") is present in the Greek, which means that a *specific washing* is meant. Paul might have in mind here the Greek marriage custom where before the marriage ceremony the bride was bathed in a stream that was sacred to some god or goddess.

Paul goes on to say, in fact, *exactly* what washing he's talking about. The text could not be clearer. As Harry Ironside put it, "The words explain themselves." Using a beautiful metaphor, Paul says that the husband cleanses his wife with the washing of water *by the word*. It's the Word of God that cleanses; it's the Word that sanctifies. Our marriages (and entire homes) should be cleansed constantly by the presence of the Word of God.

Scriptures for Study: What do Psalm 119:9 and John 17:17 declare in regard to our study today?

Word

rhēma

While we've mentioned one word translated **word** several times (*logos*; see Feb. 5, Mar. 16, see July 10), there's another that in one way is even more significant. While *logos* (3056) often refers to a "Christian proclamation as a whole in the [NT], *rhēma* (4487) usually relates to individual words and utterances."[261]

Among its some seventy occurrences, it appears in John 3:34 to refer to Jesus coming to "[speak] the words of God." In 8:47 Jesus Himself declares to the religious leaders, "He that is of God heareth God's words: ye therefore hear them not, because ye are not of God." Yes, the religious leaders knew much about the *Word* of God, that is, the OT, but they knew nothing of the *words* of God. Paul uses *rhēma* in Romans 10:17, "So then faith cometh by hearing, and hearing by the word of God." He uses it three times in Ephesians: first, in reference to the truth of salvation; second, in reference to the Christian husband sanctifying his wife by the Word (5:26; see yesterday); and third, in 6:17, where part of the Christian's spiritual armor is "the word[s] of God."

In all these verses, then, the emphasis is not to the entire body of Scripture per se, but rather, to *individual utterances* that proclaim various truths. It is, indeed, the *words* of God that comprise the sword of the Spirit!

Let us repeat, words mean things, and that's why they are my personal passion. Evangelicals say, "Oh, yes, we believe in the Word of God," but the real question is, do we believe the *words* of God, every one them, every jot and tittle? I lovingly submit that if the *words* of God really mattered to us, we wouldn't have near as many problems as we do today, such as the diluted Gospel, the seeker-sensitive movement, and various other methods of ministry.

I would also dare to interject that an emphasis on the *words* of Scripture makes the whole concept of "Dynamic Equivalence" very troubling. This approach to Bible translation replaces the concept of a *word-for-word* translation with a *thought-for-thought* translation. In other words, as long as we get across the *thought* of the author, then the *exact* words aren't really important. While that approach is popular, it should deeply trouble those who cherish the *words* of Scripture.

Scriptures for Study: Read the following verses, noting the significance of the use of the word *rhēma*: John 5:46–47; 6:63; 8:47; 17:8; 2 Peter 3:2; etc.[262]

Spot [and] Wrinkle

spilos [and] *rhutis*

Today we'll ponder three synonyms, each of which is significant for Christian living. **Spot** is *spilos* (4696), which literally refers to a spot or stain and so metaphorically to a moral flaw. The verb form *spiloō* (4695, to stain or defile) appears in James 3:6 to describe the tongue: "And the tongue is a fire, a world of iniquity; so is the tongue among our members, that it defileth [*spiloō*] the whole body, and setteth on fire the course of nature; and it is set on fire of hell." What a challenge to be careful what we say!

The noun *spilos*, then, occurs only twice in the NT, and the meaning in both is figurative. Peter calls ungodly people "spots," that is, moral defects (2 Pet. 2:13). Paul's use is a little more unique, in that he writes that the sanctifying love of the Christian husband for his wife is a love that is *without* spot, that is, any moral stain (Eph. 5:27). That certainly prevents adultery, pornography, and other stains that destroy so many marriages.

In the same verse, Paul adds that such a marriage is also without **wrinkle**. This is *rhutis* (4512, from an obsolete verb *rhuoō*, to draw together), which is "indicative of age or disease."[263] The picture this paints is that no matter how many years the couple has been married, the relationship has "no wrinkles," that is, no appearance of age. Yes, we get old and show the ravages of age, but our marriage does not. I've spoken to couples who have been married many years but who continue to say, "We're still on our honeymoon." Praise the Lord for such an attitude.

Not satisfied, Paul also adds the words "or any such thing," which will then give the end result of a marriage that is "without blemish." This is again *amōmos* (299, see Jan. 18), which Paul uses in 1:4 and means "spotless, free from faultiness." This word occurs in the Septuagint in Leviticus 22:21 to show that a sacrificial animal was to have no spot or blemish.

This is how we are to live—pure in attitude and action, a "living sacrifice" (Rom. 12:1). Why did God choose us in Christ before the foundation of the world? Not just so we could go to heaven, but rather so we *could* be and *would* be holy in *position* and *practice*.

Scriptures for Study: Read the following verses, noting the pure life that the Christian is to live (*amōmos*): Colossians 1:22 ("unblameable"); 1 Thessalonians 3:13 ("unblameable"); Hebrews 9:14 ("without spot"); Jude 24 ("faultless").

Cherish

thalpō

While we're on the subject of the Christian husband, let's note another word Paul uses in Ephesians 5:29; he says the godly husband will **cherish** his wife.

The Greek *thalpō* (2282), "to impart warmth, to cherish and nurse," paints a beautiful scene. While the world says to men, "Be macho," this word actually pictures a bird imparting body heat upon the nest. The husband (and father) is to provide the soft, warm place of comfort and nourishment. Yes, the wife adds the feminine touches and dresses up that nest, but it is the husband who provides it. And yes, God *ultimately* provides all that, but He does it through the man of the house. This was God's original design in creation, but the Fall shattered it, and it's up to each of us, through Spirit-filling (see Aug. 30ff.), to restore what was destroyed. Let each husband ask, "Do I nourish and cherish my wife?"

Dr. Robert Seizer, in his book *Mortal Lessons*: *Notes in the Art of Surgery*, provides a beautiful illustration of such sensitivity. He tells of performing surgery to remove a tumor in which it was necessary to sever a facial nerve, leaving a young woman's mouth permanently twisted in palsy. In Dr. Seizer's own words:

> Her young husband is in the room. He stands on the opposite side of the bed, and together they seem to dwell in the evening lamp light, isolated from me, private. Who are they, I ask myself, he and this wry-mouth I have made, who gaze at and touch each other so generously, greedily? The young woman speaks. 'Will my mouth always be like this?' she asks. 'Yes,' I say, 'it will. It is because the nerve was cut.' She nods, and is silent. But the young man smiles. 'I like it,' he says. 'It is kind of cute.' All at once I know who he is. I understand, and I lower my gaze. One is not bold in an encounter with a god. Unmindful, he bends to kiss her crooked mouth, and I, so close, can see how he twists his own lips to accommodate to hers, to show her that their kiss still works. It is possible to love your spouse as your own body. Practically, this means that the husband must do all he can to understand her world.[264]

Scriptures for Study: *Thalpō* appears only one other place in the NT (1 Thess. 2:7). What is the picture there? 🕮 Read the story of Jacob finding a wife in Genesis 29 (especially vv. 16–30), noting how much he must have cherished Rachel.

Fear (1)

phobos, phobeō

The words in this group actually come from a verb that does not even appear in the NT, *phobomai*, which literally means "to flee" and was used mostly by Homer. Later it refers to the physical emotion of *fear*, terror, and anxiety. It sometimes means respect, awe, and reverence, as in veneration for the gods. It is, of course, from this word group that we get the English *phobia*, an irrational fear of something.

All those meanings, except "to flee," appear in both the OT (e.g., Jon. 1:10, 16) and the NT. This word group, in fact, is common in the NT, appearing some 158 times. There are two fundamental ways these words are used, so we'll meditate on both, the first today and the second tomorrow.

The first way the verb *phobeō* (5399) and the noun *phobos* (5401) are used is in the general sense of actual fear and terror. The shepherds in Luke 2:8–9, for example, were "sore afraid" when the angel of the Lord appeared to announce the Messiah's birth, prompting the angel to say, "Fear not" (v. 10). After Jesus healed the demon-possessed man in the country of the Gadarenes, the people were terrified ("taken with great fear") and asked Him to leave (Luke 8:37). Even the disciples cried out in fear when they saw Jesus walking on the water (Matt. 14:26). Tragically, while unbelievers *should* be afraid of God's wrath and the judgment that awaits, "there is no fear of God before their eyes" (Rom. 3:18).

For the believer, however, such fear no longer exists. As Paul wrote, "For ye have not received the spirit of bondage again to fear; but ye have received the Spirit of adoption, whereby we cry, Abba, Father" (Rom. 8:15). The Christian no longer fears God because there is now a new relationship.

Another way that fear evaporates in the Christian life is that no longer is there a fear of death. As Paul assures us, "To be absent from the body [is] to be present with the Lord" (2 Cor. 5:8), for "to live is Christ, and to die is gain" (Phil. 1:21, 23).

Finally, neither does the Christian fear men or what they might do to him for Christ's sake. As Peter encourages, "But and if ye suffer for righteousness' sake, happy are ye: and be not afraid of their terror, neither be troubled" (1 Pet. 3:14; cf. Matt. 10:28).

Scriptures for Study: Which emotion "casts out fear" in 1 John 4:18? 🕮 What outlook does this then produce (Acts 21:13)?

Fear (2)

phobos, phobeō

The second way the verb *phobeō* (5399) and the noun *phobos* (5401) are used in the NT is in the moral sense of awe, reverence, and honor.

A perfect example of this appears in Acts 9:31: "Then had the churches rest [from persecution] throughout all Judaea and Galilee and Samaria, and were edified; and walking in the fear of the Lord, and in the comfort of the Holy Ghost, were multiplied." At the very heart of worship is the attitude of awe and reverence for God. This same attitude also drives the true believer to "cleanse [himself] from all filthiness of the flesh and spirit, perfecting holiness in the fear of God" (2 Cor. 7:1) and to "[submit himself] one to another in the fear of God" (Eph. 5:21).

Puritan Charles Bridges perfectly defines this "fear of the Lord" when he writes: "It is that affectionate reverence by which the child of God bends himself humbly and carefully to his Father's law. His wrath is so bitter, and His love so sweet; that hence springs an earnest desire to please Him, and—because of the danger of coming short from his own weakness and temptations—a holy watchfulness and *fear*, 'that he might not sin against Him.'"[265]

Many a Bible student has been puzzled by the phrase "fear and trembling." It appears, for example in Ephesians 6:5, where the slave (or employee) is to obey his master (or employer) with "fear and trembling." This attitude is not cowering in fear of our employer, but rather, a respect for his position and authority.

Deeper than this, however, is the thought of our fear of neglecting our responsibility and in so doing disobeying the Lord. In 1 Corinthians 2:3, Paul writes that he came to the Corinthians in "fear and trembling." This was a fear of failing both the Corinthians and the Lord.

The same thought appears again in Philippians 2:12, where Paul writes, "Work out your own salvation with fear and trembling." Notice that the verse does not say to work *for* salvation, but to work *out* salvation. As believers we work out the salvation we possess; that is, we *manifest* it, we *prove* it to others. We do all that with the attitude that we do not want to fail our Lord.

Scriptures for Study: What did his "fear and trembling" drive Paul to do (1 Cor. 2:3–5)? 🕮 Likewise, what does our reverence for God drive us to do (Heb. 12:28)?

Joined

proskollaō

The Greek *proskollaō* (4347) is a graphic word in the NT. It's used, for example, three times in the context of marriage, and surely no other word better describes what God meant marriage to be.

Quoting Genesis 2:24, our Lord Himself declares in Matthew 19:4–5, "Have ye not read, that he which made them at the beginning made them male and female, and said, For this cause shall a man leave father and mother, and shall cleave to his wife: and they twain shall be one flesh?" He adds in Mark 10:5–9 that this was always God's design "from the beginning of the creation."

Joined is *proskollaō*, a beautiful word that means "to glue or cement together" and pictures the most intimate union possible. When we glue or cement things together, is it not our intention that they stay together? That truly underscores the tragedy of divorce, which is the ripping apart of what has been glued together.

The same basic concept is true of the Hebrew behind the word *cleave* in Genesis 2:24 (*proskollaō* in the Septuagint). *Cleave* translates *dēbaq* (1692H), which means to cling to, join with, stay with. It's used, for example, in Job 41:17 of the great sea creature Leviathan, whose scales are tightly fastened together, and of clods of earth being stuck together in 38:38. Most significant is that it's also used in Numbers 36:7 for someone holding on to an inheritance. How vivid that is! As we would hold on to an inheritance and never let it go, we hold on to our marriages as if they are our very life, which in a sense is exactly what they are. So, God's design is for marriage to be permanent.

Proskollaō is also used, however, for every Christian in his or her relationship with God. Acts 11:23 declares that each of us is to "cleave unto the Lord." The imagery is again right out of the OT. Most notable is Deuteronomy 30:20: "That thou mayest love the Lord thy God, and that thou mayest obey his voice, and that thou mayest cleave unto him: for he is thy life, and the length of thy days" (cf. 10:20; Josh. 22:5; 23:8).

Let us, indeed, be "glued" to our Lord and His Word.

Scriptures for Study: What is the key principle of marriage, according to Malachi 2:14? (See tomorrow's reading.) 🕮 What does true love for the Lord imply (Matt. 16:24–25)?

Marry [and] Marriage

gameō [and] *gamos*

We have mentioned the word **marriage** many times up to now, so this would be a good place to deal with it specifically. The verb behind **marry** is *gameō* (1060), which is derived from the root *gam* (or *gem*), "to fit together, to pair," and so means "to marry, celebrate a wedding, have sexual relations." The noun **marriage** (1062), then, refers to a wedding, a marriage, and even the consummation of a marriage.[266] It's from these words, of course, that we derive such English words as *bigamy* and *monogamy*.

Interestingly, and contrary to what one might think, monogamy actually dominated the Greek world, in spite of the fact that we see polygamy referred to many times in the Greek myths. The hero in Homer's writing, for example, was monogamous and faithful. Still, however, the Greek husband was free to have concubines or even relations with harlots with no stigma attached.

While these Greek words seldom appear in the OT Septuagint, when they do they always refer to monogamy *and* faithfulness in that marriage, as adultery was punishable by death (Lev. 20:10; cf. Exod. 20:14). We should also note that while polygamy was practiced by Abraham and others, which is the model used by Mormonism to defend this practice, God merely tolerated it; it was never His design.

What, then, is marriage in God's design? The key principle of marriage, according to Malachi 2:14, is that it's a **covenant** (see Dec. 27), often called "the covenant of companionship." A companion is one with whom we are united in goals, values, affections, and, in the case of marriage, even body. So, when the "covenant of companionship" is made, each partner promises to love the other with an *agapē* **love** (see Jan. 19), to take away each other's loneliness, to meet each other's sexual needs, to honor and be faithful to the other, to bear children as God dictates, and many other things as well.

As wonderful as marriage is—as I write this, I've been married for thirty-two years, and we're still newlyweds—when we get to heaven there will be no marriage (Matt. 22:30), for there we will know far greater glories. In the meantime, however, let us have marriages that are all that God wants them to be.

Scriptures for Study: What counsel does Paul give concerning marriage and remaining single in 1 Corinthians 7:8–9? 📖 What does the teaching of mandatory celibacy reveal in 1 Timothy 4:1–3?

Obey

hupakouō

The word **obey** is one of the words from which most of us recoil. By nature none of us wants to obey. From the time we are children to the time when we are "old and set in our ways," we don't want anyone telling us what to do. As we mature, of course, we finally realize that obedience is necessary. Without it, there would be chaos everywhere.

This Greek verb *hupakouō* (5219) is a compound comprised of *hupo* (5259), meaning "under," and *akouō* (191), meaning to "hear, listen." To obey, then, doesn't just mean to "follow orders," like most of us think. Rather, obeying means "to get under the authority of someone and listen."

Of the some twenty-one occurrences of this word (fifteen more for the noun *hupakoē*, 5218, "obedience"), Ephesians 6:1 is one of the most pointed, as children are to obey their parents. God demands that children get under the authority of their parents and listen to them. They are not just to "do what they are told," but they are to listen and assimilate what they hear. While young people sometimes doubt it, parents actually know more than their children think they do. They, too, were kids once upon a time. They have been through the same troubles, pressures, and temptations.

Similarly, slaves (and employees) are to obey their masters (and employers). They are to get under the authority of the employer and heed his orders.

Even more significant, every believer is to obey God and His Word. We are, in fact, to be "as obedient children, not fashioning [ourselves] according to the former lusts in [our] ignorance" (1 Pet. 1:14), and we are to "[purify our] souls in obeying the truth" (1:22). Further, our "every thought" is to be toward "the obedience of Christ" (2 Cor. 10:5). So serious is *not* obeying God's Word that Paul wrote, "And if any man obey not our word by this epistle, note that man, and have no company with him, that he may be ashamed" (2 Thess. 3:14).

Paul praised the believers in Rome for their obedience, as it had become a testimony to others (Rom. 16:19). Can you also be noted for your obedience?

Scriptures for Study: What should the Christian *not* obey, according to Romans 6:12? What principle does Paul then lay down in verses 16 and 17?

Honor

timaō

The verb *timaō* (5091) means to estimate worth, hold in respect, **honor**, revere. In Classical Greek the noun *timē* (5092) means the worth that one ascribes to a person. This concept was carried over into the NT, and it truly underscores what it means to honor someone (and what it means if we *don't* honor them). To honor someone means to recognize that they're worth something. Who, then, are we to honor?

First, we are to honor God. Quoting Isaiah 29:13, our Lord declared, "Well hath Esaias prophesied of you hypocrites, as it is written, This people honoureth me with their lips, but their heart is far from me" (Mark 7:6). While many people say they "love God" and offer other lip service, in reality they think Him worthless and are far from being true Christians (cf. Matt. 7:21–23).

Our Lord again says, "That all men should honour the Son, even as they honour the Father. He that honoureth not the Son honoureth not the Father which hath sent him" (John 5:23). He says elsewhere that we in turn will be honored if we serve him: "If any man serve me, let him follow me. . . . If any man serve me, him will my Father honour" (John 12:26).

Second, children are to honor their parents. Paul not only said that children are to *obey* their parents, but they are also to honor them (Eph. 6:2). Where did he get that idea? From God's Law (Exod. 20:12) and from the Lord Jesus Himself (Matt. 15:4).

Third, a husband is to honor his wife. While *timaō* is not directly used in this way, the principle is certainly present in Proverbs 31:10: "Who can find a virtuous woman? for her price is far above rubies." The Christian husband cherishes his wife (Eph. 5:29).

Fourth, we are to honor widows in the church, that is, those who "are widows indeed" (1 Tim. 5:3–5). A "widow indeed" is a widow who has no means of support, such as family members. So, one of the specific ministries of the local church is to support such godly widows.

Fifth, we are to honor every person. As Peter wrote, "Honour all men" (1 Pet. 2:17). While we certainly don't approve of certain things men do and say, life is worth something, and our desire is to reach the lost for Christ.

Scriptures for Study: Besides honor, what else belongs to God (Rev. 7:12)? 🕮 Who will eventually honor God (5:13)?

Chastening, Instruction

paideia

In Classical Greek, the noun *paideia* (3809), and other words in this group (*paideuō*, 3811, and *paideutēs*, 3810), originally referred to the instruction of children (as the root *pais* means child or boy). It "denotes the upbringing and handling of the child which is growing up to maturity and which thus needs direction, teaching, instruction and a certain measure of compulsion in the form of discipline or even chastisement."[267] This word group truly characterizes Greek culture because education was central.

Paul reflects this attitude in Ephesians 6:4, where it's predominantly the father who is responsible to "bring [children] up in the nurture [*paideia*] and admonition of the Lord." At the very foundation of the family, and ultimately all society, is the instruction of children. This not only involves teaching, but discipline and even punishment. As Proverbs 13:24 declares: "He that spareth his rod hateth his son: but he that loveth him chasteneth him betimes [i.e., diligently, immediately]." By nature a child will not listen and obey because he or she is depraved and self-centered. A child must be forced to obey.

So foundational was this principle that Deuteronomy 21:18–21 tells us that a habitually rebellious child was stoned to death. Of course, that was for extreme and habitual rebellion and was part of social law that is not true today. But it still vividly demonstrates that a child who does not learn discipline is absolutely worthless to everyone, even society, a fact that is certainly not believed today.

These words are also used, however, for *every* Christian (regardless of age). Most notable is 2 Timothy 3:16, where the profits of Scripture are its "doctrine," "reproof," "correction," and "instruction" (*paideia*). One of the functions of Scripture is discipline and rebuke of wrong. Hymenaeus and Alexander, for example, had to be rebuked and "learn [*paideuō*] not to blaspheme" (1 Tim. 1:20; cf. see July 22). Chastening, in fact, is proof that God loves us, and we should not despise it but actually be thankful for it (Heb. 12:5–6; cf. Rev. 3:9).

Tomorrow we'll examine a related word that further underscores the Christian's training.

Scriptures for Study: According to 1 Corinthians 11:32, what is one purpose of chastening? 🕮 What does Paul tell every pastor to be "teaching" in Titus 2:12–13?

Admonition

nouthesia

As mentioned yesterday, there is another important NT word that emphasizes proper training. It's the word *nouthesia* (3559), which is translated **admonition** in its three NT occurrences (the verb *noutheteō*, 3560, appears eight additional times).

In Ephesians 6:4, Paul says that children must also be raised in the "admonition" of the Lord. While one Greek source says that *nouthesia* and *paideia*, as used here, are "more or less identical," that seems unlikely. For one thing, it's difficult for us to imagine Paul being redundant; for another, *nouthesia* never means punishment.

Additionally, another Greek authority goes deeper into the matter when he says that *nouthesia* is the milder term and pictures training through encouragement and warning, while *paideia* pictures training by act and discipline.[268] To simplify, *paideia* is training by *act* while *nouthesia* is training by *word.* So, by word and act, parents are to train their children in every area of life.

There is one other aspect of the Greek *nouthesia*, namely, "giving a warning." Parents are to warn their children of the pitfalls of life and the consequences for rejecting God's Word. Many a parent has wept when their child went bad, but a little counsel quickly uncovers that they never really taught them what God's Word says, nor the consequences of disobeying God's Word. We must warn our children of the consequences of rejecting God and the authority of His Word, an unsurrendered life, the wrong values and priorities, and unfaithfulness to God in general.

Is it not odd that parents engrain in their children the danger of a hot stove but never warn them of the far greater peril of neglecting God and His Word? As Albert Barnes writes, "If a man does not teach his children *truth*, others will teach them *error*." Puritan John Flavel wrote, "If you neglect to instruct them in the way of holiness, will the devil fail to instruct them in the way of wickedness?"[269]

Nouthesia is also used for every believer. As Paul wrote the Corinthians, Israel's rebellion and consequent wilderness wanderings serve as an example for us and are "written for our admonition" (1 Cor. 10:11). Likewise, during his three-year ministry in Ephesus, Paul "ceased not to warn every one [about false teachers] night and day with tears" (Acts 20:31).

Let us learn God's Word!

Scriptures for Study: Read the following verses, noting the use of *noutheteō*: Romans 15:14; 1 Corinthians 4:14 ("warn"); Colossians 1:28; 3:16; 1 Thessalonians 5:12.

Singleness, Simplicity

haplotēs

In Classical Greek, *haplotēs* (572) carried a numerical meaning of "single" in contrast to "double" (*diplous*, 1362). In the ethical sense, it came to mean straightness, openness, speaking without a hidden meaning. This developed into the NT usage of sincerity, without duplicity, and "uncomplicated simplicity."[270]

Of its eight NT occurrences, Ephesians 6:5 refers to slaves (or employees) obeying "in singleness of your heart, as unto Christ." One expositor writes, "Obedience was to be rendered, not in formality, pretence, or hypocrisy, but in inward reality and sincerity, and with an undivided heart."[271] It does little or no good to do work with complaint, a negative attitude, or hypocrisy. One might get the job done, but he has really failed in the overall task.

Haplotēs also occurs in the context of the "spiritual gift" (see Feb. 15) of "giving" in Romans 12:8. The person with this gift gives "with simplicity," that is, without ulterior motives, such as wanting something in return or even expecting thanks or recognition. The same idea is present in 2 Corinthians 8:2, 9:11, and 13. As one Greek authority concurs, while *haplotēs* is translated either "liberality" or "bountifulness," that is "not exactly so."[272] Rather, the idea again is giving out of the right motive, namely, sincerity and without a hidden agenda.

There's a fascinating occurrence of the similar form *haplous* (573) in Matthew 6:22–23, where our Lord declares: "The light of the body is the eye: if therefore thine eye be single [*haplous*], thy whole body shall be full of light. But if thine eye be evil, thy whole body shall be full of darkness" (cf. Luke 11:34). William MacDonald wonderfully comments:

> The application is this: The good eye belongs to the person whose motives are pure, who has a single desire for God's interests, and who is willing to accept Christ's teachings literally. His whole life is flooded with light. He believes Jesus' words, he forsakes earthly riches, he lays up treasures in heaven, and he knows that this is the only true security. On the other hand, the bad eye belongs to the person who is trying to live for two worlds. He doesn't want to let go of his earthly treasures, yet he wants treasures in heaven too. The teachings of Jesus seem impractical and impossible to him. He lacks clear guidance since he is full of darkness.[273]

Scriptures for Study: Read the verses noted today, examining your own drives and motives in Christian service.

Eyeservice [and] Menpleasers

ophthalmodouleia [and] *anthropareskos*

As we considered yesterday, some folks give or do other service with the ulterior motive of getting something in return. There are others, however, who do it for a different reason, namely, to be recognized or praised.

Paul mentions this in only two verses, which are both in the context of the labor of slaves (or employees), but they apply to every Christian. In Ephesians 6:6, he writes, "Not with eyeservice, as menpleasers; but as the servants of Christ, doing the will of God from the heart" (cf. Col. 3:22).

Menpleasers is *anthropareskos* (441), from *anthropos* (444), "man," and *areskō* (700), "to please." Augustus Strong offers the most graphic meaning of "man-courting, i.e., fawning." How many people there are today who fawn over someone else to get their approval or praise. **Eyeservice**, then, is *ophthalmodouleia* (3787), which is comprised of *ophthalmos* (3788), "eye" (English *ophthalmologist*), and *douleia* (1397), "service, slavery, bondage," and means that one serves only when someone else has their eye on him, only serves for the sake of appearance.

But the godly employee doesn't do that. He doesn't look busy only when the boss is around; he doesn't just do the minimum of work to get by; he doesn't need to be constantly watched; he doesn't even do his work to please his boss, to get commended by his boss, or even to get a raise in pay. In short, *he's not trying to please men*! His incentive is to please the Lord, to "[do] the will of God from the heart" (Eph. 6:6). One expositor well says:

> Mark how this motive sweetens, sanctifies, ennobles our earthly work. It then becomes a part of our worship. Animated by such a thought, the school boy diligently, joyfully applies himself to his task. The clerk needs no other master's eye over him to keep him to his work. The tradesman carefully executes his orders to the last stitch, when he feels that he works not merely for men, but for Christ. The merchant no longer sells spurious or adulterated goods, when he feels that he sells, not to men, but to the Lord Himself. The minister, the physician, the lawyer, are no longer content with a formal or perfunctory discharge of duty. The creditor, presenting his account, asks no more than is really due, and the debtor faithfully pays it.[274]

Scriptures for Study: Read the following verses, noting Paul's motive in service: Galatians 1:10; 1 Thessalonians 2:4. 🕮 Note this attitude also among the Philippians (2:12).

Wrestle

palē

The apostle Paul gives us one of the gravest warnings in all of Scripture when he writes, "We wrestle not against flesh and blood, but against principalities, against powers, against the rulers of the darkness of this world, against spiritual wickedness in high places" (Eph. 6:12).

Wrestle is *palē* (3823), which occurs only here in the NT. One Greek authority tells us that this refers to "a contest between two in which each endeavors to throw the other, and which is decided when the victor is able [to] hold [his opponent down] with his hand upon his neck."[275] Paul writes something very similar to Timothy, "Fight the good fight of faith" (1 Tim. 6:12). Timothy immediately understood that Paul was saying that spiritual warfare is savage. History tells us why.

Both ancient boxing and wrestling were horrendously brutal. In boxing matches, the "Greeks fought almost to the death with gloves reinforced at the knuckles with an iron band three quarters of an inch thick." The head was the only target, and "there was no rule against hitting a man who was down." There were no rest periods or rounds. The fight continued until one surrendered or was incapacitated. As the brutality increased in Greek times, wrestling and boxing were combined into a new contest, the *pankration*—from *pas* (3956), "all," and *kratos* (2904; April 12), "power," so literally, "game of all powers." Anything except eye gouging and biting was permitted, even kicking in the stomach. Some famous competitors won by breaking the opponent's fingers. One was noted for striking so viciously "with straightened fingers and strong sharp nails that he pierced the flesh of his adversary and dragged out his bowels."[276]

That's why Paul says we are at war! As graphic and barbaric as the ancient *pankration* was, he says that we "wrestle" against an even greater spiritual foe. Are we getting the picture? Paul mentions this again in his last letter, saying of himself, "I have fought a good fight, I have finished my course, I have kept the faith" (2 Tim. 4:7). Timothy immediately understood Paul's meaning. This fight is, indeed, "for keeps." It's not a "police action," a minor skirmish, a border dispute, or any such thing. It's an all-out war to the death. The devil has declared war on us, and we must do the same to him.

Scriptures for Study: Read the following verses, noting the struggles and victory that come in the Christian life: 1 Corinthians 9:25–27; Colossians 1:29; 2 Timothy 2:5; Hebrews 12:1–4.

Drawn Away [and] Enticed

exelkō [and] *deleazō*

James provides us with a sober warning: "But every man is tempted, when he is drawn away of his own lust, and enticed" (James 1:14): **Drawn away** is *exelkō* (1828). The root *helkō* (1670) basically means "to draw," "tug," or, in the case of persons, "compel." Jesus uses this word, for example, of irresistibly drawing souls to Himself (John 6:44; 12:32). The prefix *ek* (1537), however, means out or away, so the picture here is the drawing, tugging, or compelling someone away from that which is good.

Even more graphic is *deleazō* (1185, **enticed**), which means to bait or entrap and pictures the idea of baiting a hook. A fisherman or trapper uses an enticing bait to draw his prey. During World War II, both German and Japanese troops would booby-trap souvenirs, such as pistols and Samurai swords. The Viet Cong did the same in Vietnam. Americans returned the favor, however; since the VC loved to scrounge U.S. supplies, when GIs vacated a campsite, they often left C-rations behind wired to a claymore mine.

All that pictures Satan and his deceptions. He draws us by using bait that looks desirable and even *profitable*. But just as the fisherman, trapper, and soldier hides the consequences of taking the bait, so does Satan. He tries to hide what sin will do. He camouflages the trap so well that only by stopping and carefully examining the situation can we see the trap. Vance Havner writes: "Satan is the Master Deceiver, the Mock angel disguised as an angel of light. He does not plow up the wheat in our Lord's parable, he plants tares that resemble wheat so closely that few know the difference and final separation is left to angels. When Moses performs miracles, Jannes and Jambres are on hand to match the performance. Our Saviour repeatedly warned against deceivers in the last days."[277]

How many Satanic deceptions there are today! There are "societal snares," such as women's liberation, the new morality, and others that continue to destroy the family and erode society. There are also countless "truth traps": cults, heresy in the church, human philosophy, mysticism, and more. The discerning Christian must be constantly vigilant in detecting and avoiding satanic deception.

Scriptures for Study: How did Satan "bait" and entice Eve (Gen. 3:1–6), Achan (Josh. 7:21), and David (2 Sam. 11:2)?

Stand [and] Withstand

histemi [and] *anthistemi*

In that well-known verse about spiritual warfare, Paul instructs us, "Put on the whole armor of God, that ye may be able to stand against the wiles of the devil" (Eph. 6:11). **Stand against** is *stēnai pros,* a military expression that means to stand in front of with a view to holding a critical position, to hold one's ground. Further, "able" is *dunamai* (1410, see Feb. 28), which can be defined as "that which overcomes resistance." By putting on God's armor, we are able to defeat any resistance Satan offers and overcome any obstacle he puts in our path.

The idea here, then, is a primarily defensive tone, that we just face the enemy and hold our ground. This is further indicated by the fact that God has given us five pieces of *defensive* (vv. 14–17a) armor while giving only one *offensive* weapon, the sword (v. 17b).

A basic military tenet is to hold the ground you already possess. One of the problems in the Vietnam War was that we held certain ground during the day while "Charlie" (the Viet Cong) held it at night. Also, terrain was often taken from the enemy only to be given back later when we pulled out of the area. This obviously caused discouragement and a sense of utter futility to many a soldier. Plus, the waste in men, material, and money in such folly was incalculable.

There is something else here, however. It's extremely significant that Paul not only says that the armor makes us able to *stand* against Satan's attacks (v. 11), but also to ***with*****stand** Satan's attacks (v. 13). The Greek is actually different here. The root behind "stand" is *histemi* (2476), while the word for **withstand** is *anthistemi* (436), which means "to set oneself against, oppose, resist." This is the same word used in James 4:7, "Resist the devil, and he will flee from you." In light of the defensive word we saw earlier, this word seems to possess a more offensive tone. Not only must we be *defensive*, holding our present ground, but we must also be *offensive*, landing blows of our own on the enemy. Militarily speaking, no battle, no war, can be won by defense alone. God not only wants us to stand our ground, but He wants us to resist and oppose and land blows of our own with the Word of God.

Scriptures for Study: Read the following verses, noting how *anthistemi* is used in each: Galatians 2:11 ("withstood"); 2 Timothy 3:8 ("resist"); 1 Peter 5:9.

Armor (1)

panoplian

Considering again Ephesians 6:11—"Put on the whole armour of God, that ye may be able to stand against the wiles of the devil"—the words *whole armour* are one word in the Greek, *panoplian* (3833), from which, of course, we get our English word *panoply*, a full suit of armor. The prefix *pas* (3956) means "all or whole" and *hoplon* (3696) means "weapon." Literally, then, the word means "all the weapons" and pictures the full **armor**, both offensive and defensive, of the heavily armed Roman soldier. We have all seen pictures or movies depicting the Roman soldier, and that is the graphic and dramatic picture Paul paints here.

Additionally, the verb **put on** is in the aorist tense, showing a once-for-all act of putting on the armor and never taking it off. It's also in the imperative mood, showing a command with a military snap, as in the term "saddle up" in the modern military, that is, get all your gear together and move out. Finally, the verb is also in the middle voice (see Jan. 18), which means that the subject participates in the results of the action or shares in the benefits of the action. So, putting on the armor of God is greatly to our benefit.

Putting all of this together, God's military command is that we put on all the armor and never take it off, so that we can not only survive, but be victorious in battle. It's not enough for a soldier to go into battle with the attitude that he just wants to survive. General Douglas MacArthur truly said, "In war there can be no substitute for victory." The spiritual application is vivid: We are not fighting to survive, but to win! Our objective is not just to come out unscathed but to inflict casualties on the enemy, Satan and his servants. General George Patton said it well: "No [one] ever won a war by dying for his country; he won it by making the other poor [soul] die for his country."

While such sentiment might appear repugnant, it must be the attitude of the Christian in the spiritual war. The only way we can be victorious is to put on all the weapons and leave them on for the duration of the conflict, a conflict that will continue until we go home to be the Lord.

Scriptures for Study: Read the following occurrences of *hoplon*, noting that the Christian life is a war: Romans 6:13 ("instrument"); 13:12; 2 Corinthians 6:7; 10:4.

Armor (2)

panoplian

In Ephesians 6:14–18, Paul elaborates on "all the weapons" (*panoplian*) of God's **armor**, which we must constantly wear if we are to survive the spiritual war in which we are engaged with Satan and his army.

First, as the "girdle" (a wide leather belt) was at the foundation of the armor, holding other pieces in place, **truth**, both the *objective* truth of God's Word and the *subjective* truth of our personal truthfulness, honesty, and candor is the foundation of our lives.

Second, as the "breastplate" (*thōrax*, 2382, from which is derived the English word of the same spelling and refers to the chest area) was worn to protect the vitals within the chest and abdomen, so the imputed righteousness of Christ, which then produces right conduct and holy living in the believer, protects our "vital areas," which include our testimony, confidence, peace, and joy.

Third, as the special "sandals" of the soldier helped him to stand his ground because of the hobnails embedded in the soles, so our feet are shod with the **preparation** of the Gospel (see Oct. 8).

Fourth, as the ancient soldier could position himself behind the large, two-and-a-half-foot-wide and four-and-half-foot-high "shield" (*thureos*, 2375) to protect himself from the "flaming arrows" shot by the enemy (see Sept. 10), faith in Christ and His Word will protect us from the temptations that Satan will shoot at us constantly.

Fifth, as the "helmet" protects the most vital part of the body, so our "salvation" protects us from Satan's attacks on the mind, such as doubt concerning our security and assurance of salvation, discouragement in our living and service, and even intellectual attacks, such as evolution, secular psychology, and socialism.

Sixth, as the ancient Roman soldier wielded the deadly short "sword" (*machaira*, 3162) with blinding speed and deadly accuracy, so the Word (*rhēma*, 4487; see Sept. 17) of God is the only offensive weapon, and the Christian soldier is skilled in using it to attack all untruth.

Seventh, as the soldier must have the energy and confidence to go to battle, so the Christian is energized for battle through **prayer** and "supplication" (*proseuchē*, 4335, and *deēsis*, 1162; see May 28), which give him the confidence in Christ to fight effectively.

Dear Christian friend, have you put on all the weapons? Tomorrow we'll see the depth of those words **put on**.

Scriptures for Study: Review the other readings referred to today, and prepare yourself for battle.

Clothe (Put On)

enduō

Taking another look at Paul's admonition about God's armor, we should note again the words **put on** (or **clothe**). As already mentioned (see Oct. 2), we are commanded to put on the armor once-for-all and never take it off because it's to our benefit.

The Greek *enduō* (1746), however, goes deeper than just "getting dressed." It's a compound comprised of the prefix *en* (1722), "in," and *duō* (1416), "to sink, go in or under, to put on." The complete idea in the word, however, going back as far as Homer, is not only the literal meaning of dressing oneself, but the figurative meaning of assuming qualities or virtues. Aristophanes, for example, said to "take courage,"[278] that is, to take on that quality of life.

This is further demonstrated by several wonderful NT pictures. In our Lord's Parable of the Marriage Feast (Matt. 22:1–14), for example, one man was not dressed in appropriate clothing for that occasion ("had not on," v. 11), showing a disregard for the requirements of attendance. That pictures the person who professes to be a Christian but is not "dressed appropriately," who does not do what God requires.

The angels of Revelation 15:6 are "clothed in pure and white linen," indicating holiness. Likewise are the saints who accompany the conquering Christ at His Second Coming "clothed in fine linen, white and clean" (19:14), for they shall reign with Him in holiness.

Paul apparently liked this word very much, since he uses it several times. He commands us, for example, to "put on the new man" in Ephesians 4:24 (see Jan. 1). And what *qualities* are we putting on? "Righteousness and true holiness."

Which brings us back to putting on God's armor. As we've seen, each piece of armor is a specific quality that we must assume before we go into battle. Yes, we're "getting dressed" to go to war, but we're doing far more. We're taking to ourselves qualities and characteristics that are now part of our very being, our very nature. We are, as Peter tells us, "partakers of the divine nature, having escaped the corruption that is in the world through lust" (2 Pet. 1:4). When we "put on Christ" (Gal. 3:27), we do indeed assume His qualities. Let us live like it.

Scriptures for Study: When we "put on Christ," what does that drive us to do (Rom. 13:14)? 📖 What qualities does Paul tell us to "put on" in Colossians 3:12?

Soldier

stratiōtēs

Since we are to "put on the armor of God" so we can fight the spiritual war, that obviously makes each of us a **soldier**. *Stratiōtēs* (4757) comes from *stratos* (not in NT), which originally literally meant "to spread," and so came to mean "to spread out camp" and finally referred to an army. This is where we get our English word *strategy*, the overall plan of a battle, from the idea of "how the battle will spread out."

While *stratiōtēs* refers, of course, to a literal soldier (e.g., Matt. 28:12; Mark 15:16; etc.), Paul called Pastor Timothy a soldier: "Endure hardness, as a good soldier of Jesus Christ" (2 Tim. 2:3; 1 Tim. 1:18). While pastors must be what we could call "Special Forces," who are given more difficult and specialized missions than other soldiers, *all* Christians are soldiers. What, then, must soldiers do?

First, a soldier must endure difficult training. As Paul says, a soldier must "endure hardness." This is a single word in the Greek, *kakopatheō* (2553), from *kakos* (2556), "evil," and *pathos* (3806), "passion," hence "to suffer evil and affliction." Being a student of military history, I've read books about Navy SEALs (SEa, Air, and Land) and have been positively amazed at the requirements and training they endure. Trainees learn quickly that, "The only easy day was yesterday," and three-fourths of those who start don't finish. Being a Christian soldier is not easy. It demands difficult preparation through study and prayer.

Second, a soldier must take orders. The soldier who does not submit to authority and the "chain of command" will not last long in the military. The Christian soldier must likewise submit to the leadership of a pastor (who is equally in submission to Christ and His Word). Pastors, in fact, will give an account for their leadership (Heb. 13:17; cf. v. 7). Sadly, some Christians think they can "be their own boss" in Christian living, but God has created His chain of command in the church.

Third, a soldier must kill the enemy. War is not about negotiation, diplomacy, or politics. It's about killing the enemy and destroying his fortifications. Likewise, "the weapons of our warfare are not carnal, but mighty through God to the pulling down of strong holds" (2 Cor. 10:3–4). So, the Christian soldier must be skillful in using the weapons (armor) God has provided for the war.

Scriptures for Study: Read 2 Timothy 2. Can you identify all seven metaphors that Paul uses to illustrate the Christian life?[279]

Rulers

kosmokratōr

While Satan is certainly our primary enemy in the spiritual war, he does not fight alone. While he is the commander, he has legions of soldiers. Ephesians 6:12 lists four levels, or ranks, in the demonic world. Of special note are the "rulers of the darkness of this world" (or "world rulers").[280]

There's special significance in the fact that these are rulers of **darkness** (see Aug. 13). What darkness is this? As theologian and commentator Charles Hodge offers, it might refer either to the "kingdom of darkness," that is, the whole realm of satanic rule, or to the darkness "of ignorance and alienation from God."[281] We would submit, however, that both are true.

First, rulers is *kosmokratōr* (2888), which appears only here in the NT. It was originally rooted in astrology, in which man and this world are supposedly controlled by the planets. Eventually it came to refer to a broader application from the Roman emperor to pagan gods. Being in a pagan culture, the Ephesian believers would no doubt have recognized the concept Paul was picturing—that there are indeed evil spiritual rulers on this earth.

Second, however, as Albert Barnes writes, it's also true that "darkness is an emblem of ignorance, misery, and sin; and no description could be more accurate than that of representing these malignant spirits as ruling over a dark world."[282] Indeed, while man brags of his advanced knowledge, amazing technology, and clever inventions, he's ignorant of truth and clueless about God.

Viewing darkness as **ignorance** (see also Aug. 16), Puritan William Gurnall writes in his wonderful classic, *The Christian in Complete Armour:* "Ignorance above other sins enslaves a soul to Satan. . . . First, ignorance opens the door for Satan to enter in with his troops of lusts. Where the watch is blind, the city is soon taken. . . . Second, it locks it up in the soul, and the soul in it. Such a one lies in Satan's inner dungeon, where no lights of conviction comes. . . . Third, [it] shuts out the means of recovery. Friends and ministers, yea, Christ himself stands without, and cannot help the creature."[283]

How sad it is that such ignorance plagues not just the world but even Christians. As long as they remain ignorant of God's Word, they are destined to fall victim to Satan's attacks. There's no other escape.

Scriptures for Study: Review the "Scriptures for Study" sections for August 13 (**darkness**) and 16 (**ignorance**).

Preparation

hetoimasia

Part of God's armor that we are to wear in the spiritual war are the "sandals of the Gospel," which provide stability as we stand and fight. Paul's specific statement is that our feet are to be "shod with the preparation of the gospel of peace" (Eph. 6:15).

Preparation is *hetoimasia* (2091), which appears only here in the NT and means "preparation both in the active sense of 'making ready' and in the passive sense of 'readiness,' 'ability,' and 'resolution.'"[284] While it's used in a secular sense in the Septuagint, it often has a spiritual sense. It refers, for example, to God's eternal throne and therefore His nature and being (Ps. 103:19). Those in turn are founded upon His righteousness and justice (Ps. 89:14). He has also "founded" the earth, "prepared" the heavens (Prov. 3:19; 8:27), "setteth fast" the mountains (Ps. 65:6), and even "prepareth" rain for the earth (Ps. 147:8). He does all this and more because his faithfulness is established in heaven (Ps. 89:2).[285]

This word, therefore, means more than just "firmness," as some translators render it. The full idea is that we are ready to do whatever is needed: stand, fight, move, climb, or whatever. Paul uses another form of the word (*hetoimos*, 2092, ready, prepared) in Titus 3:1 to exhort believers "to be ready to every good work."

Why, then, does Paul say we must have our feet shod with the "readiness" of "the gospel of peace"? For what purpose? As many commentators agree, Paul is not speaking here of preaching or even personal witnessing, as some teachers assume. Rather, because the entire context concerns our conflict and battle with Satan, he's saying that we are ready to do whatever is needed because of the Gospel of peace; the Gospel of peace helps prepare us for the battle.

The term "gospel of peace" refers first to the good news that believers are at peace *with* God. Because of Christ, we're no longer at war with God. Christ is truly the "Eternal Peace Treaty" (Eph. 2:14; Rom. 5:1). Further, we also have the peace *of* God. While peace *with* God is *judicial*, the peace of God is *experiential*. No matter what our circumstances might be, no matter what the conflict or turmoil, we have a peace of mind and heart that the world can never understand. While the world is in turmoil, we can feel relaxed, assured, and confident.

Scriptures for Study: What challenge does our Lord give in Matthew 24:44 ("ready" is *hetoimos*)? 📖 Read Romans 5:1 and Philippians 4:6–7 and meditate on the peace *with* God and *of* God that you have in Christ.

Unrebukeable [and] Unreproveable

anepileptos [and] *anegkletos*

Back on January 18 (cf. see Sept. 18), we examined *amōmos*, which is variously translated as **blameless** (Eph. 1:4), "unblameable" (Col. 1:22), "without spot" (Heb. 9:14), and "without blemish" (Eph. 5:27). Today we examine two other words that are also sometimes translated "blameless," but are more vividly translated elsewhere.

In 1 Timothy 6:14, for example, Paul challenges Timothy to keep God's Word "without spot, unrebukeable, until the appearing of our Lord Jesus Christ." **Unrebukeable** is *anepileptos* (423), which literally means "not able to be seized," so figuratively, unrebukeable, irreproachable, and irreprehensible. In other words, there's nothing about this man that an adversary can observe and then seize upon to base a charge.

Similarly, Paul tells the Colossians that because they were reconciled to God through Christ, they were now "unreproveable in His sight" (Col. 1:22). **Unreproveable** is *anegkletos* (410), which carries both ideas of acquittal in court *and* being unaccusable, free from legal charge.

As many commentators agree, the quality of "blamelessness" is without question the pivotal character requirement in the list of qualifications for church leadership authoritatively listed by the apostle Paul in 1 Timothy 3:1–7 and Titus 1:5–9. We see both of these words, in fact, in those lists. "Blameless" is *anepileptos* in 1 Timothy 3:2 and *anegkletos* in Titus 1:6.

I recently had the honor and joy of writing a letter of recommendation to an ordination council concerning a longtime friend of mine who was training for entering full-time ministry. Because I've known him for twenty years and even traveled with him in ministry for over two, I was asked for my opinion of his character. A form of the paragraphs above appeared in that letter because they describe his character. There is nothing about his character that I could for a single moment call into question, nor could I imagine anyone else being able to do so. I see in him the highest moral character and a Christian man, husband, and father who ever strives for Christlikeness.

These words, therefore, challenge every one of us to be above accusation or even suspicion. When there is in us a true Christlike character (Gal. 5:22–23), no one will be able to level a charge against us.

Scriptures for Study: What other church office demands a man to be "blameless" (1 Tim. 3:10, *anegkletos*; cf. Acts 6:3)?

Patience

hupomonē

The old tongue-in-cheek adage, "I want patience, and I want it right now," reflects the difficulty of developing **patience**. Patience doesn't come overnight, and it doesn't come without **tribulation**, as we'll see tomorrow.

The Greek *hupomonē* (5281) is a compound word formed from *menō* (3306; see June 2–4), "to remain in one place, at a given time, with someone," and *hupo* (5259), "under." The idea then is to "remain under," that is, "to stay behind, to stand one's ground, survive, remain steadfast." In Classical Greek, it was "used frequently in military contexts,"[286] meaning to dig in and hold ground.

We find two fascinating occurrences of *hupomonē* in Revelation 2:2–3. In verse 2, our Lord praises the Ephesian believers for their patience, that they endured every obstacle that came into the path of their Christian service, stood their ground, and persisted through it all; they never gave an inch.

Our Lord then uses the same word again in verse 3. But while the first occurrence refers to *service,* it now refers to *suffering*. Most of the seven churches of Revelation 2 and 3 experienced persecution to one degree or another, and so it was with those in Ephesus, as recorded in Acts 19. They patiently endured without complaint.

Of the many occurrences of *hupomonē* in the NT, Hebrews 12:1 is among the most challenging: "Wherefore seeing we also are compassed about with so great a cloud of witnesses, let us lay aside every weight, and the sin which doth so easily beset us, and let us run with patience the race that is set before us." When we examine that great "Hall of Faith" in Hebrews 11, how can we not be challenged to patience?

Puritan Thomas Adams offers this encouragement: "Patience to the soul is as bread to the body . . . we eat bread with all our meats, both for health and relish; bread with flesh, bread with fish, bread with broths and fruits. Such is patience to every virtue; we must hope with patience, and pray in patience, and love with patience, and whatsoever good thing we do, let it be done in patience."[287]

Scriptures for Study: Coupled with the "comfort of the Scriptures," what does patience produce (Rom. 15:4)? 🕮 Read Hebrews 11, noting the patience of each of those great saints.

Tribulation

thlipsis

Tribulation translates *thlipsis* (2347), a graphic word that literally means "to crush, press, compress, squeeze" and "is from *thlaō*, to break."[288] Another form of this word, *thibō*, appears in Matthew 24:21, which describes the future Tribulation Period, when there "shall be great tribulation, such as was not since the beginning of the world to this time, no, nor ever shall be."

A vivid occurrence of *thlipsis* appears in our Lord's praise of the church at Smyrna: "I know thy works, and tribulation, and poverty, (but thou art rich) and I know the blasphemy of them which say they are Jews, and are not, but are the synagogue of Satan" (Rev. 2:9). As mentioned yesterday, most of the seven churches in Asia Minor endured persecution to one extent or another. The church at Smyrna, however, was under even greater persecution, no doubt because it took a stand against many things when other churches would not. Historically, those believers stood against three falsehoods: emperor worship (as Smyrna was the center of the Roman imperial cult that declared, "Caesar is God"), pagan worship (as many pagan cults existed there), and false religious worship (typified by the expression "the synagogue of Satan").

The Greek *thlipsis*, in fact, appears many times in the NT to indicate that tribulation, hardship, affliction, distress, and other difficulties are simply an everyday part of Christian living. Further, much of that tribulation will be a direct result of our standing for the Word of God. In the Parable of the Sower, for example, the "stony ground hearer" is excited at first but when tribulation and persecution come "because of the word," he withers away (Matt. 13:20–21). Paul often writes of the tribulation that he suffered because of his preaching the truth (2 Cor. 1:8 ["trouble"]; 4:17 ["affliction"]; 7:4; Col. 1:24; etc.).

Finally, what is the value of tribulation? What good does it do? As Paul encourages us, "We glory in tribulations also: knowing that tribulation worketh patience" (Rom. 5:3). Mark it down: You will never truly grow deep in your Christian life without tribulation, so you might as well rejoice in it.

Scriptures for Study: How did the Thessalonians react to affliction (1 Thess. 1:6)? 📖 What will God do to those who afflict His people (2 Thess. 1:6).

Repent

metanoeō

The word **repent** translates *metanoeō* (3340), "to change one's mind." Not surprisingly, this word is rarely found in Classical Greek because "Greek society never thought of a radical change in a man's life as a whole, of conversion or turning around." In fact, the whole concept of conversion is not found in Greek thought, but is derived from the NT.[289]

The idea in this word, then, is to turn around, change one's mind, relent, and in the theological sense involves "regret or sorrow, accompanied by a true change of heart toward God."[290]

A growing trend in "Christian" teaching today is a progressive diluting of the Gospel. As we've observed before, the Gospel is being defined in whatever nebulous terms each person desires, in whatever terms make him feel comfortable. Christianity has been reshaped to be more alluring. "Easy Believeism," "No-Lordship Salvation," the "God is love" philosophy, and other perversions of the Gospel make Christianity into just another feel-good religion that meets your social, emotional, and even economic needs.

Nowhere is this trend seen more clearly, in fact, than in the fashionable idea that repentance is not needed in order to "come to God." After all, since sin is really not an issue, there's nothing to repent from. As noted way back on January 18, however, sin *is* the issue, and repentance is therefore right at the core of salvation.

At the birth of the church, for example, Peter preached, "Repent, and be baptized every one of you in the name of Jesus Christ for the remission of sins, and ye shall receive the gift of the Holy Ghost" (Acts 2:38). He likewise preached in the temple, "Repent ye therefore, and be converted, that your sins may be blotted out, when the times of refreshing shall come from the presence of the Lord" (3:19). Even more basic, our Lord clearly declared that the reason he came was to "call . . . sinners to repentance" (Matt. 9:13). We also read how he commanded five of the seven churches in Asia Minor to repent of their sin (Rev. 2:5; 2:16; 21–22; 3:3, 19).

Mark it down, any so-called gospel that does not preach repentance is not the true Gospel, because God "now commandeth all men every where to repent" (Acts 17:30).

Scriptures for Study: Read the following verses concerning the Tribulation, noting what men will *not* do during that time: Revelation 9:20–21; 16:9, 11.

Remember

mnemoneuō

In His challenge to the Ephesian believers, who had abandoned their first love for the Lord, Jesus commanded, "Remember therefore from whence thou art fallen, and repent" (Rev. 2:5). The Greek behind **remember** (*mnemoneuō*, 3421) refers not only to the mental capability to recall something, but also "to be mindful" of it and "take [it] into account."[291] This is also in the present tense, yielding the idea of "keep remembering." The Lord Jesus wanted the Ephesians to constantly take into account from "whence [they were] fallen," which implies two principles.

First, our Lord says in effect, "Remember where you came from." One of the most beautiful verses in all of the Word of God appears in Isaiah 51:1: "Hearken to me, ye that follow after righteousness, ye that seek the Lord: look unto the rock whence ye are hewn, and to the hole of the pit whence ye are digged." To the nation of Israel, God then said in essence, "Remember your past; remember where you came from; remember that your nation exists only because of My power that created that nation from an old man and an old woman who were beyond the age of child-bearing" (vv. 2–3). Let us also remember what we were—lost, hell-bound sinners! But God loved us, had mercy on us, and sent His only begotten Son to die in our place. As Paul told the Ephesians of their riches in Christ in chapters 1–3 of his epistle to them, we should make a habit of reading those chapters in our Christian life to remember what we have in Him.

Second, our Lord also says in effect, "Remember the relationship you used to have." Dear Christian, do you remember the joy, the thrill, and the peace you felt when you first came to Christ? Do you remember the hunger and thirst you had to know more about what God's Word says? Many Christians have left that behind in favor of the values and priorities of the world. Others have abandoned it for the new and novel, leaving behind doctrine and chasing after entertainment in the church service. Still others have allowed their Christian life to become "old hat," just going through the motions.

Would that your relationship with the Savior continue to be as close and personal today as it was on the day of your conversion! In fact, it should be even more so.

Scriptures for Study: Read the following verses, noting in each what we should remember: Luke 17:32; John 15:20; 2 Timothy 2:8; Hebrew 13:7.

Poverty

ptocheia

One Greek word for **poverty** is *penēs* (3993) and occurs only once in the NT (2 Cor. 9:9). It speaks of a "pauper," one who doesn't have much and works very hard for what he does have.

Another word translated **poverty**, however, is the noun *ptōcheia* (4432), which occurs (along with the adjective *ptōchos*, 4434, and verb *ptocheuō*, 4433) about forty times in the NT. This refers to a beggar, someone who was completely destitute, having nothing. This is the word our Lord uses to describe the "poor widow" who gave all she had to God (Mark 12:42–43). Paul also used it to describe the "poor saints which [were] at Jerusalem," for whom he was taking an offering as he traveled (Rom. 15:26).

A dramatic occurrence of *ptocheia* is in Revelation 2:9, where our Lord again speaks of the believers in Smyrna (see Oct. 11). Materially, those believers were destitute. Standing for Christ in Smyrna meant no job, no money, and few possessions. (How many of us today would be willing to stand for Christ if it meant that kind of destitution?)

Further, however, what are true **riches** anyway? As we considered back on January 28, true wealth is not in *material* things but in *spiritual* things. And as the Lord goes on to say to the Smyrnan believers, "[Even in your] poverty . . . (thou art rich)." Paul referred to his own hardships in the same way: "As poor, yet making many rich; as having nothing, and yet possessing all things" (2 Cor. 6:10).

The reverse of this is also true. In dramatic contrast to the Smyrnans, who were materially poor but spiritually rich, the Laodicean believers were materially "rich . . . increased with goods, and [had] need of nothing" but spiritually were "wretched, and miserable, and poor, and blind, and naked" (Rev. 3:17).

There is great encouragement and challenge here for every believer. Which type of riches do we desire: material or spiritual? Would we rather be rich in man's eyes or in God's? Are we willing to be materially destitute for the cause of Christ?

Scriptures for Study: Read and meditate on James 2:2–6. What is James teaching us?

Nicolaitanes (Nicolaitans)

Nikolaitēs

An interesting sect is referred to twice in Jesus' letters to the seven churches of Asia Minor (Rev. 2–3). The sect was called the **Nicolaitanes** (or **Nicolaitans**, *Nikolaitēs*, 3531). While the Ephesian believers did not tolerate the teaching of this group (2:6), those in Pergamum did (2:15), and although there is some ambiguity about this sect, there is some fairly good evidence as to its teaching.

The Nicolaitan heresy was founded either by Nicolas (who is mentioned in the list of the first deacons in the early church, Acts 6:5), or by someone who merely perverted something that Nicolas taught. Either way, as several early church fathers concur, this sect had turned "liberty" into "license." They no doubt argued, "The Law is done with; we now live in grace and liberty to do as we will." The result was self-indulgence and uncleanness.

Commentator William Barclay well sums up their teaching from the church fathers:

> Irenaeus says of the Nicolaitans that 'they lived lives of unrestrained indulgence' (*Against Heresies*, 1.26.3). Hippolytus says that he was one of the seven and that 'he departed from correct doctrine, and was in the habit of inculcating indifference of food and life' (*Refutation of Heresies*, 7:24). *The Apostolic Constitutions* (6:8) describe the Nicolaitans as 'shameless in uncleanness.' Clement of Alexandria says they 'abandon themselves to pleasure like goats . . . leading a life of self-indulgence.' But he acquits Nicolaus of all blame and says that they perverted his saying 'that the flesh must be abused.' Nicolaus meant that the body must be kept under; the heretics perverted it into meaning that the flesh can be used as shamelessly as a man wishes (*The Miscellanies* 2:20). The Nicolaitans obviously taught loose living.[292]

Obviously, anyone who believes in such license is not a true Christian. Yet, many Christians today, while not believing in "license," take liberty too far in thinking that it allows them to do whatever they wish, even if it causes another believer to stumble. Paul, however, denounces such an attitude in no uncertain terms in 1 Corinthians 8:4–13. We must always "take heed lest by any means this liberty of [ours] become a stumblingblock to them that are weak" (8:9).

Scriptures for Study: Read 1 Corinthians 8:4–13, noting Paul's concern about Christians offending one another.

Manna

manna

Most of us recall the story of God feeding the children of Israel in the wilderness, according to Exodus 16:1–35. There's an odd statement, however, in verse 15 of that passage. When the people woke up that first morning of the provision, they saw "a small round thing" lying on the ground (v. 14) and then said, "It is manna: for they [knew] not what it was." Isn't that odd? How could they call it something if they didn't know what it was?

The answer lies in the meaning of the word **manna**. This is a transliteration of the Hebrew *mēn* (4478H), which literally means, "What is it?" Young's *Literal Translation*, in fact, reads, "And the sons of Israel see, and say one unto another, 'What is it?' for they have not known what it is." Moses goes on to tell them all they need to know about it: "This is the bread which the Lord hath given you to eat" (v. 15).

That is, indeed, all any of us need to know when it comes to God's provision. Skeptics have tried to explain this substance by making it refer to natural substances in the desert, such as lichen growing on rocks or insect-excreted granules on tamarisk thickets. But all such explanations come from an unbelieving heart that ignores the supernatural provision of God.

It's significant that manna is also mentioned in the NT. In John 6:31–35 our Lord likens Himself to that very provision of God. Recounting how God fed their forefathers with manna, the people asked Jesus for a sign of who He was. He answered that He was "the true bread from heaven" and "the bread of life."

Likewise, in His letter to the believers in Pergamos, He writes that to those who overcome, he will give "hidden manna" (Rev. 2:17). What manna is that? It is the Lord Jesus Himself, the Bread of Life that is hidden from the unbelieving world. Think of it! Christ Himself is viewed as our spiritual food. We are nourished by communion with Christ and His Word. This hidden manna is Christ and His Word! Let us feed on that daily!

Scriptures for Study: Read the following verses, noting the promise of God's provision in each: Deuteronomy 8:3 (Matt. 4:4); Psalm 23:1–5; Matthew 6:25–34; Philippians 4:19. Is there ever a reason to doubt?

Hold Fast

krateō

While the Greek *katechō* (2722; see Aug. 16) means "to hold down, quash, or suppress," there is a subtly different picture in the word *krateō* (2902). It means to "lay hold of, seize, adhere to." Herod, for example, "laid hold" of John the Baptist and put him in prison (Matt. 14:3), and the Roman guard "laid hands" on the Lord Jesus in the Garden of Gethsemane (26:50).

Even more significant, the idea of adhering to something is reflected in Matthew 28:9, for example, where the disciples "held [Jesus] by the feet, and worshipped him." We read this idea also concerning the Pharisees, who adhered to the tradition of men instead of the commandments of God (Mark 7:8).

This brings us to perhaps the most vivid occurrence of *krateō*. In his letter to the church at Thyatira, our Lord commands, "But that which ye have already hold fast till I come" (Rev. 2:25). Here is a challenge to all believers to **hold fast**, to adhere to and never let go of that which they have. And what is it that we have? The *Lord Jesus Christ*. We are to cling to Him until He comes to take us home.

This is actually the first mention of Christ coming for the church in the book of Revelation. We should also point out that the verb tense here is the aorist (punctiliar action). The significance of this is that these believers had "let go" of certain truths and needed first to grab hold of them again and then never let go. How we need to grab on to the truth! How we need to cling to the Savior, not the world and its philosophies!

Another instance of this word provides an additional challenge: "Therefore, brethren, stand fast, and hold the traditions which ye have been taught, whether by word, or our epistle" (2 Thess. 2:15). The greatest desire of the Christian should be to grow in grace and in the knowledge of Christ (2 Pet. 3:18). The driving force of our lives should be to know and adhere to biblical doctrine, not human **tradition** (see Oct. 19) or anything else.

Scriptures for Study: To what do we hold fast and adhere to in Hebrews 4:14 and 6:18?

Keep

tēreō

Today we encounter another word that is translated **hold fast** once in the AV (Rev. 3:3) but more often as **keep** (or "kept") and sometimes as "observe" and some form of "watch."

The Greek *tēreō* (5083) is derived from *tēros* (a warden or guard; not found in the NT) and hence means to keep an eye on, watch over, observe attentively, and even guard protectively. It's used plentifully in the NT, appearing some seventy times. In the literal sense, it's used in Acts 12:6, for example, where Paul is in prison and the guards "kept the prison."

It is the figurative use, however, that provides us with great encouragements and challenges. One of the greatest proofs of genuine salvation, for example, is recorded in 1 John 2:3–5: "And hereby we do know that we know him, if we keep his commandments. He that saith, I know him, and keepeth not his commandments, is a liar, and the truth is not in him. But whoso keepeth his word, in him verily is the love of God perfected: hereby know we that we are in him" (cf. John 14:23–24). John uses *tēreō* no less than three times to demonstrate the attitudes that the true child of God has toward the Word of God: He gazes on it intently, obeys it faithfully, and even guards it protectively. John even goes on later to add that keeping God's commandments makes us more effective in **prayer** (1 John 3:22; see May 28–29).

Other occurrences of *tēreō* encourage us in another area of Christian living, namely, purity of life. As Paul told Timothy, and by implication all believers, "keep thyself pure" (1 Tim. 5:22). James echoes that mandate when he writes, "Pure religion and undefiled before God and the Father is . . . to keep himself unspotted from the world" (James 1:27). Indeed, to stay pure in the wicked world in which we live demands that we keep an ever-vigilant eye on our lives and guard ourselves from that which will defile us.

Let us each desire that when we come to the end of our lives we can say with Paul, "I have fought a good fight, I have finished my course, I have [observed attentively and guarded protectively] the faith" (2 Tim. 4:7).

Scriptures for Study: What is the promise of John 8:51? 🕮 What did Jesus pray for us in John 17:15?

Tradition

paradosis

The word **tradition** is a touchy one. We all like certain traditions, whether they're ones that only our family observes or ones that are national holidays, and we all tend to get very defensive if someone attacks or criticizes one of our traditions.

That said, however, we must still submit to the truth that traditions must come under the same scrutiny and discernment (see July 15) that anything else must undergo. This is nowhere better illustrated than with the Pharisees, with whom our Lord battled on many occasions.

Matthew 15:1–9, for example, is perhaps the most vivid example. The Pharisees came to Jesus and asked Him why the disciples did not wash their hands before they ate. Jesus' answer, however, makes it clear that this was simply one of their legalistic traditions that had nothing whatsoever to do with a commandment of God.

Throughout their history, especially during the Babylonian Exile and the Intertestamental Period, Jewish rabbis added thousands of man-made traditions to God's Law and made them equal to it. The value of the ceremonial rinsing in view here, for example, was held so high that one rabbi insisted that "whosoever has his abode in the land of Israel and eats his common food with rinsed hands may rest assured that he shall obtain eternal life." Another rabbi taught that it would be better to walk four miles out of the way to get water than to eat with unwashed hands. But the Law of Moses contained no commandment about washing one's hands before eating (except for priests who were required to wash before eating holy offerings; Lev. 22:6, 7).

The Greek *paradosis* (3862) is derived from *paradidōmi* (3860; see Nov. 4), which in this sense means "to deliver in teaching." The idea then in *paradosis* is "a tradition, doctrine, or injunction delivered or communicated from one to another, whether divine or human."[293] Oh, the danger of human **tradition**! We must take great care that we do not "transgress the commandment of God by [our] tradition" (Matt. 15:3). Let us never violate God's Word by any tradition that we embrace. We must test them carefully.

In stark contrast are the traditions (doctrines) of God's truth. As we noted two days ago, 2 Thessalonians 2:15 declares: "Therefore, brethren, stand fast, and hold the traditions which ye have been taught, whether by word, or our epistle."

Scriptures for Study: Read the following verses, noting either the positive or negative use of *paradosis* in each: Matthew 15:1–9; 1 Corinthians 11:2 ("ordinances"); Galatians 1:14; Colossians 2:8; 2 Thessalonians 3:6.

Life (1)

zōē

There is no more dramatic contrast between two words than there is between *death* (see **dead**, see Feb. 12) and **life**. That is the ultimate contrast.

The Greek behind **life** (*zōē*, 2222), as well as "live" (*zaō*, 2198), is where we get English words such as *zoology* and *protozoa*. The idea is to have life or existence in contrast to death and nonexistence. In the thinking of the ancient Greeks, life was not a thing, but *vitality*. For that reason, *zoē* can't be used in the plural. In other words, we don't possess several "lifes" like we could possess several books or shoes; rather, life is a singular, vital, and active reality.

This word (along with *zaō*) appears some 278 times in the NT. This stands to reason since life is not only a fundamental concept, but *spiritual* life is what Scripture is all about. That universally known verse, John 3:16, is a typical example. Scripture not only speaks about *physical* life but, far more importantly, *everlasting* life. While physical life comes to an end, everlasting life is just what it says—it's forever. What, then, does John 3:16, and all Scripture, say about such "everlasting existence and vitality"?

First, everlasting life is in contrast to everlasting death. John 3:16 clearly says that without Christ a person will "perish." Paul also makes this clear in his opening words to the Romans: "For the wrath of God is revealed from heaven against all ungodliness and unrighteousness of men, who hold the truth in unrighteousness" (1:18). Without Christ, a person will spend eternity under God's wrath in hell (John 3:36; Rom. 6:23; Rev. 20:15; 21:8; etc.).

Second, everlasting life comes only through "Him," that is, Jesus Christ. As Jesus said of Himself elsewhere: "I am the way, the truth, and the life: no man cometh unto the Father, but by me" (John 14:6). The definite article ("the") makes it clear that Jesus is the only way to life.

Third, everlasting life comes by **faith**, as indicated by the word "believeth" (*pisteuō*; see Feb. 8). Salvation does not come by works (Eph. 2:8–9; Titus 3:5) or human merit. It comes by trusting in the finished work of Christ alone.

Oh, how we should rejoicing in the everlasting vitality we have in Christ!

Scriptures for Study: Read John 6:1–69. How many references to life can you count in this passage alone?

Life (2)

bios

In the same way that English has only one word for **love** while Greek has four (see Jan. 19–21), it also has only one word for **life** while Greek has two. (Interestingly, even Latin has only one: *vita*.) While some teachers view *zōē* (2222) and *bios* (979; English, *biography*, *biosphere*, etc.) as basically synonymous, that's not the case, and viewing them as such misses some very important truths.

As one Greek authority details, *zōē* refers to *intensive* life, that is, "life by which we live" (Latin, *vita qua vivimus*), while bios refers to *extensive* life, that is, "the life which we live" (Latin, *vita quam vivimus*).[294] In simpler terms, *zōē* speaks of the *reality* of life, that is, life itself, while *bios* speaks of the *duration*, *means*, and *manner* of life. For example, in the Parable of the Prodigal Son (or more accurately, "The Parable of Two Rebellious Sons and One Joyful Father"), the younger son demanded his inheritance immediately, and the father gave the son his "living" (*bios*), that is, the means for living; the son then squandered all that means for living (Luke 15:30).

Most profound, however, is how *bios* is used to picture one's *manner* of life. Paul writes Timothy, for example, "For kings, and for all that are in authority; that we may lead a quiet and peaceable life in all godliness and honesty" (1 Tim. 2:2). In what manner is the church to conduct itself? As much as possible, it is to remain quiet (from internal disturbances) and peaceable (from external disturbances). While it must never compromise truth, it is never to be disruptive, either in its local community or on the national scene.

Another usage of *bios* is again to Timothy: "No man that warreth entangleth himself with the affairs of this life; that he may please him who hath chosen him to be a soldier" (2 Tim. 2:4). Here's a challenge to pastors that their manner of life is not temporal things but the things of Christ and His Word.

The ultimate example of the use of *bios* in this sense is in 1 John 2:16, where we read of "the lust of the flesh, and the lust of the eyes, and the pride of life." Such things most certainly are not to be the manner in which the believer lives.

Scriptures for Study: Note the significance of *bios* in each of the following verses: Luke 8:14, 43; 21:4.

Watch

grēgoreuō

The word **watch** often translates *grēgoreuō* (1127), which is derived from *egeirō* (1453; "to arise, arouse") and literally means "to watch, to refrain from sleep." It eventually changed in meaning from that literal sense to the metaphorical and religious sense of attention, watchfulness, and vigilance.

We find this word several times in the NT, and each one is significant. In His Olivet Discourse, for example, our Lord speaks of His Second Coming: "Watch therefore: for ye know not what hour your Lord doth come" (Matt. 24:42; cf. 25:13). Since we do not know when He will return, we are to be watching carefully and remaining attentive to the things of God.

In Matthew 26:36–41, we then witness a shameful scene. Here we find Jesus in the Garden of Gethsemane, where he asks His disciples to sit with Him and support Him as He goes off to pray. But when He returns, he finds them asleep and asks, "Could ye not watch with me one hour?" (Matt. 26:40). He then further challenges them, "Watch and pray, that ye enter not into temptation: the spirit indeed is willing, but the flesh is weak" (v. 41). In both instances "watch" is *grēgoreuō*. Yes, we all have physical infirmities, but we must live above them. It's imperative that we be ever vigilant and stand with the Lord.

In one of the most important passages in the NT on the duty of pastors in the church, Paul first outlined those responsibilities to the Ephesian elders at Miletus and then declared, "Therefore watch" (Acts 20:17–31). How imperative it is today that pastors watch *everything* so as to protect the sheep!

Grēgoreuō also appears in 1 Corinthians 16:13: "Watch ye, stand fast in the faith, quit you like men, be strong." To be a Christian means to be attentive to spiritual things, to stand for Christ at all times, never giving an inch concerning the Christian faith; we are to stay strong and never quit.

Still another occurrence of this word is 1 Peter 5:8: "Be sober, be vigilant [*grēgoreuō*]; because your adversary the devil, as a roaring lion, walketh about, seeking whom he may devour." We must constantly be watching our Christian walk so as not to fall into one of Satan's snares (see Oct. 1).

Scriptures for Study: Read the following verses, noting the use of *grēgoreuō*: Colossians 4:2; 1 Thessalonians 5:6, 10.

Door

thura

As one might assume, the meaning of the word **door** is pretty obvious. The Greek *thura* (2374) referred to a house door, the "outer door" that led from the street to the courtyard, the door of a walled sheepfold, the door of a single room or prison cell, the gate of a city, and even the rough-cut door of a cave or sepulcher.

Obviously, those literal meanings are found in the NT. The most striking examples are the three "door miracles" in the book of Acts, where Peter and John (5:19), Peter alone (12:6–11), and Paul and Silas (16:26–31) were miraculously released from prison.

It's again the figurative meanings, however, that capture our attention. One such use is our Lord's statement that entering His Kingdom requires us to go through a door, but when that door is closed in judgment, there's no more opportunity for those who knock because the owner never knew them (Luke 13:24–25; cf. Matt. 7:21–23).

Most significant of all, our Lord Himself is called "the Door." Among many other metaphors for Christ—the Bread of Life (John 6:31–35), the Light of the World (8:12), the Vine (15:5), and others—this one, too, paints a vivid picture. Again speaking of Himself, our Lord declares in John 10:1–10 that the true shepherd of the sheep enters through the door. He goes on to say, however, that false shepherds try to enter the fold and try to steal the sheep (or at least fleece them). As a safeguard, Jesus says in verse 5, "And a stranger will they not follow, but will flee from him: for they know not the voice of strangers."

While that safeguard works with literal sheep, it tragically does not with many Christians today because *they simply are not listening to the Shepherd*. Where does the Shepherd speak? Nowadays it's claimed that He speaks through visions, dreams, inner urgings, and other such subjective means. Such sincere folks think they're hearing the Shepherd, *but they are not*. He speaks through Scripture alone, and because people don't recognize that fact, they don't even know what His voice sounds like. As a result, they mistake the voice of false shepherds for the true Shepherd and are led into error and even destruction.

Let us "tune our ears" to the voice of the Shepherd and recognize His voice alone. We'll examine another figurative use of the word door tomorrow—the **open door**.

Scriptures for Study: What is the obvious application of Matthew 6:6? 🕮 What is our Lord telling us in Matthew 28:2?

Open Door

thuran aneōgmenēn

In His letter to the godly church at Philadelphia, our Lord makes a marvelous statement: "Behold, I have set before thee an open door, and no man can shut it" (Rev. 3:8). **Open** is *anoigō* (455), "to open," and is used most frequently with *thura* (2374) in the NT to signify an **open door**.

Here is a beautiful reference to opportunities to witness and proclaim the Word of God. The door is, indeed, wide open! Paul spoke of this over and over again. When he and his colaborers returned to Antioch (his home church, which sent him out as a church planter), we're told that "when they were come, and had gathered the church together, they rehearsed all that God had done with them, and how he had opened the door of faith unto the Gentiles" (Acts 14:27). He wrote to the Corinthian believers, "For a great door and effectual is opened unto me, and there are many adversaries" (1 Cor. 16:9). He again wrote, "When I came to Troas to preach Christ's gospel, and a door was opened unto me of the Lord, I had no rest in my spirit . . . I went from thence into Macedonia" (2 Cor. 2:12–13). He encouraged the believers at Colossae to pray "that God would open unto us a door of utterance, to speak the mystery of Christ" (Col. 4:3). This challenges each of us to look for open doors for *witness* with our *lips*, and *testimony* with our *life*.

While there are other aspects of Christian service, the real heart of service is *witnessing*. Acts 1:8 records the commission that has been given to every believer: "But ye shall receive power, [when] the Holy Ghost is come upon you: and ye shall be witnesses unto me both in Jerusalem, and in all Judaea, and in Samaria, and unto the uttermost part of the earth."

How tragic it is when we fail to see an open door of opportunity when God provides it. In his exposition of Revelation 3:8, commentator Lehman Strauss observes that after World War II, Japan was a wide-open door to Christian work. General Douglas MacArthur, in fact, called upon Christians in America to send 5,000 missionaries through that open door. But we failed to answer that call.

Let us not fail in the opportunities God gives us.

Scriptures for Study: Read the following verses, noting again the commission that is given to every believer: Matthew 24:14; 28:19–20; Romans 10:14.

Cold [and] Hot [and] Lukewarm

psuchros [and] *zestos* [and] *chliaros*

The words of Revelation 3:15–16 are among the most graphic in Scripture: "I know thy works, that thou art neither cold nor hot: I would thou wert cold or hot. So then because thou art lukewarm, and neither cold nor hot, I will spue thee out of my mouth." Yes, that's pretty graphic!

The problem in the church at Laodicea was "lukewarmness," but what exactly *is* lukewarmness? To understand this, we must carefully examine all three terms our Lord uses.

First, note the term **cold**. The Greek here is not *psuchos* (5592) "cold," but *psuchros* (5593), "frigid cold, sluggish, inert with cold." As we know, our bodies shiver when we are out in cold weather because that's the body's way of trying to generate heat. But as someone is freezing to death, his body becomes inert, unable to move. Cold, then, is used here in a metaphorical way to picture a complete aloofness to Christianity. In other words, the person who is spiritually cold is lost and does not even care that he's lost.

Second, note the word **hot**. The Greek *zestos* (2200; English *zest*) means "to boil, be hot, be fervent" and pictures that which is boiling hot. Therefore, the word *hot* is used metaphorically to show fervency for spiritual things. One example of such spiritual fervency was Zacchaeus (Luke 19:2–9), who after receiving Christ was, according to Jewish law, willing to restore fourfold to anyone from whom he had wrongfully taken money. We could also note, of course, the unequaled fervor of the apostle Paul.

Third, we come to **lukewarm**. This is *chliaros* (5513), which appears only here in the NT and means "tepid, warm, a mixture of cold and hot." This picture was especially meaningful to the Laodiceans because the city had hot water piped from the famous hot spring of Hieropolis and cold water piped from Colossea (which was known for its pure, cold water). But often the water from each source was lukewarm by the time it reached Laodicea. Such tepid water was nauseating.

So, the picture of the Laodiceans is vivid indeed—many professed Christianity but were not Christian at all. Herein is a perfect description of what is called *apostasy: professed Christianity but a denial of its basic truths.*

Which one of these words describes you? We'll continue tomorrow.

Scriptures for Study: Read 2 Timothy 3:1–4:4, noting the characteristics of apostasy that exist in our day.

Laodiceans

Laodikeus

In light of yesterday's reading, the question arises, What caused the apostasy in the **Laodiceans** (Rev. 3:15–16)? Why were these people **lukewarm**? A probable answer is actually found in that name. **Laodiceans** is *Laodikeus* (2994), which is comprised of two words: *laos* (2992) meaning "people" and *dikē* (1349) meaning (depending upon the context) "law, right, custom, and even prescribed punishment." The idea in this word, then, is "the law or custom of the people" or simply "the people ruling."

You see, the society of that day (and today, may we add) was *people-centered*. People had become the authority instead of the Word of God being the authority. May I dare add, this is true even in the church today. *Never before in church history* has the church been as "people-centered" as it is now. We build entire churches and ministries based solely upon what people want. If that's not "people ruling," what is it?

We would do well to consider these words from John R. W. Stott, written in 1980: "Perhaps none of the seven letters [in Revelation 2–3] is more appropriate to the twentieth-century church than this. It describes vividly the respectable, sentimental, nominal, skin-deep religiosity which is so widespread among us today. Our Christianity is flabby and anaemic. We appear to have taken a lukewarm bath of religion."[295]

We are, indeed, living in the "Laodicean Age" of church history, the age of humanism, in which "man is the center of all things" and has set himself up as the final authority on every subject and question. This philosophy is so prevalent, permeating, and pernicious that it has infiltrated every aspect of human society.

In *social* life, the "chief god" today is self-indulgence, which is fed by money and material things. In *political* life, people scream to be heard and demand a "democracy" (i.e., mob rule) instead of the representative republic established by America's founding fathers. Even in *religious* life, the Word of God is not the sole authority. Not only do liberal theologians deny the fundamentals of the faith, but even many Christians are more impressed with the answers given by Dr. Phil or other "psychological gurus," than those given by God. Instead of the exposition of Scripture, they want entertainment.

Let us not be driven by what *we want*, but by what *God says*.

Scriptures for Study: Read Exodus 32, observing what happens when "the people" (v. 1) get what they want.

Supper, Sup

deipnon, deipneō

Many years ago, when my wife and I traveled extensively in ministry, we stayed in many Christian homes and often ate meals in different homes every day. We quickly discovered that the meaning of the words *dinner* and *supper* depended upon local custom. So, to prevent miscommunication (and probable embarrassment), we came to use the terms *noon meal* and *evening meal*.[296]

Among the Jews, Greeks, and Romans, however, **supper** (*deipnon*, 1173) referred to the main meal of the day, which was eaten at or toward evening and often extended into the night (e.g., Luke 14:16–17; John 12:2–4; etc.).

An extremely significant occurrence of the verb *deipneō* (1172), "to eat or have supper," appears in Revelation 3:20, where our Lord writes again to the **Laodiceans**, "Behold, I stand at the door, and knock: if any man hear my voice, and open the door, I will come in to him, and will sup with him, and he with me." What has always struck me about this scene is that the Lord is here pictured as being outside of His own church, asking to come back in. How true it is today! Apostates have thrust the Lord out of that which belongs to Him.

To those who will obey, however, He will come in and eat with them. Meals were an intimate affair in the ancient world. Especially significant were meals where a guest was present; a guest was always honored. As one authority recounts, "By [NT] times the *triclinium* was beginning to come into use. This was an arrangement of three tables set around a square, with access to the middle gained through the open side of the square so that servants could come and go to bring in food and to take away the left-overs. Couches were arranged on the outside of the three tables, close to one another, so that the guest could recline to eat. The guest was given a cushion and lay on his left arm with his head towards the table, leaving his right arm free to take what he wished. This made it possible for servants to rinse the feet while the guests continued the banquet. Jesus was therefore probably using a couch at a *triclinium* when his feet were washed (Luke 7:46)."[297]

Let us each search our hearts and ask, "Is the Lord being honored in my church or is He standing outside asking to come in?"

Scriptures for Study: Read about the Marriage Supper of the Lamb to which we all look forward (Rev. 19:1–10).

Lord's Supper

Kuriakon deipnon

While we've already examined both words in today's reading—*kurios* (see Apr. 8) and *deipnon* (see Oct. 27)—the words *Kuriakon deipnon* are the exact reading of the Greek in 1 Corinthians 11:20 and demand our attention.

The scene in the context is the perversion of the Lord's Supper by many believers in the Corinthian church. They had turned it (and the so-called love feast) into self-indulgent, gluttonous, and even drunken revelry. For that reason Paul writes that this was not truly the Lord's Supper at all because it could not possibly honor Him.

As verses 24–25 go on to say, the Lord's Supper is, a memorial ("a remembrance"), a celebration, in fact, of what our Lord accomplished on the cross. It's *not* a saving act (see also May 28), but rather, an act of worship to praise God for Christ's finished work. It was part of the fourfold activity of the church, according to Acts 2:42: "And they continued stedfastly in the apostles' doctrine and fellowship, and in breaking of bread, and in prayers."

It has amazed me for many years that there is a controversy over how often we should observe the Lord's Supper, when the glaringly obvious NT precedent is that we should do so every Lord's Day. Consistency dictates that *all four* of the activities of Acts 2:42 should still be practiced each Lord's Day. While it's argued that Scripture doesn't *command* the frequency of the Lord's Supper, may we ask, When there is a clear *precedent*, why would we need anything else?

Paul adds, "For as often as ye eat this bread, and drink this cup, ye do shew the Lord's death till he come" (1 Cor. 11:26). "Show" is *kataggellō* (2605), to announce publicly, proclaim. It's a derivative of *kerux* and *kērussō* (2783 and 2784; see May 18), which spoke of the imperial herald announcing the wishes of the king, as when Paul told Timothy to "preach the word" in 2 Timothy 4:2. So, each time we observe the Lord's Supper, we are proclaiming the Gospel. Should this not, then, be practiced each Lord's Day?

While that has, in fact, been the practice of the church throughout its history, and while many great men of the faith have emphasized that importance,[298] for some odd reason, the change occurred after the Reformation. And we are missing much with that omission.

Scriptures for Study: Read 1 Corinthians 11:17–29, meditating on the glorious significance of the Lord's Supper.

Fellowship (1)

koinōnia

There is in Christianity a "common bond" among true believers that is unequaled in the world's clubs, organizations, unions, and secret societies. The Word of God calls this bond **fellowship**. The word *koinōnia* (2842) speaks of a partnership, close union, and brotherly bond. It was used in secular Greek to refer to a common enterprise, a business partnership or association, and even to marriage, since it suggested a powerful common interest that could hold two people together.

The NT usage of *koinōnia* is perhaps best expressed by Greek scholar Kenneth Wuest: "joint participation in a common interest or activity."[299] The idea is that of partnership, a sharing of something in common.

A tremendously significant occurrence of this word is in Acts 2:42, which outlines the fourfold activity of the church: "And they continued stedfastly in the apostles' doctrine and fellowship, and in breaking of bread, and in prayers." One of the essentials of any local church, then, is a partnership, a close communion with other believers. Second only to the foundational element of doctrine and teaching, it's crucial that Christians fellowship with one another.

So, what exactly is fellowship in practice? While some view fellowship as Christians getting together for coffee after church, going to a ballgame together, or other such activities, true Christian fellowship goes far deeper. It involves a true union and bond in thought, desire, and goal.

In his letter to the Philippians, for example, Paul writes of his thankfulness for that group of believers and tells them that he prays for them and is joyful for their "fellowship in the gospel" (1:3–5). He was, indeed, thankful and joyful for their partnership and participation in the Gospel. This was evident in the fact that they had given sacrificially to his ministry and had sent support to him several times (4:16).

Greatest of all is our fellowship with Jesus Himself. As Paul again wrote the Philippians: "That I may know him, and the power of his resurrection, and the fellowship of his sufferings, being made conformable unto his death" (3:10). To be a partner with our Lord, to have a common bond with Him, even in suffering, should be our greatest desire. When it is, it will also be our greatest comfort.

Scriptures for Study: Concerning fellowship, what are the challenges of 1 John 1:6–7?

Fellowship (2)

koinōnia

In light of *true* Christian **fellowship**, it's equally vital to consider the other side of fellowship, that is, with what we should *not* have fellowship. Paul went into detail about this in 2 Corinthians 6:14–7:1 (I would encourage you to read that passage before continuing).

Paul's first metaphor is based upon Deuteronomy 22:10 (cf. Lev. 19:19), which commanded not to yoke together an ox and a donkey in plowing for the simple common-sense reason that their step and pull is uneven. Paul's other metaphors build on that with increasingly graphic and even more contradictory comparisons. The point is unambiguous: It's *impossible to bring such opposites together; they can have nothing to do with one another.*

Deeper, Paul uses several graphic words that describe a relationship. Besides *koinōnia* (translated "communion" here), **fellowship** is *metochē* (3352), meaning sharing, participation. Next is "concord," *sumphōnēsis* (4857; English *symphony*), meaning unison and agreement. Next is "part," which is *meris* (3310), a share or portion of something. Finally, "agreement" is *sunkatathesis* (4783), an accord or a consensus.

Can there be any doubt as to the importance of the Christian's separation from the world? Paul heaps one word upon another so there will be no misunderstanding about the Christian forging too close a bond with the non-Christian.

Those graphic words provide several obvious applications concerning separation. First, it's *never* right for a Christian to marry a non-Christian. Of all relationships, in fact, that one is the most unthinkable. It's even unwise to date an unbeliever since there can't be a common interest, and one will not be tempted to marry someone he hasn't dated. Second, a Christian should not make a business partnership with an unbeliever; there will certainly be different values, methods, motives, and goals. Third, a Christian should not be a member of a secret lodge or other such organization. Such organizations (e.g., the Masons) are *not* Christian, as even the *briefest* examination of their literature reveals.

Why make such an issue of the matter? Because God wants us to be pure, to "be separate" and "touch not the unclean thing" (v. 17). He does not want us to be defiled by evil or by fellowship with those who do evil. Further, if we do fellowship with evil, we break fellowship and communion with God. He can only "receive us" when we are separate from this world.

We'll add to this tomorrow.

Scriptures for Study: Read the following verses, noting the repeated principle of not forging a close bond with unbelievers: Proverbs 1:1–15; 4:14–15; 13:20; 24:1–2; 1 Corinthians 5:9; 15:33; James 4:4.

Keep Company (Company With)

sunanamignumi

Again in the matter of **fellowship**, let's consider another related NT word. So important is right company that Paul repeats in 1 Corinthians 5:9–10 what he had already written to those believers in another letter that no longer exists. He wrote "not to company with" fornicators, those who are covetous, extortioners, or idolaters. He then goes on to say, "But now I have written unto you not to keep company, if any man that is called a brother be a fornicator, or covetous, or an idolater, or a railer, or a drunkard, or an extortioner; with such an one no not to eat" (v. 11).

The words "to company with" (v. 9) and "to keep company" (v. 11) translate a single Greek word, *sunanamignumi* (4874), a compound from the root *anamignumi* (not in the NT), "to mix together," and *sun* (4862; see July 10), which means "together" and intensifies the root. The full idea, then, is "to mix together." Hippocrates, the famous fifth-century BC founder of scientific medicine, used it in the sense of mixing various ingredients together for medication. The fourth-century BC scholar Theophrastus uses it of different weeds that spring up and intermingle with the grain.

The application is again inescapable. The Christian is not to intermingle or have a close relationship with those who practice such serious sin. This very passage (vv. 9–13), in fact, deals with church discipline. If a Christian persists in such sin, he is to be put out of the church, and other Christians are to have nothing to do with him. Why? Because sin "rubs off." It's a communicable disease. Yes, we will have *contact* with the world, as Paul implies in verse 10, but we are not to *company* with it.

Abraham is a perfect example of this principle. Hebrews 11:9 says of him, "By faith he sojourned in the land of promise, as in a strange country, dwelling in tabernacles with Isaac and Jacob, the heirs with him of the same promise." What is most significant here is that he didn't live with the natives of that land, but rather, with "Isaac and Jacob." While he certainly had contact with them, he still remained a stranger to the pagans around him and lived instead with his godly family. In stark contrast, Lot "pitched his tent toward Sodom" (Gen. 13:12) and ended up *in* Sodom.

Let us be challenged each day to be careful of our company.

Scriptures for Study: What did our Lord pray in John 17:15 concerning the Christian's relationship to the world? 📖 Likewise, what is Paul's command in 2 Thessalonians 3:14?

Provoke

paroxusmos

Before leaving the subject of **fellowship** and Christian **company**, let's consider one more related word. Besides helping us when we need to move a refrigerator or mow our lawn while we're gone on vacation, what good are Christian friends?

The answer lies in Hebrews 10:24: "Let us consider one another to provoke unto love and to good works." **Provoke** translates an extremely strong Greek word, *paroxusmos* (3948; English *paroxysm*, a fit or outburst). The root *oxunō* (3961) means to sharpen, incite, or irritate, and the prefix *para* (3844) pictures movement toward a certain point. The idea then is to impel, incite, or rouse someone toward something.

Used in a bad sense, it speaks of sharp contention, or even an angry dispute (i.e., inciting to anger). Sadly, for example, when Paul did not want to take John Mark on his second journey—and rightly so since Mark had abandoned them during the first journey (Acts 13:13)—the "contention" was so sharp between Paul and Barnabas that they split up (Acts 15:36–40).

We also find this word in Acts 17:16, where Paul's "spirit was stirred [*paroxusmos*] in him, when he saw the city wholly given to idolatry." He was incensed to see how truly and totally pagan the city was. This reminds us again that God simply will not tolerate paganism, especially when it's mixed in and blended with His name and worship. Would that Christians today were incensed at any and every form of idolatry and paganism.

Used in a good sense, however, *paroxusmos* literally means "a sharpening," so figuratively, to spur on, stimulate, and encourage. Each of us, therefore, should seek ways that we can be an encouragement to other Christians, to impel others to do right in any given circumstance; we should look for ways to show our love and concern for their well-being and spiritual life. Hebrews 10:25 goes on to emphasize the essential nature of the church assembly.

That is what Christian friends are for. They are there to aid us in our Christian walk. Such friends can include a spouse, a fellow worker, or another Christian in the church assembly who will encourage and challenge us to holiness, perhaps even monitor us if needed.

Do you have such a Christian friend? If not, pray and ask God to bring one to you.

Scriptures for Study: Read 2 Corinthians 8:12–18 for an example of the value of such mutual encouragement.

Supply

epichoregia

In Philippians 1:19, the apostle Paul writes a glorious truth: "For I know that this shall turn to my salvation through your prayer, and the supply of the Spirit of Jesus Christ." Paul is not talking here about the "salvation" of his soul. The Greek *sōtēria* (4991; see Apr. 7) means safety, deliverance, and preservation from danger or destruction. He is, therefore, talking about his deliverance from prison, since that is where he is as he writes this letter. The means that God will use for that deliverance, Paul goes on to say, is twofold: the *supplications* of God's people and the *supply* of the Holy Spirit.

Supply is *epichoregia* (2024), a compound word comprised first of the root *chorēgeō* (5524), which is derived from *chorēgos* (not in the NT), "the leader of the ancient chorus who supplied the chorus at his own expense."[300] *Chorēgos*, in turn, is from *choros* (5525; English, *chorus*), "the chorus, a dance," and *hēgeomai* (2233), "to lead." The prefix *epi* (1909), "upon," gives the fuller meaning "further supply upon." Whenever a Greek city was going to put on a special festival, someone had to pay for the singers and dancers. The donation had to be a generous one, so this word came to refer to a generous, lavish, bountiful supply.

So, Paul didn't depend upon his own weak, dwindling resources. He depended upon the strength and generous, lavish, bountiful resources of God provided through the indwelling Holy Spirit. While the **prayer** (see May 28–31) of other believers is vitally important and helpful, Paul depended most on the spiritual resources in Christ through the Spirit.

So, what are those practical resources we have through the Holy Spirit? He directs (Rom. 8:14), calls to special service (Acts 13:2, 4), guides in service (8:27–29), illumines God's Word (1 Cor. 2:10-13), teaches the Word (John 16:13–14), empowers for service (Acts 1:8), produces Christlike character (Gal. 5:22–23), and makes all communion with God possible through prayer (Jude 20; Rom. 8:26–27), worship (Phil. 3:3), and thanksgiving (Eph. 5:18–20).

Is there any wonder that Paul reveled in "the supply of the Spirit of Jesus Christ"?

Scriptures for Study: Read each verse cited above, noting each resource carefully.

Striving

sunathleō

We examine a word today with which every athlete can identify. To the Philippians, and to us, Paul wrote: "Only let your conversation be as it becometh the gospel of Christ: that whether I come and see you, or else be absent, I may hear of your affairs, that ye stand fast in one spirit, with one mind striving together for the faith of the gospel" (Phil. 1:27).

Striving translates *sunathleō* (4866), which is used only by Paul in the NT. The root *athleō* (118) is, of course, where we get such English words as *athlete* and *athletics* and means to strive or contend, to be a champion in the public games, such as wrestling, boxing, or the *pankration* (see Sept. 30). This graphic word, therefore, pictures a completely dedicated, single-minded striving that would equal that of a committed athlete.

As we have noted in previous studies, the Christian life is, indeed, a struggle that demands total commitment. We **wrestle** (see Sept. 30) against Satan and his cohorts, and we **earnestly contend** (see Dec. 26) against those who would attack "the faith which was once delivered unto the saints" (Jude 3).

But with the prefix *sun* (4862; see July 10 and Oct. 31), "together," Paul adds the idea that Christians are to "strive and contend *together*, as would a team." As only a unified team can be effective, so must there be unity among God's people, as the context indicates. Here is a great indictment against the church today. What we need today is teamwork. There is so much bickering, pettiness, and self-righteousness that we're losing against Satan's team.

Think of it! If we would strive together in one spirit and one mind, as do the athletic teams we see today, the world would begin to notice the church as it does those teams. And would that Christians would get as *excited about* and would be as *loyal to* God's team and work as they do about their favorite sports team.

And again, for what are we striving? "The faith of the Gospel." As in Jude 3, *faith* is a noun and refers to the whole body of truth contained in God's Word, that is, historical, evangelical Christianity. Our responsibility is the *preservation*, *propagation*, and *proclamation* of God's Word.

Scriptures for Study: Read the following verses, noting the striving in each: Philippians 4:3 ("laboured" is *sunathleō*); 2 Timothy 2:4–5 ("strive" is *athleō*).

Deliver (Give, Gave)

paradidōmi

We meditate today on a strong word indeed. The Greek *paradidōmi* (3860) occurs some 120 times in the NT and is translated most often as **deliver** (or a similar form), although at times as give, gave, and betrayed.

The root *didōmi* (1325) means "to give of one's own accord and with good will."[301] The prefix *para* (3844) adds the idea of alongside or over to, providing the full meaning, "to deliver over to the power of someone." It was used in Classical Greek as a legal term for delivering a prisoner to the court. Likewise, the basic NT meaning is to deliver someone over to judgment and death. In Matthew 4:12, it's used of John the Baptist when he was "cast into prison" with the ultimate end of death.

With that in mind, it's noteworthy that most occurrences of *paradidōmi* refer to the Lord Jesus being delivered over for certain death. This was the whole reason He came to earth in His first advent. He did not come to live or even to "judge the world" (John 12:47); He came to die that sinners might be saved. We see this in every stage of his final days on earth: He was "betrayed" into the hands of men (Matt. 17:22), "betrayed" to the High Priest (20:18), "delivered" to the Gentiles (20:19), "delivered" to Pilate (27:2), "delivered" to the death sentence (Luke 24:20), and "betrayed" for crucifixion (Matt. 26:2).

It's also significant that *paradidōmi* is used of the Christian's response to what Christ did for them. Acts 15:25–26 describes Paul, Barnabas, and other "chosen men . . . that have hazarded [*paradidōmi*] their lives for the name of our Lord Jesus Christ." Can each of us say this of ourselves? Are we willing to "hand ourselves over" to whatever might come in the cause of Christ?

There is one other important meaning of *paradidōmi*. It's also used in the sense of "to hand down, pass on instruction from teacher to pupil"[302] This meaning is again vivid in Jude 3, as noted yesterday, where Jude writes that every believer "should earnestly contend for the faith which was once delivered unto the saints." As "the faith" is the preaching and teaching of the apostles that was handed down and passed on, it is that faith that comprises historical, evangelical Christianity and is the faith we are to continue to hand down.

Scriptures for Study: Note the challenge to the believer in 2 Corinthians 4:11. 📖 Read 1 Corinthians 11:2 and 23, noting again the handing down of God's Word.

Name

onoma

The Greek *onoma* (3686) is the root of the fascinating English word *onomatopoeia*, the naming of a thing or action by using a sound associated with it, such as "buzz" or "hiss." To the superstitious ancient Greeks, to know someone's name was to have power over them. In later Greek thought, especially among the Stoics, names were linked to the character or nature of the object. This led to the idea that the higher a god stood, the more names he had.

How important is a **name**? As one writer offers, "There was and is a world-wide belief that the name of an object, man, or higher being is more than a mere label only incidentally associated with the one who bears it. The name is an indispensable part of the personality."[303]

That was certainly true in OT use, as names were very significant in Jewish thinking, *onoma* appearing some 1,000 times in the Septuagint. Nabal, for example, was a fool, and his name reflects it (1 Sam. 25:25). Likewise, the name *Eve* means "the mother of all living" (Gen. 3:20), *Isaac* means "he laughs," which is a reminder of his parent's laughter at the thought that they could conceive a child in their old age, and *Babel* means "confusion," hence the name of the tower where God confounded earthly languages.

Turning to the NT, we again see *onoma* many times (228). Of men, for example, names reflect character. *Paul* means "little," and that's what he thought of himself (Eph. 3:8). The surname *Boanerges* (transliterated from the Chaldean *bēn*, 1123H, *son*, and *regesh*, 7285H, *tumult*, *thunder*) is ascribed to James and John as "the sons of thunder" (Mark 3:17).

Most significant of all, of course, are the names ascribed to God. *All* his names are significant: **God, Jesus, Christ, Savior, Lord, I Am, the Alpha and the Omega, Almighty** (see Apr. 3–6, 8–12), etc.

We, too, have significant names ascribed to us: **saint** (see Jan. 9), **servant** (see Feb. 11), **friend** (see Nov. 18), **Christian** (see Nov. 29), **stranger, foreigner,** and **fellowcitizen** (see Dec. 2). God always lives up to his name. Are we living up to ours?

Scriptures for Study: What does Philippians 2:9–10 declare about Christ's name? 🕮 What's spoken of as "better" in Hebrews 1:4? (We'll see more about the "betters" of Hebrews on Dec. 10.)

Inspiration

theopneustos

Without doubt, the issue of **inspiration** is the pivotal doctrine concerning the Bible. The first key scripture, of course, is 2 Timothy 3:16–17: "All scripture is given by inspiration of God, and is profitable for doctrine, for reproof, for correction, for instruction in righteousness: That the man of God may be perfect, thoroughly furnished unto all good works."

While **revelation** (see Feb. 17) refers to the act of God of making known His truth and to the content of that truth, **inspiration** refers to the *way* God makes His truth known. In the next few days, we'll examine this great subject.

Technically, the term *inspired* actually comes from the inferior Latin Vulgate (*divinitus inspirata*) and speaks of a "breathing *in*." The Greek *theopneustos* (2315), however, which appears only here in the NT, literally means "God-breathed," that is, breathed *out*. It is a compound comprised of *theos* (2316; see Apr. 3), "God," and *pneō* (4154), "to breathe hard, or blow."

The best way to understand these words is to contrast them with two others. One is *psuchō* (5594), "to breathe naturally." In contrast, *pneō* speaks of a forceful expiration of air. In the NT, in fact, it's "used only of the 'blowing' of a dangerous wind or of the south wind which brings heat (Matt. 7:25, 27; John 6:18; Luke 12:55) or the destructive winds in Rev. 7:1."[304] Another word is *aēr* (109), "to breathe unconsciously," while *pneō* speaks of a conscious breathing.

All this provides a clear definition of inspiration: *Inspiration is the forceful and conscious exhaling of God into the Scripture writers*. That definition clearly reflects what is meant when we say the Scriptures are "God-breathed." It's the "expiration" of God, that is, with all His energy He "blew" His very words into the writers of Scripture, while still allowing for the writer's personality and style. *That* is the miracle of inspiration.

As we'll see in coming days, it's inspiration that makes Scripture accurate, authoritative, and admonitory. Why? *Because it's what God has said*. In fact, the Bible declares hundreds of times that God Himself is speaking, using such phrases as: "saith the Lord" (854), "the Lord said" (219), "Jesus said" (65), "Jesus saith" (43), "God said" (46), and "God saith" (4).[305]

Scriptures for Study: Read the verses leading up to 2 Timothy 3:16–17 (vv. 1–15). Why is inspiration needed?

Correction [and] Thoroughly Furnished

epanorthosis [and] *exartizō*

Paul goes on to tell us in 2 Timothy 3:16–17 that because of **inspiration**, Scripture is profitable (*ophelimos*, 5624), that is, "useful, beneficial, advantageous," for five things. Having already examined "**doctrine**" (see May 22)—nothing is more profitable than that—"reproof" (**reprove**, see Aug. 23), and "**instruction**" (see Sept. 26), we come to a *fourth* profit, **correction**.

The Greek *epanorthōsis* (1882; only here in NT) is interesting and actually consists of three words. The root *orthos* (3723) means "upright, straight, correct" and is where we derive such English words as *orthodontist* (who corrects and straightens teeth), *orthopedics* (the correcting of bone injuries, deformities, and diseases), and *orthodox* (conforming to correct doctrine or belief). Add to this the prefix *epi* (1909), "to" or "upon" and the prefix *ana* (303), denoting repetition (as in the word "again"), and the result is "to set upright again, to straighten again."

The idea in this marvelous word, then, is bringing things back to where they should be. That is, indeed, what correction is. Sin is first exposed, rebuked, and punished, and then comes restoration. That is what the Word of God does: It sets things right, improves, restores, and brings us back to where we're supposed to be.

Fifth and finally, the Word of God makes us **thoroughly furnished**. The Greek *exartizō* (1822), which has the root *artios* (739), "complete, capable, or fit" (also translated "perfect" in our text; only here in NT), is reemphasized with the prefix *ek* (1537), "out." So, God gives us His Word so we can be "fitted out, altogether fitted, or fully fitted."

In western states such as Colorado, hunting, fishing, and camping are part of life. "Outfitters" are people who pack horses with all the needed equipment and provisions, sometimes even providing a guide, to take hunters or campers into the mountains for a week or more. As those campers are "fully fitted" for their task, so the Word of God fully fits us for our task, which is living and ministering in the world.

The words "man of God" refer directly to the **pastor-teacher** (see June 30). Specifically, he must be fully fitted, and when he is, he will be capable of "equipping the saints for the work of the ministry" (Eph. 4:11–12). By application, when the Word rules in each of our lives, we too will be fully fit, fully capable for every good work, that is, worship, holy living, and Christian service.

Scriptures for Study: Read the following verses, noting what we are to be prepared for in the Christian life: 2 Timothy 2:21; 2 Corinthians 9:8; Ephesians 2:10; Titus 3:1.

Sure

bebaios

Another pivotal text concerning the doctrine of **inspiration** is 2 Peter 1:19: "We have also a more sure word of prophecy; whereunto ye do well that ye take heed, as unto a light that shineth in a dark place, until the day dawn, and the day star arise in your hearts."

First, the Word of God is *accurate*. "Prophecy" refers, of course, to the OT Scriptures. In verses 15–18, Peter writes about his witnessing of Christ's transfiguration, but now he declares that there is something much surer than "personal experience." How important that is in light of how many Christians today speak of their "experience." Peter declares here that he, too, had an experience but that it cannot compare with the "more sure word of prophecy," that is, *the written Word of God*.

Sure is *bebaios* (949), which means "fit to tread on, having a firm foundation, durable, unshakeable, sure, reliable, and certain." Used in a legal sense, it meant "valid and legal." As one authority writes, "Thus the hope and confidence of man is firmly secured as by an anchor, when the object of the trust is the Word of God, which He has legally confirmed with an oath (Heb. 6:16, 19)."[306] As another adds, this word "in the NT is not used of persons but objects (Heb. 6:19), that which does not fail or waver, immovable, and on which one may rely."[307] So, as long as we cling to the Word, we will be firm, unshakable, sure, and certain. The reason for this "surer proof" is because the Word of God came by inspiration, as Peter goes on to write in verses 20–21.

Second, the words "take heed" teach us that the Word of God is *admonitory*. The Word of God is challenging and helpful in all things. How we so desperately need to listen! As our text says, it is the light that shines in darkness, and our world today is dark, indeed. There is, in fact, only one other thing that outshines the light of the Scripture: Christ's Second Coming ("the day dawn").

Third, *bebaios* clearly demonstrates that the Word of God is *authoritative*. Authority lies not in human reason nor in the church and its traditions, but in Scripture alone. Only it is **sure**.

Scriptures for Study: What makes us sure in Romans 4:16? 🕮 What are we to make sure in 2 Peter 1:10?

Private [and] Interpretation

idios [and] *epilusis*

As 2 Peter 1:20 goes on to declare, "No prophecy of the scripture is of any private interpretation." While the words "private interpretation" (*idias epiluseōs*) are controversial, they're really not difficult at all in light of language and context. **Private** is *idios* (2398), which means "pertaining to oneself or one's own." It appears 114 times in such verses as John 10:3 ("own"), 1 Corinthians 3:8, and 1 Peter 3:1.

Likewise, how many people there are today who sit in private and alter God's Word to suit *their own* purposes! How many there are who sit in private and twist the Word of God to fit their lifestyle and justify their actions and attitudes!

Interpretation, then, is *epilusis* (1955; only here in the NT). One Greek authority is weak here: "'A loosening, unloosing', *metaphorically* 'interpretation.'" Much stronger is Spiros Zodhiates: "*Epilusis*; genitive *epiluseos*, feminine noun from *epiluō*, to solve. Exposition, interpretation. In 2 Pet. 1:20, 21, it indicates that no prophecy comes from any private source, referring to the exposition of the will and purposes of God by the prophets themselves."[308] Another adds, "*Epiluō*, *epilusis*. Literally meaning 'to release,' *epiluō* [1956] means 'to resolve' (an issue) in Acts 19:39 and 'to explain' in Mk. 4:34. *Epilusis* means 'exposition' or 'interpretation' in 2 Pet. 1:20."[309]

So, "interpretation" is not a *metaphorical* meaning, but rather, it is *the* meaning. The emphasis here is that the prophets themselves did not *originate* ("unloose") the Scriptures or even *interpret* the words God gave them to write.

This point is vitally important in light of a common expression we often hear when it comes to the Bible. We all have heard people say after we quote the Bible, "Well, that's just your interpretation of the Bible; everybody has their own interpretation."

As mentioned in our "Mining Word Riches" chapter later in this book ("A Word of Caution on 'Interpretation'" section), an essential principle of biblical interpretation is *allowing Scripture to interpret itself.* This principle is called *analogia scripturae*, "the analogy of Scripture," that is, comparing Scripture with Scripture. The way to "interpret" the Bible is to take it as it reads. What matters is not how men *interpret* God's words, but what God's words plainly *say.*

Scriptures for Study: Read 1 Peter 1:10–12, noting how Messianic prophecies were especially not of men's own reasoning. 🕮 Read 2 Timothy 3:16–17 again and be reminded that this is true of "all Scripture."

Moved

pherō

Second Peter 1:21 is the capstone, the climax to what Peter has been writing on the subject of the **inspiration** of Scripture: "For the prophecy came not in old time by the will of man: but holy men of God spake as they were moved by the Holy Ghost." Scripture didn't come by anyone's experience. It didn't come from anyone's private interpretation. It didn't even come from the men who wrote it. From where, then, did it come? Holy men of God were moved by the Holy Spirit of God.

The Greek behind **moved** is the same one used for "came" in verses 17 and 18. It's *pheromenoi*, the present passive participle of *pherō* (5342). In both secular and NT Greek, *pherō* means "to bring, bear, or carry" with the added pictures of "to bear with the idea of motion" and "to bear with the idea of motion to a place."[310]

Luke used this word to describe how a ship is carried along by the wind (Acts 27:15, 17). Peter apparently loved this word, for he uses it six times in his two epistles (also translated "came" in our text). Being an outdoorsman, he wanted to paint a picture, and what a picture it is! Men today are moved, motivated, and mastered by many things, but the men whom God used were controlled only by one thing, the Holy Spirit.

This is further underscored by the verb tense. Because it's passive, "holy men" (the subject) were being acted upon by the Spirit, and because it's present, this action was continuous. Those "holy men," therefore, were being "continually carried along" by the Holy Spirit. Perhaps Peter was thinking, "It's as though the Scripture writers raised their sails and allowed the Holy Spirit's breath to carry them along, to drive them to their destination."

That is what is meant by the theological term *verbal, plenary inspiration*. "Verbal" means that the Holy Spirit guided the choice of the words, and "plenary" means full or complete. The Bible, therefore, is the full, complete revelation of God. All this gives us a conclusive definition of **inspiration**: *the activity of God by which He superintended the reception and the communication of His message, even in the specific words used, while still allowing for the style and personality of each writer, with the result being the Word of God.*

Scriptures for Study: Read the other four instances of Peter's use of *pherō*, noting the picture he paints in each: 1 Peter 1:13 ("brought"); 2 Peter 1:17 ("came"); 1:18 ("came"); 2:11 ("bring").

Jot [and] Tittle

iota [and] *keras*

Our Lord Himself declares the wondrous truth: "For verily I say unto you, Till heaven and earth pass, one jot or one tittle shall in no wise pass from the law, till all be fulfilled" (Matt. 5:18).

Jot is the Greek *iota* (2503), which refers to the Hebrew letter *yod*, the smallest letter in the Hebrew alphabet. Our Lord is, therefore, saying that not even the smallest letter of God's Word will pass away until all of it is fulfilled.

Even that is not enough, however, for our Lord also uses the word **tittle**, the Greek *keraia* (2762). This word comes from *keras* (2768), which was used to refer to the horn of an animal (e.g., Rev. 13:11) and to the projections on altars. This word was, therefore, used to refer to the small lines or projections on Hebrew letters that would change the entire meaning of words. So, not only is every *letter* and every *word* important, but so is *every little stroke of the pen*. Not one stroke of the pen will "pass away," that is, vanish or perish. Our Lord again says in John 10:35, "The scripture cannot be broken." What stronger language could be used? Indeed, there is no doubt, no question; the Word of God is God-breathed.

This text is, in fact, the final nail in the coffin of the higher critic. Evangelicals are criticized for "circular reasoning" when they argue that the Bible speaks of itself as being inspired. "After all," they argue, "suppose 2 Timothy 3:16–17 and 2 Peter 1:19–21 are not authentic; suppose they were penned by some second-century successor to the apostles and merely reflect his view of the Scriptures; while these verses tell us that the inspiration of Scripture was the teaching of the early church, they still don't prove the reality of claim." But our text (and many others) shows without question that Jesus Christ himself declared the inspiration of Scripture.[311]

Scriptures for Study: Read the following verses, noting what each declares about Scripture: Psalm 119:89, 90, 102; Isaiah 40:8; 1 Peter 1:25.

Study

spoudazō

In 2 Timothy 2:15, Paul writes, "Study to shew thyself approved unto God, a workman that needeth not to be ashamed, rightly dividing the word of truth."

Study is *spoudazō* (4704), a verb derived from the noun *spoudē* (4710), meaning speed, haste, diligence. In Classical Greek, this verb means "'to make haste' and is thus closely related to 'to be zealous, active, concerned about something.'"[312] The usual idea in NT usage is "zealous effort."

Concerning our text, many think that newer Bible translations that read, "Be diligent" (NASB), or "Do your best" (NIV, which is a terrible translation), are better. One popular commentary says: "'Study' (KJV) is obviously too narrow a term, usually referring today to the studying of books." On the contrary, we submit that the beauty of the AV's Old English actually says much more. In his unabridged dictionary, Webster says that "study," "to be diligent," and "to be eager" are all "akin," and then defines *study* as "a state of absorbed contemplation." Now, in all honesty, isn't that better?

Indeed, our attitude and approach to the interpretation of Scripture must be "absorbed contemplation." How much slip-shod, shallow, and sentimental Bible interpretation there is today! Many think they can just read a few verses, make a quick "application," and then hurry on to their next activity. Many preachers do likewise in their sermon preparation, spending an hour or two in the Word and coming away with a shallow, topical "sermonette for Christianettes." Sadly, some Bible colleges are the guiltiest because that is the approach they teach.

Another deadly danger to honest interpretation is the common practice of formulating a preconceived idea, opinion, or position and *then* going to Scripture to try to defend it. The story is often told of the preacher who said, "I've got a really good sermon in mind; all I need is a Scripture verse to go with it." That might be humorous, but it's more common than you think. This is also common among folks who have held a certain position all their lives and refuse to consider any other teaching.

If I may be frank, we must get out of the way and allow God to speak. We must lay aside whatever *we think*, and then approach the Scripture to find what *God says*.

Scriptures for Study: Read the following scriptures, noting the use of *spoudazō*: Ephesians 4:3 ("endeavouring"); 2 Peter 3:13–14 ("diligent"); 1:10 ("diligence" is *spoudē*).

Workman [and] Rightly Divide

ergatēs [and] *orthotomeō*

Second Timothy 2:15 goes on to declare that the careful pastor (and by application, every Christian) is to be "a workman that needeth not to be ashamed, rightly dividing the word of truth."

Workman is *ergatēs* (2040; see also **working**, see July 27), which spoke of "a worker as the member of a class (frequently a slave) or of an occupational group (in particular farm-labourers)."[313] Here is, indeed, the true NT picture of the pastor, for Paul is writing to a pastor. He is to labor over the Word of God as a slave or a farmer labors in his tasks.

The words "to shew thyself approved unto God" reemphasize this fact by showing that the workman is totally dedicated to God and His Word. This is first and foremost the responsibility of the pastor, who is called by vocation to do this and has the time to devote to this. By application, however, all Christians can (and should) study the Word under the guidance of their pastor; they will, of course, not have the time or tools to devote to this, but they can do basic **study**.

Often we incorrectly think that the reason and goal for studying the Scriptures is knowledge. While it's true that we want knowledge (**truth**, Feb. 1–3), our chief goal should be to "rightly divide the word of truth." **Rightly divide** is *orthotomeō*, a compound comprised of *orthos* (3723; see Nov. 7), "straight," and *temnō* (not in NT), "to cut or divide." The word was used in ancient times for cutting a straight furrow, something that a farmer is always concerned about as he plows. Similarly, a carpenter is concerned about making a straight cut on a board, and a seamstress is concerned about sewing a straight seam.

That, then, is the goal of the student of Scripture: to cut it straight, to rightly divide it so that it is clearly understood and accurately applied. Our goal is spiritual, not intellectual. How, then, do we accomplish this? Again, it takes work, *hours* of laborious study; there is no substitute, no shortcuts. We will not properly interpret if we grab a verse here and a principle there. We must labor to rightly divide. That must be our goal and passion.

Scriptures for Study: What warning does 2 Corinthians 4:2 give concerning the handling of Scripture? 🕮 What was Paul's further mandate to Timothy concerning his ministry in 1 Timothy 4:12–16?

Heart

kardia

In Matthew 22:37–38, our Lord declares, "Thou shalt love the Lord thy God with all thy heart, and with all thy soul, and with all thy **mind**. This is the first and great commandment."

Heart is *kardia* (2588), from which, of course, medical terms such as *cardiac* and *cardiologist* are derived. Its significance is enormous. It was used in secular Greek both in the literal and figurative sense, but the figurative was the most profound, picturing the heart as the seat of emotions and spirituality. In Homer's time (eighth century BC) and onward, however, it took on the even more significant meaning of both spiritual and *intellectual life*, including man's will and decision-making.

These meanings flowed naturally into NT usage and provide us with striking applications. *Kardia* appears in Jesus' Beatitudes, for example: "**Blessed** are the pure in heart: for they shall see God" (Matt. 5:8). Who is blessed (see Jan. 12)? The one who is pure in feeling, thought, and will.

Here in our text, then, Jesus' words are pointed indeed. Most people, even Christians, equate the heart with only emotion, which in turn produces "up and down" emotional living and even a desire for emotionalism and entertainment in the church service. But the Christian life is a life not only of feeling, but a life of the mind and will. In fact, as one Greek authority points out, there is a closeness of meaning in the NT between heart (*kardia*) and mind (*nous*; see Apr. 2).

The principle, therefore, of our loving the Lord with all our heart is truly the "heart" of living the Christian life. If we really love him with our feelings, our thoughts, and our decisions, that will drive everything we do and say. If we really love him, we'll live holy, we'll desire His Word, we'll obey Him, we'll edify and serve others, and the list goes on.

Start today by asking yourself, "Do I really love the Lord?"

Scriptures for Study: In light of *kardia*, what does Romans 1:21 tell us about man's sinfulness? 🕮 What does Romans 10:9–10 declare about salvation?

Angel

angelos

The term *angel* is obviously a transliteration of the Greek *angelos* (32). As far back as Homer, it simply refers to "a messenger," but the role of such a messenger was sacred, and he was supposedly under the special protection of the gods.[314]

While such pagan concepts have no basis in Scripture, neither do some of the misconceptions that arose in Judaism. Many Jews, for example, believed that angels form a council that God consults before doing anything. Many also believed that various angels control the stars, seas, rain, snow, and other such things. Still others believed that "recording angels" write down everything people say and that every nation and child has a "guardian angel."

The latter idea is still popular in our day, no doubt as a result not only of Jewish **tradition** (see Oct. 19), but also from the writings of Thomas Aquinas, who was notorious for mixing human philosophy (especially Aristotle) with Christian thought. In his view, prior to birth each person is protected by the mother's guardian angel and then has his or her own assigned at birth.[315]

Scripture, however, nowhere says such things. What it *does* say, we find in Hebrews 1:14, for example: "Are they not all ministering spirits, sent forth to minister for them who shall be heirs of salvation?" We also read in Matthew 18:10: "Take heed that ye despise not one of these little ones; for I say unto you, That in heaven their angels do always behold the face of my Father which is in heaven." What we see here is that angels serve believers collectively (as the pronoun "their" is collective). The picture is that they are always looking at the face of God so as to hear His command to help believers.

The beloved Henry Morris (who went home to be with our Lord during the writing of this book) well sums up: "They accomplish their ministry on behalf of the heirs of salvation in various ways, including: instruction (Acts 10:3–6), deliverance (Ps. 34:7; 91:11), comfort (Matt. 1:20; Luke 22:43) and, finally, reception at death (Luke 16:22). They were created to be ministering spirits, continually sent forth to minister (that is, serve) those who shall be heirs of salvation."[316]

Scriptures for Study: Read the verses cited above, noting the ministry of angels. 🕮 The point of Hebrews 1:4–14 was to show Jews that Christ, among other things, was better than angels. Read that passage and note the author's arguments.

Disciple

mathētēs

Disciple is *mathētēs* (3101) and means more than is commonly thought. While it comes from *manthanō* (3129), "to teach," it means more than just being a student or learner. *Manthanō*, in fact, is comparable to *epignōsis*,[317] "a full and thorough knowledge" (see Feb. 19).

In Classical Greek, *mathētēs* is what we would call "an apprentice," one who not only learns facts from the teacher but other things, such as his attitudes and philosophies. In this way the *mathētēs* was what we might call a "student-companion," who doesn't just sit in class listening to lectures, but rather, who follows the teacher to learn life as well as facts.

While the same basic idea is present in NT usage, *mathētēs* goes even deeper. Interestingly, while it appears over 260 times, those occurrences are only in the Gospels and Acts. It pictures total attachment to the Lord Jesus, a connection that goes even further than the idea of an apprentice. Being a disciple of Christ means that we are, like the twelve disciples were, with him night and day, day in and day out. Being His disciple means that we are true followers, true believers, imitating all He does and quoting all He says.

While some teachers make a distinction between a "**Christian**" (see Nov. 29) and a "committed disciple," that idea is a modern invention and is foreign to Scripture. They are clearly synonymous (Acts 6:1–2, 7; 11:26; 14:20, 22; 15:10).

One of the many significant occurrences of *mathētēs* is its first appearance: "And seeing the multitudes, he went up into a mountain: and when he was set, his disciples came unto him: And he opened his mouth, and taught them" (Matt. 5:1–2). What follows in chapters 5–7, of course, has been called the "Sermon on the Mount." Its first outstanding feature is that it's addressed not to the multitude, but to disciples, true believers. It does not deal with salvation, but with how the true follower of Christ lives. From that time on, the disciples could not only remember the words Jesus spoke, but they would also see those words lived out in His life.

At the opposite end of our Lord's earthly ministry, we see the verb form in the "Great Commission" He gave to His disciples: "Go ye therefore, and teach all nations . . ." (Matt. 28:19). "Teach" is *matheteuō* (3100), so the disciples are now "making disciples of" others, who in turn make other disciples. That is, indeed, our commission.

Scriptures for Study: Over the next few days, read the Sermon on the Mount and be challenged with what it means to be Jesus' disciple, a true Christian.

Follow

akoloutheō

The Greek *akoloutheō* (190) is from *akolouthos* (not in NT), "attendant, follower," which in turn comes from *keleuthos* (not in NT), "path," and the collative prefix *a* (1), showing unity (see Nov. 28). It therefore means "to accompany, go somewhere with someone, go behind, follow." Besides the literal meaning, it also carries the metaphorical meaning in Classical Greek of "follow the drift, understand (Plato), follow someone's opinion, agree (Plato), [or] adapt oneself (Thucydides)."[318]

While there are instances in the NT where *akoloutheō* does not involve being a true **disciple**, such occurrences concern crowds who followed Jesus but who had no conviction or commitment (Matt. 4:25; 8:1; 21:9; Mark 10:32).

In contrast, the word has special significance when used in the context of individuals, especially when it involves Jesus' call to follow Him. When Jesus called Matthew, for example, He said, "Follow me," and Matthew's response was that he, indeed, "followed him" (Matt. 9:9). What, then, does following Christ involve?

First, we follow Christ in *salvation*. To come to Christ means true conversion, commitment, and change. As illustrated by the rich man (Matt. 19:21–22) and the man who supposedly had to bury his father first (Luke 9:61), salvation is a forsaking all to follow Christ. As Peter testified, "Behold, we have forsaken all, and followed thee" (Matt. 19:27).

Second, we follow Christ in *separation*. When Jesus called Peter and Andrew, "they forsook their nets, and followed him" (Mark 1:16–18). They not only *left* it all behind, but it *stayed* behind. Jesus declared, "I am the light of the world: he that followeth me shall not walk in darkness, but shall have the light of life" (John 8:12). The true believer is separate from the world and no longer follows the works of darkness.

Third, we follow Christ in *service*. While the words "follow me" are a different Greek word in Matthew 4:19 (*deute*, 1205, "Come hither!"), the challenge to be "fishers of men" remains the same. To be a *follower* of Christ is to be a *proclaimer* of Christ.

Fourth, we follow Christ in *suffering*. "Whosoever will come after me," Jesus declared, "let him deny himself, and take up his cross, and follow me" (Mark 8:34). To follow Christ means to suffer, and perhaps even die, for Him. That is why He also said that anyone "that taketh not his cross, and followeth after me, is not worthy of me" (Matt. 10:38).

Scriptures for Study: Read the scriptures mentioned in the four points above, meditating on how, as one writer puts it, "Discipleship is much more than simply strolling with the Savior."[319]

Friend

philos

Our dear Lord uses a word in John 15:15 that should warm our souls like few words can: "Henceforth I call you not servants; for the servant knoweth not what his lord doeth: but I have called you friends; for all things that I have heard of my Father I have made known unto you."

While we are still "servants" of God (see Feb. 11), our Lord here makes the startling statement that as His disciples we are also His *friends*. **Friend** is *philos* (5384) and simply means friend, that is, someone for which there is "tender affection" (see also Jan. 21).

At various stages in Classical Greek, *philos* referred to "'followers' of a political leader," "'clients' who cluster around a prominent and wealthy man," and even "legal assistants and political supporters." Later it took on a much deeper meaning in that "the supreme duty of a friend is to sacrifice himself for his friend even to the point of death."[320]

It's that latter picture that lays the foundation for the NT usage of *philos*. As verse 13 declares, in fact, "Greater love hath no man than this, that a man lay down his life for his friends." Our Lord did, indeed, give His life for us out of His true, perfect, selfless love (*agapē*; see Jan. 19). Likewise, *philos* appears in the Septuagint in such verses as Proverbs 17:17: "A friend loveth at all times, and a brother is born for adversity."

So, my dear Christian friend, if I may use that term sincerely, what is your relationship to your Lord? Can you be called, as was Abraham according to James 2:23, "the Friend of God"? (Cf. 2 Chron. 20:7; Isa. 41:8.) Why was Abraham called the friend of God? Because of his obedience, which brings us right back to John 15:14: "Ye are my friends, if ye do whatsoever I command you."

While we all have many acquaintances, a smaller number of closer relationships, and perhaps even a smaller cadre of associates or colleagues, we will have very few *true* friends (Prov. 18:24). But the Friend who cannot be equaled by any other is our Lord.

Scriptures for Study: What might allegiance to Christ cost you, according to Luke 21:16–17? 🕮 What kind of friendship means enmity with God (James 4:4)?

Vine

ampelos

Looking again at John 15, as we did yesterday (see also June 3–4), in verses 1–5 our Lord paints a graphic picture of our relationship with Him by referring to Himself as the **Vine** (*ampelos*, 288).

Viticulture is among the oldest, if not *the* oldest, of all agricultural forms. As far back as Noah we read, "Noah began to be an husbandman, and he planted a vineyard: And he drank of the wine, and was drunken; and he was uncovered within his tent" (Gen. 9:20–21). It's significant that Noah illustrates both the positive and negative metaphors that the vine provides: fertility and growth on the one hand and debauchery through drunkenness on the other.

The vine was a very important image in the OT. In Isaiah 5:1–7, for example, where Israel is pictured as a vineyard, God is the Vinedresser, and the harvest consists of wild grapes that are not fit to use for anything and ultimately have to be laid waste.

The vine is, therefore, a pivotal image here in John 15. Most significantly, and in dramatic contrast to Israel, our Lord says of Himself, "I am the true vine" (v. 1). As we noted on April 10, Jesus equated Himself with God using the words **I Am** and declares that He is self-existent and without beginning. This declaration is, in fact, the last of seven "I am" statements of Christ in John's gospel that declare His deity.[321]

The vine, therefore, provides us with at least three practical pictures.

First, there is *life* in the vine. "Without me ye can do nothing," our Lord says (v. 5). That is because He *is* life: "In him was life; and the life was the light of men" (John 1:4). And that, of course, is because He is the Creator, the Originator of Life (1:1–3).

Second, there is *longevity* in the vine. As we considered back on June 2–4, as the branches have continued life because they **abide** in the vine, so we have life because we abide in the true Vine.

Third, there is *luscious fruit* in the vine. This, too, we've examined before (**fruit**, see Aug. 19–22), but it bears repeating. Every true believer either bears *fruit*, bears *more* fruit, or bears *much* fruit, and it is all because he or she abides in the true Vine.

Scriptures for Study: Read John 15:1–11 once again, and rejoice that you are part of the Vine.

Apprehended

katalambanō

Among the most challenging verses in Scripture is Philippians 3:12: "Not as though I had already attained, either were already perfect: but I follow after, if that I may apprehend that for which also I am apprehended of Christ Jesus."

A chief problem about living the Christian life is that we can easily become satisfied and content with the spiritual level we have attained. One reason for this is that we tend to compare ourselves with other Christians, who also are not making much progress. A second reason for this is that while we might *evaluate* ourselves (again in comparison to others), we seldom truly *examine* ourselves (2 Cor. 13:5).

The Christians in the church at Sardis (Rev. 3:1), for example, *evaluated* themselves and had made quite a name for themselves, but Jesus said they were dead. Likewise, those in the church at Laodicea (3:17) *evaluated* themselves and thought they were rich, but upon close examination, Jesus said they were "wretched, and miserable, and poor, and blind, and naked."

When Paul *examined* himself, however, he realized that he had not yet **apprehended**. The Greek is *katalambanō* (2638), "to lay hold of, to seize with eagerness," so figuratively, "to fully understand and comprehend." There is a clear allusion here to the Greek games in strenuously contending for the prize and an eagerness to seize it.

Here, then, is the apostle Paul, who, even though he has been a Christian for some thirty years, has planted numerous churches all over the known world, and has written several God-breathed letters that will become part of sacred Scripture, still says, "I haven't arrived yet. I haven't reached the prize. I don't even fully *comprehend* the prize. I therefore continue to reach forth, to **press** [see June 21] toward, to pursue, to go after the **prize** [see June 22] of the knowledge of Christ" (vv. 13b–14).

What an encouragement! If Paul could say such a thing, what about us? Each of us should have what we could call a "spiritual dissatisfaction." Never should we be satisfied with our spiritual level. There's *always* more.

Scriptures for Study: What does Paul challenge us to "comprehend" in Ephesians 3:18? 🕮 Review our February 20–23 readings in this context.

Born (Again)

gennaō (anōthen)

One Greek word translated **born** is *tiktō* (5088), "to bring forth, bear, bring" (e.g., Luke 2:11). More commonly, however, is *gennaō* (1080), from which, of course, are derived English words such as *generation* and *genetic*. Used in the literal sense, it speaks of men begetting (e.g., Matt. 1:1–16a) and women bearing children (16b).

It's the metaphorical sense, however, that is most significant. One aspect of this is the Jewish way of using the word *begetting* as a picture of the relationship between a teacher and his **disciple** (Nov. 16). In Jesus' day, for example, it was customary for a rabbi to address his pupil, or even any member of the community, as "my son."

Another aspect of the metaphorical sense is "God begetting in a spiritual sense, which consists in regeneration, sanctifying, quickening anew, and ennobling the powers of the natural man by imparting to him a new life and a new spirit in Christ (1 John 5:1)."[322] That is what is meant by being "born of God" (1 John 3:9) and being the "sons of God" (Rom. 8:14).

Most significant of all is the term **born again** (John 3:3, 7). **Again** translates *anōthen* (509), which is comprised of *ano* (507), "above, upwards" (see June 20), and the suffix *then*, which denotes "from." The literal idea, therefore, is "to be born from above," which is how Young's *Literal Translation* renders it. "Born again," however, is still correct because this birth is a new birth that can come only from God (Tyndale's 1534 translation renders it "born anew"), and Nicodemus clearly recognized that this is "second" birth (v. 4).

Another wondrous Greek word that is rendered **born again** is *anagennaō* (313), which occurs only twice in the NT. While it's translated "born again" in 1 Peter 1:23, it's rendered even more literally in 1:3: "Blessed be the God and Father of our Lord Jesus Christ, which according to his abundant mercy hath *begotten us again* unto a lively hope by the resurrection of Jesus Christ from the dead" (emphasis added). Here is the doctrine of "regeneration" in a nutshell. We have new life in Christ because we have been "begotten again." What else is there to say besides *hallelujah*?

Scriptures for Study: What is the contrast in Galatians 4:28–29? 📖 What do foolish questions give birth to ("gender" is *gennaō*) according to 2 Timothy 2:23? 📖 What's the promise of 1 John 5:4?

Way

hodos

In over 100 NT occurrences we find the word *hodos* (3598), which means a **way**, road, highway, or street in their many possible forms. To the Greeks, this could refer to "the narrow path trodden by those who have gone before, or the broad roads made for traffic, on which chariots can travel, troops can march, and processions can be held."[323]

Perhaps our Lord had that very contrast in mind when He declared in His Sermon on the Mount (see Nov. 15): "Enter ye in at the strait gate: for wide is the gate, and broad is the way, that leadeth to destruction, and many there be which go in thereat: Because strait is the gate, and narrow is the way, which leadeth unto life, and few there be that find it" (Matt. 7:13–14).

While we hear such statements today as, "There are many roads to heaven," and we must be "broad-minded" and "all-inclusive," that is *not* what Jesus taught. He was very narrow in His statement about who will be saved. Yes, the popular teaching is that "eventually everyone will be saved," but Jesus says the exact opposite, that comparatively few will be saved.

Understanding this word enables us to fully grasp John 14:6. In answer to Thomas's question in verse 5, "Lord, we know not whither thou goest; and how can we know the way?" Jesus answers, "I am the way, the truth, and the life: no man cometh unto the Father, but by me." This is the sixth of seven "I Am" statements by our Lord in the gospel that declares His deity (see Nov. 19). As the definite article ("the") precedes "life," showing that Jesus is the only life, the article also precedes "way," showing that Jesus is the only way to that *life*.

This verse does indeed declare the ultimate, threefold self-revelation given by Christ. While men think there are many ways to God—morality, humanitarianism, religious observance, sacraments, and all manner of things under the sun—there is one and only one way, and that is Jesus Christ alone. To those who would say, "That sure is narrow-minded thinking," we reply, "You're absolutely right. It *is* narrow, because the *way* is narrow." The way to Christ is about sin, righteousness, judgment, and repentance, and few people want to take that route.

Scriptures for Study: What is the "new and living way" spoken of in Hebrews 10:19–23? 🕮 What is the sobering warning of 2 Peter 2:21?

NOVEMBER 23

Blaspheme, Blasphemy

blasphēmia, blasphēmeō

Our English words **blaspheme** and **blasphemy** are obviously direct transliterations of the Greek noun *blasphēmia* (988) and verb *blasphēmeō* (987). In secular Greek, these refer not only to "abusive speech," but also to "the strongest form of personal mockery and calumniation." They're almost equal, in fact, to *loidoria* (3059), railing in harsh, insolent, and abusive speech[324] (note "reviled" for *blasphēmeō* in Matt. 27:39 AV).

What is most significant about these words is that while our English word means speaking evil of *God*, the Greek means speaking evil of *anyone*. As one source outlines, we find, in fact, no less than six usages in the NT for the objects of blasphemy.[325]

First and foremost, of course, there is blasphemy against God. The ultimate blasphemy against God will come from the Antichrist (Rev. 13:5–6). Here is monstrous blasphemy as he glorifies himself, mocks God, and denies His work. The Antichrist will even enthrone himself in the temple (2 Thess. 2:4), making himself "God." Likewise, anyone can blaspheme God by speaking against Him in any way, as did Paul, for example, before his conversion (1 Tim. 1:13), and as do countless people today through false religion.

Second, there is blasphemy against Christ, as when the people mocked His messianic claims (Matt. 27:39; Mark 15:29), as the thief on the cross did as well (Luke 23:39).

Third, there is blasphemy against the Holy Spirit, which is even spoken of as the "unpardonable sin" (Mark 3:28–29). While there's debate about how one commits that sin, one Greek authority puts it very well: "This can hardly refer to the mere utterance of a formula in which the word [*Spirit*] appears. It denotes the conscious and wicked rejection of the saving power and grace of God towards man."[326]

Fourth, there is blasphemy against the Word of God. A disregard for or rebellion against God's Word actually blasphemes it, as declared in 1 Timothy 6:1 and Titus 2:5.

Fifth, there is even blasphemy against angels. First-century Gnostics despised the idea of angels, and Jude 8 seems to refer to such teachers who "speak evil of dignities," as does 2 Peter 2:10–11.

Sixth, there is also blasphemy against people. As Paul was treated "slanderously" (1 Cor. 4:13, "defamed;" 10:30, "evil spoken of"), we should expect the same (1 Pet. 4:1–4, "speaking evil of").

Scriptures for Study: Read the scriptures mentioned in today's study, noting the seriousness of blasphemy, regardless of the object.

Heresy (1)

hairesis

Heresy is another transliterated word from the Greek. The literal meaning of the noun *hairesis* (139) is truly interesting. In Classical Greek, it means "seizure, taking, acquisition, choice, desire for something, and purposeful decision." Later in Hellenistic Greek, it "denotes the teaching or the school of a particular philosopher with which a person identifies himself by his choice."[327] In the Septuagint, it speaks of choice, as it translates the Hebrew *nedēbēh* (5071H) in Leviticus 22:18 and 21 ("freewill offering").

The NT usage of *hairesis*, then, follows that of Hellenism and the Septuagint. Heresy is a choice, a deliberate decision to "seize" upon a particular teaching that is not orthodox. Acts 5:17, for example, mentions "the sect [*hairesis*] of the Sadducees," a Jewish faction that denied the doctrine of resurrection. Acts 15:5 refers to another sect, the Judaizers, who taught salvation by works, such as adding circumcision as a requirement. That issue prompted the Jerusalem Council, as the following verses describe, which definitively stated the principle of salvation by grace alone through faith alone.

There has always been the plague of false teaching and teachers. That is why **discernment** is so crucial (see July 15–22). The main thrust of Peter's second epistle is a warning against false teachers who will infiltrate the church. That is best summarized in 2:1: "There shall be false teachers among you, who privily shall bring in damnable heresies, even denying the Lord that bought them, and bring upon themselves swift destruction." We see here at least three principles.

First, false teaching is *deceitful*. "Privily" is *pareisagō* (3919), to bring in by the side of, to bring something in by smuggling it. False teaching has to be "brought in the side door" lest someone see it for what it really is.

Second, false teaching is *degrading*. False teachers deny the Lord and His work in one way or another and in so doing degrade and **blaspheme** Him.

Third, false teaching is *destructive*. "Damnable" is *apōleia* (684), to destroy fully. False teaching not only destroys right doctrine and the lives of its victims, but it also destroys the propagators themselves ("swift destruction").

We'll continue these important thoughts tomorrow.

Scriptures for Study: What other "works of the flesh" are listed with "heresies" in Galatians 5:19–21? 🕮 What command does Paul give concerning heretics (*hairetikos*, 141) in Titus 3:10?

Heresy (2)

hairesis

Before leaving the word **heresy**, we should note that it has taken on a slightly broader meaning in our day when compared with another word—*apostasy*. While there's a fine line between the two, there is a distinction.

Apostasy, which is illustrated by "cults," is a departure from Christian truth in general; it's *professed* Christianity but actually a denial of it. This might consist of all Christian truth or just a single truth (such as Christ's deity or salvation by grace) that's so pivotal that it results in the destruction of all biblical truth. *An apostate is not a Christian*. One historical example is Arius, a fourth-century parish priest in Alexandria who taught that Jesus was not coequal with God and was, in fact, a created being. Arianism has existed in various forms ever since (see July 22).

Heresy, however, as used today, is somewhat broader and can be committed by a true Christian. It occurs when, while holding to the foundational doctrines of Scripture, one deviates on a particular doctrine. One example is the use of images in church history. While any use whatsoever of images was *never* used by the early church *because God forbid it*, they slowly came into use through emblems such as the dove, fish, anchor, vine, and lamb. Gradually this increased through paintings, sculptures, and jewelry that depicted biblical events, items, saints, martyrs, and even Christ Himself.

So, while some folks get upset by this observation, such practices of hanging pictures of Jesus on the wall, plastering Christian symbols on our cars, and wearing jewelry with religious symbols is actually heresy. It violates a *very specific* command of God to make no images (Exod. 20:3–5; cf. Matt. 22:36–38; see also Dec. 9).

There are many such examples. The so-called Christian Crusades were based on the heretical teaching that Christians can use force against unbelievers. There's the heretical teaching that God demands poverty from Christians, as well as the other extreme, "prosperity teaching," that God returns our "investment" and makes us rich. The "seeker-sensitive" movement that appeals to people's "felt needs" to lure them into the church is heresy; the NT nowhere teaches that approach. The spirit of "tolerance" in the church today is heretical, because God commands that we discern **truth** from error and strongly condemn false teaching in no uncertain terms.

Yes, these are "hard sayings" (cf. John 6:60ff.), but as Puritan John Trapp wrote, "Truth seldom goes without a scratched face."[328]

Scriptures for Study: As you so desire, review our study of **discernment** (see July 15–22) to be reminded of its crucial importance.

Treasure (1)

thēsauros

Once again we see an English word that comes directly from the Greek, and in this case it's almost the same spelling—the Greek is *thēsauros* (2344), and the English is *thesaurus*.

In NT times, in both pagan and Jewish culture, it was common practice to have a treasury right in the religious temple, in which gifts and taxes were stored. In Greek culture, in fact, this practice goes back as far as 700 BC. This treasury was called the *thēsauros*, "treasury, treasure box, storehouse." Later it came to refer to the **treasure** itself. That meaning makes perfect sense of our English *thesaurus*—it is a "treasury of words."

We see this word (along with the verb *thēsaurizō*, 2343, "to lay up or store for future use") some twenty-six times in the NT. The Magi, for example, brought "treasures" to the infant Savior (Matt. 2:11), and Moses chose rather to suffer with the Israelites, "esteeming the reproach of Christ greater riches than the treasures in Egypt" (Heb. 11:25–26). In the Parable of the Rich Fool, what made the man a fool was that he "[laid] up treasure for himself, and [was] not rich toward God" (Luke 12:21).

Most significantly, Matthew 6:19–21 provides the same challenge: "Lay not up for yourselves treasures upon earth, where moth and rust doth corrupt, and where thieves break through and steal: But lay up for yourselves treasures in heaven, where neither moth nor rust doth corrupt, and where thieves do not break through nor steal: For where your treasure is, there will your heart be also."

The imagery is truly graphic here, as our Lord uses *thēsauros* five times. Literally, verse 19 says, "Treasure not up treasures for yourselves upon earth." Holding, hoarding, and hiding earthly riches benefits no one, and they can be devalued and stolen. Verse 20 then declares, "Treasure up treasures for yourselves in heaven." True **riches** (see Jan. 28), true wealth is not in *material* things but is in *spiritual* things.

Finally, where your "treasure" is, that is, what you value most, indicates the kind of heart you have. You will have either a heart for greed or generosity, a heart for hoarding or helping, a heart for money or ministry.

Scriptures for Study: What contrast does our Lord make in Luke 6:45? 🕮 What great treasures are hid in Christ (Col. 2:3)?

Treasure (2)

thēsauros

One of the most significant occurrences of *thēsaurizō* is in 1 Corinthians 16:2: "Upon the first day of the week let every one of you lay by him *in store*, as God hath prospered him, that there be no gatherings when I come" (emphasis added). We see here at least four principles of Christian giving.

First, there is the *period* for giving. The words "upon the first day of the week" leave no doubt about the day God's NT people are to meet for worship (cf. Acts 20:7). They also specify that giving is a part of worship. The absence of the definite article ("the") further demonstrates that giving is not on "*the* week," such as "Lenten Sunday," "Faith Promise Sunday," or other such artificial, man-made events. Giving is to be regular, on each Lord's Day.

Second, there are the *people* who give. "Every one of you" leaves no one out of this important practice. Every Christian is to give to the support of God's work.

Third, there is the *place* for giving. The words "upon the first day of the week" and "lay by him in store" underscore the fact that the local church is where God's people are to give. The imagery of the ancient "treasury" could not be clearer. While not a popular view, there's no other place spoken of in Scripture for giving than the local church, with the exception of giving to someone who is in need (James 2:15–17).

Fourth, there is the *proportion* of giving. The words "as God hath prospered him" should encourage us to forever delete the word *tithe* from our vocabulary. Several "tithes" were prescribed in the Mosaic Law, which, when totaled up, amounted to about 23 percent.[329] These were not freewill offerings, but rather, taxes to operate the government.

Christians are likewise required to pay their taxes (Rom. 13:6), but their giving to God is not calculated by percentages. What dictates our giving is how God has prospered us. "Prospered" is *euodoō* (2137), which comes from *eudos* (not in NT), "easy to travel through," and literally means "to prosper, make good one's journey." The idea then is not just money, but a good journey in general. Has God given us a good journey? We, therefore, should give accordingly—systematically, sacrificially, and sublimely.

Scriptures for Study: What model does the poor widow in Mark 12:41–44 provide for our giving? 📖 What did Paul praise the Corinthians for in 2 Corinthians 8:2?

Brother

adelphos

Brother translates *adelphos* (80; English *Philadelphia*, city of brotherly love), a compound made from *delphus* (not in the NT), "a womb," and the prefix *a* (1). Not only is this prefix used as the "alpha negative," which makes a word mean the exact opposite (e.g., see Apr. 1), it's also used in a "collative" manner, signifying unity.

The picture in *adelphos*, then, is "one born from the same womb." Originally, it referred to a physical brother (or sister with the feminine *adelphē*, 79). Later it came to refer to any near relative, such as a nephew or even a brother-in-law. Finally, there are several examples in the Septuagint where *adelphos* is used to refer even to fellow Israelites (e.g., Exod. 2:11; Lev. 19:17), showing a close relationship without any physical heritage.

Besides the obvious physical meaning (e.g., Peter and Andrew [Matt. 4:18]), it's that very practice of **brother** being used to refer to fellow Israelites that was carried over into the NT. As one authority observes, the idea of fellow Christians being brothers appears some thirty times in Acts and 130 times in Paul's epistles,[330] so this concept carries tremendous importance. Let's meditate on the significance of being a brother (or sister, 1 Cor. 7:15) in Christ.

First, it means we have the same parentage. As noted on November 21, the Christian has been **born again** ("born from above") and has been "born of God" (1 John 3:9). We now see the deeper principle that we all have the same Father, the Sovereign God of the Universe. As Malachi asked, "Have we not all one father? hath not one God created us?" (2:10). Likewise, Paul often mentioned God being "*our* Father," that is, all Christians collectively (Rom. 1:7; Gal. 1:4; 1 Cor. 1:3; Eph. 1:2; etc.).

Second, being brothers in Christ shows a family relationship. In such verses as Romans 16:14 (and context) and 2 Timothy 4:21, Paul speaks collectively of several believers, wonderfully illustrating the family that every local church should be.

Third, being brothers in Christ shows closeness. So close is the relationship of Christian brothers that each would lay down his life for another (1 John 3:16).

Fourth, being brothers in Christ means a future inheritance. While earthly siblings might receive different portions when the father's will is read, all Christians have the same "riches of the glory of his inheritance in the saints" (Eph. 1:18).

Scriptures for Study: Read the apostle John's emphasis on the attitudes and actions of true Christian brothers and sisters: 1 John 2:9–11; 3:10–17; 4:20–21.

Christian

Christianos

Appearing only three times in the NT (Acts 11:26; 26:28; 1 Pet. 4:16), **Christian** is an obvious transliteration of *Christianos* (5546) and literally means "of the party of Christ." Calling someone by the name of a teacher or leader was not unusual, as the followers of Herod were called Herodians (*Herodianos*, 2265; Mark 3:6).

While one Greek authority says that "the term was first used by non-Christians" but that "does not have to imply that it was meant derisively,"[331] that seems unlikely. The word was commonly used by *non*-believers, since believers spoke of themselves using such terms as *brethren* and *saints*. While Peter uses the term, he does so in the context of persecution. As another authority therefore comments, "Being applied to Christians by outsiders, it contained an element of ridicule and that in this it did not differ from the description *Nazarēnos*"[332] (see **Nazarene**, see Apr. 14).

While it's fashionable nowadays to be called a "Christian," and while in many circles one can believe just about anything he wants and still be considered a "Christian," that was not the case when the term originated. To be a Christian meant something. It immediately described one who acted like Christ, one who stood for righteousness, condemned false religion, and didn't just "fit in" with everyone else. It was a term that invited persecution, not acceptance. It, indeed, meant to be a **disciple** (see Nov. 16).

To be called a "Christian" is to be greatly honored, but it's a term that we must live up to. The story has been told that Alexander the Great had a certain namesake, but not one who honored him. One of his soldiers was brought before him for court-martial. After listening to the charges, he turned to the soldier and asked, "What is your name?" "Alexander!" was the reply. Again the emperor questioned, "What is your name?" And the second time the soldier answered, "Alexander!" With a cry of rage, the emperor roared, "I say, what is your name?" When the soldier answered for the third time, "Alexander!" the great general angrily replied, "You say your name is Alexander? You are found guilty of your crime as charged, and now you must pay the penalty. Either change your conduct or change your name, for no man can bear the name of Alexander, my name, and do the things that you have done."[333]

Scriptures for Study: Read the three instances of *Christianos* and meditate on the challenge to live up to that name.

Temptation

peirasmos

Temptation is an often-misunderstood subject. Many of us tend to think that temptation is sin, that temptation is the problem with living the Christian life. On the contrary, as Puritan Thomas Watson wrote, "The devil tempts, that he may deceive; but God suffers [i.e., allows] us to be tempted, to try us. Temptation is a trial of our sincerity."[334]

That quotation hits the nail on the head. The noun *peirasmos* (3986) comes from the verb *peirazō* (3985), "to make trial of, to test," so the idea is "a test, a trial." It was used in Classical Greek, for example, to refer to a medical test, which would prove either health or disease. We are, therefore, tested to see if we are sincere, that is, whether we really are who we profess to be. As James makes clear, God never tempts us, but rather, we are tempted by our own lusts (James 1:12–16), as well as Satan (1 Cor. 10:9) Paul adds, and the test is to see if we will remain faithful to the truth. So, *temptation* isn't sin, but rather, *yielding* to temptation is sin.

To go a little deeper, what are we *really* being tested to do? Are we just being tested not to do wrong? While that's certainly part of it, we would submit that the more important part of the test is not only to see if we will prove to be sincere, but to see *how* we will prove it. In other words, how do we get victory over temptation? Is it by some psychological technique or sheer willpower?

The answer lies in the temptation of our Lord (Matt. 4:1–11). In every one of Satan's tests—the first from the **lust** (see May 11) of the flesh (vv. 2–3), the second from the lust of the eyes (vv. 8–9), and the third from the pride of life (vv. 5–6)—*our Lord had victory because He quoted the Word of God* (v. 4, Deut. 8:3; v. 7, Deut. 6:16; Deut. 6:13–14).

We submit, therefore, that the real test in temptation is *to see if God's Word will rule*. That is the promise of 1 Corinthians 10:13. Not only does God not allow any temptation that will overwhelm us, but He also "[makes] a way to escape." And what way is that? *His Word.*

Mark it down: The more Scripture you know, the harder it will be to sin.

Scriptures for Study: Read Matthew 4:1–11 and observe how our Lord won the victory. 🕮 You might also want to review our March 10 and 11 readings.

Heal

therapeuō

Our English word *therapeutic* refers to the treatment of disease and is rooted in the Greek *therapeuō* (2323). Interestingly, its original meaning in early Classical Greek had nothing to do with medicine; it meant "to wait upon, minister to, render voluntary service." Plato, for example, used it in the sense of slaves ministering to their masters. Later, also in Plato and others, it acquired the sense of caring for the sick, treating medically, and curing.[335]

During the writing of this book, I had a health issue arise and needed to visit our local clinic, which had recently been "reorganized." As I stood at the check-in window, I looked over to see a sign that partially read, "Notice to our customers." Sadly, no longer are we patients in need of care, much less people in need of service or ministry, but rather, customers to feed a business. Like abortion, that attitude is a long way from the original intent of the Hippocratic Oath.

In stark contrast, *therapeuō* speaks of service and ministry, which is actually at the foundation of medical care. While money certainly has to be charged to support the system, that should be only secondary to what the practice of medicine was originally about.

We see this clearly when we turn to the NT usage of *therapeuō*, which appears some forty-three times, forty of which appear in the Gospels and Acts. In all of those the meaning is healing (except Acts 17:25, where the point is that God doesn't require temples to be "worshipped").

Further, only twice (Luke 4:23; 8:43) does *therapeuō* refer to ordinary healing by medical means. In all the rest, healing comes by miraculous means. At the heart of Jesus' earthly *ministry* was *healing*, which served not only as a confirming sign of His claim to be the Messiah (Luke 4:40–41; John 2:11; cf. Matt. 12:38–40), but also pictured the greater spiritual healing that only He could provide.

After healing the woman with an issue of blood, who out of faith touched the hem of Jesus' garment, He said to her, "Daughter, be of good comfort: thy faith hath made thee whole; go in peace" (Luke 8:43–48). She went away not just healed of her physical illness, but healed "in full," healed spiritually in Christ.

Let us rejoice throughout this day in the true healing we have in the Great Physician.

Scriptures for Study: Read Matthew 8:5–13. Like the account of the woman with an issue of blood, what is the point of this incident?

Strangers, Foreigners, [and] Fellowcitizens

zenos, paroikos, [and] *sumpolitēs*

While we mentioned *paroikos* in passing back on June 10, a closer look will be a great encouragement to our Christian walk. In Ephesians 2:19, Paul writes, "Now therefore ye are no more strangers and foreigners, but fellowcitizens with the saints."

Paul mentions this again by using two terms, **strangers** and **foreigners**, and there's a true gem of truth in understanding them. While synonymous, there is a subtle distinction.[336] **Strangers** translates *xenos* (3581), which in Classical Greek referred to a foreigner who did not belong to the community, and is in direct contrast to *politēs* (4177, a "citizen" of the country), *epichōrios* (an "inhabitant" of the land; not in NT), and *endēmos* (a "native" of the country; not in NT). It could even refer to a wanderer or a refugee. To the Greeks, a *zenos* was the same thing as a barbarian. This is, of course, where we get our English word *xenophobia*—a fear and hatred of strangers or foreigners or of anything that is strange or foreign.

Foreigners is *paroikos* (3941), a compound comprised of *para* (3844, by or alongside) and *oikos* (3624, house), so therefore, "by the house," "next to the house," or "one who has a house alongside others." This was a foreigner who lived beside the people of a country, one who was a neighbor that enjoyed the protection of the community (the natives) but one who had no citizen rights because his citizenship was elsewhere. He was a "resident alien," a licensed sojourner, one who paid an "alien tax" to live in the area without being naturalized.

Paul was therefore telling the Ephesians that they were no longer either *zenos* or *paroikos*, neither passing strangers nor licensed immigrants. Rather, he calls them **fellowcitizens**, *sumpolitēs* (4847). The root *politēs* (4177) referred to a citizen, an inhabitant of a city, a freeman who had the rights of a citizen. Adding the prefix *sum* (4862, "together with") yields the idea of a citizenship with others.

Putting all this together, Paul tells the Ephesians that they all have a common citizenship in Christ. This would have made a deep impression in their minds. Their thoughts might well have gone something like this, "If a Roman citizen has great privileges, what greater ones we must have in Christ! Indeed, we are citizens of a far greater country than Rome." May this make a deep impression on us as well.

Scriptures for Study: Read Ephesians 2:12–18. To what were we "aliens" and "strangers"? What has the blood of Christ accomplished?

Strangers [and] Pilgrims

paroikos [and] *parēpidemos*

Building on yesterday's reading (and again June 10), Paul elsewhere uses some of the same terms to picture that the Christian is a "stranger," "foreigner," and even a "pilgrim," but this time *in regard to the world* because our true citizenship is now in heaven. Referring to the Jews in Egypt but extending that to the Christian, he preached to those in Antioch that the people were "strangers [*paroikia*] in the land of Egypt" (Acts 13:17).

Likewise, in that great "Hall of Faith" in Hebrews 11, he wrote concerning all those faithful souls, "These all died in faith, not having received the promises, but having seen them afar off, and were persuaded of them, and embraced them, and confessed that they were strangers [*zenos*] and **pilgrims** on the earth" (v. 13). **Pilgrims** here is *parēpidemos* (3927), which is similar to *paroikos*, referring more or less to a temporary resident without the license.

Peter also used the term in his first epistle as he wrote "to the strangers [*parēpidemos*] scattered throughout Pontus, Galatia, Cappadocia, Asia, and Bithynia" (1 Pet. 1:1). In 2:11 he encourages them "as strangers [*paroikos*] and pilgrims [*parēpidemos*]" to "abstain from fleshly lusts, which war against the soul."

What a challenge and encouragement this is to the Christian! As wonderful as life is, as blessed as American citizenship is, it all pales to insignificance in light of the fact that we are only temporary residents of this earth. We're just passing through. Our citizenship is in the Heavenly City.

Sadly, many preachers today don't emphasize this truth enough, preferring to put their emphasis on political reform and social change. Thank God, however, for those like seventeenth-century English churchman Jeremy Taylor, who put it so well: "Faith is the Christian's foundation, hope is his anchor, death is his harbor, Christ is his pilot, and heaven is his country."[337] And as I once heard the beloved Vance Havener say: "We are not citizens of this world trying to get to heaven; rather, we are citizens of heaven just trying to get through this world."

Scriptures for Study: Read Psalm 119:19 and 54, meditating on what shall be our comfort during our pilgrimage.

Cross

stauros

The **cross**. When we say those words, we state the very focal point of history. The OT *points* to it, the NT *presents* it, and the Christian *proclaims* it. It is the cross that is our salvation. A study of the cross as used in crucifixion is a sobering exercise. We learn much even by a brief look.

Crucifixion was, without question, the cruelest, the most disgraceful, barbaric, and excruciating execution ever devised by a depraved mind. It was probably invented by the Persians, who used it because it would not defile the ground, which they consecrated to their god Ormuzd. Alexander the Great introduced it to Egypt and Carthage, and the Romans seem to have picked it up from the Carthaginians and "perfected" it. It was reserved for slaves, foreigners, revolutionaries, and the vilest of criminals.

While practices varied in specific cultures, archaeology indicates that the Romans preferred the "low Tau" cross. Unlike the traditional shape, this cross looked like a "capital T," with the upright post called the "stipes" and the crossbar called the "patibulum." The patibulum alone, which our Lord was forced to carry in his already greatly weakened state, weighed from seventy-five to one hundred pounds.

At the crucifixion site, the stipes was secured while the victim was thrown to the ground with his arms outstretched along the patibulum. While some cultures tied the victim, the Romans preferred to use "nails," tapered iron spikes approximately five to seven inches long and about three-eighths of an inch in diameter. History further confirms that the spikes were driven not through palms of the hands, which could not support a man's weight, but through the wrists (see **hand,** Dec. 24), causing unimaginable pain as the large median nerve was crushed or severed. The patibulum was then lifted onto the stipes and the feet were then nailed to it through the heels, causing the knees to bend and rotate to one side as the man's weight hung on his wrists.

The most fiendish aspect of all this was that the man's weight locked the intercostal muscles in the state of exhalation and paralyzed the pectoral muscles so he could not lift himself up to breathe. This brought on hypercardia, spasms, and asphyxia.

It is indeed significant that our English word *excruciating* comes from the Latin *excruciatus*, "out of the cross." That, and much more, is what our Savior endured for us.

Scriptures for Study: Read the following verses, noting the significance of the cross in each: Matthew 16:24–25; 1 Corinthians 1:18; Ephesians 2:16; Philippians 3:10.

Hour

hōra

As one might think, the word *hōra* (5610) denotes a specific increment of time. While it can refer to a year, day, moment, season, or even stage of life, it comes relatively close to our English word **hour**. When Jesus healed the boy that the disciples could not, for example, Matthew tells us that "Jesus rebuked the devil; and he departed out of him: and the child was cured from that very hour" (17:18; cf. 15:28). We, therefore, see several meanings in this word.

First, it's used, of course, in *telling* time. Mark tells us, for example, that at Jesus' crucifixion, there was darkness from the sixth to the ninth hour, which was odd because that was the middle of the day (noon until three p.m., Jewish time).

Second, *hōra* is used for a *set* time. We see several examples of set times in the NT: a time of prayer (Acts 3:1), the time of Jesus' suffering (John 12:27), the time for a meal (Luke 14:17), and the time for Christ's judgment (Rev. 14:7).

Third, *hōra* is used for a *prearranged* time, that is, a time when something must occur. Jesus' glorification, for example, was prearranged to occur at the crucifixion, which was fixed before the world was even created (cf. John 2:4; 12:23; 17:1).

Fourth, *hōra* is used for an *expected* time. Jesus also spoke of hope and expectation using this word, as He told the Samaritan woman that "the hour cometh, when ye shall neither in this mountain, nor yet at Jerusalem, worship the Father. . . . But the hour cometh, and now is, when the true worshipers shall worship the Father in spirit and in truth: for the Father seeketh such to worship him" (John 4:21, 23). He also told His disciples to expect persecution as they proclaim Him (John 16:2).

Fifth, *hōra* is used for a *prophetic* time. Most notable here are Jesus' words, "Be ye also ready: for in such an hour as ye think not the Son of man cometh" (Matt. 24:44). So, He went on to declare, "Watch therefore, for ye know neither the day nor the hour wherein the Son of man cometh" (25:13). It is *that* hour to which we all look.

Scriptures for Study: What did Paul say that it's time to do in Romans 13:11? 🕮 In the context of time, what is Paul's point in Galatians 2:4–5?

Rock

petra

In Classical Greek, *petra* (4073) refers to a large rock, such as a boulder, cliff, bedrock, or even a mountain chain. It (with *petros*, 4074, a smaller stone that a man can throw) is, of course, where we get English words such as *petrify* (turning organic matter into rock) and *petroleum* (oil that comes from the earth or even from rock, as in the case of oil shale). It also carries the figurative meaning, as Homer used it in his *Odyssey*, of firmness and immovability of character. Aeschylus and Euripides also used it to denote hardheartedness.

Similarly, while *petra* is not used often in the Septuagint, when it does appear, it has the following meanings: a literal rock or cliff (Exod. 17:6; Num. 20:8), a figurative name for the Messiah (Isa. 8:14), unbending character (Isa. 50:7), a hardened heart (Jer. 5:3), and a name for God (2 Sam. 22:2).[338]

Undoubtedly, the most outstanding NT appearance of *petra* is Matthew 16:18, where our Lord declares to Peter, "Thou art Peter, and upon this rock I will build my church; and the gates of hell shall not prevail against it." While this verse has been twisted by Roman Catholic dogma into a theology of error, this is a simple play on words. Our Lord is clearly saying that He will build His church, not on Peter (whose name is *Petros*, a throwable stone), as Catholicism teaches, but on Himself, Who is the large rock, the bedrock, the foundation stone (cf. **cornerstone**, see July 9). He then adds that it's because of that foundation that nothing will ever "prevail against" (*katischuō*, 2729, "overcome, overpower, vanquish") His church.

A wonderful passage that also contains *petra* is Matthew 7:24–25, where our Lord again speaks: "Whosoever heareth these sayings of mine, and doeth them, I will liken him unto a wise man, which built his house upon a rock. And the rain descended, and the floods came, and the winds blew, and beat upon that house; and it fell not; for it was founded upon a rock." We live in a day of shifting sand (see vv. 26–27), where "truth" is constantly changing and is supposedly different for each person. Those who build on that will see their "house" fall. But when we build on the **truth** (see Feb. 1–3) of God's Word, we will stand forever.

Scriptures for Study: Read the following verses, noting the use of *petra* in each: Romans 9:33; 1 Corinthians 10:4; 1 Peter 2:8.

Crowd

ochlos

We encounter today an extremely interesting and practically significant word. **Crowd** translates *ochlos* (3793), which in Classical Greek, while referring militarily to a company, troop, or army, most often pictures a crowd of people milling around, a throng, confused multitude, or rabble. Even more graphic was how Plato used it to denote a "leaderless and rudderless mob . . . where the people have no power of judgment."[339]

Of its some 174 appearances in the NT, it's that idea of an unorganized crowd that we see most often. In its very first occurrence, for example, Matthew tells us that "great multitudes of people" followed the Lord Jesus, but "seeing the multitudes, he went up into a mountain" to get away from the crowd and instruct His disciples by way of His greatest teaching, the Sermon on the Mount (4:25–5:1ff.).

We see such *ochlos* over and over again in the gospel record to refer to such crowds (e.g., Matt. 8:1, 18; 9:8, 33; etc.). Most significant is John 6, where John states plainly that "a great multitude followed him, *because they saw his miracles*" (v. 2, emphasis added). Most people followed Jesus only out of curiosity and/or to see what they might get from Him.

As that chapter develops, we witness the feeding of the five thousand, the people wanting to make Him king by force, and His departure into the mountains to be alone (vv. 5–15). On the next day the "people" (v. 22, *ochlos*) were gathered again, at which time our Lord delivered His discourse on the Bread of Life, in which He presented a very narrow statement that only He is the way to eternal life (vv. 26–59). We then read that many regarded what He said as a "hard saying" and that ultimately "from that time many of his disciples went back, and walked no more with him" (vv. 60, 66).

The practical application of this is very pointed. It is sad, indeed, that many churches today are comprised merely of *ochlos*, multitudes of people who are identical to the multitudes who followed Jesus. By appealing to what people want through entertainment, emotional excitement, and other such fleshly means, we're gathering big crowds, but Christ and His truth are pushed to the background or even expunged altogether. Instead of being "Savior-centered," we have become "seeker-sensitive."

Scriptures for Study: Read John 6:22–71, prayerfully noting the tragedy of that scene.

Hypocrite

hupokritēs

Coming directly from the Greek *hupokritēs* (5273) is our English word **hypocrite**, a terrible word in any language. A compound comprised of *hupo* (5259), "under" (denoting secrecy), and *krinō* (2919), "to judge," the hypocrite is a pretender, one who professes to be something he is not. In Classical Greek, it originally meant to explain or interpret something but later came to be used in the theatre—the *hupokritēs* was "the 'answerer' who appeared on stage and turned the self-contained speeches of the chorus into dialogue form, or the 'interpreter' who explained the situation to the audience."[340]

Interestingly, however, the Classical meanings of *hupokritēs* never appear in the NT; it's the figurative idea that we find every time. The hypocrite is one who "plays the part," who says the right words, who convincingly acts the role, but who is not what he claims to be.

Of its some twenty-one NT occurrences, it appears only in the Gospels, especially the synoptics, and *always* from the lips of our Lord Himself. Of special significance is Jesus' quotation of Isaiah 29:13 in Matthew 15:7–9: "Ye hypocrites, well did Esaias prophesy of you, saying, This people draweth nigh unto me with their mouth, and honoureth me with their lips; but their heart is far from me. But in vain they do worship me, teaching for doctrines the commandments of men."

While *hupokritēs* appears only in the gospels, the related noun *hupokrisis* (5272) does appear in the epistles. Most serious was Paul's record of Peter's *hupokrisis* (translated "dissimulation") in Galatians 2:11–13. For some reason, perhaps for unity or expediency, Peter had actually compromised the Gospel by withdrawing from Gentile believers and making himself appear to the Judaizers (see Apr. 2; July 4; Nov. 24) that he agreed with them about the necessity of Gentiles keeping the **Law**, when he knew that that was not so. Paul had to rebuke him for such compromise. Tragically, the same error is still with us today among some Christian teachers who insist on strict observance of the Law, *while that very error is exactly what most of the letter to the Galatians is about.*

As Paul also warns Timothy, hypocrisy will grow worse, along with other error, during the last days (1 Tim. 4:1–2ff). We must carefully guard against hypocrisy and live what we profess.

Scriptures for Study: Read Matthew 23, noting our Lord's scathing and intolerant condemnation of hypocrisy.

Law

nomos

In light of yesterday's mention of the Judaizers, today we consider the debated issue of **law**. The noun *nomos* (3551), which in turn is derived from the verb *nemō* (not in NT), "to deal out, distribute, apportion." *Nomos*, then, "originally referred to distributing and what follows from it . . . [namely] custom, usage, statute, law, especially in the context of distribution of goods, and of law and order."[341]

Some Bible teachers talk about the "law" of the OT and the "grace" of the NT. That is a little misleading because **grace** has *always* been in operation and law is *still* in operation, although a *different* law is now in force.

What do we mean by that? Jesus Himself said, "Think not that I am come to destroy the law, or the prophets: I am not come to destroy, but to fulfil" (Matt. 5:17). He even summarized the *entire* law into two: love God and your neighbor, on which "hang all the law and the prophets" (Matt. 22:36–40).

So, if the old Law was fulfilled, what law is in operation now? *The law of love*. As Paul wrote, "He that loveth another hath fulfilled the law. . . . Love worketh no ill to his neighbour: therefore love is the fulfilling of the law" (Rom. 13:8, 10). He also told the Galatians, "For all the law is fulfilled in one word, even in this; Thou shalt love thy neighbour as thyself" (Gal. 5:14). He adds that as we "bear one another's burdens," we "so fulfil the law of Christ" (6:2).

This new law is, in fact, *far* superior to the old. Jesus provides several examples in Matthew 5. While the old law said to not commit adultery, the new says to not even look with lust (vv. 27–28; cf. Exod. 20:14). While the old said to not swear falsely, the new says, "Swear not at all," that is, carelessly or profanely (vv. 33–34; cf. Lev. 19:12). While the old said "an eye for an eye," the new says "turn the other cheek" (vv. 38–39; cf. Exod. 21:24).

As Galatians 3:1–3 declares, it's not the old law that makes us "perfect" (mature, *teleios*, see July 14); rather, the Holy Spirit does so through the law of Christ. While the old law was the "schoolmaster," Christ now is the teacher (v. 24).

Scriptures for Study: Read Galatians 5:16–26, noting the great superiority of walking in the Spirit over following "the weak and beggarly elements" of the old law (4:9).

Sacrifice

thusia

In keeping with yesterday's meditation, we can't mention the **Law** without also mentioning **sacrifice**, for that concept was central to the OT covenant. From Homer onward, *thusia* (2378) has always referred to a sacrifice, specifically, in fact, "a smoking or burnt sacrifice." Later it came to include the idea of the slaying of the animal for sacrifice.

In the Septuagint, of course, this word was used to refer to the Jewish levitical sacrificial system. The point of sacrifice was the taking away of sin and the pointing to the perfect sacrifice that would come in Christ.

When we then come to the NT, we see *thusia* some twenty-nine times to emphasize sacrifice in one way or another. In Matthew 9:13, for example, our Lord quotes Hosea 6:6 to show that the outward *ritual* of sacrifice apart from inward *repentance* was meaningless. Our Lord went on to make clear that He was the fulfillment of the Mosaic system, that His blood was the "blood of the new [covenant], which is shed for many for the remission of sins" (Matt. 26:28).

As the book of Acts and early church history go on to confirm, the sacrificial system was no longer necessary and was abandoned. The emphasis in the NT epistles is that Christ's sacrifice was the perfect sacrifice, the only one that could be the **propitiation**, the complete taking away, of our sin (Rom. 3:23–25; see tomorrow's reading).

By far the most significant NT use of *thusia* appears in Hebrews, where we find it fifteen times. If there is one word that sums up Hebrews, it's the word *better*. Everything in it is better: a better priesthood (*Christ*; 2:17; 5:1–9), a better sacrifice (*Christ*; 7:27), a better living (*Christ*; 9:9–14), a better intercession (*Christ*; 10:1–12). Indeed, as 10:1 declares, the Law with all its sacrifices and rituals was but "a shadow of good things to come." Thank God we no longer need the *shadow*, for we have the *substance*. No longer do we need the *pictures*, for we have the *Person*. No longer do we need the *Law*, for we have the *Living Savior*.

Are there *any* sacrifices still going on today? Yes, actually, there are. Each of *us* is to be "a living sacrifice, holy, acceptable unto God, which is [our] reasonable service" (Rom. 12:1). Holiness in our daily living is a constant reminder that sin has been dealt with in Christ.

Scriptures for Study: Read the Hebrews passages listed above, rejoicing in all that is better in Christ.

Propitiation

hilastērion

Before leaving the subject of Law and the OT sacrificial system, let us consider one other significant word, **propitiation**. Both the noun *hilastērion* (2435) and the verb *hilaskomai* (2433) have as their root *hileōs* (2436), "appeased or merciful" when speaking of gods and "cheerful, favorable, or merciful" when speaking of men. In ancient Greek, then, *hilastērion* conveyed the idea of bringing a gift to the gods to appease them and receive mercy.

This word was, therefore, used in the Septuagint in reference to the levitical system. It's used, in fact, to translate the Hebrew word for "mercy seat" (*kappōreth*, 3727H) in Exodus 25:17–22, where the high priest would sprinkle blood on the Day of Atonement for the sins of the people.

It is then in the NT that we read the wondrous statement of the apostle Paul in Romans 3:25: "Whom God hath set forth to be a propitiation through faith in his blood, to declare his righteousness for the remission of sins that are past, through the forbearance of God." Paul makes the startling declaration that Christ Himself was the True Mercy Seat, that the Ark of the Covenant pointed to none other but Him, Who would also not only as the High Priest *bring* the sacrifice, but who would as the **Lamb** (see Dec. 17) *be* the sacrifice.

Again Hebrews makes careful note of all this: "Neither by the blood of goats and calves, but by his own blood he entered in once into the holy place, having obtained eternal redemption for us" (9:12). Unlike the OT sacrifices that had to be perpetually repeated uncounted times over the centuries, Christ's sacrifice was once-for-all and forever (10:10). No one has stated it better than theologian A. A. Hodge:

> The sacrifices of bulls and goats were like token-money, as our paper promises to pay, accepted at their face-value till the day of settlement. But the sacrifice of Christ was the gold which absolutely extinguished all debt by its intrinsic value. Hence, when Christ died, the veil that separated man from God was rent from the top to the bottom by supernatural hands. When the real expiation was finished, the whole symbolical system representing it became *funetum-officio*, and was abolished. Soon after this, the temple was razed to the ground, the ritual was rendered forever impossible.[342]

Scriptures for Study: Read the following verses, noting how the apostle John was also captivated by the truth of Christ's propitiation: 1 John 1:7; 2:1–2; 4:10.

Promise

epaggelia

In Classical Greek, the original idea in *epaggelia* (1860) was simply to announce something. It was also used in a legal manner to denote a summons or promise to do or give something. Homer, for example, used this word to speak of a public announcement or statement of intent.

A profound change in the word came in NT usage. While in Greek literature it was always men who promised something to the gods and never the other way around, in the NT it's usually God who makes the promise. In fact, while this word group occurs often, rarely does it speak of promises made by men to God.

How profound that is! An early occurrence of this word is in Luke 24:49, where our Lord speaks of the coming Holy Spirit: "And, behold, I send the promise of my Father upon you: but tarry ye in the city of Jerusalem, until ye be endued with power from on high" (cf. Acts 1:4; 2:33). As we've studied previously, Paul also writes of this in Ephesians 1:13: "In whom ye also trusted, after that ye heard the word of truth, the gospel of your salvation: in whom also after that ye believed, ye were sealed with that holy Spirit of promise." What a promise!

Even before that, Acts 13:23—"Of this man's seed hath God according to his promise raised unto Israel a Saviour, Jesus"—recounts the promise God made to David in 2 Samuel 7:11–12 of the coming kingdom. Ephesians 6:2–3 remind us of the first of God's commandments that had a promise attached to it: "Honour thy father and mother . . . That it may be well with thee, and thou mayest live long on the earth" (cf. Exod. 20:12).

What a blessing it is to know that God will always deliver on His promises (Heb. 6:17; 2 Pet. 3:9)! Our **faith** (see Feb. 8) is never misplaced when it's set on His promises.

Scriptures for Study: Who shares in the promise God made to Israel in Ephesians 3:6? 🕮 How are the promises of God inherited (Heb. 6:12, 15)?

Lamp (Candle)

luchnos

Today and tomorrow we compare two words because of their seeming similarity; in reality, however, there is an important distinction. As one noted Greek scholar makes clear, *luchnos* "refers to an oil-fed hand-lamp," and *lampas* refers to "a torch."[343]

We find *luchnos* (3088), for example, in Matthew 5:15–16: "Neither do men light a candle [*luchnos*], and put it under a bushel, but on a candlestick [*luchnia*, 3087, lampstand]; and it giveth light unto all that are in the house. Let your light so shine before men, that they may see your good works, and glorify your Father which is in heaven." While *candle* and *candlestick* are close translations, more precise is **lamp** and *lampstand*. Oil is used in Scripture as a symbol of the Holy Spirit, so the picture here is that we do not *hide* the light of Christ or *hoard* it for ourselves, but rather, empowered by the Holy Spirit, we display it for all to see.

We find the same truth in Revelation 1:12, 13, and 20, where the seven churches are likened to "candlesticks," that is, "lampstands." The churches themselves do not create light; rather, each church bears the light of Christ through the power of the Holy Spirit.

Also significant is 2:5, where our Lord tells the Ephesian church that if they do not repent of their sin, He would remove their "lampstand" (*luchnia*). As commentator Adam Clark puts it, "Take away my ordinances, remove your ministers, and send you a famine of the word."[344] That is a frightening warning. And tragically there is today a famine of the Word of God in countless churches. Our Lord's words vividly picture the fact that He would remove their light, which would also mean that real life and vitality would disappear.

Our Lord paid a great tribute to John the Baptist by declaring that "he was a burning and a shining light" (John 5:35). **Light** is *luchnos*, again giving us the picture of the "oil" of the Holy Spirit empowering him as a witness for the coming Christ. Significantly, our Lord goes on to say that He was an even "greater witness than that of John" (v. 36). As we've noted before, in fact, He is the "Light of the World" (see **light**, *phōs*, June 15–16).

Let us be the "oil-fed hand-lamps" we should be.

Scriptures for Study: What marvelous truth do we read about in Revelation 21:23 ("light") and 22:5 ("candle")? 🕮 What "light" is referred to in 2 Peter 1:19?

Torch

lampos

As noted yesterday, there is a difference between *luchnos* (an oil-fed hand-lamp) and *lampas* (2985), a **torch**. While our English word *lamp* comes from *lampas*, that's where the similarity ends.

Perhaps the most vivid example of this contrast appears in Revelation 4:5, where we read of John's vision of God's throne in heaven: "And out of the throne proceeded lightnings and thunderings and voices: and there were seven lamps [*lampas*, torches] of fire burning before the throne, which are the seven Spirits of God."

While a **lamp** (*luchnos*), an image John used back in 1:12, 13, and 20, gives off a softly glowing light, a torch (*lampas*) is a fierce, blazing fire. As the number seven is used throughout Scripture as the number of perfection, this describes the Holy Spirit's perfect and diverse, sevenfold ministry. And what is that ministry? Isaiah 11:2 tells us: "And the spirit *of the Lord* [showing deity] shall rest upon him, the spirit of *wisdom* and *understanding*, the spirit of *counsel* and *might*, the spirit of *knowledge* and of the *fear of the Lord* [showing reverence; emphasis added]."

Added to those, however, our text depicts the Holy Spirit's judgment. A torch often pictures war in Scripture (e.g., Judg. 7:16, 20; Nah. 2:3–4). Here, then, we see God preparing to make war on sinful, rebellious man, and we see the Holy Spirit as His "war torch." While the Holy Spirit was originally sent by Christ to be the *Comforter* of those who *received* Him (John 14:16; etc.), that same Spirit will come as the *Consumer* of those who *rejected* Him.

Another graphic use of *lampas* appears in the familiar Parable of the Ten Virgins (Matt. 25:1–13). The point of the parable, of course, is the importance of being ready for the Lord's return. While five of the virgins (i.e., bridesmaids) were ready for the bridegroom's arrival, pictured by their having oil for their lamps in case he arrived later than expected, five of them were not ready and had no oil. The application is clear that the latter five represent only *professing* believers.

What's noteworthy here is that "lamps" is *lampas*, not *luchnos*. The picture, therefore, is not small lamps, but rather, blazing torches. As one Greek authority notes, in eastern culture, torches as well as lamps were fed by oil.[345]

How many people do you know who are not ready for the Bridegroom's arrival?

Scriptures for Study: Read John 18:3 ("torches") and Revelation 8:10 ("lamp"), noting the true image that *lampas* gives.

Seek

zētеō

From Homer onward, the idea in *zēteō* (2212) is to **seek** for something. It became "a technical term for striving after knowledge, especially philosophical investigation." It was also used occasionally for judicial investigation.[346]

Amazingly, *zēteō* occurs some 400 times in the Septuagint, usually translating the Hebrew *bēqash* (1245H), "to seek, try to attain." It's used both in the general sense of looking for something, as Joseph looked for his brothers (Gen. 37:16), but also in the spiritual sense of seeking after God, as in Isaiah 9:13, where the people did *not* seek after God, and in Jeremiah 29:13, where those who *do* seek Him will find Him "when [they] shall search for [him] with all [their] heart."

The NT usage of *zēteō* follows those same concepts in some 120 occurrences. When we study this word closely, however, we are profoundly struck by the fact that the will is at the heart of the seeking. In such cases, for example, as the merchant looking for the perfect pearl (Matt. 13:45), the woman searching frantically for a lost coin (Luke 15:8), and even Judas looking for just the right moment to betray Jesus (Matt. 26:16), we see the will in control.

This provides us with today's powerful application. *Of central importance is our seeking God.* While before conversion no man "seeketh [*ekzēteō*, 1567, 'to seek out'] after God"—so God is the one who really did the seeking (Luke 19:10)—the true believer can and *must* seek God diligently. Our Lord Himself declared in Matthew 6:33 (and context), "Seek ye first the kingdom of God, and his righteousness; and all these things [i.e., temporal needs] shall be added unto you."

Further, because God seeks "true worshippers" who will "worship [him] in spirit and in truth," it should be our overwhelming desire to praise His glory, exalt His name, glorify His nature, and seek His will. In a day when most people seek their own interests and desires, it is for us to "seek . . . the things which are Jesus Christ's" (Phil. 2:21), to "seek those things which are above, where Christ sitteth on the right hand of God" (Col. 3:1).

Scriptures for Study: What did Paul *not* seek in Galatians 1:10 and 1 Thessalonians 2:6? 🕮 What else should we seek, according to 1 Corinthians 14:12?

Conscience

suneidēsis

Puritan John Trapp reminds us, "Conscience is God's spy and man's overseer," as well as "the domestic chaplain."[347] On the lighter side, someone else offers, "Conscience is what makes a boy tell his mother before his sister does."[348]

The Greek *suneidēsis* (4893), from *sun* (4862), "together," and *eidō* (1492), "to know," has an interesting development. Originally, it focused on knowledge as one looks back on his past and his evaluation of what he sees as being good or evil. Gradually it took on the present idea of moral conscience. Interestingly, in ancient Greek literature, it almost always refers to a *bad* conscience, while the Romans (especially Cicero) usually spoke of a "good," "clear," or even "best" conscience. It was then in NT times (even in the Roman statesman Seneca) that conscience came to be regarded as "a watchman, bestowed by God upon the individual."[349]

Concerning the NT usage of *suneidēsis*, one Greek authority puts it perfectly: "Conscience is the testimony of the Spirit in man's heart concerning his obligation to God."[350] The apostle Paul makes several strong points with this word, using it some nineteen times (excluding the book of Hebrews). He admonishes the Corinthians, for example, that while they have liberty in Christ to engage in a particular practice, they should refrain if it would violate a weaker brother's conscience (1 Cor. 8:7, 10, 12).

In stark contrast to someone who would dishonestly manipulate the Scriptures to deceive people, as he was accused of doing, Paul called upon people's own consciences to show them, by God's power, that the Gospel was true (2 Cor. 4:2).

Most notably, Paul painted the grave picture in 1 Timothy 4:2 that man's "conscience [has been] seared with a hot iron." As noted on August 17, "seared" is *kauteriazō* (English, *cauterize*). Just as nerve damage accompanies scar tissue, man's "spiritual nerves" have been cauterized by sin. His conscience is so deadened that it no longer feels anything.

In contrast, what a blessing it is to know that we can "draw near with a true heart in full assurance of faith, having our hearts sprinkled from an evil conscience, and our bodies washed with pure water" and that we can "hold fast the profession of our faith without wavering; (for he is faithful that promised)" (Heb. 10:22–23).

Scriptures for Study: What could Paul without question claim to the Jewish leaders (Acts 23:1 and 24:16)? 📖 Read 1 Peter 3:16–17 and meditate on Peter's challenge.

Lamb

arnion [and] *amnos*

Originally, the Greek *probaton* (4263) was a generic term for all four-footed animals, especially tame, domestic ones. It was later restricted to full-grown "sheep" only, and is so translated in all its some forty-one NT occurrences. In contrast, *arnion* (721, diminutive for *arnos*) refers to a young lamb, a "little lamb." Both of these words appear in Jesus' recommissioning of Peter in John 21 ("lambs" in v. 15 is *arnion*, and "sheep" in vv. 16–17 is *probaton*). Later *arnion* became synonymous with *amnos* (286), a young sheep, frequently one year old, used for sacrifice.

The first of four NT appearances of *amnos* is that striking scene in John 1:29 (and 36) where John the Baptist heralds, "Behold the Lamb of God," which literally means, "*The* [not just *a*] Lamb provided by God." Luke pictures Christ as the submissive lamb before the shearers (Acts 8:32), and Peter declares that Jesus is the "lamb without blemish and without spot" (1 Pet. 1:19). *Amnos* is also used in the Septuagint for a sacrificial lamb (e.g., Exod. 29:38ff.).

Interestingly, however, while John uses *amnos* only twice, he adopts *arnion* later in his gospel (21:15) and then throughout the entire book of Revelation (twenty-nine times). Why the difference in terms? One Greek authority offers, "*Amnos tou theou* [the Lamb of God] denotes God's offering, Christ, whom he destined to bear the sin of the world, while *arnion* emphasizes the fact that He who is eternal Lord is also Christ crucified for us."[351] In other words, *arnion* pictures Christ as *both* Redeemer *and* Ruler.[352]

In His wonderful book, *The Master Theme of the Bible*, the late and beloved J. Sidlow Baxter traces the theme of the Lamb through the Bible, noting ten passages where the Lamb is specifically mentioned: 1) Genesis 4:3–7a proves the *necessity* of the Lamb. 2) Genesis 22:6–8 presents the *provision* of the Lamb. 3) Exodus 12:3–23 records the *slaying* of the Lamb. 4) Leviticus 16 describes the *character* of the Lamb. 5) Isaiah 53:6–8 establishes the *personality* of the Lamb. 6) John 1 reveals the *identity* of the Lamb, Jesus. 7) Acts 8 declares that that Lamb named Jesus is the *Promised Messiah*. 8) First Peter 1:18–21 confirms the *resurrection* of the Lamb. 9) Revelation 5:6–8 shows the *enthronement* of the Lamb. 10) Finally, Revelation 21–22 proclaim the *everlasting kingship* of the Lamb.[353]

There's only one word we can add: *Hallelujah!*

Scriptures for Study: Over the next few days, read the texts cited by Baxter and meditate on that *Master Theme of the Bible*.

Lion

leōn

In startling contrast, while Jesus is called the "**Lamb**," He is also called the "**Lion**." We'll return to that thought later.

Our English word **lion** actually comes from the Greek *leōn* (3023), which is found in writings all the way back to the time of Homer. Not only does it refer to the literal animal, but it also carries a figurative sense, such as the constellation or a brave or violent man. Of all animals, the lion is seen most often in ancient fables, usually as a symbol of power and courage.

The lion is mentioned some 150 times in the Septuagint, usually in a comparative way. Ezekiel 1:10, for example, describes the cherubim as having heads like a lion, picturing power.

A fascinating feature of the NT use of *leōn* is that every occurrence (there are nine) alludes to the OT. Paul, for example, writes to Timothy about being "delivered out of the mouth of the lion" (2 Tim. 4:17), that is, mortal danger, an allusion to Daniel's ordeal in the lion's den (Dan. 6:22). The same reference to Daniel occurs in Hebrews 11:33. (Note today's "Scriptures for Study" for another example.)

Turning to Revelation, in 4:7 we again see the cherubim of Ezekiel 1 and then see images using the figure of a lion (9:8, 17; 10:3; 13:2).

The greatest image of all, however, is in Revelation 5:5, where we read, "Behold, the Lion of the tribe of Juda, the Root of David, hath prevailed to open the book, and to loose the seven seals thereof." Looking back to Genesis 49:8–10, one of the "elders" before the heavenly throne refers to the chief member of the tribe of Judah, the Lord Jesus Himself, who is of the "Root of David," that is, He who fulfills God's covenant with David (cf. Isa. 11:1, 10). He is also pictured there as holding a scepter, as He will become the King of Israel, and will rule the world.

Before the King comes to rule, however, He must judge. The image pictured here occurs just before the judgments of the Tribulation begin in chapter 6 and continue through chapter 18. While Christ came the first time as a *Lamb* to the *slaughter*, He will come the second time as a *Lion* to *devour*. "Even so, come, Lord Jesus" (22:20).

Scriptures for Study: Read Peter's warning about apostasy in 1 Peter 5:8, and then note how he, too, alludes to the OT (Ezek. 22:25; Hos. 13:8).

Book (1)

biblos [and] *biblion*

The Greek *biblos* (976) is "on loan" from the Egyptian language. It originally referred to the papyrus plant and then its fibrous stem, which was exported to Greece through the port of Byblos in Syria. There, the plant was prepared by splitting the stems and then pressing and gluing two layers together to form a sheet. A series of sheets were then joined together to form a scroll that was rolled from both ends. Because papyrus was not very durable, becoming brittle with age, and rotting with moisture, it was eventually replaced by "vellum," which was made from animal skins, such as calf, antelope, sheep, or cow.

The word *biblos*, then, came to be used not just in its literal reference to papyrus, but for any writing material. It finally came to mean a scroll, **book**, letter, or just writing. The word *biblion* (975) is the diminutive of *biblos*. It became more common in both the Septuagint and NT Greek. In secular Greek these came to refer to any holy book, and this carried over into the writings of Josephus and Philo, who called the OT *hierai bibloi* (holy books). Our English word *Bible*, then, comes from the Latin *ta biblia*.

One Septuagint use of *biblion* (Hebrew *sēpher*, 5612H) that always sticks out is Nehemiah 8. Verse 1 begins: "And all the people gathered themselves together as one man into the street that was before the water gate; and they spake unto Ezra the scribe to bring the book of the law of Moses, which the Lord had commanded to Israel."

The scene here is the return of the Israelites from seventy years of captivity in Babylon and the completion of the reconstruction of the walls of Jerusalem. It should strike us profoundly that, unlike what might occur in our day, they didn't ask for a pageant, a stage play, a music concert, a motivational talk, or a ten-minute devotional that appealed to their feelings. *They cried out for God's Book.*

Further, they then *stood for six hours* while the Law was read. Since they now spoke Aramaic instead of Hebrew, the Law had to be explained, that is, "exposited" to them, providing us an unmistakable picture of expository preaching (see May 18). A pulpit was even constructed for that purpose (v. 4).

Mark it down, historically, no revival has ever come apart from the preaching of God's Book. May that be our desire today!

Scriptures for Study: Read Nehemiah 8, noting four principles that the people realized concerning God's Word: its *sacredness* (v. 1), its *seriousness* (vv. 3–8), its *security* (vv. 9–12), and their *submission* (vv. 14–18).

Book (2)

biblos [and] *biblion*

As mentioned yesterday, like the Septuagint, the NT uses the diminutive *biblion* far more often than *biblos* (thirty-four times vs. ten). We see it first in Matthew 19:7, where it's used to refer simply to "a writing." When Jesus went to the synagogue, "There was delivered unto him the book of the prophet [Isaiah]," from which He reads 61:1–2 and declares that He is its fulfillment (Luke 4:16–20).

Most outstanding of all its NT appearances are those in the book of Revelation. In 1:11, for example, the Lord Jesus commands John, "What thou seest, write in a book, and send it unto the seven churches which are in Asia." And what a Book it is! It's a Book that has never been out of print, a Book that details what God is going to do in the future, how He will complete "His Story."

Perhaps the most dramatic scene of all appears in 5:1–9, where John is in heaven beholding these future events and sees "in the right hand of him that sat on the throne a book written within and on the backside, sealed with seven seals" (v. 1). Scrolls were also used in ancient times for a will, a contract, and a deed to a parcel of land. The latter is the case here but with a significant twist. While this "book" is a "title deed," it's not just for a *parcel* of land, but for *all* land, the entire earth, which belongs to He who made it, Jesus Christ (John 1:1–3).

In keeping with ancient legal custom, the scroll had writing on the inside *and* outside. On the inside were all the details of the deed, but the outside had enough information to make clear what land it referred to and its rightful owner. It was then sealed and stored in a safe place until the time came for the owner to open it.

A unique feature of this book, however, is that instead of detailing *what* the owner will rightfully inherit, this one details *how* He will go about getting it. What are those details? Revelation 6–19 tell us. It is there that we read of the judgments that will come upon a rebellious race and how the Owner will then redeem the earth, followed by His setting up His Kingdom upon it for 1,000 years (chapter 20).

What a Book!

Scriptures for Study: What other book does Revelation mention in 20:12 and 21:27? 🕮 What warning does 22:19 give to those who would alter God's Book?

Wept

dakruō [and] *klaiō*

There is an important difference between the two words translated **wept** in the NT, *dakruō* (1145) being the much milder one. It means to "shed tears" or even a "a tear." This is actually the word used in John 11:35, where Jesus is said to "shed a tear" (not "wept," as most translations read) for the dead Lazarus. In contrast, *klaiō* (2799) is a weeping and wailing out of overwhelming grief. That is what Mary and those with her were doing in verse 33, but not the Lord Jesus. He merely shed a tear for Lazarus and those who were grief-stricken, for He knew that He was about to raise Lazarus from the dead.

The only time *klaiō* is used of the Lord Jesus, in fact, is when he wept over the city of Jerusalem in Luke 19:41, which only Luke mentions in the gospel record. Our Lord grieves over the true shallowness of the people, who while now cheering His entry into the city, would soon be crying, "Crucify him, crucify him" (23:21).

Another occurrence of this word is in Luke 22:62, where as a result of his denying His Lord, "Peter went out and wept bitterly." "Bitterly" is *pikrōs* (4090), from *pikros* (4089), "bitter, pungent," and is used figuratively here for violent, uncontrolled wailing.

In light of yesterday's look at the **book** referred to in Revelation 5:1–9, another example of overwhelming grief was when the apostle John "wept much, because no man was found worthy to open and to read the book, neither to look thereon" (v. 4). Why was John wailing? He wept over an earth that appeared to him to be hopelessly cursed, to be forever locked in sin and death because there was no one who could open the book and redeem the earth from its bondage.

While John's grief was certainly understandable, it was unnecessary, for "one of the elders saith unto [him], Weep not: behold, the Lion of the tribe of Juda, the Root of David, hath prevailed to open the book, and to loose the seven seals thereof" (v. 5).

While there is much weeping and wailing now as we, too, grieve over sin and death, there will come the day when our Lord will open that "title deed" and redeem this fallen world.

Scriptures for Study: Read that wondrous scene in Revelation 5:1–14, noting again the **Lion** (Dec. 18) and the **Lamb** (Dec. 17), who we now see is the only one worthy to claim the "title deed" to all creation.

Only Begotten

monogenēs

In that verse of verses we read, "For God so loved the world, that he gave his only begotten Son, that whosoever believeth in him should not perish, but have everlasting life" (John 3:16).

Along with the great truths of this verse, such as God's **love** (*agapē*, see Jan. 19–20) for His own, and the eternal life that comes by **faith** (*pisteuō*, see Feb. 8) in Christ, it is strikingly unique because the apostle John is the only Scripture writer who uses the term *monogenēs* (3439) to describe the relationship of Jesus to the Father. Several modern translations (ESV, NRSV, NLT, CEV, and GWT) replace "only begotten" with "only" or "one and only" (NCV and NIV). Such readings, however, clearly do not mean the same thing as "only begotten," so, which is correct, or does it really matter?

Monogenēs is a compound, of course, comprised of *monos* (3441; English *monograph*), "only, alone, without others," and *genos* (1085; English *gene*), "offspring, stock." The clear idea then is "only offspring," "only physical stock," or, as one commentator puts it, "only born-one."[354] In ancient Greek, this word was used to refer to a unique being.

So, to say "only son," or worse, "one and only son," is simply not so and is, quite frankly, serious error. Jesus is *not* the *only* Son of God, else Paul was wrong when he wrote that Christ is "the firstborn among many brethren" (Rom. 8:29). Who are those brethren? We are! We, too, are sons of God by the sovereign act of God in **adoption** (see Jan. 2). Jesus, however, is, as one translator renders it, "the uniquely begotten one."[355]

John actually makes this point earlier in his gospel when he writes that Christ is "the only begotten of the Father, full of grace and truth" (1:14) and is "the only begotten Son, which is in the bosom of the Father" (v. 18). He writes again in his first epistle "that God sent his only begotten Son into the world, that we might live through him" (4:9). Sadly, the above mentioned translations repeat their error in all three verses.

One Greek authority says it well: "[John] here understands the concept of sonship in terms of begetting. For [Jesus] to be the Son of God is not just to be the recipient of God's love. It is to be begotten of God."[355]

Scriptures for Study: Read the following verses, noting the clear idea of "uniqueness" and "only begotten" in each: Luke 7:12; 8:42; 9:38; Hebrews 11:17.

Defense (Answer)

apologia

When we do something that offends or hurts someone, we "apologize" or "make an apology," which is an admission of error. The source of these English words, however, has a very different meaning. The Greek *apologia* (627) is comprised of *apo* (575; e.g., see Feb. 17), "from," and *logos* (3056; see Feb. 5, Mar. 16, July 10) "speech." In Classical Greek, it was used as a legal term referring to an attorney presenting a defense for his client.

That idea is carried over into the NT. Paul, for example, made a *defense* before the people of Jerusalem for his speaking against the Law in Acts 22:1. He also "answered" Festus in defense of his faith 25:8 (cf. v. 15), as well as Agrippa in 26:1.

Every Christian is challenged to "be ready always to give an answer to every man that asketh you a reason of the hope that is in you with meekness and fear" (1 Pet. 3:15). That doesn't mean "arguing religion," but rather, telling someone why he or she is a Christian, to thoughtfully articulate the Gospel.

One cannot mention this word, however, without also addressing the subject of "apologetics," the branch of theology devoted to the defense of Christianity. There are two basic schools of thought.

First, there is "evidential" apologetics, which teaches that by reasoned arguments and the presentation of evidence we can prove God's existence and prove the Bible to be true.

Second, there is "presuppositional" apologetics, which maintains that instead of *proving* God, we must *presuppose* Him; that is, we must start with God or we can know nothing, for it is only in Him and His Word that we find truth. While "evidentialism" accuses "presuppositionalism" of being guilty of circular reasoning and undermining the "reasonableness" of the Christian faith, the latter criticizes the former for starting with man and then trying to get to God, and thereby trying to argue people into heaven.

This is certainly not the place to debate the issue, but whichever approach is correct, each of us must be ready to proclaim the facts concerning the Lord Jesus. One "apologist" writes, "Some people say the best offense is a good defense, but I say unto you that the best defense is a good offense. . . . The best defense of Christianity is a clear, simple presentation of the claims of Christ and Who he is in the power of the Holy Spirit."[357]

Scriptures for Study: Read the following verses, noting the use of *apologia* in each: Philippians 1:7, 17; 2 Timothy 4:16.

Hand

cheir

Hand is *cheir* (5495; English *chiropractic*), a truly ancient word, appearing as early as the Mycenaean period of Greek history (1600–1200 BC). It originally referred not only to the "hand," but to the entire arm from the fingers to the shoulder. That's why it is not contradictory to say that Jesus was nailed to the cross through the wrists, not the palms (see **cross**, Dec. 4; cf. John 20:25).

It's the figurative meaning of *cheir*, however, that stands out. As a person's activity is said to be the "work of the hands," the hands become a symbol of power. In Greek mythology, for example, in the "hands of the gods" there was protection of individuals and intervention in earthly events. Asclepias, the god of healing, supposedly healed by touching the sick with his hand.

In the Septuagint, falling into someone's hands means to come into their power, as in Judges 2:14, where because of Israel's idolatry, God "sold them into the hands of their enemies." Most significant, however, is that in over 200 instances we see "the hand of Yahweh," a reference that is "always to God's activity by which He shows Himself mighty in creation and work"[358] (Exod. 7:4; Isa. 45:11–12; etc.).

We see the same picture throughout the NT. Further, however, it's not only "Yahweh" who is in view, but Christ. As John 3:35 declares, "The Father loveth the Son, and hath given all things into his hand" (cf. 13:3). Our Lord Himself declares in 10:28: "And I give unto them eternal life; and they shall never perish, neither shall any man pluck them out of my hand." What a comforting promise of security!

Further, throughout the NT we see "God's hands" picturing numerous aspects of His activity: creation (Acts 7:50; Heb. 1:10); sovereignty (Acts 4:28); righteous punishment (Heb. 10:31); special care (Luke 1:66); empowering the proclamation of the Gospel (Acts 11:21); and our humble submission to His providence (1 Pet. 5:6).

What challenge does all this leave for us? Not only do we rejoice in it, but God also leaves us something to do with *our* hands. Let us each be "working with [our] hands the thing which is good" (Eph. 4:28).

Scriptures for Study: Read the verses concerning God's activity cited above, rejoicing in all He accomplishes.

Idol

eidōlon

Our English word **idol** is derived from the Greek *eidōlon* (1497). Homer used *eidōlon* for phantoms and apparitions. In later Classical Greek, it carried the other non-religious meanings of picture, copy, or "any unsubstantial form, an image reflected in a mirror or water, an image or idea in the mind."[359]

In the Septuagint, however, *eidōlon* is used to translate some fifteen Hebrew words and always refers to the images of heathen gods and the gods themselves. God's second commandment in the Law, for example, prohibited making any "graven image" (Exod. 20:4; cf. Deut. 5:8). Among many recurrences of idolatry, Ezekiel prophesied God's judgment upon Israel for that abomination: "Your altars shall be desolate, and your images shall be broken: and I will cast down your slain men before your idols. And I will lay the dead carcases of the children of Israel before their idols; and I will scatter your bones round about your altars" (6:4–5).

Turning to the NT, we see the Septuagint usage of *eidōlon* carried over, as we discover many restatements of the repugnance of idols. To both the Corinthians and the Thessalonians, for example, Paul specifically contrasts how they used to worship idols but were converted from it. He praised the Thessalonians that they had "turned to God from idols to serve the living and true God" (1 Thess. 1:9). Likewise, in his introduction to his teaching concerning "spiritual gifts" (Feb. 15), he reminded the Corinthians that they used to be "carried away unto these dumb idols" (1 Cor. 12:2), and in his second letter he mentions the total contradiction that exists between "the temple of God" and "idols" (2 Cor. 6:16).

We then read John's crystal-clear command to God's "little children," that they "keep [themselves] from idols" (1 John 5:21). As commentator Albert Barnes observes, an idol is not only "an image or representation of the Deity" but is also "the making of [anything] an object of adoration instead of the true God."[360] Men do this in countless ways, making gods of money, possessions, success, and even other people.

It's good for us to be reminded, especially at this particular time of the year, who God really is and how easily we can make other gods that come before Him, replace Him, or even subtly undermine Him.

Scriptures for Study: What incident is being recounted in Acts 7:41 and its context? 📖 What was one of James' recommended guidelines that should be given to Gentiles at the Jerusalem Council in Acts 15:20?

Earnestly Contend

epagōnizomai

One of the most dominant and tragic characteristics of our day is an almost total disinterest in **truth** (see Feb. 1–3). And, as Puritan William Gurnall rightly pointed out over 350 years ago in his classic exposition of Ephesians 6:10–20, *The Christian in Complete Armor*, "Not to desire [truth] is to despise it." As we've mentioned before (see Feb. 19, June 2), relativism rules the day. Most people think that truth is different for each person. What might be true for one might not be true for another. Each person must find his or her own truth, what's good for them. Absolutes have virtually disappeared entirely.

Even more tragic, however, is that many professed Christians think exactly the same way. To many of these, doctrine doesn't really matter and truth is relative, totally open to everyone's "interpretation" of the Bible.

It's for that reason that godly Christians need to be challenged to *love* **truth**. Nothing should be *more* important, or even of *equal* importance, than truth. As Gurnall writes again: "[Truth] is the great treasure, which God delivers to His saints, with a strict and solemn charge to keep against all that undermine or oppose it. Some things we trust God with, some things God trusts us with. . . . That which God trusts us chiefly with is His Truth."[361]

There is no better proof of that statement than Jude 3 (see Nov. 3–4), where Jude exhorts us, "Earnestly contend for the faith which was once delivered unto the saints." "Faith" here is not a verb that refers to the act of believing, but rather, it is a noun that refers to the body of revealed truth that constitutes historical, evangelical Christianity.

The words **earnestly contend** are a single word in the Greek, *epagōnizomai* (1864), which appears only here in the NT. At the heart of this compound word is the root *agōn* (73; English *agony*), which means "strife, contention, [a] contest for victory."[362] It, along with the verb *agōnizomai* (75), originally referred to the fighting and struggle involved in the Greek games. By adding the prefix *epi* (1909, "for"), Jude is telling us that we must fight for the faith. Like Paul in Ephesians 6:10–20 (see Sept. 30ff.), Jude uses graphic imagery to show us the spiritual war in which we are engaged, an all-out war that gives no quarter to error or those who propagate it.

Scriptures for Study: Read the following verses, noting the use of *agōnizomai* in each: 1 Corinthians 9:25 ("striveth"); 1 Timothy 6:12 ("fight"); 2 Timothy 4:7 ("fought").

Covenant

diathēkē

Covenant is *diathēkē* (1242), which in Classical Greek refers to a will or testament and, therefore, denotes an irrevocable decision that cannot be cancelled by anyone.

The covenant concept is, of course, dominant in the OT. *Diathēkē*, in fact, appears some 270 times, usually translating the Hebrew *beriyth* (1285H), a broad word covering several types of agreements, including a covenant between friends (1 Sam. 18:3) and rulers (1 Kings 5:12; "league"). As noted back on September 23, **marriage** is also spoken of as a covenant, a covenant, in fact, that is meant to be permanent.

Most important, however, are the covenants that God made with various individuals, such as: Noah (Gen. 6:18), Abraham (2 Kings 13:23), and Moses (Exod. 19:5–6ff.). Each of those covenants also extended to the descendants of the man.

Of special significance, of course, was the Mosaic Covenant, a "conditional covenant" in which God blessed the people if they obeyed Him. Given only to Israel, it consisted of the Commandments (moral; Exod. 20:1–6), the judgments (social; Exod. 21:1–24:11), and the ordinances (religious; Exod. 24:12–31:18). The whole point of the Law was to reveal man's sin (Rom. 3:20) and point him to the coming Christ, who would fulfill all the symbols and pictures contained in the Law (Matt. 5:17).

The book of Hebrews is a glorious book, where we find *diathēkē* no less than fourteen times. As noted back on December 10, the word *better* sums up its message like no other word. As 7:22 declares, "Jesus made a surety of a better testament." And what is that "new testament" (or covenant)? Jesus Himself told us when He instituted His Supper: "This cup is the new testament in my blood, which is shed for you" (Luke 22:20). Again Hebrews declares: "He obtained a more excellent ministry, by how much also he is the mediator of a better covenant, which was established upon better promises" (8:6).

Let us rejoice in 9:13–15: "For if the blood of bulls and of goats, and the ashes of an heifer sprinkling the unclean, sanctifieth to the purifying of the flesh: How much more shall the blood of Christ, who through the eternal Spirit offered himself without spot to God, purge your conscience from dead works to serve the living God? And for this cause he is the mediator of the new testament. . . ."

Better! What a word!

Scriptures for Study: Read Hebrews 9:13–28, noting the contrast between the Old Covenant and the New.

Mediator

mesitēs

Mediator is *mesitēs* (3316), which is derived from *mesos* (3319), "in the middle, in the midst," and therefore means "one who finds himself in the middle between two parties or bodies." In Classical Greek, *mesos* became a legal term denoting neutrality (hence the Latin and English *neuter*, "neither of two"), as in one who sits between two conflicting parties to arbitrate and settle a matter. The man who sits in the middle, then, is the *mesitēs*.

While the concept of a mediator is not found in the OT—although Paul refers to Moses and the Law as a mediator in a negative sense (Gal. 3:19–20)—its use in the NT is extremely significant.

One such occurrence is in 1 Timothy 2:5: "For there is one God, and one mediator between God and men, the man Christ Jesus." The backdrop of that statement is the pagan Greek concept of multiple gods and goddesses. In contrast, Paul tells Timothy how vital it is that he proclaim the one and only God who can be reached by the one and only Mediator, Jesus Christ. The same message is desperately needed today as well. Not only do men worship many gods, but false religions such Roman Catholicism teach that a "priest" is a necessary "mediator" between men and God. But Paul makes it clear that it is Christ alone who mediates through His death and resurrection.

Most noteworthy again, however, are the uses of this word in the book of Hebrews. As noted yesterday, Christ "obtained a more excellent ministry, by how much also he is the mediator of a better covenant, which was established upon better promises" (8:6). Once again, Christ is *better* than all things and, therefore, most certainly is an infinitely better mediator than the Law (cf. 9:15 and 12:24).

We should also note that while *mesitēs* itself appears only six times, the concept of Christ as Mediator is reflected many more times. Could the concept be clearer than it is in John 14:6, where Christ is the *only way* to God? And it is Hebrews again that speaks of Christ as our Great High Priest who goes to the Father on our behalf (4:14–16; 7:25). Likewise, John declares that He is our Advocate, our wonderful Defense Attorney, who constantly pleads our case (1 John 2:1).

Once again, let us rejoice that Christ is *better*.

Scriptures for Study: Read the scriptures cited today, as well as Matthew 11:25–30, and rejoice in your Mediator.

It Is Finished

teleō

The words **it is finished** (John 19:30), which our Lord spoke from the cross, state a profound truth. The Greek is *teleō* (5055), which is derived from *telos* (5056), which "originally meant the turning point, hinge, the culminating point at which one stage ends and another begins; later, the goal, the end." Several things were looked upon as being an end, or a goal, such as marriage, physical and intellectual knowledge, and, of course, death. *Teleō*, then, means "to bring to a *telos,* to complete."[363]

Teleō appears, for example, in Revelation 20:5–7, which refers to "when the thousand years are expired," that is, when the Millennium comes to its culmination, ushering in the final events on earth.

Among other instances of this word, however, **it is finished** is the greatest. That statement declares that the goal of redemption had been reached, that salvation by Jesus' sacrifice was completed. This was the purpose that Jesus Himself spoke of in John 4:34: "My meat is to do the will of him that sent me, and to finish [*teleioō*] his work" (cf. 17:4; Acts 13:29). This word was actually rooted in ancient culture. As Charles Ryrie writes, "Receipts for taxes found in the papyri have written across them this single Greek word, which means 'paid in full.'"[364] Indeed, Christ paid the full price for our sin. Nothing else either *need* be paid or *could* be paid. Salvation is by **grace** (see Feb. 13–14) alone.

Further, the actual construction in the Greek text (*tetelestai*) is in the perfect tense, which describes an action that took place in the past with the results of the action continuing into the present. Since it has no direct equivalent in English, it's often translated as "has," "have," or "hath." Young's *Literal Translation*, for example, reads, "It hath been finished." The significance, then, is clear. While the actual *work* of Calvary occurred some 2,000 years ago, the *results* have not diminished one iota through the ages. So, when Jesus uttered those words, **It is finished**, the work of redemption was accomplished for all time.

Take some time today to meditate on and rejoice in a salvation that is truly finished in Christ.

Scriptures for Study: According to Romans 10:4 (cf. Gal. 3:13), what else came to an "end" (*telos*) through Christ's work? 🕮 In our Christian walk, what will keep us from fulfilling ("fulfil," *teleō*) the lust of the flesh (Gal. 5:16)?

Hallelujah

allēlouia

What joy comes with a study of this word! The Greek *allēlouia* (239) is a transliteration of two Hebrew words: *hēlal* (1984H), "to praise," and *Yēh* (3050H), a shortened form of "Yahweh" (3068H), a name so sacred to the Jews that they would not even utter it and translated it **Lord** (*kurios*, April 8–9) instead of "God" in the Septuagint. How tragic it is, however, that while they practiced such outward observance, inwardly they rebelled and blasphemed the very God they supposedly revered.

We should also interject that since the Hebrew is *hēlal*, the Greek and English should actually have the "h" sound, as in **Hallelujah**.[365]

This word, therefore, means "praise ye Yah," or "praise the Lord." We find this word some twenty-four times in the book of Psalms. Except for 135:3, it always appears at the beginning or ending, "suggesting that it was a standardized call to praise in temple worship."[366] This is further seen as it was "associated with the ministry of the Levites who praised God morning and evening (1 Chron. 23:30)."[367] Other psalms, such as 106 and 117, use this word, as one commentator observes, "to set forth the spirit of millennial anticipation and praise."[368]

It's in that latter usage, in fact, that we find *allēlouia* only four times in the NT, all in Revelation 19, in glorious anticipation of the Millennium. We see in those verses four things for which God is to be praised.

First, in verse 1, He is praised for His *rescue*: "And after these things I heard a great voice of much people in heaven, saying, Alleluia; Salvation, and glory, and honour, and power, unto the Lord our God."

Second, in verses 2–3, He is praised for His righteous *retribution*: "For true and righteous are his judgments: . . . And again they said, Alleluia. And her smoke rose up for ever and ever."

Third, in verse 4, He is praised for His *reputation*, that is, simply because of Who He is: "And the four and twenty elders and the four beasts fell down and worshipped God that sat on the throne, saying, Amen; Alleluia."

Fourth, in verse 6, He is praised for his *reign*: "And I heard as it were the voice of a great multitude, and as the voice of many waters, and as the voice of mighty thunderings, saying, Alleluia: for the Lord God omnipotent reigneth."

There is nothing more to say except, *Hallelujah*!

Scriptures for Study: Read Psalms 145–150, noting their praise (other psalms include: 104–106; 111–113; 115–117; 135).

Amen

amēn

Here is a word that is often overlooked in Bible study when it's actually quite significant. **Amen** is merely a transliteration of the Hebrew *ēmēn* (543H). One purpose of the word is to confirm a statement, and it could be translated in various ways: "so be it," "so it is," "there you have it," and even "verily" (truly). It's noteworthy that in all the NT, as one authority observes, "only the Lord Jesus uses *amēn* at the beginning of a sentence as a word of affirmation." Further, as *amēn* is equivalent to *alēthos* (truly, really, in truth), the Lord Jesus uses it to say that He Himself is **truth** (see Feb. 1–3). John 1:51, for example, could be rendered, "I who am the Amen [truth itself] tell you as a most certain and infallible truth."[379]

Another use of *amēn*, however, was originally one of *response* by the listeners or readers who were present when truth was given. Two other Greek authorities tell us that a certain custom, which passed from the synagogue to the Christian assemblies, was that when someone closed a solemn prayer, others present responded with "Amen" and thus made all that was said their own.[370]

How thrilling! We find it several times in the OT, for example, as the people responded in praise while listening to the choir (Ps. 41:13; 72:19; 89:52) and to other declarations of truth (1 Chron. 16:36; Neh. 8:6; Ps. 106:48).

This challenges us to say "Amen" to the truths of God's Word, to make them our own. In Romans 11:36, for example, in response to the statement, "For of him, and through him, and to him, are all things: to whom be glory for ever," we can say with Paul, "Amen." Also with Paul in his prayer closing the first half of Ephesians, we can say a hearty "Amen" (3:21) to all the grand truths of those chapters. And in answer to our Lord's promise, "Surely I come quickly," in Revelation 22:20, we can, with the entire church, affirm the promise with "Amen" (v. 21).

Dear Christian friend, let *amen* become an important word in your Christian vocabulary. The author and publisher of this book pray that you have been richly blessed by these studies and have been able to say "Amen" many times. May God richly bless you as you go forth *in* His power and *for* His glory.

Amen.

Scriptures for Study: Read the following verses, noting what truth is being affirmed in each: Matthew 5:18; 17:20; 18:3; John 3:3; 8:51, 58; 16:23.

***Soli deo gloria*—to God alone be the glory.**

Mining Bible Word Riches

While the studies in this book cover many NT words, it's certainly not exhaustive; there are countless more jewels to mine. The student might even want to go a little deeper into some of the words covered in this book. This chapter, therefore, presents some principles and procedures, as well as some language tools, that will equip the student to examine NT Greek words.

Basic Study

For many students, the following basic tools for studying NT words will be enough.

First, the foundational tool is a concordance. One such concordance, of course, is the universally known *Strong's Exhaustive Concordance of the Bible*. It's available not only in book form, but virtually every computer Bible program includes it. It gives each word as it is used in the AV followed by a listing of the Scripture references, and a short portion of the verse where that word appears, along with a number that Baptist minister and theologian Augustus Strong (1836–1921) assigned to that word. This number can then be used to look up the word in the dictionary in the back of the book. Here is an example listing for the word **love** as the lines actually appear:

Love

Mt	6: 5	for they **l** to pray standing in the	*5368*
	24	he will hate the one and **l** the other;	*25*

The corresponding dictionary definitions, then, are as follows. Numbers in italics are for Greek words, while normal print numbers are for Hebrew words. Also note the helpful phonetic spelling for each word.

25. **ἀγαπάω agapaō**, *ag-ap-ah'-o*; perh. from **ἄγαν agan** (much) [or comp. 5689]; to *love* (in a social or moral sense):—(be-) love (-ed). Comp. *5368*.

5368. **φιλέω phileō,** *fil-eh'-o*; from *5384*; to *be a friend to* (*fond of* [an individual or an object]), i.e. *have affection for* (denoting *personal* attachment, as a matter of sentiment or feeling; while *25* is wider, embracing espec. the judgment and the *deliberate* assent of the will as a matter of principle, duty and propriety: the two thus stand related very much as *2309* and *1014*, or as *2372* and *3563* respectively; the former being chiefly of the heart and the latter of the *head*); spec. to *kiss* (as a mark of tenderness):—kiss, love.

Strong's definitions and numbers are, therefore, extremely helpful to the student. The numbers are, in fact, so universally used that most Greek tools available today are keyed to those numbers, enabling the student to quickly find what he needs. Every Bible student is deeply indebted to Strong's efforts.

On the other hand, while *Strong's Exhaustive Concordance of the Bible* is very useful, Young's *Analytical Concordance to the Bible*, written by Scottish Free Church theologian Robert Young (1822–1888), uses a little different approach and is in some ways superior in analyzing Greek words. Here are two entries for the same words mentioned above:

LOVE, to —
5. *To love,* ἀγαπάω *agapaō*
Matt. 5.43 Thou shalt love thy neighbor, and hate
5.44 I say unto you, love your enemies, bless
5.46 For if ye love them which love you, what
6.24 either he will hate the one and love the

7. *To be a friend,* φιλέω *phileō*
Matt. 6: 24 for they love to pray standing in the syn.

This approach is a little "cleaner" than Strong's, listing all the references for a particular Greek word in its own separate section, instead of having numbers intermingled in one long list. While Strong's provides longer definitions, Young's, though short, are right in front of you. Especially helpful is Young's "Index-Lexicon" in the back of the book. This lists each Greek word along with the different ways that word is translated in the AV and the number of instances that translation appears. Here are the entries for the words for **love** we've been using:

AGAPAO ἀγαπάω
love 135
Pass. ptc. beloved 7.

PHILEO φιλέω
kiss 3
love 22

Some entries reveal that a particular word is actually translated in several ways. The reason for this is usually the context in which the word appears; the context will often give a word a little different shade of meaning. A good example is the Greek *dunamis*, which we examined in our February 28 reading. It's actually translated by no less than fourteen words. Here is its entry in Young's "Index-Lexicon":

DUNAMIS δύναμις
ability 1
abundance (M. power) 1

meaning 1
might 4
mighty deed 1
mighty work 11
miracle 8
power 77
strength 7
violence 1
virtue 3
wonderful work 1
worker of miracles (M. power) 1
mighty (*gen.*) 2 (M. power 1)

So, when it comes to a concordance, Young's is the most useful (in the author's opinion). Strong's is really needed only for its numbering system since the many other tools available today are keyed to its numbers and provide more in-depth explanations. It actually can be replaced totally, in fact, with *The Complete Word Study New Testament*, which we'll examine next.

Second, the aforementioned *The Complete Word Study New Testament* (AMG Publishers) edited by Dr. Spiros Zodhiates is a must-have tool for NT Greek study. It contains the entire NT text (AV) with a Strong's number above each word. Numbers in normal type correspond to the Strong's dictionary included in the back of the book, while numbers in bold face *also* correspond to the "Lexical Aids" section, which provides more detailed definitions. Also appearing above each word are letters that refer to the grammatical construction of the Greek word and which are explained in the "Grammatical Notations" section. The letters "pfip," for example, appear above the words "It is finished" in John 19:30 (see December 29 reading), indicating the perfect indicative passive construction. This wonderful tool also has several other features, including, among others: book introductions, explanatory footnotes, and a Scripture index.

Third, for a little deeper study, the student needs a good Greek word dictionary, and I cannot recommend *The Complete Word Study Dictionary*: *New Testament*, compiled by Dr. Zodhiates, highly enough. Keyed to Strong's numbers, every NT word is defined and explained. Key features include: word derivation, exegetical commentary, word history and etymology, and synonym and antonym list (also with Strong's numbers). These books by Dr. Zodhiates, as well as others, are also available for your computer in AMG's *Bible Essentials CD-ROM Software*. Another dictionary worth having is the classic *Vine's Expository Dictionary of Old and New Testament Words* (Nelson).

Those three (or four) books will provide most students with all the tools they'll need to adequately study and understand the words used in the NT.

Fourth, the student might also want one or more word-study books. A classic tool here is the four-volume *Word Studies in the Greek New Testament* by Kenneth

Wuest (Eerdmans). While not every NT book is covered, many are: Mark, Romans, Galatians, Ephesians, Colossians, Philippians, Hebrews, the Pastoral Epistles, Peter's epistles, and John's epistles. There are also numerous other word studies in various sections and fairly good indexes.

Another classic is the four-volume *Word Studies in the New Testament* (Eerdmans) by Presbyterian scholar M. R. Vincent (1834–1922). This does cover the entire NT, although not every verse. Wuest often quotes from Vincent, so buy Vincent only to cover what Wuest does not.

I would also interject that while some Bible teachers also recommend A. T. Robertson's *Word Pictures in the New Testament* (Broadman), I do not. I find it very weak in comparison to the tools already mentioned and not worth the investment.

Advanced Study

The tools mentioned below are only for students who wish to go much deeper into the study of NT words and are not for the faint of heart. These tools are either older works that are a little harder to read or are so detailed that many students would be overwhelmed. Also mentioned last are Greek grammars for interested students.

First, there is *Trench's Synonyms of the New Testament* by Irish scholar Richard Trench (1807–1886). While sort of in the middle between basic and advanced, I list it here because it tends toward complexity, although many English readers can handle it. Its main use is to examine differences between similar words. Chapter 51, for example, explains the several words translated "prayer" (see our May 28 and 29 readings).

Second, the large four-volume *The New International Dictionary of New Testament Theology* (Zondervan) is an indispensable tool for deeper study of NT words. It examines the Classical Greek usage, OT (Septuagint) usage, and then NT usage of each word. While not exhaustive, it covers words that have important theological significance, and was used extensively in the writing of this book.

Third, there is the mammoth ten-volume (9,212 pages!) *Theological Dictionary of the New Testament* (Eerdmans), edited chiefly by German scholar Gerhard Kittle (1853–1948), which was also used often in writing this book. It, too, presents the Classical, Septuagint, and NT usage (especially the Jewish background), but in much greater detail. One should have at least a working knowledge of Greek before tackling this work. I would also add that this work demands theological *discernment*; there are some instances that demonstrate a liberal point of view, so the user should be adequately grounded in sound biblical theology. There is also an abridged, one-volume version of this work, which is affectionately referred to as "Little Kittle."

Fourth and finally, for the student who wants to actually learn Greek grammar, there are numerous tools. A classic is J. Gresham Machen's, *New Testament Greek for Beginners*, but there are easier works, such as Ian MacNair's lighter-styled *Teach Yourself New Testament Greek* (Thomas Nelson Publishers). Some teachers will not appreciate the downplaying of the importance of accent marks (p. 115), but this is an excellent basic grammar. For advanced study, and only for the very serious student, there is *Greek Grammar Beyond the Basics: An Exegetical Syntax of the New Testament* by Daniel Wallace (Zondervan).

A Word of Caution on "Interpretation"

Let it be clearly stated, *word study is only one aspect* of "rightly dividing the word of truth" (2 Tim. 2:15). Basing interpretation solely on a word's etymology, isolating a word from the verse in which it appears, or separating it from the whole of Scripture are all dangerous, to say the least. Besides the "Grammatical Principle," which we outlined earlier, there are several other principles of correct biblical interpretation that must *always* be followed. Here is a very brief summary of the most important ones.

First, there is the "Plain Principle." To interpret "plainly" (or "literally") is to explain the original sense of the speaker or writer according to normal, customary, and proper usage of words and language. Some of the most heinous heresies in history have come by "allegorizing" or "spiritualizing" Scripture. The Bible, therefore, is to be taken in its plain meaning unless it makes it clear that it is to be taken otherwise. When Scripture is speaking figuratively, it makes it plain that it is doing so either in the immediate context, the larger context of Scripture, or through historical reference.

Second, there is the "Contextual Principle." Probably the most violated principle of biblical interpretation is the ripping of verses from their context. This principle, therefore, involves examining the words that surround the word in question, the verses that surround that verse, and the basic theme of the book where the verse appears. I don't know whom to credit for this thought, but it has been well said, "A text without a context is pretext."

Third, there is the "Comparison Principle." No Scripture verse stands by itself. Comparing Scripture with Scripture is absolutely essential to arriving at the proper interpretation of a given text. This principle is called *analogia scripturae*, "the analogy of Scripture," that is, comparing Scripture with Scripture.[371] In other words, we allow Scripture to interpret itself.

Fourth, there is the "Historical Principle." It is vitally important to understand the social customs, historical names and events, political climate and rulers, and even geographical references that might be pertinent to a given text. No study of Scripture is complete (or honest) without the historical context.

Fifth, there is the "Illumination Principle." As we study the Word of God, we must ever remember that what we are doing is not some intellectual exercise. Our ultimate purpose is not intellectual, but spiritual. Therefore, no matter how much we study the Word, no matter what tools we use, no matter how many principles we employ, nothing can substitute for the illumination of the Holy Spirit.

Sixth and finally, there is the "Practical Principle." By this we don't mean that we sit back and say, "What is the Bible saying to me?" That is practiced quite often in the church today, even to the extent of people supposedly "receiving new revelation." What we mean here is that we simply ask, "In light of my diligent study of what the Bible *says,* what does it now *demand* of me?" There is nothing mysterious about this, for once we go through the interpretation process, the application reveals itself. We don't have to *look* for the application; it becomes self-evident.

May God richly bless you as you mine the infinite riches of His Word.

Notes

[1] Robert McCrum, William Cran, and Robert MacNeil, The Story of English (New York: Elisabeth Sifton Books, Viking Penguin, 1986), p. 51.

[2] Ibid, p. 20 (emphasis in the original).

[3] Barclay, pp. 12–13.

[4] Gleason L. Archer in Merrill C. Tenney (Editor), *Zondervan Pictorial Encyclopedia of the Bible* (Grand Rapids: Zondervan, 1975), vol. III, p. 870.

[5] Trench, p. 15.

[6] Cited in Mal Couch, *An Introduction to Classical Evangelical Hermeneutics* (Grand Rapids: Kregel Publications, 2000), p. 55.

[7] Trench, p. 233 (emphasis in the original).

[8] Kittle, Vol. I, p. 360.

[9] This is the reading of the Traditional Text and the Majority Text, but *not* the Critical Text, the latter of which, as John Eadie (*A Commentary on the Greek Text of the Epistle of Paul to the Ephesians* (Eugene, OR: Wipf and Stock Publishers, 1998; reprint of 1861 edition) points out (p. 237), relies only on two manuscripts, Sinaiticus and Vaticanus.

[10] Zodhiates, #1573. (All references to Zodhiates's *The Complete Word Study Dictionary*: *New Testament* use the Strong's number instead of a page number.)

[11] Thayer, #1573. (All references to *Thayer's Greek-English Lexicon of the New Testament* use the Strong's number instead of a page number.)

[12] *The Bible Exposition Commentary* (Wheaton: Scripture Press Publications, 1989). Electronic edition by Logos Library Systems, comment on Ephesians 1:1.

[13] Zodhiates, #3107.

[14] Ibid.

[15] Zodhiates, #1679.

[16] Brown, Vol. 2, p. 239.

[17] Cited in William Barclay, *Daily Study Bible: The Letters to the Galatians and Ephesians* (Westminster John Knox Press, 1982), electronic edition, comment on Ephesians 2:12.

[18] J. Sidlow Baxter, *Explore the Book* (Grand Rapids: Zondervan, 1960), Vol. 6, p. 165 (emphasis in the original).

[19] "Little Kittle," p. 7 (Kittle, Vol. I, pp. 36–37).

[20] "Little Kittle," pp. 8–9 (Kittle, Vol. I, p. 48).

[21] Zodhiates, #4183, and John Eadie, p. 141.

[22] Trench, p. 58.

[23] Trench, p. 290.

[24] Brown, Vol. I, p. 697.

[25] Zodhiates, #4678.

[26] Brown, Vol. 2, p. 616.

[27] Brown, Vol. 2, p. 296.

28 Charles Hodge, *A Commentary on the Epistle to the Ephesians* (London: Banner of Truth Trust, 1964), p. 37.

29 Cited in Brown, Vol. 3, pp. 840-841, based on the writings of Aristotle (*Politics*, 1, 9, p. 1256b-1258a, 8; 2, 9, p. 1269a, 34f) and Plato (*Republic* 7, 521a; 8, 547b; *Phaedo* 279c).

30 Eadie (*Ephesians*), p. 68.

31 Kittle, Vol. I, p. 238.

32 William Barclay, *The Letters to Timothy, Titus, and Philemon* (Philadelphia: Westminster, 1975), p. 89.

33 Zodhiates, #331.

34 Zodhiates, #4100.

35 "Little Kittle," pp. 849, 854. References in brackets added by the author. Fuller discussion in Kittle, Vol. I, p. 205.

36 Zodhiates, #1401.

37 Eadie (*Ephesians*), p. 120-121.

38 Thayer, #5485.

39 Brown, Vol. 2, p. 115.

40 Warren Wiersbe, *The Bible Exposition Commentary* (Wheaton, IL: Victor Books, 1997), electronic edition, comment on Ephesians 1:17.

41 Thayer, #1922.

52 Zodhiates, #4114.

43 "Little Kittle," p. 1242 (Kittle, Vol. VIII, p. 605).

44 John R. W. Stott, *God's New Society*: *The Message of Ephesians* (Downers Grove, IL: Intervaristy, 1979), p. 137.

45 Zodhiates, #3788.

46 Brown, Vol. 3, p. 127.

47 Cited in Albert Barnes, *Barnes Notes on the New Testament* (Grand Rapids: Kregel Publications, 1974, and electronic edition in *The Online Bible*), comment on Ephesians 1:18.

48 Earle, p. 295.

49 Eadie (*Ephesians*), pp. 94–95.

50 Eadie (*Ephesians*), pp. 95.

51 Martyn Lloyd-Jones, *The Unsearchable Riches of Christ* (Grand Rapids: Baker Book House), p. 306.

52 Brown, Vol. 2, p. 606.

53 Cited in Brown, Vol. 2, p. 611, from *Luther's Works*, XXXI, 1957, 344.

54 *Calvin's Commentaries*. See also *Sermons on Ephesians* (pp. 122-3). This is also the view of Martyn Lloyd-Jones, William Hendrickson, R.C.H. Lenski, Charles Hodge, and others.

55 Joseph Excell (editor), *The Biblical Illustrator* (originally published in 1887; electronic edition by Ages software), from comments on Ephesians 5:18.

56 For further study see Brown, Vol. 3, pp. 585–586 and Trench, pp. 245–247.

57 William Barclay, *Daily Study Bible*: *The Letter to the Romans* (Westminster John Knox Press, 1982), electronic edition.

58 *God's Way of Reconciliation*: *Studies in Ephesians Chapter 2* (Grand Rapids: Baker, 1979), pp. 21–22.

[59] Wuest, *Ephesians*.

[60] Brown, Vol. 3, p. 719.

[61] Brown, Vol. 2, p. 470.

[62] Zodhiates, #2372.

[63] M. R. DeHaan, *Windows on the Word* (Grand Rapids: Radio Bible Class, 1984), p. 11.

[64] Brown, Vol. 3, p. 377.

[65] Brown, Vol. 3, p. 1081.

[66] Zodhiates, #3004.

[67] Eadie (*Ephesians*), p. 357.

[68] Brown, Vol. 2, p. 99.

[69] Hunter Mead, *Types and Problems of Philosophy*, Third Edition (New York: Holt, Rinehart, and Winston, 1959), p. 62.

[70] Cited in Paul Lee Tan, *Encyclopedia of 7,700 Illustrations* (electronic edition in Logos Library Systems).

[71] A. T. Robertson, *New Testament Word Pictures* (electronic edition in Online Bible), comment on Ephesians 4:31.

[72] Martyn Lloyd-Jones, *Darkness and Light* (Grand Rapids: Baker Book House), pp. 282–283.

[73] Brown, Vol. 2, p. 105.

[74] Zodhiates, #5543.

[75] Thayer, #5543.

[76] DeHaan, *Windows on the Word*, p. 88.

[77] Thayer, #1656.

[78] William Hendrickson, *New Testament Commentary*: *Ephesians* (Grand Rapids: Baker Book House), p. 117 (emphasis W.H.).

[79] Trench, p. 75.

[80] Thayer, #4891.

[81] Brown, Vol. 3, pp. 587–589.

[82] Zodhiates, #5424.

[83] Thayer, #40.

[84] Cited in James Montgomery Boice, *Foundations of the Christian Faith* (Downers Grove, IL: InterVarsity Press, 1986 revised edition), p. 674. I should point out that Boice does *not* agree with this definition. On the contrary, he criticizes it and shows how the church has fallen into "secularism."

[85] Zodhiates, #1.

[86] Baker and Carpenter, #7706. (All references to Baker and Carpenter's *The Complete Word Study Dictionary*: *Old Testament* use the Strong's number instead of a page number.)

[87] John Philipps, *Exploring Revelation*, rev. ed. (Chicago: Moody, 1987; reprint, Neptune, N.J.: Loizeaux, 1991), pp. 22–23.

[88] Baker and Carpenter, #6055.

[89] *Metropolitan Tabernacle Pulpit*, sermon #3479.

[90] Martyn Lloyd-Jones, *God's Way of Reconciliation*, p. 133.

91 Walter L. Liefeld, *Ephesians* (Downers Grove, IL: InterVarsity Press, 1997), electronic edition, Logos Library Systems.

92 *Confessions*, Book X, chapter 8.

93 Kittle, Vol. II, p. 704.

94 M. R. Vincent, p. 851.

95 Brown, Vol. 3, p. 130.

96 Zodhiates, #4920.

97 Zodhiates, #3850.

98 Brown, Vol. 4, p. 259.

99 Josh McDowell, *More Than a Carpenter* (Wheaton, IL: Living Books, 1977), p. 89.

100 Both cited in McDowell, pp. 97–98.

101 *Antiquities of the Jews*, 15.11.5; *The Wars of the Jews*, 5.5.2; and 6.2.4.

102 Brown, Vol. 2, p. 722 (emphasis added).

103 Brown, Vol. 3, p. 591.

104 Zodhiates, #1199.

105 Trench, p. 163.

106 Eadie (*Ephesians*), p. 225.

107 M. R. Vincent in Wuest.

108 Thayer, #2644.

109 Thayer, #575.

110 "Little Kittle," p. 40. Kittle, Vol. I, p. 254.

111 "Little Kittle, p. 41. Kittle, Vol. I, p. 258.

112 Brown, Vol. 1, p. 232.

113 Matt. 3:1; Mark 1:4, 7; Luke 3:3; Acts 10:37.

114 Matt. 4:17, 23; 9:35; 11:1; Mark 1:14, 38-39; Luke 4:44; 8:1; 1 Pet. 3:19.

115 Matt. 10:7; 24:14; 26:13; Mark 3:14; 6:12; 13:10; 14:9; 16:15, 20; Luke 9:2; 24:47; Acts 8:5; 9:20; 19:13; 20:25; 28:31; Rom. 10:8, 14-15; 1 Cor. 1:23; 9:27; 15:11–12; 2 Cor. 1:19; 4:5; Gal. 2:2; Col. 1:23; 1 Thess. 2:9; 1 Tim. 3:16; 2 Tim. 4:2.

116 Zodhiates, #3874.

117 Alford in Wuest.

118 Cited in "Does The Truth Matter Anymore?" Taped study by John MacArthur (Word Pictures; Boca Raton: CrossTV).

119 Brown, Vol. 2, p. 92.

120 Brown, Vol. 2, pp. 92, 95.

121 *Calvin's Commentaries*: *Isaiah* (electronic edition; *Online Bible*).

122 Zodhiates, #3454.

123 Brown (Vol. 2, p. 643) cites the following: Eros (*Symposium*, 189c-193d; 202d-212a); creation (Timaeus, 29d-92b); the world to come (*Gorgias*, 523a-524a); the judgment of the dead (*The Republic*, 10, 614a-621d).

124 Zodhiates, #3454.

125 Trench, p. 202.

126 Zodhiates, #2171.

127 Trench, pp. 201–202 and Zodhiates, #155..

128 Berry, p. 59.

129 Zodhiates, #89.

130 Brown, Vol. 3, p. 1147.

131 Kittle, Vol. II, p. 653.

132 Brown, Vol. 3, p. 224.

133 *Calvin's Commentaries*: *Isaiah* (electronic edition; *Online Bible*).

134 Respectively: *hamartanei* (present indicative active) and *hamartanōn* (present indicative participle).

135 Jamieson, Fausset, and Brown, *A Commentary: Critical, Experiential, and Practical*, 3 vols. (Grand Rapids: Eerdmans Publishing Company, reprint 1993), Vol. 3, p. 435 (emphasis in the original).

136 Zodhiates, #1506.

137 Zodhiates, #1710.

138 Brown, Vol. 3, p. 943.

139 Kittle, Vol. I, p. 238.

140 Brown, Vol. 2, p. 490.

141 Jacob Neusner, *The Mishnah*: *A New Translation* (New Haven: Yale University Press, 1988), Sukkah 5:2-4.

142 Zodhiates, #3767.

143 Brown, Vol. 3, p. 348.

144 Brown, Vol. 1, p. 271.

145 1 Cor. 15:9; 10:27, and three quotations from the LXX: Rom. 9:7 (Gen. 21:12); Rom. 9:25 (Hos. 2:23, 25); Rom. 9:26 (Hos. 1:10). Brown, Vol. I, p. 275.

146 Brown, Vol. 2, p. 187.

147 Walter Elwell (editor), *Baker Theological Dictionary of the Bible* (Grand Rapids: Baker Book House, 1996), p. 138.

148 Cited in Detzler, p. 33.

149 Zodhiates (#908, p. 314) well says, "The whole paragraph, Eph. 4:1–5, is indicative of Paul's desire that there should be unity of the Spirit in the body of Christ. No reference is made to water baptism at all. The verse says, 'One Lord, one faith, one baptism.' This baptism must be, therefore, the spiritual baptism, the baptism in the Spirit that was promised by John the Baptist that the One coming after him would accomplish (Matt. 3:11; Mark 1:8; Luke 3:16; John 1:33) and Jesus Christ Himself promised in Acts 1:5. This took place in Acts 2. . . . The purpose of this Spirit baptism is shown in 1 Cor. 12:13 as the incorporation of all Believers into the body of Christ, the Church (Eph. 1:22, 23)."

150 Brown, Vol. 3, p. 1078.

151 (1) No more than three, and preferable only two, were to speak; (2) they were not to speak simultaneously; (3) everything said had to be interpreted by a single interpreter; (4) if no interpreter was present, the would-be speaker was not even to speak; (5) everything was to be done without confusion or disorder; and (6) women were to keep silent, that is, were not to exercise speaking gifts within the public forum of worship. While the last two are specifically in the context of prophecy, they obviously are universal principles in church order.

152 Zodhiates writes, "In the NT *prophētēs* corresponds to the person who in the OT spoke under divine influence and inspiration. This included the foretelling future events or the exhorting,

reproving, and threatening of individuals or nations as the ambassador of God and the interpreter of His will to men (Ezek. 2). Hence the prophet spoke not his own thoughts but what he received from God, retaining, however, his own consciousness and self–possession (Exod. 7:1; 2 Pet. 1:20, 21; especially 1 Cor. 14:32). . . . In Eph. 2:20; 3:5, the prophets, named side by side with the Apostles (meaning the Eleven and those who were commissioned by Jesus directly) as the foundation of the NT church, are to be understood as exclusively NT prophets. They are listed in Eph. 4:11 between apostles and evangelists (see 1 Cor. 12:28). NT prophets were for the Christian church what OT prophets were for Israel. They maintained intact the immediate connection between the church and the God of their salvation. They were messengers or communicators. Such prophets were not ordained in local churches nor do they have successors" (#4396, pp. 1244–46).

153 Martyn Lloyd-Jones, *Christian Unity An Exposition of Ephesians 4:1-16* (Grand Rapids: Baker, 1982), p. 189.

154 As Dr. John MacArthur puts it, "There is no [actual] mention of the latter two gifted offices replacing the first two, because in New Testament times all were operative. But the fact is that, as they continued to serve the Church, the evangelists and [pastor-teachers] did pick up the baton from the first generation apostles and prophets" (*The Macarthur New Testament Commentary: Ephesians* [Chicago: Moody Press, 1986], p. 142).

155 Louis Sperry Chafer, *Systematic Theology* (Dallas: Dallas Seminary Press, 1947), Vol. III, p. 20.

156 Brown, Vol. 3, p. 564.

157 Brown, Vol. 3, pp. 766, 768.

158 The Granville-Sharp's Rule: ". . . When there are two nouns in the same case connected by *kai* (and), the first noun having the article [the], the second noun not having the article, the second noun refers to the same thing the first noun does and is a further description of it" (cited by Kenneth Wuest, *The Pastoral Epistles in the Greek New Testament* [Grand Rapids: Eerdmans, 1952], p. 195). He again writes, "This construction requires us to understand that the words 'pastors' and 'teachers' refer to the same individual, and that the word 'teacher' is a further description of the individual called a 'pastor.' The expression, therefore, refers to pastors who are also teachers, 'teaching pastors'" (Kenneth Wuest, "Chapter IV, Greek Grammar and the Deity of Christ," *Treasures from the Greek New Testament* [Grand Rapids: Eerdmans, 1945]).

159 Charles Hodge, *Ephesians* (London: Banner of Truth Trust, 1964), pp. 120–121.

160 *Teach* (1 Tim. 1:3; 2:12; 3:2; 4:11; 6:2, 3; 2 Tim. 2:2, 24; Titus 2:4); *teaching* (Titus 1:11; 2:12); *preach* (1 Tim. 4:2); *preaching* (2 Tim. 4:7; Titus 1:3); *speak* (1 Tim. 2:7; Titus 2:1; 2:15 [1 Tim. 5:14 and Titus 3:2 not appropriate]); *exhort* (1 Tim. 2:1; 6:2; 2 Tim. 4:2; Titus 1:9; 2:6, 9, 15); *doctrine* (1 Tim 1:3, 10; 4:6, 13, 16; 5:17; 6:1, 3; 2 Tim. 3:10, 16; 4:2, 3; Titus 1:9; 2:1, 7, 10); *rebuke* (1 Tim. 4:1; 5:20; 2 Tim. 4:2; Titus 1:13; 2:15); *reprove* (2 Tim. 4:2).

161 M. R. Vincent, *Word Studies in the New Testament*, one volume edition (Grand Rapids: Associated Publishers and Authors, Inc).

162 Matthew Henry, *Matthew Henry's Commentary on the Whole Bible* (Wilmington, DE: Sovereign Grace Publishers, 1972), electronic edition in *The Online Bible*, comment on 1 Timothy 5:17.

163 *Faith of the Early Fathers*, Vol. 2, p.194.

164 Brown, Vol. 1, p. 715.

165 Brown, Vol. 3, pp. 349–351.

166 R. C. H. Lenski, *Commentary on the New Testament*: *Galatians*, *Ephesians*, *Philippians* (Peabody, MA: Hendrickson Publishers, 1937, 2001), p. 454.

167 Zodhiates, #3056.

168 As Martyn Lloyd-Jones puts it in *God's Way of Reconciliation*, p. 362.

169 *Vine's Expository Dictionary.*

[170] Zodhiates, #837.

[171] Zodhiates, #2233.

[172] Brown, Vol. 2, p. 59.

[173] Brown, Vol. 1, p. 412.

[174] Brown, Vol. 3, p. 943.

[175] Thayer and Wuest respectively.

[176] *The Sword and the Trowel*, March 1887 issue.

[177] Augustus Strong.

[178] Zodhiates, #4152.

[179] Brown, Vol. 2, p. 362.

[180] Brown, Vol. 2, p. 362.

[181] John Gill, *The New John Gill's Exposition of the Entire Bible*. Originally completed in 1766. Modernised and adapted for the computer by Larry Pierce of *The Online Bible*. Comment on 1 Thessalonians 5:22.

[182] *The Da Vinci Code* by Dan Brown (Doubleday, 2003). While seemingly just another thriller novel set in the present day, it has a hidden agenda that makes it far more. Starting with the murdered curator of a Paris museum, the hero and heroine of the story must decipher the clues left behind by the murdered man and thereby uncover an ancient and sinister plot. *And what is this ancient secret?* The supposed "true" story that Christianity has been trying to hide for 1,600 years, namely, that Jesus was just another man who actually ended up marrying Mary Magdalene. Not only is it Arianism and Gnosticism in a new wrapper, but it's also full of countless historical errors that reveal the author to be either incredibly ignorant or just a blatant liar. For example, referring to the Council of Nicea in 325, Brown claims that "until that moment in history, Jesus was viewed by His followers as a mortal prophet . . . a great and powerful man, but a man nonetheless." *But that simply is not so*. History proves beyond doubt that early Christians overwhelmingly worshiped Jesus Christ as their risen Savior and Lord. Before the appearance of complete doctrinal statements, early Christian leaders wrote summaries of doctrine called the "Rule" or "Canon" of faith that stated this fact. The canon of well-known second-century bishop Irenaeus, for example, was prompted by 1 Corinthians 8:6: "But to us there is but one God, the Father, of whom are all things, and we in him; and one Lord Jesus Christ, by whom are all things, and we by him." There is no doubt that those early Christians viewed our Lord as God.

[183] Robert H. Schuller, *Self-Esteem*: *The New Reformation* (Waco, TX: Word Books, 1982), pp. 98, 99.

[184] *Expositor's Greek Testament* in Kenneth Wuest (*Ephesians*).

[185] Respectively: Calvin; *Expositor's* in Wuest; Jamieson, Fausset, and Brown; Lloyd-Jones; and Hendrickson.

[186] Brown, Vol. 3, p. 877. The remainder of the quotation is: "However, sometimes *alētheuō* means to prove true; or in the passive, to be fulfilled (Xenophon, *Institutio Cyri* 4, 6-10)." But neither of these meanings would make sense in the context.

[187] Albert Barnes, *Barnes Notes on the New Testament* (Grand Rapids: Kregel Publications, 1974, and electronic edition in *The Online Bible*), comment on Ephesians 4:15.

[188] Attributed to Spurgeon in *The Biblical Illustrator*, but that could not be confirmed.

[189] John Phillips, *Exploring Ephesians and Philippians* (Grand Rapids: Kregel Publications, 1993, 1995), p. 122.

[190] Joseph Excell, ed., *The Biblical Illustrator* (originally published in 1887; electronic edition by Ages software), from comments on Ephesians 4:15.

[191] Brown, Vol. 1, p. 262.

192 Zodhiates, #2038.

193 William Barclay, *Daily Study Bible: The Letters to the Galatians and Ephesians* (Westminster John Knox Press, 1982), electronic edition, comment on Ephesians 5:1.

194 Credited to Charles Caleb Colton (1780-1832), *The Lacon; cited in Bartlett's Familiar Quotations*, sixteenth edition (Boston: Little, Brown, and Company, 1882, 1992), p. 393.

195 *Metropolitan Tabernacle Pulpit*, Vol. 29, Sermon #1725.

196 Zodhiates, #151.

197 Zodhiates, #3049.

198 Kittle, Vol. IV, pp. 284, 288; Brown, Vol. 3, p. 824.

199 John Eadie, *A Commentary on the Greek Text of the Epistle of Paul to the Philippians* (Eugene, OR: Wipf and Stock Publishers, 1998; reprint of 1858 edition), p. 253.

200 *Matthew Henry's Commentary on the Whole Bible*, electronic edition in *The Online Bible*, comment on Philippians 4:8.

201 William Hendrickson, *New Testament Commentary*: *Exposition of Philippians* (Grand Rapids: Baker Book House), p. 198.

202 John Eadie, *A Commentary on the Greek Text of the Epistle of Paul to the Philippians* (Eugene, OR: Wipf and Stock Publishers, 1998; reprint of 1858 edition), p. 255.

203 Ralph P. Martin and Gerald F. Hawthorne, *Word Biblical Commentary*: *Philippians*, *Revised* (Nashville: Thomas Nelson, 2004), p. 251.

204 J. B. Lightfoot, *Philippians*: *The Crossway Classic Commentaries* (Wheaton, IL: Crossway Books, 1994, 1998), electronic edition, Logos Library System, comment on Philippians 4:8.

205 John Phillips, *Exploring Ephesians and Philippians*, p. 169.

206 Kittle, Vol. II, p. 237.

207 Brown, Vol. 2, p. 44.

208 Thomas Watson, *A Body of Divinity* (Carlisle, PA: The Banner of Truth Trust, 1992 reprint of 1692 edition), p. 15.

209 Note also the opposite Hebrew word *iy-kēbōd* (350H, literally, "there is no glory") in 1 Samuel 4:21–22 ("Ichabod").

210 John Gill, *The New John Gill's Exposition of the Entire Bible*, comment on Hebrews 1:3.

211 Zodhiates, #541.

212 Brown, Vol. 1, p. 421 (emphasis added).

213 Eadie, *Ephesians*, p. 379.

214 Diogenes Laertius, *Lives of Eminent Philosophers*, Bk. II, sec. 31. Cited in *Bartlett's*, p. 70.

215 *The Inn Album* [1875], II. Cited in *Bartlett's*, p. 468.

216 In Memoriam [1850], Prologue, st. 7. Cited in *Bartlett's,* p. 457.

217 Brown, Vol. 2, p. 288.

218 Paul uses it to describe the misery of nature, and Peter uses it to describe apostates.

219 "Their alienation had its cause, not in something external, casual, or superficial, but *in themselves*—in a culpable ignorance in their own nature or heart" (Kenneth Wuest, *Ephesians*, emphasis added).

220 Brown, Vol. 2, p. 406.

221 Brown, Vol. 2, p. 153. Also Kenneth Wuest (*Ephesians*): "the covering with a callous."

222 R. C. H. Lenski, *Commentary on the New Testament: Galatians, Ephesians, Philippians* (Peabody, MA: Hendrickson Publishers, 1937, 2001), pp. 556–7.

223 Brown, Vol. 1, p. 722.

224 *The New John Gill's Exposition of the Entire Bible*, comment on Philippians 1:13.

225 Brown, Vol. 2, p. 140.

226 Trench, pp. 29, 30.

227 *Calvin's Commentaries: Ephesians* (electronic edition; *Online Bible*), comment on Ephesians 5:11.

228 Kent Hughes, *Ephesians: The Mystery of the Body of Christ* (Wheaton, IL: Crossway Books, 1990), electronic edition, Logos Research Systems.

229 Zodhiates, #1453.

230 The Latin term is *limbus patrum*, that is, "limbo of fathers." The literal idea of *limbus* is "fringe or border," and the basic idea in the word *limbo* is "a state or place of confinement." So, the teaching in the term *limbus patrum*, which was chosen in the Middle Ages, refers to a place on the border of hell that, as the *Catholic Encyclopedia* puts it, was the place where "the just who had lived under the Old Dispensation, and who, either at death or after a course of purgatorial discipline, had attained the perfect holiness required for entrance into glory, were obliged to await the coming of the Incarnate Son of God and the full accomplishment of His visible earthly mission. Meanwhile they were 'in prison'" . . . awaiting "the higher bliss to which they looked forward" ("Limbo" in *Catholic Encyclopedia*, Classic 1914 Edition [http://www.newadvent.org/cathen]).

We might also interject that a similar teaching is called *limbus infantium* ("children's limbo"), which, according to Catholic teaching, is the place where unbaptized infants go; since they weren't baptized, they can't go to heaven, but because they have done no wickedness, they go to a place of happiness and no "positive pain." This is why infant baptism is so strongly emphasized to parents, so that they will be able to see their children again in heaven.

231 Martyn Lloyd-Jones, *Christian Unity*, p. 153.

232 There is obviously a slight discrepancy between Psalm 68:18 and our text. The psalm reads "*received* gifts *for* men," but Paul writes "*gave* gifts *unto* men." The liberal critic immediately sees a contradiction here, which he thinks argues against the inspiration and infallibility of Scripture. But there is no problem because our Lord did *both*: He received and gave. On the one hand, the Son received them from the Father, and on the other, the Son gave them to the church. As a victorious king would first receive the spoils of war and then distribute them to those who aided in the conquest, so the King of kings received of his Father and distributed to his church.

233 Brown, Vol. 3, p. 839.

234 Kittle, Vol. III, p. 455.

235 See Strong (#1805), Brown (Vol. 1, pp. 268–9), Kittle (Vol. I, p. 125); Zodhiates (#1805), etc.

236 R. C. H. Lenski, *Ephesians*, p. 614.

237 Eugene Ehrlich, *Amo, Amas, Amat and More* (New York: Harper and Row, Hudson Group, 1985), p. 136.

238 M. R. Vincent in Wuest (*Ephesians*).

239 Zodhiates, #810.

240 Wuest (*Ephesians*).

241 Louis Sperry Chafer, *Major Bible Themes* (Grand Rapids: Zondervan Publishing House, Revised Edition, 1974), p. 115.

242 Brown, Vol. 3, pp. 671–672.

243 Harvey Marks, *The Rise and Growth of English Hymnody* (New York: Fleming H. Revell Company, 1938), p. 29.

244 Brown, Vol. 3, p. 668.

245 Zodhiates, #5215.

246 Zodhiates, #5603.

247 J. Ligon Duncan, from his address "God-Centered Music," delivered at Ligonier Ministries' 2004 Pastor's Conference in Orlando, Florida.

248 Vance Havner, *Moments of Decision* (Grand Rapids: Baker Book House, 1985; formerly printed by Fleming H. Revell, 1976), p. 50.

249 Duncan, *op. cit.*

250 Brown, Vol. 3, p. 671.

251 Brown, Vol. 3, p. 109.

252 Zodhiates, #4570.

253 Brown, Vol. 1, p. 474.

254 Louis Sperry Chafer, *He That Is Spiritual*, revised edition (Grand Rapids: Zondervan, 1971), pp. 91–92 (emphasis in the original).

255 Earle, p. 402 (quoting Walter Lock, *A Critical and Exegetical Commentary on the Pastoral Epistles*, p. 85).

256 Zodhiates, #2776.

257 Brown, Vol. 2, p. 157. As Kent Hughes reports: "Dr. Wayne Grudem, in a careful study of 2,336 instances of *kephalē* from classical Greek literature—all the non-classical references from Philo, Josephus, the Apostolic Fathers, the Epistle of Aristias, the Testaments of the Twelve Patriarchs and Aquila, Symmachus, and Theodocian—says, 'No instances were discovered in which *kephalē* had the meaning source, origin'" (*The Role Relationship of Men and Women, ed.* George W. Knight III [Chicago: Moody Press, 1985], pp. 65–69).

258 A. W. Tozer, "The Waning Authority of Christ in the Church," *God Tells the Man Who Cares* (Harrisburg: Christian Publications, 1970), p. 163.

259 R. C. Sproul, *Chosen by God* (Wheaton: Tyndale House, 1986), pp. 209–210.

260 As Zodhiates (#3067) points out, "Unfortunately Strong in his dictionary attributes the figurative meaning of baptism." See Zodhiates, #908 (section XIV, C) and #3067 for his excellent discussions of this word and verse.

261 Brown, Vol. 3, p. 1121.

262 Others: Acts 2:14; 10:44; 11:14, 16; 26:25; 1 Cor. 12:4; Heb. 1:3; Jude 17; Rev. 17:17; etc.

263 Eadie, *Ephesians*, p. 421.

264 Richard Seizer, *Mortal Lessons*: *Notes on the Art of Surgery* (New York: Simon and Schuster, 1976, pp. 45–46). Cited in R. Kent Hughes, *Preaching the Word*: *Colossians and Philemon—The Supremacy of Christ* (electronic edition in Logos Library Systems), comment on Colossians 3:19.

265 Charles Bridges, *Exposition of the Book of Proverbs* (Grand Rapids: Zondervan, 1959), pp. 3–4.

266 Brown, Vol. 2, p. 575.

267 Kittle, Vol. V, p. 596.

268 Trench, p. 126. As R. C. H. Lenski submits (*Ephesians*, p. 650), Trench's discussion of these synonyms is still the best. Zodhiates (#3559) agrees with Trench: "*Paideia* is instruction and training by act and discipline. *Nouthesia* is the milder term without which *paideia* would be incomplete."

269 I. D. E. Thomas, *The Golden Treasury of Puritan Quotations* (Carlisle, PA: The Banner of Truth Trust, 1989 reprint), p. 204.

270 Brown, Vol. 3, p. 572.

271 *Expositor's Greek Testament.*

272 Zodhiates, #572.

273 William MacDonald, *Believer's Bible Commentary* (Nashville: Thomas Nelson Publishers, 1995), p. 1226.

274 W. Grant in *The Biblical Illustrator*, commenting on Ephesians 6:6.

275 Thayer, #3823.

276 Will Durant, *The Story of Civilization, Vol. II, The Life of Greece* (New York: Simon and Schuster, 1939, 1966), pp. 214–15; *Vol. III, Caesar and Christ*, p. 382.

277 Vance Havner (compiled by Dennis Hester), *The Vance Havner Notebook* (Grand Rapids: Baker Book House, 1989), p. 272.

278 Brown, Vol. 1, p. 314.

279 A son (v. 1); a soldier (vv. 3–4); a runner in the games (v. 5); a farmer (v. 6); a workman (v. 15); a vessel (v. 21); and a bondservant (v. 24).

280 This seems to refer to those demons that specialize in infiltrating political systems. Daniel 10:13 speaks of "the prince of the kingdom of Persia," which was the spiritual force behind the physical ruler. Such a power has been behind every wicked ruler of history.

281 Charles Hodge, *A Commentary on the Epistle to the Ephesians*, electronic edition from Logos Library Systems, comment on Ephesians 6:12.

282 Albert Barnes, *Barnes Notes on the New Testament*, comment on Ephesians 6:12.

283 William Gurnall, *The Christian in Complete Armour* (Carlisle, PA: Banner of Truth Trust, 1974 reprint of the 1864 edition from the original 1665 edition), Vol. I, pp. 161–162.

284 Kittle, Vol. II, p. 704.

285 Brown, Vol. 3, p. 117.

286 Brown, Vol. 2, p. 772.

287 I. D. E. Thomas, *The Golden Treasury of Puritan Quotations* (Carlisle: The Banner of Truth Trust, 1989 reprint), p. 204.

288 Zodhiates, #2347.

289 Brown, Vol. 1, p. 356.

290 Zodhiates, #3340.

291 Brown, Vol. 3, p. 230.

292 William Barclay, *Daily Study Bible*: *The Revelation of John* (Westminster John Knox Press, 1982), electronic edition, comment on Revelation 2:15.

293 Zodhiates, #3862.

294 Trench, p. 107.

295 John R. W. Stott, *What Christ Thinks of the Church* (Grand Rapids: Eerdmans, 1980), p. 116.

296 There was actually a similar ambiguity in the Greek *ariston* (712), which literally means "without boundaries, indefinite," and referred to a meal taken at no particular time; to the Jews it sometimes corresponded to our breakfast or sometimes our lunch (see Luke 11:38 and especially 14:12 where *ariston* and *deipnon* appear together).

297 Ralph Gowers, *The New Manners and Customs of Bible Times* (Chicago: The Moody Bible Institute of Chicago), p. 1987.

298 William MacDonald, *Believer's Bible Commentary* (p. 1588); H. A. Ironside, *1 Corinthians* (pp. 350–353, 342); John Calvin, *Institutes* (Book IV, Ch. 14, Section 44); Francis Turretin, *Institutes of Elenctic Theology* (Vol. 3, p. 445); Matthew Henry, *Commentary* (1 Cor. 11:26); A. C. Gaebelein, *Acts* (pp. 344, 67); Louis Sperry Chafer, *Systematic Theology* (Vol. VII, p. 229); John Murray, *Collected Writings* (Vol. 2, pp. 376, 380); Wayne Grudem, *Systematic Theology* (p. 999). See the author's full-length article on this issue at *www.TheScriptureAlone.com.*

299 Kenneth Wuest, *Word Studies in the Greek New Testament*, electronic edition by Logos Library Systems, comment on Philippians 2:1.

300 Zodhiates, #5524.

301 Zodhiates, #1325.

302 Brown, Vol. III, pp. 772–773.

303 Kittle, Vol. V, p. 243.

304 Kittle, Vol. VI, p. 452.

305 Counts done using *QuickVerse 4.0* on the AV.

306 Brown, Vol. I, p. 658.

307 Zodhiates, p. 331.

308 Spiros Zodhiates, *The Complete Word Study Dictionary: New Testament* (Chattanooga: AMG Publishers, 1992), p. 630.

309 "Little Kittle," p. 544.

310 Zodhiates, #5342.

311 For an excellent presentation of this, see the discussion in Laird Harris' *Inspiration and Canonicity of the Bible* (Grand Rapids: Zondervan Publishing House, 1957), pp. 45–71. While I think his points on this are excellent, I do disagree with him on his comments concerning textual criticism and manuscript evidence.

312 Kittle, Vol. VII, p. 559.

313 Brown, Vol. 3, p. 1147.

314 Kittle, Vol. I, p. 74.

315 *Summa Theologica*, Part 1, question 113.

316 Henry Morris, *Defender's Study Bible* (Grand Rapids: World Publishing, 1995), comment on Heb. 1:14.

317 Zodhiates, #3129.

318 Brown, Vol. 1, p. 481.

319 Detzler, p. 162.

320 Kittle, Vol. IX, pp. 147, 153.

321 The other six are: "the Bread of Life" (6:35); "the Light of the World" (8:12); "the Door" (10:9); "the Good Shepherd" (10:11); "the Resurrection and the Life" (11:25); "the Way, the Truth, and the Life" (14:6).

322 Zodhiates, #1080.

323 Kittle, Vol. V, p. 42.

324 Kittle, Vol. I, p. 621.

325 Five of these points are very loosely adapted from Detzler, pp. 42–43. We also added the fourth point.

326 Kittle, Vol. I, p. 624.

[327] Brown, Vol. 1, p. 533.

[328] I. D. E. Thomas, *The Golden Treasury of Puritan Quotations* (Carlisle, PA: The Banner of Truth Trust, 1989 reprint), p. 300.

[329] Note the 10 percent of Leviticus 27:30 for the Levites, the 10 percent of Deuteronomy 14 used to support the national feasts and holidays, and the 10 percent collected each third year for a benevolence fund according to Deut. 14:28–29.

[330] Kittle, Vol. I, p. 145.

[331] Kittle, Vol. IX, p. 537.

[332] Brown, Vol. 2, p. 343.

[333] Cited in Paul Lee Tan, *Encyclopedia of 7,700 Illustrations,* electronic edition in Logos Library Systems.

[334] I. D. E. Thomas, *The Golden Treasury of Puritan Quotations* (Carlisle, PA: The Banner of Truth Trust, 1989 reprint), p. 295.

[335] Kittle, Vol. II, pp. 128–129.

[336] Gleaned from Barclay, *New Testament Words*, pp. 281–288, Brown, Vol. 1, pp. 686–691, Detzler, pp. 362–363, and Earle, p. 305.

[337] Cited in Detzler, p. 363.

[338] Kittle, Vol. VI, p. 95.

[339] Kittle, Vol. V, p. 583.

[340] Brown, Vol. 2, p. 468.

[341] Brown, Vol. 2, p. 439.

[342] Cited in Augustus Strong, *Systematic Theology* (New York: Fleming H. Revell Company, 1954), p. 728, from A. A. Hodge, *Popular Lectures on Theology*, p. 247.

[343] Trench, p. 179.

[344] *Adam Clarke's Commentary on the Whole Bible*, electronic edition in *Online Bible*, comment on Revelation 2:5.

[345] Trench, p. 179.

[346] Brown, Vol. 3, p. 530.

[347] I. D. E. Thomas, *The Golden Treasury of Puritan Quotations* (Carlisle, PA: The Banner of Truth Trust, 1989 reprint), p. 59.

[348] Cited in Detzler, p. 91.

[349] Brown, Vol. 1, pp. 348–349.

[350] Zodhiates, #4893.

[351] Brown, Vol. 2, p. 412.

[352] Kittle, Vol. I, p. 341.

[353] J. Sidlow Baxter, *The Master Theme of the Bible* (Wheaton: Tyndale House, 1973), pp. 21–34.

[354] John F. Walvoord and Roy B. Zuck, *The Bible Knowledge Commentary* (Wheaton: Scripture Press Publications, 1983, 1985).

[355] *Wuest's Expanded Translation* (Grand Rapids: Eerdmans Publishing Company, 1961).

[356] Kittle, Vol. IV, p. 741.

[357] Josh McDowell, *The New Evidence that Demands a Verdict* (Nashville: Thomas Nelson, 1999), p. xxxi.

[358] Kittle, Vol. IX, p. 427.

[359] Brown, Vol. 2, p. 284.

[360] Albert Barnes, *Barnes Notes on the New Testament*, comment on 1 John 5:21.

[361] William Gurnall, *The Christian in Complete Armor*, vol. I, pp. 294 and 306 respectively.

[362] Zodhiates, #73.

[363] Brown, Vol. 2, p. 59.

[364] *The Ryrie Study Bible* (Chicago: Moody Press,1978).

[365] As Lehman Strauss offers, "Allelujah, without the initial 'h,' is a misspelling, having been robbed of its initial aspirate" (*The Book of Revelation* [Neptune, NJ: Loizeaux Brothers, 1964], p. 315).

[366] Zodhiates, #239.

[367] Baker and Carpenter, #1984.

[368] William R. Newell, *The Book of Revelation* (Chicago: Moody Press, 1935), p. 292.

[369] Zodhiates, #281.

[370] Thayer, #281. See also Brown, Vol. 1, pp. 97–99.

[371] This is further explained by the principle: *Scripturam ex Scriptura explicandam esse* ("Scripture is to be explained by Scripture"). This principle is related to another: *Analogia Fide* ("Analogy of Faith"), i.e., Bible doctrine is to be interpreted in relation to the basic message of the Bible, which is the Gospel, the content of faith, or simply "The Faith" (cf. 1 Cor. 2:13; 15:1–4; Jude 3).

Bibliography

Notes are keyed to this bibliography.

Archer, Gleason, Laird Harris, Laird, and Bruce Waltke. *Theological Wordbook of the Old Testament.* Chicago: Moody Bible Institute, 1980.

Baker, Warren and Eugene Carpenter. *The Complete Word Study Dictionary: Old Testament.* Chattanooga: AMG Publishers, 2003.

Barclay, William. *New Testament Words*. Louisville: Westminster John Knox Press, 1964, 1974.

Berry, Harold J. *Gems from the Original*. Lincoln, NE: Back to the Bible Broadcast, 1972.

Brown, Colin, gen. ed. *The New International Dictionary of New Testament Theology* (3 vol.). Grand Rapids: Zondervan, 1975.

Detzler, Wayne A. *New Testament Words in Today's Language*. Wheaton: Victor Books, 1986.

Earle, Ralph. *Word Meanings in the New Testament*. Peabody, MA: Hendrickson Publishers, 1997.

Hodges, Zane C. and Arthur L. Farstad. *The Greek New Testament According to the Majority Text.* Nashville: Thomas Nelson Publishers, 1985.

Kittle, Gerhard, ed. *Theological Dictionary of the New Testament.* 10 vol. Grand Rapids: Eerdmans, 1964. Reprinted 2006.

Roberson, A. T. *Word Pictures in the Greek New Testament*. Electronic edition in *The Online Bible*.

Strong, James. *Strong's Exhaustive Concordance*. Updated electronic version by *The Online Bible*.

Thayer, Joseph. *Thayer's Greek-English Lexicon of the New Testament*. Grand Rapids: Associated Publishers and Authors, n.d.

Trench, Richard. *Synonyms of the New Testament*. Peabody, MA: Hendrickson, 2000.

Vincent, M. R. *Word Studies in the New Testament* (one-volume edition). Grand Rapids: Associated Publishers and Authors, n.d.

Vine, W. E. *An Expository Dictionary of New Testament Words*. Old Tappan, NJ: Fleming H. Revell Company, 1966. Electronic edition, Logos Research Systems.

Wuest, Kenneth. *Word Studies in the Greek New Testament* (4 vols.). Grand Rapids: Eerdmans, 1966.

Young, Robert. *Young's Analytical Concordance to the Bible.* Peabody, MA: Hendrickson Publishers, n.d.

Zodhiates, Spiros. *The Complete Word Study Dictionary: New Testament*. Chattanooga: AMG Publishers, 1992.

Scripture Index

Mark

Luke

John

Acts

Romans

1 Corinthians

2 Corinthians

Galatians

Ephesians

Philippians

English Word Index

Greek and Hebrew Word Index

(Hebrew words are followed by an "H")

Strong's Number Index

(Hebrew numbers are followed by an "H")